75 ¢

The Rodale
Herb Book

The Rodale Herb Book

HOW TO USE, GROW, AND BUY NATURE'S MIRACLE PLANTS

Edited by William H. Hylton

With Chapters By

Nelson Coon

Louise Hyde

Bonnie Fisher

Marion Wilbur

Barbara Foust

Heinz Grotzke

William H. Hylton

AN ORGANIC GARDENING AND FARMING BOOK

RODALE PRESS BOOK DIVISION
Emmaus, Pa. 18049

Standard Book Number
0-87857-076-4
Library of Congress Card Number
73-18902
PRINTED IN THE UNITED STATES OF AMERICA

OB-729

TENTH PRINTING – AUGUST 1976

Library of Congress Cataloging in Publication Data

Hylton, William H
  The Rodale herb book.

(An Organic gardening and farming book)
Bibliography: p.

1. Herbs. 2. Herb gardening. 3. Cookery (Herbs). 4. Materia
medica, Vegetable. 5. Aromatic plants. 6. Dye plants. I. Coon,
Nelson. II. Title. III. Title: How to use, grow, and buy nature's
miracle plants.

SB351.H5H94   635'.7   73-18902
ISBN 0-87857-076-4

CONTENTS

INTRODUCTION

Where to begin is the hardest thing in learning about herbs. There is so much to the subject that it seems easier to remain ignorant. There are so many books and articles on the subject—all that lore, the mystique, and the odd names. It seems that the best you can hope for is an inviting spot along the vista that prompts you to stop and study the herbal landscape. Once you get to know a few landmarks, the whole project becomes easier, if only because you've discovered how engaging and entertaining herbs can be.

Perhaps this book will be that inviting vista for you. Or perhaps it will be only a new overlook along an already-familiar panorama. Whichever it is, I think you will find this book of value.

Let me assume that you are vaguely familiar with herbs. You know what an herb is—until someone asks you to define the term. You know that some cooks use herbs for seasoning. Then you recall the storied herb lady who cured ailments with concoctions made chiefly of plants. Or you have seen dried-up old plants hanging by the hearthside in historic homes visited on vacation.

The many minds that helped me find out about herbs will help you find out about herbs, too. These minds were set to thinking about the matter of herbs, not for my benefit but for yours, through the initial efforts of M. C. Goldman, better known as Lee, a managing editor of *Organic Gardening and Farming*. Lee created a plan for a book, lined up knowledgeable writers, and passed the project along. He got the herbs together; it was for me to make a garden of them.

I think everyone will find something of interest in the herb garden that has grown out of our efforts. Your first steps into our garden will show you what herbs are. You'll see highlights from their past. You'll learn the rudiments of botanical nomenclature, something the herbalist should be familiar with. Finally, you'll meet your garden tour guides. These guides, each in charge of a special area of the garden, will show you the many uses of herbs, whet your appetite, then show you how to grow your own, where-ever you live. The tours can be taken in sequence, or, you can pick and choose with the flip of a few pages.

In the end, you'll be free to roam our dictionary of 50 engaging herbs, ranging from the herbs everyone knows—like peppermint, thyme, sage, and rosemary—through the oddly-named mugwort and beebalm to some you may not have thought of as herbs like horseradish, garlic, and scented geraniums. Roam these pages and get to know these striking herbal personalities. If you go further, you'll meet many other plants that are a part of the herb landscape and learn where you can go to get to know them better.

This garden is yours to work and enjoy. I think you will.

WHO WILL GUIDE US?
NELSON COON

With the long history of herbs as medicinal plants, it is per-haps somehow appropriate that the oldest contributor to our herbal garden is the author of our herbal chapter. Nelson Coon is a spry old duffer who dashes more than he duffs. At least that's the appearance he presented to me during a short but busy visit I made to his Martha's Vineyard home.

I was met on the wharf by a man nearly 80 years old, but he wasn't the sort of fellow I expected. From the first wave of the hoe to the final wave of the hand two hours later, Nelson Coon never really stopped moving. The hoe had been snatched from a nurseryman cultivating the shrubs at the ferry parking lot—"It's a project of mine," he said; "I designed the planting"—and waved to attract our attention. As he ferried us through the island's midsummer crush of tourists with the adroitness of the New York cabbie, he provided a commentary on the points of interest between the ferry slip and his home, a very short distance.

As our visit ran its course, we rushed from garage to drive-way plantings, to houseside shrubs and trees and herbs, to compost heap and coldframe, to vegetable garden, to greenhouse, to the

Nelson Coon

table, and finally to the Coon study. As long as Nelson Coon's life has been, it's apparently only this frenetic pace that's enabled him to accomplish as much as he has.

He is at base a horticulturalist, albeit a self-taught horticulturalist. He worked at a whole slew of jobs in New York and New England, most of them related to growing plants. Then he retired to Martha's Vineyard and began a new career as an author, writing a half-dozen books, on garden fragrance, on weeds, on healing plants. For relaxation, he and his wife annually lead garden-loving tourists on a grand tour of Europe's outstanding gardens, with the arrangements handled by a New York travel agency.

Coon characterizes himself as a researcher and writer. Noting that Euell Gibbons is an acquaintance (Gibbons cites his indebtedness to Coon's scholarship in *Stalking the Healthful Herbs*), he told me that he isn't like Gibbons, who actually goes out and forages for the plants he writes about. "I do my foraging in here," Coon said, his arm sweeping along his shelves of books. Though he may be a book searcher, his searching is not done in ignorance, not after his horticultural career, not with his greenhouse and gardens. It's just that when you get to be nearly 80 you don't do all the things you did when you were younger. You slow down a bit, when you can find the time.

BONNIE FISHER

If Nelson Coon represents the wisdom of the ages, Bonnie Fisher represents the enthusiasm and curiosity of youth. She's the youngest of our contributors, but that, of course, doesn't mean she doesn't know what she writes about. She and her husband, David, are developing an herbal-based business, with aromatic products main items in the Hickory Hollow line. And if the aromatic products hadn't measured up in the marketplace, their business would have folded long ago.

The Hickory Hollow herbal products come from Bonnie's expanding herb garden. It isn't sprouting every herb imaginable or dozens of variations on a single genus. It is, rather, representative of the sort of herb garden that anyone at all interested in herbs and in gardening might easily cultivate in the backyard —though it is certainly on a larger scale. It was developed much the way you might develop yours; some plants were grown from purchased seed, others were grown from cuttings provided by friends who also have some herbs. (This latter is typical of the relationship among herb people, among gardeners in general.)

Bonnie didn't start big, rather she started with the old reliables. The last few years, she's been experimenting with mulches. If business goes well, the garden might expand.

The harvest, of course, is on a similar plane. Bonnie, knife in hand, basket by her side, cuts her herbs. Those slated for drying are hand tied and hung in the attic. Eventually they find their way into homes across the country in bottles of salad dressing and vinegar, jars of seasonings and boxes of tea, all made on the same small, personal scale.

All of it is in part a reaction, for the Fishers represent a phenomenon we at Rodale Press have been aware of for quite some time—a rising revulsion with the modern synthetic way of life. When Bonnie and David got married, they set up housekeeping in their native Ohio, he working as an engineer with one of Akron's major industries, she teaching art in that area's public schools. But the revulsion was rising, and they determined to leave. In carefully studying demographic, economic, environmental, and sociological characteristics of various potential destinations, they weren't particularly typical of their generation's drop-outs. For the Fishers were not dropping out so much as changing their life-style.

Currently established on a 112-acre mountain-side farm in a peaceful corner of West Virginia, the Fishers are determinedly pursuing their goals. They are depending directly on their own skills, and whatever help they can recruit from neighbors. Thus, their fruits and vegetables are raised on their own land, their poultry products come from their own chickens, and the improvements to their house and outbuildings are the work of Dave's and Bonnie's hands. It isn't a life-style based on ease, but on satisfaction. Their home might be considered remote, but they are neither remote from each other nor the earth. The satisfaction is there.

Bonnie Fisher

MARION WILBUR

Marion Wilbur too has left the city for the country. In early 1973, she, her husband Leonard, and the other members of the family packed their belongings and departed the Los Angeles area for Day's Creek, Oregon, for some peace and a new challenge. Like the Fishers, the Wilburs are homesteading, but unlike the Fishers, they were deeply involved in it before ever thinking about leaving their half-acre homestead in Tustin, a Los Angeles suburb.

Mrs. Wilbur wrote about landscaping with herbs, and she has some rather unusual landscaping experience. She has the usual herbal book-learning, and knows about the old traditional forms, knot gardens and mazes and labyrinths and other stiff formal exercises in horticulture that many people associate with herbs. But for the Wilburs, this sort of formality wouldn't do. Like many organic homesteaders, Marion and her family are unconventional.

Though their half-acre homestead in California had a fairly typical ranch home constructed on it, the home was surrounded

Marion Wilbur

by a greenhouse, goat and rabbit pens, compost heaps, vegetable gardens, fruit trees, and, of course, herbs. The inventory suggests everything was cheek-by-jowl, but the Wilburs pulled it off very successfully, thanks to a well-planned and executed landscape design. (In Oregon, the goats, rabbits, plants, and people have more room.) The design was successful enough to earn a few jobs in the area, tasks the Wilburs took on between tending their own gardens and animals and supplying some produce, seed, and herbs for paying customers. The place was called "Casa Yerba," and that's the name the business adopted.

A prime line for the Casa Yerba business was the herbs. Being a gardener first and an herb gardener second, Mrs. Wilbur wanted to work the herbs into her garden. She's a companion planter, and the herbs keep her vegetables and flowers relatively free of insect pests. And this was her selling point: the herbs repelled insects.

Increasingly, herbs have become significant in the lives of Marion Wilbur and her family: a source of garden beauty and fragrance first, a source of protection in the garden second, and finally a source of income.

BARBARA FOUST

Barbara Foust is just turning to her herbal hobby as a source of income. Barb is a vegetable dyer, which means she uses plant matter as dye for wool and other textiles. She lives in an old Pennsylvania German fieldstone house with her husband Earnest, a professor of English at nearby Kutztown State College, and their family. The setting of the place invites Barb Foust's sort of people and herbal sorts of plants. In a sense, it was the setting that got Barb started as a vegetable dyer. "I had 70 acres of weeds to work with," she'll laugh. She discovered that, like herb gardening, using herbs and other plants for dyeing can quickly become a driving force.

She started on a small scale, as an experiment, and soon her life revolved around herbs and dyeing. Barb Foust started going to auctions because she needed some enamelled pots for dyeing. Then she asked for scales and pots for her birthday or Christmas.

Barbara Foust

And, Barb Foust got a lamb so she doesn't have to keep buying that store's brand of wool (and so she can dye in-the-wool).

Barbara Foust has gotten so involved that she appears annually at the famous Pennsylvania Dutch Folk Festival in Kutztown to demonstrate dyeing for the cognoscenti, dilettantish festival-goers, and simple tourists alike. She gets out the hulking brass pot her family gave her and the tripod her husband and son built to hang the pot from, the dye materials and the wools and yarns, and of course the festival mufti. For ten days or so she sets up shop under the big old tree just down from the draft horse tent and up from the balloonist's jumping-off point, lights the fire under the old pot and just dyes. Like her home environment, she fits right in.

Now that she's been a festival participant for several years, and now that she's written about her dyeing, going into business seems to be the next logical step. It isn't one that you would necessarily take, but, as with other contributors, it's a part of her herbal experience.

LOUISE HYDE

Louise Hyde has a lot in common with Barbara Foust; they're friends, they're both herb lovers, they're both very involved in their avocation, to the point that they're dropping the initial "a" from it.

Louise Hyde, with her husband, Cyrus, runs Well-Sweep Herb Farm, a rapidly growing New Jersey enterprise. In addition to her share of the summertime's long daily stint in the herb patches, Louise is chief cook, producing major quantities of herbal vinegars, salad dressings, jams, and the like to supplement the farm's line of teas, seasonings, and plants. Her culinary contribution to this book is as natural a thing as her culinary contribution to Well-Sweep.

The Hydes and Well-Sweep are their own unique situation, a variation on the herb-centered life. Cyrus Hyde is an herbalist. His interest and knowledge of herbs spring from his family's interest and traditions. "Generations of my family have passed down their knowledge of herbs and their uses," he said. "When we were kids and got sick, my mother and grandmother used herb

Louise Hyde

remedies that they had learned from their mothers." For a number of years he worked as the herbalist at the Waterloo Village Restoration in Stanhope, N. J.

But during that time, he and Louise were restoring their small place in Port Murray. When they moved in in the mid-sixties, the house was rundown, the land a clutter of rocks and brush. In six years, Well-Sweep has been transformed into a bright, orderly home business. There are a couple greenhouses, formal gardens arranged around a sundial, working gardens—in all the Hydes have over 200 varieties of herbs, including eight varieties of sage, five of rosemary, 24 of thyme, 22 of scented geraniums, and nine "flavors" of mint—a drying and storage shed, and their home. In six years, the sales of plants and seeds, seasonings, and Louise's other culinary herbal products have necessitated Cyrus' full-time presence and, in season, the hiring of a good half-dozen other hands.

The hours can be long, but the rewards of honest toil and the independent life are what Louise and Cyrus Hyde were after. And knowing that, it doesn't surprise you to learn they are organic. "The Bible says that as you give, so shall you receive," says Cyrus. "We farm organically; we give the soil what it needs, and it pays us back. When you farm with chemicals, you're not giving anything back to the earth, you're destroying it."

Such an attitude strikes me as being typical of the people I worked with on this book, and it seems surely to go hand-in-glove with the herbal mystique. As ye sow, so also shall ye reap. It is a force in the Hyde's care for their home, their business, their customers; as busy as they are in season, there's always time for a tour, for an exchange of herb lore. So too with herbs. The best care and handling, both before and after the harvest, ensure the finest quality herbs, for tastes, scents, tonics, or other uses. Only a natural grown plant can offer a scent of nature, or a native flavor, or a pure, nonartificial health.

HEINZ GROTZKE

As well as anyone, Heinz Grotzke knows about reaping what you sow. He runs his business on that basis. Quality is the hallmark of his Meadowbrook Herb Garden. It begins with the soil

Heinz Grotzke

and extends through the range of the operation to the packaging and marketing. He gets a quality herbal product by growing quality herbs. In this book, his subject is growing, and he passes along the points he's determined are salient through his long years as an herb grower.

Grotzke is a European, a Teuton. As such it is not surprising that he is a proponent of the Bio-Dynamic system, which has its roots in the work of Rudolf Steiner, an Austrian philospher and educator. Bio-Dynamicists place great emphasis upon quality, upon building and maintaining the innate character of the soil, upon developing top-quality composts. As a European, it is not surprising that Grotzke is an herbalist, for the roots of herbs are deep in Europe.

Meadowbrook's herbs are widely regarded as among the best available. The quality begins with the soil, which Grotzke has been building since he started Meadowbrook in the mid-sixties. (He came to the United States originally in the fifties and managed an organic farm in Pennsylvania for several years. Then he turned to herbs, managing the justly-famous Greene Herb Garden of Greene, Rhode Island, for a number of years before striking out on his own in nearby Wyoming, Rhode Island.) The quality is thus built into the plant.

It is maintained through careful harvesting, drying, and storage. The herbs are clipped by hand, spread in large screen racks in two special rooms that can be heated to over one hundred degrees, and, when dry, stored in special voluminous paperboard barrels.

The packaging and marketing, too, are crucial to product quality in Grotzke's eyes. Only a small quantity of packaged items —about 60 jars of each kind of herb seasoning, for example—are inventoried at Meadowbrook; most of the herbs are stored in those barrels, where they will stay fresher longer. The products are sold only to retailers and through the mail. Selling to wholesalers would undercut product quality by requiring Grotzke to expand, thus surrendering a measure of his personal control over each aspect of the operation and by permitting the warehousing of huge quantities of packaged items, the freshness of each slowly being vitiated.

The process and the business tells you a lot about the owner and his personal standards. The product does too.

WILLIAM HYLTON

There is one other major contributor to this book, a contributor who can claim none of the expertise vested in the other six. The contributor is me. The contribution (in addition to the assembly of the book and the next chapter you read) is the chapter on using plants to control garden pests.

The subject is one that has grown not so much out of herbal lore as out of gardening lore. Herb gardeners may have observed the insect-repelling character in a great number of herbs, but the characteristic probably meant little to them. It *did* mean something to the vegetable gardener, however, for insects have long been a hazard of his undertaking.

I view myself as primarily a journalist: a writer and an editor. My stock in trade is putting words on paper, ideas in sequence. My editorial work in the past several years has centered on gardening and the organic idea. And I have been practicing what I've been writing about in a family vegetable garden.

Things have a way of happening, and when we got down to the wire, there was no expert to write about herbs in the vegetable garden. There were ideas, a raft of magazine articles, and a deadline. So I wrote it. Primarily, I drew on Jeff Cox's two-part article on companion planting which appeared in the February and March 1972 issues of *Organic Gardening and Farming,* an article by Richard Merrill of the New Alchemy Institute in the April 1972 *OGF,* several *OGF* articles by Ruth Tirrell, a New England gardener and herbalist, the basic book of companion planting, called *Companion Plants* (published by Devin-Adair) and information provided by Marion Wilbur.

Writing the chapter was a learning experience for me, as putting together this book has been, although as a gardener I already knew some things about herbs in the vegetable garden. A most exhilarating aspect of journalism is the challenge of taking up a new subject and immersing oneself in it sufficiently to become if not an expert, at least a skilled hand. So it has been, not only with herbs in the vegetable garden, but with the whole subject of herbs.

In the end, this project has to be regarded as one of learning and enjoyment. For several months, I was taking a full-time crash course in herbs, with six expert teachers, a reading list of fascinating and challenging resource books, a lot of visual aids, and some field trips besides. I won't claim we have the definitive herb book here, but I will claim that it answered the questions I raised and gave me enough herb project ideas to keep me going for years. It is, frankly, a reconstruction of my tour through the herbal lore. I enjoyed it and hope you do too.

Now, let's start at the beginning.

—*W.H.H.*

HERBAL
BEGINNINGS

by William H. Hylton

ONE

AN HERB ISN'T ALWAYS AN HERB

As you approach our herb garden, you are going to want to know how to characterize the plants we have in it. Herbs are herbaceous, suggesting that anything herbaceous is an herb.

If we tell you that not only is herbaceousness not the key, but that an herb isn't even always an herb, you're going to be back where you started, and you're going to be annoyed. A few minutes with a good dictionary should clarify the word games we are playing here. Herbaceousness is a botanical quality, and in our consideration of "herbs," we are not necessarily speaking in botanical terms.

The primary definition given the word herb by the dictionary is: "a seed-producing annual, biennial, or perennial that does not develop persistent woody tissue but dies down at the end of a growing season." This is the botanical definition of an herb. But this definition would eliminate from our herbal landscape plants that are traditionally regarded as herbs—rosemary or thyme, for example—as well as some plants historically regarded as herbs —like poplars and sunflowers. Tied to this definition of herbs are such words as herbaceous and herbage, which relate to the absence of woody tissue as a plant characteristic. However, the herbaceous character of a plant doesn't make it an herb for our purposes, and, since some of the plants we will be considering herbs do have woody tissues, these terms can only loosely be applied to herbs.

All of this hasn't helped us reach the definition of herb we want. The definition we want is: "a plant or plant part valued for its medicinal, savory, or aromatic qualities." The term "herb" as defined here includes a broad spectrum of plants—trees, shrubs, and herbage.

Nevertheless, this definition doesn't suit all. I've heard of a very knowledgeable herb grower, a fellow who makes his living at it, who prefers the botanical definition. But the Herb Society of America, as good an arbiter of such things as any, has always held that an herb was "any plant that may be used for pleasure, fragrance, or physic," or some variation on that theme. Our guides through this herbal maze came up with several variations of their own with perhaps the best coming from Heinz Grotzke. "My definition of herbs embraces all plants," he wrote, "that can be used for culinary and flavoring purposes, and for medicinal and veterinary uses, and that lend themselves to dyeing, smoking, cosmetics, or similar uses . . . To set herbs apart from spices, I like to limit the geographical area for herbs to the northern temperate zones around the earth."

Historically, most plants that can be categorized as herbs make it on the basis of some medicinal concoction derived from root, leaf, bark, flower, or fruit. Paging through an old herbal (which properly is a book dealing with the medicinal aspects of plants) you will find the names of hundreds of plants; some you may never have heard of, others you may have thought were weeds, still others you considered trees or shrubs (and you frankly never considered a hundred-foot poplar an herb). Could such a definition take in too many plants?

Henry Beston, in his short but delightful book *Herbs and the Earth* suggested just that. He said:

> In its essential spirit, in its proper garden meaning, *an herb is a garden plant which has been cherished for itself and for a use* and has not come down to us as a purely decorative thing. To say that use makes an herb, however, is only one side of the story. Vegetables, quasi-vegetables, herbal what-nots, and medicinal weeds are not "herbs" and never will be "herbs," for all the dictionaries. It is not use which has kept the great herbs alive, but beauty and use together. Clumsy food plants, curlicue salad messes and roots belong in the kitchen garden, in the *jardin potager,* and not with the herbs. They spoil the look of an herb garden, taking from it its inheritance of distinction; they confuse it; they destroy its unique atmosphere.

Beston's remarks advance imposing standards, although beauty,

Herbs are one of nature's many gifts to man. Throughout history, this gift has continually blessed man with its varied virtues, not the least of which is its beauty.

in the eye of the beholder, can encompass even "vegetables, quasi-vegetables, herbal what-nots, and medicinal weeds."

Euell Gibbons, in his book on wild herbs, *Stalking the Healthful Herbs,* offers a more extensive commentary on using herbs, and he suggests that a great utility of herbs stems from the beauty of these plants. "Everyone appreciates the conspicuous and flamboyant beauty of the larger wildflowers," he notes, "but how many have thrilled to the sheer beauty of the thrice-pinnate foliage of the common yarrow that grows by every roadside? How many," Gibbons continues, "have ever seen the intricate beauty of the many wildflowers that are so tiny they must be studied under a magnifying glass? Once the eye is trained to see these things, one finds that nature has surrounded us with breath-taking beauty that largely goes unobserved and unappreciated."

Gibbons *does* find beauty and utility in what-nots and weeds, and he cherishes them for themselves. And as our guide to landscaping with herbs will show you in Chapter Eight, even what-nots and weeds find utility and place in a garden of conscious design. I think Beston is too selective in establishing his standards of bloodlines, breeding, and character, for he is advocating an horticultural aristocracy. We organic gardeners tend to be more homefolks, and we opt to embrace as herbs all sorts of plants with utility, beauty, and a measure of domesticity.

BY WHAT NAME?

There is another aspect of what herbs are, and that is what you call them individually. It's fine to know what they are, but if you can't distinguish each particular kind of plant with exactitude, you are at a disadvantage.

The botanists have a system of naming plants, and many herbalists, professionals and aficionados alike, use their system. The system may put you off, partly because it seems confusing, but all the more so because many people advocate using the system without explaining how it works. However, there are good reasons for knowing the system, not so much to be able to rattle off those two-worded Latinate names, but to be able to function with the basics of the system should the need arise. The need may be sooner than you think.

Say you want to purchase thyme. If you approach a competent herb grower, you are going to be asked which thyme you want. There are dozens of varieties, but you will probably end up with *Thymus vulgaris,* the most common variety. Or suppose you are speaking to someone about herbs. You are talking about valerian. But the other party to the discussion is talking about garden heliotrope. Without the common ground the botanical names provide, you may never know you are speaking of one and the same plant, *Valeriana officinalis.*

What the botanists have done is really quite remarkable, for they have achieved an international accord establishing a uniform system for classifying and naming plants. Botanists everywhere speak the same language. There are disagreements and points of controversy, but in the main, the system works well.

The classification system includes several levels and ranges of categories, beginning with the tremendously broad divisions—there are only two—and descending with increasing specificity through classes, orders, families, and genera to species, the particular plant. Occasionally there is some slight variation within a species of plant, and the system includes a compensating factor —an extra word or two or three added to the botanical plant name.

A botanist in classifying a plant will describe the plant, becoming more and more specific, using its characteristics to move it through the categories and ultimately into a species designation. The initial step is to separate plants with flowers from plants without flowers. Plants without flowers are put in Division I and called Cryptogams; plants with flowers in Division II are called Phenerogams. The Phenerogams, which interest us, are segregated in accordance with the method of carrying the ovules, or female cells which will ultimately become the seeds. Plants, such as pines, firs, and other cone-bearers, which carry the ovules exposed are called Gymnosperms, Subdivision I, while those which carry the ovules enclosed in a fruit or other protective capsule are called Angiosperms, Subdivision II. Next there are two classes, based on the development of the seed itself at germination. Class I are the Monocotyledons, plants producing a single seed leaf, and Class II are the Dicotyledons, plants which pro-

In 1640, European settlers were beginning to spread over a new land called America, taking with them the multi-virtued plants they brought with them from Europe and discovered in their new home. This garden at the John Whipple House in Ipswich, Massachusetts, is typical of those planted in the dooryards of homes throughout Europe and America in the sixteenth and seventeenth centuries. In addition to their visual contribution to the home landscape, the herbs were valued for their fragrant, dye, culinary, and healing virtues.

duce two seed leaves. The distinctions continue, as the plants are slipped into subclasses, then orders and families, and finally into genera and species. For our purposes, it's only really necessary to understand the genera and species designations, but it may be of interest to you that a large number of the regal herbs fall into five families. These families are: Labiatae, Compositae, Umbelliferae, Boraginaceae and Cruciferae.

The common characteristics of the Labiatae (mint) family are square stems and mostly irregular, two-lipped flowers having four stamens. The fruit is small, with four nutlets (seeds). Familiar members of the mint family include peppermint, spearmint, and all the other mints, of course, but also basil, lavender, sage, rosemary, and thyme.

All members of the Compositae (Composite or sunflower) family are sun-lovers. They have either a disc flower or a ray flower. The fruits are dry and hard, a type known to botanists as achenes. The fruits often have plumes of hairs to aid in wind dispersal. Among the family members are the artemisias (southernwood, mugwort, wormwood, tarragon), tansy, calendula, chicory, and santolina.

The Umbelliferae or parsley family members often have hollow stems and flowers in flat-topped clusters called umbels. Caraway, dill, coriander, fennel, lovage, of course parsley, angelica, and chervil are all parsley family members.

Members of the Boraginaceae or borage family all have tubular flowers, mostly in curved racemes, and have five stamens attached to the tube. The ovary is superior, usually forming a fruit composed of four nutlets. The namesake of the family is probably the most famous family member.

The last, and I think least, of our five important herbal families is the Cruciferae or mustard family. Members of this family have flowers with four petals forming a square cross, four long stamens and two short ones, and the ovary is superior. Cruciferae may be important, but in our encyclopedia of significant herbs, which we compiled somewhat arbitrarily though drawing heavily upon the writings of our tour guides, only a few herbs of that family are included. Herbs of the Liliaceae family, such as garlic, chives, and Egyptian onion, appear, as well as a number of other families, such as Rutaceae, Rubiaceae, Valerianaceae, Verbanaceae, and Rosaceae. Incidentally, there are 250-300 families in the classification system, depending on what source you consult. *Gray's Manual of Botany* lists only 168.

The generic (for genus) and specific (for species) names are the heart of the Binomial System of identifying plants. The system was first proposed by Carl von Linne, a Swedish biologist and botanist who is better known by the Latinized form of his name, Carolus Linnaeus. In a sense, the Binomial System is like the bureaucratic system for handling people's names—last name first, first name last. Or more correctly, genus name first, species name second.

The generic name of a plant loosely corresponds to the family or surname of a person. Within botanical families, which might be said to loosely correspond with humanity's clans, there are groupings of similar plants, all given a generic name to identify them as to group membership. In the family Compositae there is the genus *Artemisia.* Just as we tell the Smiths apart by giving them different first names, the botanist tells the *Artemisias* apart by giving them additional names, only these names come second. So we have *Artemisia vulgaris* (mugwort), *Artemisia dracunculus* (tarragon), *Artemisia abrotanum* (southernwood), *Artemisia absinthium* (wormwood), and others.

The generic name is often derived from the Greek language, but other languages are represented as well. Sometimes the name is representative of the original plant name, of the person who discovered the genus, the place in which it was discovered, some hero of Greek mythology or ancient legend, or whatever else flitted through the mind of the person giving the name. Thus we have the *Artemisias* named for Artemis, daughter of Zeus, and the *Achillaes,* named after Achilles, the fellow with the bad heel. The genus name *Rosemarinus* is constructed of the Latin for dew or spray, *ros,* and for the sea, *marinus,* to denote the seaside habitat of the plant.

The specific names are supposed to describe the plant, but this ideal is sometimes missed. Occasionally, the name commemorates the name of the discoverer or the area to which the plant is native. Especially among the herbs, we see many plants with a specific name *officinalis* or *officinale,* which means that the plant had some commercial value, generally to the apothecary. *Vulgaris* or *vulgare* describes the species as being the common or ordinary variety of the genus.

When a variation occurs within a species, the variation is described in a word and that word is tacked on the binomial name with a "var." in roman type. Thus a variety of the common yarrow which has red, rather than white, blossoms is name *Achillae millefolium* var. *rubrum.*

Three of the vagaries of the system that can be puzzling are the variations in some of the common specific names, like *vulgare* and *vulgaris,* or *officinalis* and *officinale,* the only occasional capitalization of a species name, and the appearance, again on occasion, of a letter or apparent abbreviation in roman type after the binomial., as *Hyssopus officinalis* L. or *Levisticum officinale* Koch or, even worse, *Anthriscus cerefolium* L. Hoffm. The first, the difference in species name, is simply a rule of Latin. The two elements of the binomial must agree in gender, and the species element is the one that must agree with the genus element. It might be worth mentioning in passing that Latin was originally selected as the standard language for the botanical classification system because, at the time Linnaeus advanced the Binomial System, Latin was the language that was almost universally understood by the better-educated classes. Even today, Latin is a basic language of scientific nomenclature.

The second puzzler was simply an example of an exception to the rule. The rule is that the specific name never be capitalized —except when the species name is a former genus name. The dual capitalization occurs when a botanist reviews a plant's classification and determines that it is in the wrong genus and moves it. He may keep the old generic name as the specific name to go with the new generic name, in which case he capitalizes both elements of the binomial. It used to be that specific names derived from a specific location or a person's name were capitalized, but that practice is dying out.

The exploration and development of America meant a new burgeoning of herbal lore. The American Indians and the new Americans added their information to the lode of European herbal knowledge, committing much of it to writing. But just as much has become a rich part of the American folklore. This is the herbal lore learned from grandparents and great-grandparents. Or from herbal lorists, such as Cyrus Hyde of Port Murray, New Jersey, who have made this lore their business as well as their pleasure. Hyde makes an annual appearance at the Pennsylvania Dutch Folk Festival in Kutztown, Pennsylvania, to show herbs and tell of their lore. He operates a family herb farm too.

At Hyde's Well-Sweep Herb Farm, he and his family and their hired help cultivate a wide variety of flowers and herbs which are sold for themselves and for their uses. The herbs are started in greenhouses, hardened off in the row of cold frames (above) before sale as live plants or transplanting into the farm's spacious gardens (below). The herbs and flowers are harvested and dried (right) before packaging or inclusion in an arrangement. Well-Sweep is as unique as the Hyde family, but not unlike dozens of small herb enterprises found across the country.

The final puzzler turned out to be what journalists might call a by-line. Those few letters spell or abbreviate the name of the botanist who coined the plant name. The letter "L" is for Linnaeus (also abbreviated Linn.). The L. Hoffm. after *Anthriscus cerefolium* means simply that at some point a botanist named Hoffman reviewed Linnaeus' classification of the plant and confirmed its correctness.

One bit of shorthand that is seen quite often is the abbreviation of the genus name to the first letter, as in *A. millefolium*. The abbreviation is only used when it is clear what the genus is and when a complete binomial is being used. One wouldn't talk about the *A.'s*, one would talk about *Artemisias*. But in listing the species in a genus, one would spell out the genus only in the first name.

The botanical system of classifying and naming plants is at base quite simple, which is the major reason it works so well. Perhaps the trouble people have with it stems from the fact that it is based on a language foreign to them. *Cochlearia Armoracia* can twist your tongue if you've never seen the words before, but the more you say it and use it, the easier it becomes.

HOW WILL WE BE GUIDED?

You have the basics now, the definition of herbs, the system of proper names. Let me now, with the help of our tour guides, get specific and show you the reasons that the blue-bloods of the herbal world have that long tradition of being cherished for a variety of uses and for themselves.

It is the purpose in this tour to show you how to grow herbs and how to use them. Because you will want to understand the utility of what it is we are urging you to grow, we'll start there, with the healing, cooking, aromatic, and colorful uses of herbs. Once you've been convinced to grow them, we'll tell you how and suggest where.

"The dried leaves [of horehound] are made into a 'tea' or other drinkable form," writes Nelson Coon in the next chapter, "and this for centuries has been known as an expectorant and

tonic. The great herbalist Culpeper says: 'It helpeth to expectorate tough phlegm from the chest;' and, of course, everyone knows
the value of 'horehound candy' for rough throats. If one has
other herbs to work with, it may be combined with hyssop, rue,
licorice, and marshmallow as an excellent cough syrup."

"Basil is the 'herb of love' and is favored by many," writes
our culinary expert, Louise Hyde in Chapter Three. "Its sweet
flavor and aroma give it infinite uses, whether for main meals or
desserts. Basil is probably best known for its use with tomatoes.
It can be sprinkled over sliced tomatoes with an oil and vinegar
salad dressing, or used to make homemade tomato or spaghetti
sauce. For seasoning pizza, basil rivals oregano for first place.
Tossed salads, salad dressings, egg and cheese dishes, vegetable
dishes, poultry, and veal, as well as rolls and breads are well
seasoned with basil. When baking apples, sprinkle a few leaves
over the apples for a delicious flavor."

Lavender is justly famous for its scent, and in our aromatics
chapter, Bonnie Fisher tells how to use it for its fragrance. To
make a sachet, she relates, "collect a small bunch of lavender
flowers. Lay the flowers in a single layer to dry. When completely
dry, grind the lavender flowers to a fine powder. You can use a
mortar and pestle, perhaps a blender, or, if you happen to have
one, a flour mill. One lavender plant should produce enough
blossoms to fill twelve two-inch-square sachets. Place in small
cloth bags and sew up the openings." And later she writes: "If
your interest is merely a sweet scent in your bath water, any one
of the dozens of fragrant herbs will do. Lavender is the favorite
of many ladies, as it has been for centuries. It's used to scent
many commercial bath articles, so why not use your own garden
lavender. Moreover, lavender is reputed to be an excellent palliative for nervousness." There are other intriguing ways of captur-
ing and using the scent of lavender, but I'll let Mrs. Fisher tell
you of them in Chapter Four.

Woad is probably the only herb which measures up both to
Beston's standards and to the rigors of dyeing. In England it
was used specifically as a dye plant. Barbara Foust reports in her
chapter on dyeing that woad was not only *"the* important dye of

the Middle Ages," but also that "its extraction, in the words of a British dyer, is 'a bit of a fiddle.' "

All these herbs have been cherished for their own beauty, in gardens both formal and informal. Perhaps the purest form in which herbs were used for themselves in the landscape were the elaborate Renaissance gardens. There were mazes and labyrinths framed in herbs, the famous knot gardens, which used herbs of various sizes, densities, textures, and colors, all carefully, artfully trimmed and pruned to depict knotted cords. Indeed, these gardens were the rage and the landed aristocrats vied with one another for the honor of having the most notable garden. While a few examples of this type of gardening still exist at occasional, mostly historical sites in the northeastern United States, most of you will have to satisfy yourselves with photographs, artists' conceptions, and the verbal descriptions.

But today's gardener need not limit himself or herself to these labor-intensive but traditional forms. Herbs deserve to be a part of your home landscape, says Marion Wilbur in the final stop of our tour, even if you restrict them to a border or ground-cover. And the blue-bloods should be among your prime candidates. Beston might be upset, but these candidates can even find a cherished spot in your vegetable patch, if you have one. As shown later in the tour, these herbs and others can benefit other plants in your vegetable garden by keeping pesty insects at bay. This is a use seldom attributed to herbs in standard herb definitions, even in those cited above, yet the plants commonly regarded as having some insect repelling qualities are also plants which fall within the purview of someone's definition of herbs.

If in reading on through our herbal tour you feel moved, as I and your other tour guides hope you will, to buy some herbs or grow some herbs for teas, seasonings, a remedy, the scent or their beauty, do be sure to get the best quality. We organic gardeners use the organic technique because we believe it produces the best quality. A tomato grown organically tastes far better than one grown with the help of some chemical fertilizer and chemical insecticides and weed killers. The same is true of herbs; the herb grown organically will be far superior in taste, smell, and insect resistance than its chemically stimulated counterpart. Furthermore, you will brew a tea or season a salad with all the assurance in the world, knowing that there's no insecticide residue to vitiate or sap your constitution.

To French healer Maurice Messegue this is an important point. For years, Messegue has successfully treated a wide variety of ailments using herbal concoctions. The quality of his herbs, he says in his book, *Of Men and Plants,* is vital, as are the moment of harvest and the procedure used in the harvesting, drying, and storage of the herbs. All of his herbs are gathered from the wild. "The first rule," he explains, "is never to pick plants along main roads, where they are poisoned by exhaust fumes, nor pick plants that grow close to cornfields or orchards or vineyards, where they can absorb the harmful spray of chemical fertilizers or insecticides. Plants must be picked as far away as possible from land under cultivation." In an appendix to his book Messegue offers instructions on cultivating certain medicinal herbs and pointedly says not to use chemical fertilizers and pest killers. "You must never use insecticides, pesticides, defoliating sprays; otherwise you'll be doing more harm than good," he says.

Research by the Henry Doubleday Research Association of England substantiates such exhortations. David Greenstock of that association has discovered that the quality of garlic, at least, is effected by the growing technique. Lawrence Hills explained in an *Organic Gardening and Farming* article on Greenstock's research (which will come up again in Chapter Seven):

> David Greenstock has discovered that the active principle of garlic, now called "allicin," is a complex mixture of substances which are mainly allyl sulfides. These are produced by enzyme activity in the bulb, where their balance and effectiveness depend on the presence of assimilable sulfur. This sulfur is produced in the soil by a number of micro-organisms, mainly certain tiny fungi that cannot grow without ample humus.
>
> It is this fact that has produced varied results in the past, with emulsions made from one batch of garlic killing a pest, and then the next one leaving it leering triumphantly at the gardener. Commercial garlic bulbs, or the expensive oil made from them, could have the wrong mixture of allyl sulfides because they were grown with chemical

fertilizers and not enough humus to support the fungi, while David Greenstock's own—or those from local peasants—would have plenty. It is possible that measuring the assimilable sulfur in garlic (and probably onions) may be the first definite test to show a clear analytical difference between organically-grown and chemically-grown produce.

In his long experience as an herb grower, Heinz Grotzke has always used organic techniques—more exactly, Grotzke is of the Bio-Dynamic school—and his herbs are universally regarded as being of highest quality. The growing techniques he has learned and perfected in his years are explained in a later stop on our tour. While his techniques may vary from those used by our other guides who grow herbs themselves—as either a vocation or avocation—there's one point from which there is no variance: all our guides are advocates of the organic method.

HERBS FROM THE BEGINNING

Historically, the oldest uses of herbs always strike me as being the medicinal uses. Perhaps this is because much of the lore of herbs is derived from the herbals—the plant medicine books—and it is to these ancient volumes that we tend to turn in determining whether or not a plant may properly be called an herb. There are, of course, other herbal uses explained, but even the culinary and aromatic qualities seem tied to the curative, salutary, or hygienic properties of the plants. Sweet-smelling pomander balls and herbal bags were used not only for the olefactory esthetics involved but for the supposedly hygienic effect of the scents in the midst of the stench of rotting garbage, putrifying sewerage, disease, and death. A cook used herbs on meat not so much because the herbal flavor was appetizing but rather because the taste of meat going bad was *not*. At least psychologically, such culinary and aromatic uses had a salutary effect.

Probably because so much of the herbal lore seems to me to derive from three Elizabethan herbalists — Nicholas Culpeper, John Gerard, and John Parkinson—I tend to associate herbs in history with the Elizabethan Age. This is one of my more parochial associations, I suppose, for herbs have a far more ranging part in history. And while there are some herbs that are native to England, just as some are uniquely American, the blue-bloods are almost all of Mediterranean ancestry. And while a rich body of lore is found in sixteenth- and seventeenth-century English herbals, at least a core of that lore is derivative of material first recorded by Greek herbalists and passed through the rise and fall of Rome into the Dark Ages, emerging in the works of monks.

I have read reports of an ancient record, the Ebers Papyrus, which said that Egypt, 2000 years before Christ, had about 2000 herb doctors. The Bible, in both Old and New Testaments, makes repeated references to herbs. These references serve to substantiate the import of the ancient papyrus: that herbs were well known in ancient Egypt.

"And ye shall take a bunch of hyssop, and dip it in the blood that is in the basin, and strike the lintel and the two side posts with the blood that is in the basin; and none of you shall go out of the door of his house until the morning." The instructions from Exodus 12:22 may stick in your mind, though the identity of the herbal brush might not (it should be noted that scholars believe the hyssop of this reference is *Origanum aegyptiacum* rather than *Hyssopus officinalis,* the latter being today's hyssop). Similarly, many will recall the story of Manna, but not its description: "And the house of Israel called the name thereof Manna; and it was like coriander seed, white; and the taste of it was like wafers made with honey" (Exodus 16:31). Other references to herbs appear in the Book of Numbers and the Proverbs.

But other than these Old Testament references and the Ebers Papyrus, much of what we know about the herb knowledge of this period is somewhat speculative. We *do* know that in later years the Greeks, as you might expect, studied the herbs and commited their observations and speculations to writing. For them, too, the herbs were well known. Aristotle had a garden of more than three hundred plants reputed to have medicinal qualities, according to Theophrastus. The latter was a pupil of the great teacher and thinker and had the opportunity to study and write about Aristotle's herbs. Four centuries later, about the time of Christ's birth, Dioscorides, a Greek physician, wrote a justly remembered herbal.

Heinz Grotzke's Meadowbrook Herb Garden is a small but prosperous business built on a few acres on the edge of Wyoming, Rhode Island. In the fields surrounding the greenhouse, drying and storage buildings, and small shop, a variety of culinary and aromatic herbs are cultivated. Planting, weeding, and harvesting are all hand-labor; no chemicals are used. Mail-order sales are the heart of the operation, quality its hallmark; the herbs that are mailed from Grotzke's shipping room have been in their packaging no more than two weeks. Operations like Grotzke's are the heart of herb culture in America. They are good sources of herbs and good classrooms for learning what herbs look like and what they are used for.

Theophrastus and Dioscorides produced the most remarkable herbals, but information about herbs and references to them appeared in the works of Pliny the Elder, Galen, Vergil, and Homer. New Testament references indicate that herbs continued to be commonplace. The Greek record was passed along to the Romans, who made extensive medicinal and culinary use of herbs. Indeed, the spread of the Roman Empire might be credited with the spread of herbs, for the Roman armies carried them everywhere, planting them inadvertently in some spots, by design in others.

Where the Romans left off, the Christians picked up. In the Dark Ages, the monasteries of Benedictine and Cistercian orders were the centers of herbal activity. Individuals all over Europe had herb gardens, much as they had vegetable gardens, but the monks of these orders collected and cultivated as many varieties as they could find, serving as the most formal vehicle for the perpetuation of the use of herbs for healing. Moreover, the monks developed a record of their lore. Most of their herbals drew heavily on the works of the Greeks, and the illustrations they provided lacked any reasonable semblance to the plant depicted. Nevertheless, the contribution of these pious men was invaluable.

As civilization struggled out of the Middle Ages, the herb garden gained a new respectability and status. It still was a part of the monastery setting, and of the kitchen garden at individual homes and manors across the land. But the garden was being formalized in the capitals of the Renaissance, and the herbs were a focal point of these elaborate ornaments. As the Renaissance continued, important new contributions were made to the existing body of herbal knowledge, which had simply been regenerating for centuries. In 1475, the first wood cuts known to be used as botanical illustrations appeared. They appeared in a work called *Das Buch der Natur*, published by Konrad von Meganberg.

Slightly over one hundred years later, in 1597, the first major new herbal appeared, and it remains one of the best-known of the many the era engendered. The book is commonly known simply as Gerard's Herball. It was the work of Englishman John Gerard. Born in 1545, Gerard was a surgeon, but he made his mark in English society serving as the superintendent of the gardens owned by Queen Elizabeth's Chief Secretary of State, Lord Burleigh, and later as the apothecary to James I. His herbal made the most lasting mark, however.

The next notable herbal of the period was written by another apothecary to James I. This writer's name was John Parkinson, and his herbal *Theatrum Botanicum* was produced in 1640. Only a few years later, sometime between 1649 and 1653, came what is perhaps the most readable of the herbals of this period, the one written by Nicholas Culpeper. Culpeper's effort was based more in superstition and folklore than the works of Gerard and Parkinson. While this did contribute to the readability of the book, it also contributed to an overstatement of the value of many of the plants.

One of the more curious superstitions recorded by Culpeper (and others before him) was the Doctrine of Signatures. "And by the icon or image of every herb, man first found out their virtues," he wrote. "Modern writers laugh at them for it, but I wonder in my heart how the virtues of herbs first came to be known, if not by the signatures. The moderns have them from the writings of the ancients—the ancients had no writings to have them from."

According to this belief, the medicinal use of a plant could be determined from some element of its appearance. The spotted, lung-shaped leaves of the lungwort indicated to the ancients that it was good for curing diseased, or spotted, lungs. The hollow stalk of the garlic showed it was a remedy for windpipe ailments. Some weeds—like dandelion, plantain, yarrow, and nettles—revealed the broadness of their healing virtues through their abundance.

Equally pervasive in Culpeper's herbal is his belief in astrology. Invariably his entries on herbs include some commentary on the influence of the moon, the planets, and the constellations on the plant. (While this is regarded as the rankest form of superstition in some contemporary herb books, it should be remembered that some very successful gardeners and farmers still plant and harvest according to the phases of the moon. And while astrology may be in scientific disrepute, it is hardly in popular disrepute.)

It is perhaps worth noting that most of Culpeper's work is

still, as of this writing, in print, being available under the title *Culpeper's Complete Herbal* (Sterling). Extensive excerpts from Gerard's herbal have been published by Dover Publications under the title *Leaves from Gerard's Herball.* Selections from many old herbals are included in a number of books written about herbs.

About the time these Englishmen were collecting their herbal lore into book form, other Englishmen were moving to the New World. They were taking, along with everything else, their healing and savory plants. As had been true with all these ages, the first settlers in the new land counted on the herbs primarily for their salutary qualities. Their healing properties combatted illness, their scents masked the poor sanitation, their flavors masked bland or spoiling food.

But the New World was just that, a new land with a population and a plant world of its own. The new arrivals discovered that the native peoples had a vast herbal knowledge of their own. They discovered that some of their plants didn't thrive in the new land, while others did quite well. The upshot was the development of a new body of herbal lore, a body recorded largely by the naturalized Americans.

The American Indians formed their herbal lore much the same way other peoples formed theirs. The doctrine of signatures that Culpeper described found practitioners in America. Similarly, the Indians, like their contemporaries around the globe, were superstitious, and they based some plant uses in superstition. And of course in every age and civilization their are experimenters. However the uses were determined, the Indians did have some use for almost every plant native to their land.

What happened as the immigrants started arriving was that the Indians passed along what they knew of their plants and learned about plants that the new arrivals brought along. And the new arrivals probably taught them a few things about the native American plants, and the Indians discovered some things about the naturalized plants that the newcomers didn't know about. Herbal knowledge was rapidly expanding.

Undoubtedly the first written record of the native American herb lore was made by Juan Badianus, a native Mexican Indian doctor. Badianus had been educated by priests and in 1552 wrote a manuscript, in Latin, recording native medical practices. The exchange of herbal knowledge between the new and old worlds was begun in the seventeenth century by two Englishmen, William Wood and John Josselyn. In 1634, Wood published in London a book titled *New England Prospect,* basically reporting on the new world as he observed it. The book included a chapter, "Of the Hearbes, fruits, woods, waters . . ." Josselyn's book was published in 1672, again in London, and its almost interminable title admirably captured the gist of the text: *New England's Rarities Discovered: In Birds, Beasts, Fishes, Serpents, and Plants of that Country. Together with The Physical and Chyrurgical Remedies wherewith the Natives constantly use to Cure their Distempers, Wounds and Sores. Also A perfect Description of an Indian Squa in all her Bravery; with a Poem not improperly conferr'd upon her. Lastly A Chronological Table of the most remarkable Passages in that Country amongst the English.*

Other writings and researches on the uses of plants followed, of course. In the late seventeenth century, the first arboretum was established in America by a Bavarian named Johann Kelpius, who was residing in Germantown, outside of Philadelphia. Kelpius was interested in testing the medicinal plants he had heard about from the Indians.

Philadelphia was also the home of the man who brought official medical recognition to the Indian herbal cures. Dr. Benjamin Rush, a respected physician, investigated the cures and published his findings. His work spawned a flurry of compilation activity and soon a variety of guides to Indian medicines was available. Perhaps the most notable and valuable of them was written by Dr. Benjamin Smith Barton, a fully accredited physician. Barton, another Philadelphian, lived from 1766 to 1815. His written work was called the *Materia Medica of the United States.*

One of the more weighty of the guides was an 800-page, $20 manual published in 1822, the work of a self-taught physician named Samuel Thomson. The New Hampshire native soon discovered that his most efficacious prescriptions were being widely

Some herbs are cultivated on a surprisingly large scale. In southern California, vast fields of safflower such as these are the basis for the safflower oil industry. In other sections of the country, herbs are grown to supply seasonings for the food industry and drug plants for the pharmaceutical industry.

duplicated and often misrepresented. In 1813, Thomson selected certain of his plant compounds, those most useful in treating easily diagnosed ailments, and had them patented. It began the era of the patent medicine, a notable though not necessarily illustrious period. For his trouble, Thomson found himself in almost perpetual litigation for the remaining thirty years of his life. Then as now the medical establishment didn't appreciate the work of non-establishmentarians.

Although it would probably have to be concluded that

Thomson failed in his attempt to protect the unwary from the unscrupulous with his medicine patents, the patenting of medicines to widen their availability did provide a major impetus to growers of medicinal herbs. Diligent though they might be, the backwoods plant foragers simply could not meet the demand. Growers stepped into the gap.

Among the most interesting of the growers were the religious communities established in various locations throughout the eastern United States by the Church of the United Society of Believers, more commonly known as the Shakers. The first Shaker medicinal herb garden was cultivated in New Lebanon, New York in 1820. Thirty-seven years later the Shakers were still cultivating medicinal plants, the New Lebanon community having marketed some seventy-five tons of plants its members raised and dried. The Shaker product list included well over 300 kinds of seeds, flowers, leaves, and barks, as well as a nearly equal number of medicinal preparations. The Shakers continued their herb-growing business into the second half of the twentieth century, giving it up only when sharply dwindling community membership forced them to.

The tendency exists to attribute such things as the decline of the Shaker herbalists to a decline in interest in plant medicines, but this is not strictly true. Scientific and technological developments in the twentieth century have led to increasing use of synthetics in pharmaceuticals, but there remain a large proportion of medicinal substances that can reasonably be derived only from plants. Nearly half of all prescriptions contain some drug derived from a plant. In 1967 alone, medicinal plants accounted for $300 million worth of pharmaceutical business. Thus there has been a steady demand for medicinal plants, a demand emphasized during and after the two World Wars, chiefly because of the embargoes and increased needs endemic to war. The wars seemed also to spawn revivals of popular interest in herbs.

One result of the first revival was a two-volume work called *A Modern Herbal.* The author, Mrs. Maude Grieve, an English-woman, was a leader in the revival and wrote a number of books. Her herbal is probably the most thorough and up-to-date book of its type. Undoubtedly, quite a number of the other herbals and herb books of twentieth century origin can be traced to one or another of the revivals.

This view of herbal history, of course, reflects a Caucasian view of civilization. But a fabulous lode of herbal lore, and the people who are perhaps today's most accomplished herbalists, are found in the Oriental half of the world. If one accepts the Oriental, predominently Chinese, herbal lore at face value, one accepts the Chinese lore as the oldest in the world. The dates traditionally given for the writing of the oldest Chinese herbal would, if true, make it nearly a millennium older than the Ebers Papyrus.

This oldest of the Chinese pharmacopoeias, *Pen-ts'ao* (or *Herbal)*, is reputed to be the work of the Emperor Shen-nung, a great cultural hero who is said to have lived from 3737 to 2697 B.C. Shen-nung is said to have compounded and self-tested hundreds of herbal preparations, aided by a transparent abdomen which enabled him to observe the workings of his internal organs. The freakish condition was undoubted a gift of legend, rather than of nature. Recorded in the *Pen-ts'ao* are 365 medical preparations, all but 51 of which are herbal.

The emperor who succeeded Shen-nung was also interested in medicine and prepared his own medical text. The book, *Huang-ti Nei-ching* or *The Yellow Emperor's Classic of Internal Medicine,* is less of an herbal and more of a comprehensive review of the state of medical arts in China. It is presented as a dialogue between the Yellow Emperor, Huang-ti, and his chief minister, Ch'i Po. Huang-ti is said to have ruled from 2697 to 2595 B.C.

The authenticity of both these works is in question, however. The ancient Chinese had a propensity for attributing their writing to older sources in hopes of bolstering their value, and such is probably the case here. Studies have placed the two in the first millennium before Christ, making them not as old as the Ebers Papyrus. Despite the discrepancies of the dates, the *Pen-ts'ao* and the *Huang-ti Nei-ching* are valuable and legitimate old herbals.

The Chinese are undoubtedly the leading contemporary herbalists. Herb remedies are a mainstay of traditional Chinese medicine, which is enjoying an officially approved revival in the People's Republic of China. Medicinal herbs are grown in small but intensive gardening operations, then dried and compounded in drug shops such as this. The mixtures of leaves, seeds, and other ingredients are infused with boiling water by the patient and taken as a tea or as otherwise prescribed.

Some time prior to the birth of Christ, the Chinese and their neighbors in India exchanged medical information, enhancing the knowledge of both peoples. Curiously, though the Eastern and Western civilizations centuries later opened trade, there was apparently never an exchange of medical information, to the extent there was here and in the contacts between the Europeans and the American peoples. Nevertheless, the herbal knowledge developed in China and other Oriental countries is almost completely compatible with that developed by the Westerners.

The first major Chinese medical work to be translated into Western languages was the *Materia Medica of Li-Shih-Chen,* a masterpiece written by Li-Shih-Chen during the sixteenth century. A great compendium of remedies, it listed 12,000 prescriptions and formulas and analyzed 1,074 plant substances, 443 animal substances, and 354 mineral substances. The book is still studied by traditional Chinese physicians, who are very important people in Chinese medicine today.

For unlike the Western nations, where the typical medical practitioner disdains intuitive folk medicine practices, the Chinese today are basing their research and practice on the traditional theories and techniques. The Chinese typically steer their own course, but during the regime of Chiang Kai-shek (1912-1949), the western influence was officially favored and traditional medicine fell into disrepute. With the ouster of Chiang in 1949 came a resurgence of Chinese nationalism. The guiding principle today has been articulated by Chairman Mao: "Chinese medicine and pharmacology are a great treasure house. Efforts should be made to explore them and raise them to the highest level."

Joining in the rise to the highest level are the herbal remedies. Herbs are widely cultivated, chiefly for their medicinal qualities. Even military installations have prominent herb gardens, each plant carefully labeled, from which plant medicines are derived and in which the soldiers are taught to identify medicinal plants, to enable them to forage for healing plants in field situations. Paramedical personnel work closely with the people, using herbal remedies to a great extent. Moreover, as one Western observer put it, "Everyone in China is a little bit of an herbalist. The housewives, the farmers, and even the school children grow herbs and learn to recognize them. Furthermore, herbs are easily available at stores, are extremely cheap, and are reasonably safe to use." Coupled with the resurgence on the popular level is the emphasis on clinical and laboratory research on the healing plants. Of course, there is some interest in this work throughout the world, but the Chinese seem to be the leaders.

In the United States today there seems, too, to be a resurgence of popular, and to some degree scientific, interest in herbs. The spread of information on the current Chinese culture may be a contributing factor. But those of us associated with Rodale Press and the organic philosophy have been observing this herbal revival for a number of years. And it is not one of interest strictly in healing plants. This revival is due to a complex of reasons, which seem to add up to a growing dissatisfaction with the synthetic way of doing things. More and more people are turning to gardening, to homesteading or part-time farming, to home crafts, to quieter and simpler pleasures. And certainly herbs are a quiet, simple pleasure, yet a pleasure that shouldn't be denied as too modest. The pleasure of herbs is a never-ending one, rooted in the fact that herbs are a way of life.

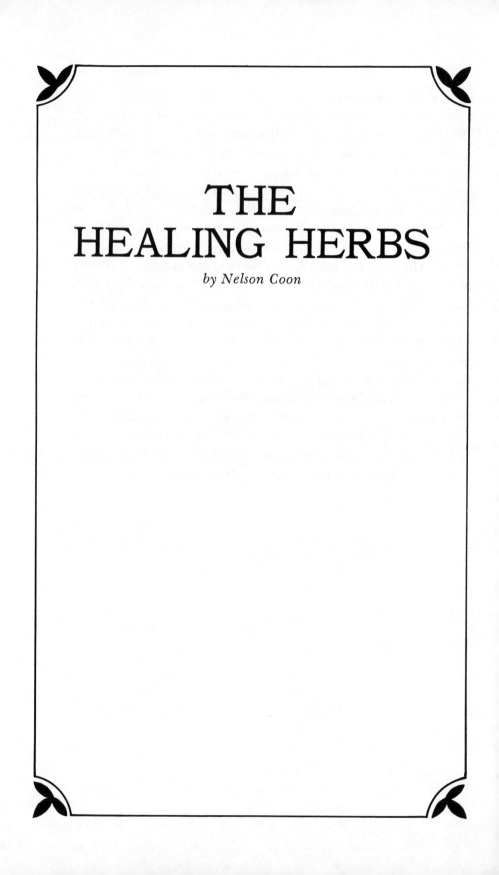

THE
HEALING HERBS

by Nelson Coon

TWO

Few indeed are the inhabitants of this world of ours who are not subject to the need, at one time or another, of medicines or of the advice from those who are accepted as knowledgeable either through local or tribal education or who, even without much education, are acknowledged by society to have "powers." Such practitioners have high status, either as influential "medicine men" or, as today in our Western Civilization where the prestige of our medical profession and the protection of "their" rights is too well known.

Yet, as these words are being written, even American doctors, with supposed total knowledge, are taking a second look at millenia-old acupuncture, and pharmaceutical companies are widely exploring the alkaloid and other property contents of as many as 40,000 plant species, looking to find those plant qualities which have for centuries made for their use as healing agents among uneducated (by our standards) primitive tribes.

It is interesting to note that the knowledge of the truly healing properties of plant materials was accepted almost immediately by those who came from Europe to settle among the long-established and herb-knowing Indians. First to do so were the Spaniards who reported to their emperor that not only did the Mexicans have a great pharmacopeia, but had medicinal-plant test gardens, actually the first in the world of such, which were to become in Europe several centuries later, places which we now know as botanic gardens. In 1552, in Mexico, the now famed Badianus manuscript was written which pictures and describes the use of hundreds of local plants, to be followed within a century by more intensive study of such uses by Hernandez. Actually, the use of these medicines is still going on as a part of modern medicine in that land below our borders.

In Canada, we find considerable early observation of the ways of the Iroquois with native medicines—medicines which then seemed to promote noticeable longevity, except as the introduced diseases of the Europeans produced epidemics and circumstances beyond their native knowledge. The Dutch in New York also recognized the values of native medicines. One member of the New Netherlands colony in 1650, identified some 30 herbs as being of basic Indian medicinal value. Nor should we fail to note the Indians' use of sassafras. which was so prominent in inviting exploration.

The adaptation of these native plant remedies into our own American medicine was perhaps retarded by the feeling of the immigrants from Europe who felt they had superior knowledge, plus the questionable (to them) nature of the rituals which the Indians often added in applying medicines. But the values of plants such as the aforementioned sassafras, of ginseng, of maidenhair fern, and finally of willow bark (containing what we have now synthesized as aspirin), these and many other practices, all made up much of our early medicinal knowledge.

Of much recent interest, however, in finding out about plant medicines, is the sending of explorers to the vast areas of the Amazon basin, to Africa, and to other places still inhabited by tribes depending on centuries of acquired knowledge, where, through intensive search, much new knowledge is being found of use to world doctors and pharmacists. I am thinking here of the great work of Richard Evans Schultes, who has written widely of his twelve years living among the Indians of the Amazon. As Professor of Biology at Harvard and director of its Botanical Museum, he has told much about the special interest of his explorations—especially of the plants which we call hallucinogens (as well as other more usual healing drugs).

In an address at the 100th anniversary of the Arnold Arboretum he told of his regrets of "the progressive divorcement of primitive peoples, to a greater or lesser degree, from dependence upon their immediate ambient vegetation." While admitting that aspirin, for instance, may be more efficient than native herbal remedies and magic, he feels that such uses may start an "astonishing disintegration of native medicinal lore." Then at the end of his address he said that "what does interest us is the almost certain loss in the next half century of the greater part of America's nature herbal lore. Our search amongst the Plant

The mortar and pestle was once an indispensible tool of the pharmacist, used to grind medicinal botanicals, among other substances, when compounding prescriptions. Though it remains a symbol of the drugs in the drug store, it is used very little today.

Kingdom's half million species for new medicines will then have lost a most valuable and promising field of exploration."

The purpose of this chapter is to list the values that have been placed on a selected few of the wild (and some cultivated) herbs, from every part of the United States, which have been used or recommended as medicinal aids. It is the hope that such a listing will encourage the reader to pursue further his study and use of such medicines, and to keep this knowledge from being lost. It is obviously not possible within the limits of just one chapter, to detail the collecting, preparation, and formularies for preparing and taking medicines. To the end of aiding the reader in pursuing his interest, an extensive bibliography has been prepared (see Appendix C). Actually the use of this or that plant for a particular medicinal need is often quite different in different parts of our country. The kind of plant used for a disease must, quite naturally, depend on the plants which grow in a district, obviously varying from Cape Cod to the Southwest desert. Every interested person, then, should arm himself with one or another extensive herbal, and as well, with one of the new regional wild flower guides, such as those published by the New York Botanical Garden.

Throughout the study of plant life, careful attention should be paid to the scientific nomenclature, even when the plant is well known by a common name or names. For, and especially with medicinal plants, considerable knowledge can be gained by studying the many specific names which have been given to the plant through the years since Linnaeus first gave scientists in every field a now accepted system of nomenclature.

For instance, one will find many plants which are named *officinale,* which means that the plant has been known as an official drug plant. Then one will discover a number of plants which bear a common name of "wort," which again indicates that they are used for healing. A common name of "healing-herb" will naturally make one stop to think of a possible use, as would "cancer-root" or "fleabane." Anything with "bane" added would likely have been used medicinally. And what would one expect from "flux root," or "horse balm," or "alum root"?

It should be noted that within the last decade, the medical "experts" are finding deleterious side effects resulting from using chemical compositions which otherwise have demonstrated known values in healing. These effects are not known to happen with the perhaps less fast-working herbal remedies which, again, may have similar but less potent values. It seems unlikely at this point that medicine will turn back to plant sources for all the needed remedies, but it is certain that there is, at present, renewed interest in the natural chemicals which are found in healing herbs. We are, it seems, entering a new period of understanding of the wonders and workings of Nature.

In presenting some samples of the many hundreds of plants which have medicinal values, it should be understood that only a selected few of the various values of plants have been listed here. The number of diseases and afflictions of mankind are manifold, and the remedies of botanical origin are truly of a staggering number. What might be used for one condition on the East Coast would differ widely from those used in the Mid-west or West.

Too, the preparation and method of using this or that plant is variable and often highly involved. It should be obvious that detailed instructions on how to prepare concoctions from each and every plant, which would run all the way from simple infusions to complicated salves, cannot be given. Neither would it be wise within the limits of such a discussion to prescribe doses of even the most simple of medicines, as both diagnosis and prescription must be done with some knowledge of immediate circumstances. Thus readers should be warned not to chew leaves, bark, or roots of plants mentioned, nor "stew them up," without full investigation of how this is done or in what quantity prepared medicines are taken. There are pharmacological books which give this information, or a good method would be to take advice from a friendly neighbor who may have had the knowledge passed down from a parent or grandparent. Or, do as I do, try to find salves and concoctions which are indicated as being of plant origin, which may come from an herbalist or the drug store. One *can* be one's own doctor with plants, but it is rarely wise.

Of course, there are simple things such as knowing that the juice of the *Aloe vera* is an instant cure for kitchen burns; that chewing peppermint is likely to aid a digestive disorder; or knowing that the eating of blackberries will modify diarrhea, just as too much rhubarb will have the opposite effect. And there are more involved things, such as the following simple instructions on how to prepare some—but not all—of the medicines discussed in the listings which follow.

The simplest of preparations is an infusion which can be mixed with juice and drunk or applied directly, depending on the injury. To make an infusion, bruise the plant and add a quart of water.

Tinctures which are used only for outside applications are made by taking one or two ounces of the powdered herb or plant and adding a quart of alcohol. Let stand two weeks.

Essences, used like tinctures, are made by dissolving one or two ounces of the essential oil (s) in a quart of alcohol.

Teas can be made to taste by simmering a cup or a pot of herbs on

the stove. Some plants will lose their potency if boiled, though, and these can be mixed with cold water until ready to use—it takes longer but tastes the same.

Naturally, not all medicines can be prepared in these basic ways, and generally, more extensive herbals should be consulted. Complete details can be found in such a standard reference as *A Modern Herbal* by Mrs. M. Grieve and a standard American pharmaceutical work such as the *Textbook of Pharmacognosy* by Heber W. Youngken (Blakiston, 1948). Other valuable and helpful books are those cited in the bibliography, but these two are "musts" for the herbal "doctor."

The listings that now follow are for the purpose of suggesting uses which have been made of many American medicinal plants, all of which the reader might explore in one way or another. Some of the plants are found in the lists of pharmaceutical plants, some are plants which once were highly regarded and have now been superseded by synthesized drugs, while a number of plants mentioned may be those which are listed as having "reputed values." Thus, in all of this matter of plant drugs, one might say in the Latin form *Caveat qui utitut* (Let the user beware).

In conclusion, it may be of interest to go back some three hundred years and see what was then said about the matter. For, as everyone knows, "history repeats itself," in many phases of our lives, and in reading this quotation think of it as something which might truthfully be said today.

THE HOME HERBALIST

In the knowledge of simples, wherein the manifold wisdom of God is wonderfully to be seen, one thing would be carefully observed . . . which is, to know what herbs may be used instead of drugs of the same nature, and to make the garden the shop; for home-bred medicines are both more easy for the parson's purse, and more familiar for all men's bodies. So, where the apothecary useth either for loosing, rhubarb, or for binding, bolearmena, the parson useth damask or white roses for

The patent medicine is one of nineteenth century America's most infamous but colorful contributions to herbal lore. Most contained a long list of herbs and were alleged to remedy an equally long list of ailments.

the one, and plantain, shepherd's-purse, knot-grass for the other, and that with better success. As for spices, he doth not only prefer home-bred things before them, but condemns them for vanities, and so shuts them out of his family, esteeming that there is no spice comparable for herbs to rosemary, thyme, savory, mints; and for seeds to fennel and carraway-seeds. Accordingly, for salves, his wife seeks not the city, but prefers her garden and fields, before all outlandish gums. And surely hyssop, valerian, mercury, adder's tongue, yarrow, melilot, and St. John's wort made into a salve, and elder, camomile, mallows, comphrey, and smallage made into a poultice, have done great and rare cures.—*A Priest to the Temple;* or the *Country Parson, his Character and Rule of Holy Life.* 1652.

PLANTS AND YOUR EARS

As with many plants which are discussed in this chapter, a number have been described in the old herbals as being good for most anything from head to foot, and in many cases, the values attributed to some plants are beyond belief. But in the instance of plants for treating affections of the ear, only one is worth mentioning and that is an ear-oil made with the leaves of the lovely roadside great mullein. The flowers are to be picked and steeped in olive oil and the extract thus made used as eardrops for an earache or discharges from the ear.

PLANTS AND YOUR EYES

The notable herbal book called *Herbal Simples* by Fernie gives a whole column of names of plants which are said to be good for alleviating eye soreness, improving the sight, or other conditions; but responsible pharmacologists do not concur in such values. One plant, which bears the interesting name of eyebright *(Euphrasia officinalis)* has been used in olden times in Europe, but does not grow here, and its value is questionable. Such kitchen garden herbs as fennel, rue, and trefoil also have such listed uses, but again their use is not recommended.

Extracts from the sagebrush of the American West *(Artemisia tridentata)* have been used for the eyes as well as from the plant called salsify *(Tragopogon porrifolius)*. Again there is considerable record of the Indians using an extract of the bark of several sorts of the maples *(Acer)* for sore eyes.

Mullein was known primarily as a remedy for respiratory ailments. Although the leaves are the primary part used, the flowers can be gathered when fully open, and when dried, are just as effective when made into a soothing infusion.

Some minor experimenting with such medicines for eyes might be done by the modern herbalist, but in view of the very delicate nature of the eyes, consult your opthalmologist before herbal treatment is undertaken.

TEETH AND TWIGS

In writing these short comments on the use of plant material for improving conditions of the teeth, my mind goes to TV advertising in which it is recommended that your dog be given some very hard chewy biscuits as food *to improve his teeth and gums.* The same advice may well be given to man. Indians are known to have used the hard crushed dogwood stems as tooth-brushes. These sticks and those of hazelnut would both be useful to chew on to exercise the gums and to help extract food from the teeth. In the case of "natural" material, there is still no better toothbrush than one made from hard natural bristles.

All authorities on uses of plants for medicine seem to agree that the acid juice of strawberries is of considerable value in dissolving tartar on the teeth. And everyone knows the value of the oil of cloves in alleviating a sudden toothache; or, in the absence of this, of getting some relief from oil of peppermint. Some Indian tribes used a chew of tobacco for this purpose, relying on what we all know to be the sedative value in tobacco. In the case of the child cutting his first teeth, some tribes used to give the children the roots of the marshmallow plant to chew on.

Among the herbal medicine-makers of the eighteenth century, one finds that mouth washes were made of a tincture of bayberry, of myrrh, and of golden seal or, in another recipe a combination of chloride of soda, of bayberry, myrrh, and essence of sassafras.

All these early uses of plants for the care of the teeth are beneficial, which tends to show the pressure we are subjected to in modern advertising to use modern pastes and powders which probably are no better (or not as good as) the old natural cures.

SOAP AMONGST THE PLANTS

It may seem strange to talk about soap among the medicinal plants, and yet cleanliness and sanitation head the list of good health. While it may not be necessary for everyone to make soap from wild plants, it is interesting to note the plants containing substances which act the same as the household soap.

One of these, in fact, is peculiar in its values and bears the name of soapwort *(Saponaria ocymoides),* which is a common and beautiful pink-flowered wild plant. The roots of this, gathered when the plant is in flower, are made into suds by pounding in water. It has long been known as a soap and is especially recommended for washing rare silks, as it not only cleans, but imparts a little sheen to silk, not otherwise obtainable. From the Indians on our East Coast we know that the flowering heads of sweet pepper bush *(Clethra alnifolia)* can be stripped off when one is in the swampy woods (perhaps blueberrying) and be used as a good soap.

In the western part of our country, a plant such as the Yucca can be made into a soap by chopping up the roots and crushing in water. The roots of *Chenopodium californicum* can be similarly used. One western plant called amole or soapplant *(Chlorogalum pomeridianum)* provides a lathery soap by crushing the heart of the plant's bulb. In another family either the

The roots of the yucca plant can be chopped and soaked in water to extract a soapy substance the western Indians used for washing. The shoots of the plant can be double-boiled to produce a winelike liquid which was used by the Indians as a stimulating tonic.

ground root or the raw ground gourds from the buffalo ground root *(Cucurbita foetidissima)* makes a soapy substance. Again a number of species of the *Ceanothus* shrub provide soapiness from the fresh flowers crushed in water.

Hence, whether one is at home or across the country, nature provides plants useful for purposes quite beyond food or medicine.

PLANTS AGAINST THE ITCH

However free from many of the diseases discussed in this chapter the reader may be, there are likely few among humans who have not been subject to an itch of some kind. And yet here, with all the thousands of plants there are in the world, only a few are recognized as a help for a plain and simple itch. Among these, only two stand out as being generally agreed to have such a value.

One plant which grows in most of the United States is *Rumex crispus,* a common narrow-leaf dock which is equally useful as a spring green, or delightful as an ornamental seed stalk for flower arrangers. For use medicinally for the itch the leaves are boiled in vinegar until the fibre is softened and then combined with lard to make a simple ointment.

In the Far West, similar values can be found in a number of species of *Grindelia,* the gum-plant, a widely found shrub, and here a fluid extract of the plant is recommended for not only the itch, but as an alleviant for cases of ivy poisoning.

Two plants which are found in older herbals as being useful for the itch are leaves of the common pansy or of the violet; while another plant from Europe, now naturalized in much of the United States is the figwort or celandine, *Ranunculus ficaria,* which has astringent properties and was once recommended for itch.

Among the household remedies for the itch is a poultice made of cornstarch, while simple fresh lemon juice may be quickly and efficaciously applied to itching spots.

For use in cases of itching in my own home, a useful ointment is made according to an old Indian formula using extracts of a number of plants of astringent qualities, which combine to produce a helpful effect.

ANTISEPTICS

Allium sativum: More and more these days that ancient vegetable, garlic, is being suggested as good medicine, certainly as a flavor for food, and because easy to grow (as well as buy), it is a basic herb. Here it is being offered as an antiseptic, for which purpose it was used in difficult times in England in World War I, when the raw juice of garlic was diluted with water and applied with sphagnum moss as a bandage.

Baptisia tinctoria: Indigo broom is one of the common wild plants with mildly antiseptic qualities.

Cornus florida: Dogwood bark contains gallic acid which when used with other constituents is valuable as an antiseptic.

Gentiana catesbaei: Extracts of the blue gentian are somewhat antiseptic.

Hamamelis virginiana: Witch hazel has long been known and used as an astringent and hemostatic and because of its sharp sting is often listed as an antiseptic.

Plantago major: The common plaintain is a medicinal plant used as a very mild antiseptic.

Quercus alba: The bark of an oak has long been known to have antiseptic qualities.

Rhus glabra: The bark of the smooth sumac is listed in many herbals as an antiseptic.

Sphagnum (various species): The living plant which dying and after centuries buried becomes the peat moss of gardening is not only a superior absorbent material, but the acid water in which it grows has definite antiseptic qualities and can be used as an emergency antiseptic.

ASTRINGENTS

An astringent, according to the dictionary, is a medicine, from plants or otherwise, which "contracts the soft organic textures and checks discharges of blood, mucus, etc." It is not, in this sense, anything such as the dried species of puffballs, which will coagulate blood; but, as it says, something "which tends to contract external or internal fleshy parts."

Many who are in touch with the common values of plant products know well that oak bark and sumac have these qualities. For internal use, a common tea is made from the dried leaves of one of the species of camellia. Blackberry is "astringent" in the intestinal tract, while witch hazel is good externally.

Beyond this, there is in the flora of our great wide America, many plants which have in their roots, bark, leaves, or seeds, similar qualities and just a few of them are reviewed below.

Arctostaphylos uva-ursi: The common, wide-spread, and attractive ground cover, the bearberry (to use one of a score of names) provides in a tea made of its dried leaves, a long used "disinfectant in urinary disorders."

Chimaphila umbellata: From the same family as the plant above, the pipsissewa, a well known wild plant, has similar values to bearberry.

Eucalyptus globulus: The eucalyptus trees have come to us from Australia, but the oil extracted is found now in many common medicines, among its values being as an astringent in throat troubles.

Cornus, various species: There are a few recommendations in herbals for the use of extractions of dogwood bark for medicinal uses including that of astringent.

Geranium maculatum: One of the wild members of the *Geranium* genus, the alum root provides in its dried rhizome (root) qualities used for cure of hemorrhoids.

Hypericum punctatum: The flux weed (note medicinal name) is known for various internal uses made of it, the name making it hard not to guess one of them.

Ilex verticillata: The bark of the black alder has astringent qualities used either externally or internally.

Myrica cerifera: The wax myrtle has other uses than in providing wax for candles, including that of medicine made of the dried root bark as an astringent for external ulcers.

Polygonatum biflorum: This plant, the hairy solomon's seal, is used along with other plants for an internal medicine with astringent properties.

Quercus, various species: Oak bark likely has astringent properties, but here the most valuable medicine is made from an extraction of the concentration of such values, found in the round oak galls (little brown balls often seen) which are really a hatchery home grown around an insect egg. Such galls are much used, especially in tanning.

Rhus glabra: The ornamental red seed heads of the smooth sumac used to be collected and dried by the Indians as a source for "winter lemonade," but incidentally, and likely known to them, there are qualities here which make the drink an excellent astringent gargle.

PLANTS FOR SORES

There are, among the wild plants of this country, many plants which in one way or another, have qualities in their "juices" which may be soothing, or astringent, or have other qualities which tend to reduce soreness in one or another exterior part of the body. Virginia Scully in her book on the uses of herbs by the American Indians lists many such plants used by one or another tribe, beginning one paragraph with:

> There were dandelion, milkweed, cinquefoil, or elder poultices for swellings or sores. Curly dock was highly favored, running a close second to the invaluable balsam root. Poultices to reduce swellings were made also from boiled lamb's quarters, chewed locoweed, or crushed fresh flax leaves, . . .

Thus in this page one can but look at a few plants which have been noted in modern herbals as being good for sores, external or internal. For instance in the case of canker sores in the mouth (or for thrush in children) medicine made from the whole plant or the roots of gold thread or mouthroot *(Coptis groenlandica)* has long been used in one way or another. One recipe calls for using one ounce of crushed root in a pint of diluted alcohol for an ulcerated mouth.

Plants such as the aloe or the houseleeks have juices recommended elsewhere for healing burns, and those also would have some value in other external sores. Another plant whose common name, healing herb *(Symphytum officinale),* indicates it is of value in sores of various kinds. It is used by beating up the whole plant to bring out the juices and then applying the material directly to the inflamed sores.

As previously indicated, the crushed seeds of flax *(Linum usitatissimum)* have long been used and applied as a poultice for sores as well as the oil (linseed) used as a part of many healing medicines.

Another plant, the seeds of which may be substituted for flaxseed, is the common plantain *(Plantago major)*, the use of which will help to rid the lawn and garden of a difficult weed. One reliable reference notes that: "Rubbed on parts of the body stung by insects, nettles, etc., or as an application to burns and scalds, the leaves will afford relief and will stay the bleeding of minor wounds."

A careful reading of all the literature on plant remedies shows, as here, that there are multiple uses of plants for medicinal purposes and, with all of the present findings of secondary effects of many synthetic drugs, it behooves everyone to know about relying on such simple uses of plants.

STINGS AND BITES

In surveying all the literature relating to the use of plants and plant products for the alleviation of pain and the effects from bites and stings, it would seem that few of the recommendations are reliable. Plants such as those with a common name like rattlesnake root or button snakeroot have but little history of results with snake bites, and the best thing in such cases is to have your doctor phone to the nearest poison control center and describe the condition.

With minor bites from bees, mosquitoes, and other small insects, one recommendation would be to rub the part with the juice from honeysuckle vines, or such herbs as rue and chamomile.

Often called knitbone for its reputed value in healing bone fractures, comfrey also has a reputation as the "healing herb." The large leaves and the root were beaten and applied as a poultice to sprains, swellings, bruises, and sores.

Plain vinegar, too, will be of possible help and so, too, would be rubbing the affected part with the juices of *Aloe vera,* as recommended for burns.

Additionally there are proprietory remedies from the drug stores which one should not hesitate to take, and as well a number of repellants which one can spray here and there where infestation and circumstances indicate. Here, whether it be snake bites or bee stings, prevention is often easier than cure.

PLANTS FOR TREATING POISON IVY

If there is one "disease" which can afflict at any age and in any part of this country, it is that of ivy poisoning, for in one species or another, plants of the poisonous forms of the genus *Rhus* are found from coast to coast. In the East, there is the species which we know as *Rhus radicans* (syn. *R. toxicodendrom*) which may be called poison ivy or poison oak, and which may be variable in foliage and growth. In eastern swamps *Rhus vernix* may be found, the poison sumach, or poison dogwood, a tall shrub with nice white fruits, fine for decorating if one dared to pick them. On the entire West Coast, one finds *Rhus diversiloba,* called there the poison oak.

The poison is in the form of an oily substance which may be effective with contact, or even from the smoke from burning brush. Whenever contact has been known, or suspected, there are a number of things to do.

First, in the East, one finds nearby growths of the jewelweed plant, *Impatiens pallida* or *biflora,* and crushes the juices from the stems on the affected parts. As a result, there is a chance of stopping the poison immediately. If operating in a camp in the woods, a quantity of jewelweed boiled down makes a good treatment for all who have been in the woods for a time. Prevention is better than cure.

A second plant which is found in barren country in the East is that of the sweet fern *(Comptonia asplenifolia)* where the oil from the "fern" seems to dissolve that of the ivy.

A third plant which has been rated to have some value here is the mugwort *(Artemisia vulgaris)* a widely naturalized plant from Asia.

For those living in the Far West, there seem to be two plants which have similar values. One is the yerba santa, *Eriodictyon californicum,* and the other is the gum-plants, various species of *Grindelia,* of which there are a number of western species. The success in use of any of these plants in alleviating the distress of poison ivy, cannot be guaranteed, varying much between persons, just as does the poisoning by the ivy itself—as some persons seem to be immune.

PLANTS FOR HEALING BURNS

Possibly the most common demand in the world is for a healing agent for the common burn. In the past a number of plants have been rated as healing for burns and various concoctions have been made. For years I have used a salve passed along by some Indians to a friend—a salve containing white oak bark, black ash bark, red sumac berries, marshmallow root, borax, and a eucalyptol. Always effective for burns and itches and the like, each plant adds some extra quality.

Today the most accessible plant for a cure for burns, is the healing aloe, which from personal experience and that of many people, is a quick and certain cure for any minor burn. The juice of the leaf applied at once, produces amazing results.

Other old-fashioned remedies are washing with (the astringency of) hot tea; applying the sticky juice which is found around quince seeds (if you can find them); or applying a salve of an extract of Irish moss *(Chondrus crispus).* Another recommended procedure would be the application of some linseed oil to which has been added a little lime water, rated to be excellent. This, of course, comes from the common flax plant, *Linum usitatissimum.* Also, the application at once to a burn of the juices of any of the various sorts of the houseleeks *(Sempervivum tectorum* and others) produces good results. In ancient times, records show that the juices of the leaves of the plant called hound's tongue *(Cynoglossum officinale)* was a reasonably good remedy.

But again, and with strong recommendation, every person reading this section should buy a nice plant of the easily grown and very pretty common aloe, which will sooth many burns quickly.

WOUND TREATMENT WITH PLANTS

It is a little difficult to decide with the word "wounds" where a wound begins and a cut, or a sore, or a bruise ends. Often all of these conditions may be a part of the "wound." Thus the reader is advised to consider plants mentioned under such other headings, where treatment is to be applied. Actually a number of plants have been suggested as having wound-healing qualities of which the following are samples.

Achillea (various species) : The yarrow is a denizen of many herb gardens, and while its action may be limited it is interesting to note that the plant was named after Achilles who perhaps should have used it on his heel.

Antennaria margaritacea (syn. *Anaphalis):* This is the pearly everlasting of the flower garden, which has a minor reputation when used as a poultice for sprains.

Cowania mexicana: A small evergreen from the rose family found in the Southwest, it is commonly called the quinine bush, and a tea made from the plant is recommended for washing wounds.

Eriodictyon californicum: This southwestern plant known as mountain balm offers material for poulticing cuts and wounds with crushed fresh leaves.

Hamamelis virginiana: Most everyone knows of the use and effects of the common witch hazel which with its astringent properties, is valuable mainly for easing the flow of blood from a wound.

Monarda (various species): All of the members of the horse-mint

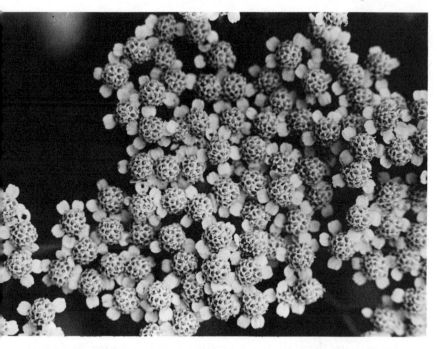

In days of old when knights were bold and during the Civil War as well, yarrow was crushed and applied to the wounds of battle to staunch the flow of blood. The multitudes of tiny flowers on each plant have been used in uterine diseases, catarrh, and as an astringent.

group, which is a member of the mint family, contain a "biting" oil which may help to relieve the sting of wounds of various kinds.

Opuntia (various species) : This member of the cactus family provides, as do other succulents, viscous juices which are healing in quality and these cacti are one of the good healers to know about in the Southwest.

Polygonatum biflorum: The hairy Solomon's seal offers a poultice for wounds when the powdered root is used.

Solidago (various species) : Some of the many species of goldenrod offer possible value when an antiseptic powder is made from the crushed leaves.

Typha latifolia: The water-loving common cattail offers aid for cuts and wounds through the soft, feathery down of the seed pods, which can be used (with other herbal preparations) in bandaging wounds.

PLANTS AGAINST BLEEDING

When one talks of bleeding, the question arises as to the source of the bleeding, and one finds in many herbal books all sorts of plants which are reputed to help in curing bleeding from the lungs, or stomach, or other internal trouble. However, one should go at once to a doctor of some repute, rather than going to the woods for a remedy.

Even in the matter of external bleeding, one finds that most of the plants which are possibly helpful in such accidental bleedings are found in among the plant genera which are rated as "astringents," all of which might be of some aid. Parts of the oak such as extract of oak bark are very astringent and the weedy Canadian fleabane *(Erigeron canadensis)* has similar properties. But here the problem is to find the plant at the moment needed.

In perhaps the only plant product which is generally agreed to be most helpful in bleeding, we must go back to one used by the American Indians, and that is the use of the black powderlike spores which are found in the ripe member of the mushroom family which we call the puff-ball. There is good evidence that Indians used to keep this powder on hand in their homes for use at any time, the action being that the powder is so fine that it causes the blood to clot very, very quickly.

This suggestion really makes sense as a valuable bit of nature-lore, but one caution should be given in that this powder is very, very explosive and should be stored with care. In the early days of photography, this powder was used for making flashes. So, be careful.

Another hemostatic which is not quite in the plant world, is the use of bunched up pieces of cobwebs for the same sort of effect, but as cobwebs are so often found on plants, perhaps the reader will pardon this suggestion.

EXPECTORANTS

To a certain extent, plants which are considered below as expectorants might well be mentioned under those for coughs and colds and the like, since the purpose of expectorants is to cause the discharge of irritating accumulations of mucous and aid thus in curing basic trouble. Yet, there are some plant medicines which seem to be particularly suitable for this effect, of which a few are discussed below.

In an American herbal medicinal book published in 1842, an interesting expectorant is recommended in which the powdered dried roots of skunk cabbage, of *Aletris farinosa* or unicorn root, of lobelia seed, and of cayenne pepper are combined with honey or molasses and "taken at bedtime." It is hard to believe that many would try such a mixture today, but perhaps it had more values than presently we would allow.

Possibly of greatest help as an expectorant is just plain honey.

Helianthus annuus: Sunflower seed is a plant product increasingly of interest and, next to corn, may be the greatest contribution of America to world foods. Medicinally it is said to have good expectorant qualities, a couple of ounces of seed being boiled down in a quart of water (to 12 oz.), then with gin and some honey added, taken three or four times a day. It is also listed as a diuretic and one writer, John H. Tobe, recommends the raw seeds eaten in quantity as an alleviant for prostate gland troubles.

Liquidimbar styraciflua: Of the exuded gum from the bark of the sweet gum or storax tree there is made, commercially, a thick liquid which, when combined with Benzoin, is a stimulating expectorant. However, it would be found difficult to produce as a "home medicine."

Marrubium vulgare: The dried leaves of horehound are made into a "tea" or other drinkable form, and this for centuries has been known as an expectorant and tonic. The great herbalist Culpeper says: "It helpeth to expectorate tough phlegm from the chest"; and, of course, everyone knows the value of horehound candy for rough throats. If one has other

The sunflower is widely grown in the United States and Russia for its seeds and the oil they yield. Though not commonly regarded as a medicinal plant, it does have a variety of healing virtues.

herbs to work with, it may be combined with hyssop, rue, liquorice, and marshmallow as an excellent cough syrup.

Eriodictyon californicum: The yerba santa is a California native plant, the dried leaf of which has been much used as an expectorant, and also as an addition to medicines of quinine to mask the bitter taste. Here we have two plants, the uses of which came to us via the cultures of the Indians of North and South America.

PLANTS FOR COUGHS

Possibly one of the most common complaints of mankind are coughs and sore throats, and, through the centuries, many plant remedies have been suggested in various cultures. One of the easiest of the natural remedies to use is a plant product, honey. Honey can be taken alone or combined with some of the plants which themselves are valuable. A selection of the most noted is discussed below.

Aralia racemosa: Indian-root or spikenard dried rhizome or roots are used and often combined as part of a "white pine" compound.

Chondrus crispus: For those who live in sea-coast areas, the dried pieces of the Irish moss are not hard to obtain. From them is easily made, by cooking and boiling them down to a jelly-like material, a substance which can be used for making puddings and is actually today found in many of our food products. It is extremely soothing to the throat, as well as having nutrient values.

Sassafras albidum: At one time considered a complete cure-all, and still found for sale in areas here as a spring tonic, the decoction made from roots of the sassafras is said to reduce fevers and help, in general, with its reputed tonic values.

Linum usitatissimum: Linseed oil, known to most persons, has the quality of soothing inflamed membranes, and could well be used in any afflictions of the pulmonary tract.

Osmunda regalis: The mucilaginous extract from the royal fern (or fern brake) rhizomes have in the past been a part of the druggists' supply, but is now of doubtful value.

Pinus strobus: White pine offers from its dried inner bark stimulating expectorant values, and when combined into cough syrups with honey and morphine or similar products, makes one of the best cures known for an ordinary cough.

Prunus serotina: The dried bark of the stems of the chokecherry tree gives a stimulating expectorant which is found today in many of the best cough syrups. The bark when soaked provides a dangerous cyanic acid, and thus the raw bark should never be chewed.

Rhus glabra: The dried, lovely red fruit heads of the common wild shrub, smooth sumac, when soaked and strained provide a little astringent quality useful in throat gargles.

Tussilago farfara: The leaf of coltsfoot, dried in early summer and made into a tea, is, when combined with honey, a very old and much used remedy for coughs and similar conditions of the throat.

COLDS AND FEVERS

Probably most readers know that one of the best ways of ridding oneself of a cold (with or without a fever) is to go to bed for a day or two, drink plenty of water and/or some hot lemonade. Possibly if the cold is accompanied by a cough or sore throat, a tea may be made of lemon, honey, and some Irish moss, which eases the soreness. While no longer a plant remedy, aspirin can be justified by the nature-user in that it was introduced to us by the Indians, who found the same properties in willow bark from which it was later synthesized. Beyond these simple things, here are some plants to add additional help.

Allium sativum: Good and anciently used garlic is a medicine prescribed for many things, and here as something promoting expectoration. One authority says of it that garlic provides "many marvelous healing powers."

The berries or "hips" of the Rosa rugosa *make a popular tea which is an excellent source of vitamin C and thus a fine beverage for cold sufferers.*

Achillea millefolium: One of the most common plants in the herb garden is yarrow, of which a tea made from dried foliage is an old cold remedy.

Aralia racemosa: Spikenard or Indian root used as a hot infusion is helpful.

Aristolochia serpentaria: Virginia snakeroot (also known by a host of other names) is a plant with much reputation for use when there is a fever with a cold.

Artemisia tridentata and *vulgaris:* Both of these species of wormwood are listed as being a cure for feverish conditions and are found widely in the United States.

Cnicus benedictus: Blessed thistle is also good for fevers and is administered through a tea made with an ounce of the dried herb to a pint of boiling water.

Cornus (several species) : The bark of various dogwoods is reputed to be good for colds.

Hyssops officinalis: Hyssop, another denizen of the ordinary herb garden, is reputed as a good curative agent for colds and fevers.

Marrubium vulgare: Horehound is a plant which gave us soothing candy when we were children, and which we know now as always good for coughs and sore throats and as something to be found almost anywhere in our country.

BRONCHIAL ASTHMA

In reading about the remedies for this distressing condition as used by the western American Indians, one finds a variety of cures tried, some of them soothing, some sedative, and varying with the plant material of the locality. One remedy quoted by Virginia Scully in her *Treasury of American Indian Herbs* says: "Skunk cabbage, onion, and honey were deemed an excellent brew . . . the Indians sometimes varying the formula with garlic."

Allium sativum: Mrs. Grieve in her book *A Modern Herbal* recommends a "syrup of garlic" as one good remedy and devotes much discussion to the other many uses of garlic.

The medical profession allows for many possible uses. Indeed uses go back to very early times.

Asclepias incarnata: Various species of milkweed have been used for curing a variety of diseases, but use by lay persons should be done with great care as there are poisons here when used in excess. One species in the Far East was possibly used as a hallucinogen, which is known in the Hindu religion as "Soma."

Chrysanthemum leucanthemum: The dried plant and even the flowers of the common daisy boiled up with some honey, have been recommended as an alleviant to attacks of asthma.

Dioscorea villosa: Pleurisy root, rheumatism root, or colic root, are the common names of the wild yam, which has often been rated as an internal medicine, the part used being the dried root (rhizome). Although of doubtful value in asthma, this plant is a good example of how common names often indicate medicinal value.

Drosera rotuniflora: Perhaps because it is sort of a magical plant, in that it gets its food by eating insects, sundew has been rated as having a number of medicinal values, including that of being an aphrodisiac. Again, beyond being listed as an asthma cure, it is said to be a "cure for old age."

Eriodictyon californicum: Here again the common names of consumptives weed and mountain balm indicate the possible values in this plant of the Far West, which, when the dried leaves are used for making a decoction, becomes a soothing expectorant, good for asthmatic conditions.

Grindelia robusta: The California gum plant is said to be a good remedy for asthma, especially when the leaves, combined with those of *Stramonium,* are smoked.

Lobelia inflata: Indian tobacco and other members of the genus were important Indian medicines and were used, among other things, for relief from asthma. Improperly used, it is poisonous.

Trifolium pratense: The ground blossoms of red clover have been used in the preparation of a cigarette to be smoked as an antiasthmatic.

CATARRH

In discussing a few plants which are rated as being good for catarrh, it should be noted that catarrhs may well be found not only in the nasal passages as commonly thought, but in internal tracts such as that of the stomach. For that reason, a number of plants which, in some other classification may be said to be useful for inflammed mucous membranes, could well be considered for catarrhal conditions in whatever area. Here are a few plants which have been used for this condition.

Borago officinalis: Borage is a common garden herb, with most lovely blue flowers, which is often planted just to attract the bees to one's garden, and one which has been used for centuries for catarrhal conditions. Infusions of it are healing to inflamed membranes, and it is thought that a known saline content provides other aids, as does a salt gargle.

Cnicus benedictus: As with so many plants, a number of healing values are given for blessed thistle including the control of fever. A plant long used by the herbalists, a simple infusion

Borage is a demulcent, acting to soften and sooth inflamed mucous membranes. As such, it has been used in catarrh and some respiratory ailments.

may be made of one ounce of the dried herb to a pint of boiling water.

Cynoglossum officinale: Hound tongue, the lovely blue-flowered member of the borage family, is grown as a lovely garden flower and has, when prepared as a medicine, a number of listed medicinal values, all of them tending to be demulcent or soothing to membranes and an alleviant to coughs.

Hydrastis canadensis: The powdered root of golden seal, a long used plant in herbal medicine, is the source of the healing qualities, but users should be certain to obtain careful instructions in preparation as overdoses are harmful.

DIGESTION

Perhaps this section might better be labeled Indigestion, rather than Digestion, for the plants discussed here often not only have some curative properties in easing stomach upsets, but also are a stimulant to encourage good eating. It is actually very interesting to note that almost every substance used in *good* cooking is for the stimulation of the appetite and is most usually a plant product. Thus, to list every plant here which is tasty or adds to the joy of eating would take a book in itself.

Here, also, it is notable that plant products made originally as medicines have sometimes come to be purely appetite-stimulants, as in the case of the much used angostura bitters, or in raw plants—the eating of parsley, watercress, horseradish, ginger, nutmeg, and sage.

But there are other less well known plants which offer an aid to digestion.

Acorus calamus: The widely growing water-plant, the sweet flag, besides having uses for rush-seating, has uses as an aromatic tonic.

Angelica atropurpurea: A common denizen of the home herb garden is angelica, which is known medicinally as a "stimulant."

Capsicum (various species): Cayenne (and similar peppers) is a stimulating stomachic.

Cnicus benedictus: Blessed thistle is a very anciently known stimulating tonic plant.

Gentiana catesbaei: The blue gentian has high rating as a source for stomachic tonic.

Grindelia (various species): This western gum plant, when a broth is made of the leaves, offers good relief from indigestion.

Humulus lupulus: The seedcase of hop plant offers an aid to digestion.

Inula helenium: Way back in Roman times, Pliny told of the fact that the use of elecampane would relieve indigestion.

Mentha (various species): It is hardly necessary to point out here that some of the mint family such as spearmint and peppermint are good to aid digestion.

Panax quinquefolium: Here is the famous ginseng which the pharmacist would call only an aromatic bitter, but which has ratings in China that it will cure anything.

Rosmarinus officinalis: A basic plant for all herb gardens is rosemary, which has been known and used for millenia as a stimulating tonic, but one which when used for cooking meats makes them much more inviting to eat.

Satureja douglasi: A plant, which the Spanish explorers in the West called yerba buena, or the good plant, provides the source for a tea of aid to digestion.

Tragopogon porrifolius: Salsify or oyster-plant, when chewed, yields a juice which is said to aid digestion.

DIARRHEA

Many of the complaints of man are uncommon and afflict only a few people, but the difficulty of diarrhea is something few people miss. One might mention among the most common of remedies which are plant-oriented, would be the drinking of strong tea, the taking of blackberry brandy, the eating of oatmeal, and always, for so many troubles, "an apple a day." Beyond this there would be possible some plants mentioned under astringents, and also from a long list of "reputed" cures the ones named below are more often mentioned.

Capsella bursa-pastoris: The native wilding, shepherd's purse, is usually found mentioned in old herbals as a simple cure for diarrhea.

Cercis occidentalis: The Judas tree species found in California was used by the native Indians for diarrhea by chewing the bark.

Geranium maculatum: Alum root or cranesbill is a reputable cure here.

Hypericum perforatum: St. John's wort, as the name "wort" implies, is a quite ancient remedy for many conditions, including that of diarrhea.

Quercus alba: A decoction of the bark of white oak is recommended in cases of chronic diarrhea. This is likely true with other oaks, as the barks of all oaks are astringent.

Rubus (various species) : As mentioned above, blackberry brandy is known as a quick aid to this trouble, and also the fresh fruit in quantity, as well as a decoction of the root bark.

Vaccinium macrocarpon: The syrup of the fruit of blueberries is said to be a good medicine for alleviation of diarrhea.

Vitis (various species) : Grape juice taken in quantity, fresh, is often listed as an aid to simple diarrhea.

LAXATIVES AND PURGATIVES

From childhood to old age the most common medicine to be administered is one or another of these, and happily for those who dislike the idea of using synthetics or who may be living in the wild, there are a number of good plants which will supply relief from constipation.

At home and somewhat outside a consideration of wild plants, there are such fruits as figs or prunes or pears, while stewed rhubarb in the spring has sure effects in cleaning out the system. Olive oil is a mild laxative, and in the purgative field one would use castor oil.

Wild plants which in one way or another and in quantities to be used according to need for mildness or strength, are as follows.

Aloe vera and *Agave americana:* These two plants from allied families and both from the Southwest, are known as laxatives in the areas where they are grown. A recent article in *Organic Gardening* magazine (October, 1972) tells in detail how juices of these plants are collected and evaporated before use.

Cornus canadensis: A widely spread low-growing plant, the bunchberry, provides a cathartic in the form of the fresh bark.

Croton corymbulosus: From the dry Southwest comes this member of the spurge family, which was once used as the source of a very strong purgative called croton oil. The common name of the plant is chaparral tea. The plant juices, as with the juices of many other members of the spurge family, are poisonous to animals.

Euonymus atropurpureus: The shrub which we know as wahoo or burning bush offers mild or strong laxatives.

Fraxinus americana: The white ash offers, in the extraction of medicine from the bark, values—either laxative or purgative.

Juglans cinerea and *nigra:* If walnuts of one or another sort are eaten in quantity, laxative effects may be noted.

Linum usitatissimum: Few do not know the many values to be found in a flaxseed poultice, or of linseed oil, which has good qualities as a laxative.

Magnolia virginiana: In the South where the magnolia grows, a number of medicinal uses are made of extracts from magnolia trees, including laxatives.

Marrubium vulgare: Horehound is a well known wild plant providing not only sources for candy and cough medicine, but also a simple laxative.

Morus rubra: The soft fruits of the common red mulberry will, if eaten in quantity, produce a mild laxative effect.

Rhamnus purschiana (and *R. californica* of the West): These wild shrubs or small trees give in their bark, dried and made into medicine, the well-known purgative cascara, which is also prescribed as a tonic in lesser doses. But in eating fruit from these plants care should be exercised, as the purgative power is very pronounced.

Horehound is most familiar as an ingredient in cough drops and syrups, but it has also been used as a mild laxative and as a tonic. The leaves and flowers are used to make a decoction, being simmered in boiling water for about ten minutes. Half-cup doses every three hours are recommended.

Taraxacum officinale: Reputed to have been used medicinally in Egypt thousands of years ago, the common and wide-spread dandelion has spring tonic and laxative values well indicated by the specific name *officinale,* meaning that for centuries it has been on the list of official drugs. A fine spring tonic plant.

TONICS

The definition of a tonic is not easy to settle on, as a tonic may be something which is just stimulating to the appetite, something which improves the activity of the organs, or something which produces a healthful feeling. Thus the plants here are to be found with various values, but all of them are noted in one book or another as being tonics.

Achillea (various species) : The yarrows are always species found in any list of valuable herbs, and in either east or west, we have what one could call a stimulating or aromatic bitter.

Acorus calamus: The water-loving sweet flag is a plant also noted as an aromatic bitter.

Artemisia: The wormwoods in one or another species are also old-time sources for stimulating, aromatic bitters, and as the basis for absinth.

Asarum canadense: Everyone knows of the appetite stimulation of the gingers, and while this American wild form is not true ginger, it can have the same effect.

Berberis: Certain principles in the barberries are bitter and said to be useful in liver and digestive disorders.

Chicorium intybus: Chicory and especially the related dandelion are both said to be good plants as spring tonics, and have been so used by southern Europeans for centuries.

Comptonia peregrina: The sweet fern has astringent and tonic properties as well as being a good plant to cure poison ivy.

Marrubium vulgare: Horehound combines taste good in candy and coughdrops. Horehound is also reputed to be of use as a nutritious tonic.

Matricaria chamomilla: One of the oldest of herbal remedies is camomile, which is often noted as a valuable aromatic bitter (and thus a tonic).

Mentha (various species) : The mints of many sorts are seemingly all good for aiding digestion, and thus of tonic value.

Nasturtium nasturtium-aquaticum: This is the long and interesting name for watercress, which everyone knows as stimulating to the appetite.

Prunella vulgaris: Named "self-heal" this plant offers itself as an astringent tonic.

Tanacetum vulgare: Tansy is an easy-to-note aromatic bitter and thus becomes "tonic."

RHEUMATISM

One reads archeological reports of ancient mummified bodies being dug up in which the condition of hands, etc. would indicate the presence of what we now call rheumatism or arthritis. Hence one can assume that when plants were the only medicine, as well as now when there are all sorts of scientific knowledge and medicines available crippling of the body from this disease was a dread condition.

One hears much that the only pain-alleviant is synthesized aspirin, which has come down to us from the once-Indian-remedy of willow bark; and now more recent various writers are suggesting that much help can also be obtained by taking Vitamin C—some of which is found in citrus fruits of various kinds. But this is not too new, for the most reliable modern herbal writer said some forty years ago that "lemon juice is highly recommended in acute rheumatism." Such medicine as any of the citrus juices, being harmless and indeed healthful in many other ways, seems to be a first choice here.

But there are a number of other plant medicines said to have anti-rheumatic values.

Betula lenta: An infusion of the bark of the black birch has been used.

Cimicifuga racemosa: Infusions and decoctions of this plant, called the black snakeroot, are variously listed as of possible value.

Chimaphila umbellata: One common name of this is rheumatism-weed. It is used by crushing the fresh leaves and applying them to affected parts. One reference says "not too reputable."

Eupatorium perfoliatum: The plant with one name of "boneset" is a much recommended herb for many conditions, and here, for muscular rheumatism, a warm infusion is recommended.

Magnolia macrophylla: In the South where the magnolia grows reports are that the mild astringent qualities of the leaves are an alleviant for rheumatism.

Phytolacca americana: The pokeweed plant which, in the spring, is a much used vegetable in the mid-South, is also through roots and seeds extremely poisonous. Yet extracts from the plant are recommended as an "alterative in chronic rheumatism."

Sambucus canadensis: The juices of the fruit of elderberry in olden times were thought to be a good remedy for rheumatism. Perhaps there is vitamin C here, as well as in lemons.

Solanum dulcamara: Bittersweet, which is related to the deadly nightshade, is the vining plant with the bright red berries, rather than the black berries of the poison form. It is just as well for those not accomplished in nature lore to keep away from using almost any wild plants in the solanum or potato family as there is a basic poison reserve in all of them. However, in the case of this bittersweet, Mrs. Grieve in her book says that for "Chronic rheumatism it has been much employed in the past, an infusion of 1 oz. of the dried herb to ½ pint of water, being taken in wineglassful doses, two or three times daily."

EMETICS

There is quite often in our lives some immediate necessity to cause ourselves or others to vomit, and almost everyone knows that a finger down a throat will usually get the needed reaction. If that is objectionable, then perhaps an overdose of salt will help, or the swallowing of soapsuds. Beyond this, a number of herbal remedies have been known and used in different cultures. These below are a few.

Brassica (various species): The use of preparations of the ground seeds of black or white mustard provides every home with not only a good condiment, but, in large doses, a good emetic.

Cowania mexicana: This plant of the Southwest called cliffrose, provides, when a strong tea is made of the leaves, an emetic known and used by the Indians in that region.

Frasera caroliniensis: The plant of the Far West called the elk-weed (a member of the gentian family) has emetic qualities when infusions from the fresh or dried root are taken.

Gratiola officinalis: The hedge-hyssop is a plant of many medicinal uses, not least as an emetic.

Ilex (various species) : Long known to the Indians of our country, some of the berries of our native hollies are violently emetic and should be used with care. Use so made of them was part of certain religious ceremonies of Indian tribes in our southern states, circumstances reported by the earliest explorers. Vomiting as a religious exercise is not, to us, an attractive thing, but neither were many earlier Christian practices.

Impatiens pallida: The plant often commonly called "touch-me-not" has a good name as, while it may be good as a poison ivy cure used externally, it is quite poisonous taken internally and even just mild use may cause vomiting.

Lonicera (various species) : Fruits of the honeysuckle vine are somewhat poisonous and also emetic.

Phytolacca americana: The common pokeweed, a fine spring vegetable used as asparagus, has very poisonous roots and berries, but this poison taken carefully has been listed as a good emetic.

Trillium (various species): The roots of the wake-robin, widely found, are known to be a powerful emetic and one used by the Indians.

PLANT STIMULANTS

The casual reader might well ask: Why discuss a stimulant as far as medicines are concerned? And what part or function would stimulation play in these days of general over-stimulation.

The plants below are those which may stimulate the sense of taste or digestion to the point where one might find interest or pleasure in using added medicines or in more delightful or digestible foods.

With a list of plants such as those below, one could well

Foxglove is often cultivated as an ornamental, but it is an important drug plant, being the source of digitalis, a heart stimulant. A potentially dangerous drug, digitalis should be used only under a doctor's guidance.

have a very stimulating herb garden and one with many uses, medicinal and otherwise.

Acorus calamus: Sweet flag is an aromatic bitter, useful medicinally.

Angelica atropurpurea: Angelica is a well known stimulating herb.

Anthemis nobilis: A common garden herb, camomile has aroma and bitterness.

Armoracia rusticana: Horseradish stimulates the appetite and even causes tears when it is grated.

Artemisia absinthium: Wormwood has been used since earliest times as a stimulating bitter.

Asarum canadense: Everyone knows the stimulation of wild ginger.

Gaultheria procumbens: Wintergreen is bright and stimulating to taste and smell.

Hedeoma pulegioides: Pennyroyal is a brightly spicy plant from the herb garden.

Juniperus (and other members of the pine family): All are aromatic stimulants.

Lavandula vera: Lavender from the herb garden or cosmetic bottle will revive almost anyone.

Liquidambar styracifolia: Storax gum is a first-class stimulating expectorant.

Magnolia macrophylla: The foliage of this and other magnolias is an aromatic stimulant.

Mentha (various species): Who does not know the palate stimulating and gastric correctiveness of almost any of the mint family? Tiny *M. requiena* in the herb garden would revive anyone.

Rosmarinus officinalis: A fine nasal and tongue stimulator is rosemary.

Sambucus canadensis: Elder-flower tea is pleasant and a stomach stimulant.

Sassafras albidum: The flavorful roots make stimulating tea and medicine.

Tanacetum vulgare: Common tansy is stimulating, if not especially pleasant.

Urtica dioica: Nettle leaves can be cooked and eaten and make a stimulating tonic.

Zanthoxylum americanum: One chews the dried bark of prickly ash to get the stimulating qualities.

SEDATIVES

In discussing this subject recently with a modern pharmacist, the comment was made that one must be very careful with sedatives recommended, for all too often any substance which may have sedative qualities is likely to be, in larger doses, a harmful or even killing opiate. One could think at once of the relaxing and sedative quality of any form of alcoholic drink, which when recommended by doctors for older people is a useful sedative, but which when abused is a killing drug.

Then there is the presently much-discussed plant called *Cannabis sativa* or marijuana, which has a centuries-old history of use for sedative and religious purposes. A research company in Cambridge, Massachusetts (as reported in *World*, December 19, 1972) says that marijuana may well "find application in the treatment of certain forms of psychiatric illness" such as depression.

Among other plants which might be mentioned as being highly valuable under proper medical supervision, although all are potent plants, would be:

Conium maculatum (poison hemlock), *Datura stamonium* (jimson weed), *Gelsemium sempervirens* (yellow jasmine), *Papaver somniferum* (opium poppy), and *Veratrum viride* (white hellebore).

Beyond these there are a few less potent plants with calmative qualities.

Ceanothus americanus: New Jersey tea got its name from the fact that the leaves of it were used as tea by the soldiers in the American Revolution, but for the purpose here it is notable that the bark of the root, properly prepared, is a mild sedative.

Collinsonia canadensis: Horse balm is a plant with sedative qualities and at one time was in the standard list of American medicines.

Humulus lupulus: It is hardly likely that the sedative qualities of seeds of the hop vine are found in ordinary beer (made in part from hops), but actually an oil made from this plant is a "reputable" sedative.

Lycopus virginicus: This member of the mint family called bugle-weed, gives, in an infusion, some mild sedative qualities.

Matricaria chamomilla: One of the most generally useful denizens of the home herb garden is that of camomile, and a tea made from the dry leaves has long been known as a pleasing sedative drink.

Valeriana officinalis: The drug valerian is used for a number of purposes and is one that has survived the onslaught of synthetic and modern chemical medicines. Among its uses is that of a nerve-soothing and calmative drug, but one to be taken under physician's orders. The common name of valerian is heal-all, which comes from the Latin word *valere*, meaning to be well.

PLANT DIURETICS

In exploring the field of plant medicine one finds many plants which are rated primarily or secondarily as having properties which promote the flow of urine. Some of these are well known such as quantities of watermelon or raw onions. Common parsley, too, has a strong reputation as a diuretic and is a common food enjoyed by all. Below are a selected few native American wild plants which reputable books rate as possible useful diuretics.

Apocynum androsaemilfolium: This plant known often by the common name of dog-bane is listed reputably as a "diuretic in dropsy."

Arctostaphylos uvi-ursi: The common acid-soil loving bearberry and another member of the same family, *Chimaphila,* have long been known and used as diuretics.

Burdock is a common wild plant, long regarded as an excellent blood purifier. A decoction of the root, the part usually used, is said to remedy chronic skin diseases. It is also a diuretic and diaphoretic.

Chichorium intybus: The common chicory with its lovely blue flowers and its usually closely-growing-neighbor, the common dandelion, *Taraxacum officinale,* have both been long used as diuretics, although they are possibly not very powerful.

Iris virginica and *versicolor:* The "flags" or irises are reputed diuretics.

Juniperus communis: The common ground juniper in extracts from bark or berries is listed as a "stimulating diuretic."

Lycopodium complanatum: Commonly known as ground pine or clubmoss, extracts from this plant are rated as "powerful" diuretics.

Menispermum canadense: The moonseed or Texas sarsaparilla is known, when taken in mild doses, as useful for promoting the flow of urine.

Pyrola (various species): Wintergreen has long been known and used as a mild diuretic.

URINARY DISORDERS

In this classification would fall such plants as are often considered diuretics and have to do with kidney ailments, bladder disorders, and the like. In no sense is the list below a complete listing of all of the plants in this category, but rather a sampling of botanical medicines, many of which have been known and used for centuries, and some of them involving knowledge given to us by the American Indians.

Achillea (various species): The yarrows are a well known herb which might be considered to be used as a minor diuretic.

Agropyron repens: The quack or couch grass is a prime pest to the gardener, but the roots of it, along with the roots of Bermuda grass, have constituents which place it among the diuretics.

Arctostaphylos uvi-ursi: Commonly known as bearberry, this plant is to be found over much of our country, usually growing in sunny acid soils. It, along with other ericaceous plants, has diuretic properties and is a mild disinfectant to the urinary tract. The dried leaves are made into a tea.

Chimaphila umbellata: From the same family as above, the pipsis-sewa is listed as a diuretic.

Curcubita (various species) : In this genus the seeds of both the pumpkin and the cucumber are "distinctly diuretic." Seeds such as this are said to contain quantities of vitamin F which is noted for aiding urinary problems, and one authority credits the eating of such seeds with retarding the development of prostate troubles in men.

Equisetum hymenale: Horsetails or scouring rush are primitive seeming plants growing in waste areas. The fresh stems chewed or made into a decoction have not only uses as a diuretic, but are readily available for scouring pots and pans, as the second name indicates.

Eupatorium purpureum: Known often as boneset or gravel root, this plant has long been used as a diuretic.

Helianthus annus: As with members of the cucumber family the seeds of the common sunflower are strongly recommended for those with urinary or prostate disorders. Two ounces of the seeds can be boiled with a quart of water. When eleven ounces are left, add Holland gin.

Hydrangea arborescens: This is the white flowered native hydrangea found on the East Coast, which was used medicinally by the Cherokee Indians as a diuretic stimulant and for other purposes. Most herbals list it as one of the valuable remedies for such a condition.

Juniperus (various species): The junipers, especially the blue berries of *Juniperus virginiana* and *communis,* contain an oil notable as a diuretic and are something which give flavor to gin. (Gin is a prevarication of the French word for juniper, genievre.)

Lycopodium complenatum: This almost "moss-like" plant known as ground-cedar is rated in good herbals as a "powerful diuretic." There are, as said, a number of plants which have properties similar to the above. One excellent authority, John L. Tobe, lists in his book on prostate troubles (beyond the ones above) such plants as broom, parsley, shepherd's purse, and wild carrot.

FEMALE DISORDERS

Or perhaps a better title than the above might be "women's problems," for there are circumstances of menstruation and other matters that relate only to women, just as the men have quite unique problems. As might well be expected in considering efforts made to correct such irregularities that do occur, the home herb-gardener in past times, who was usually a woman or perhaps an Indian squaw who knew about plant values, did a lot of experimenting with concoctions from the plants she knew best, and often with satisfactory results. Teas made from Solomon's seal roots, from parsley, from yarrow, from juniper berries, and a lot of others were used, according to the new *Treasury of Indian Herbs.* There were, indeed, plants suitable for almost any need including that of contraception.

In the quite reliable story of plant drugs by Fernie called *Herbal Simples,* written in England at the turn of the century, the listing of "Plants to promote the monthly flow" goes to some thirty names, with a similar list for other special problems in this area. All are, quite frankly, too many to be fully explored here.

Dr. Youngken, in his pharmacological survey, mentions some of the same plants known of old, of which these are:

Achillea millefolium: The quite common yarrow seems to be of prime value.

Berberis (various species): Preparations made from the barberry are referred to as reliable "anti-periodics."

Caulophyllum thalictroides: In the barberry family, the dried roots of the blue cohosh are recommended pharmaceutically.

Hedeoma pulegioides: Pennyroyal, an ancient denizen of the herb garden, appears in almost every list of valuable herbs.

Ruta graveolens: A warm infusion of rue is a remedy used for centuries.

Trillium erectum: Among a number of plants said to aid in

childbirth, medicine made from the purple trillium has some reputation.

Readers of all the above should understand, as with every other condition discussed here, that the circumstances of recuperation are variable, that detailed instructions for preparing and taking medicines should be carefully studied, and that the trusted physician should be consulted in anything other than mild disorders. But, just as our modern doctors are now beginning to discover that the Orientals have something not to be overlooked in ancient acupuncture, so too must reconsideration often be given to the use of much of the millenia-old knowledge held by the herbalists.

MALE DISORDERS

Men, as well as women, have problems which are peculiarly theirs.

In the matter of the prostate condition, for instance, the noted authority in this field, John L. Tobe, has proposed in his book on the subject, that among other cures is the eating of foods which are high in vitamin F, a list of which would include such things as sunflower seeds, pumpkin and melon seeds, wheat germ, and safflower and soybean oils. In one chapter he lists a number of other plant drugs which are used, and generally suggests that there are possible cures for this condition other than an operation. It is pointed out that herbs which assist in urination are also of benefit in this and other conditions.

VENEREAL DISEASE

The subjects of syphilis and gonorrhea are a matter of great concern to far too many citizens today. As a resident of Martha's Vineyard, such a subject is of prime historical interest to me, since in 1603 the English explorer Gosnold, first found and named this Island when he was out with a ship looking for forests of sassafras trees, the roots of which might be used as medicine for the cure of syphilis (and of almost any other disease). Now there is not known to be any real medicinal value in sassafras, but at least it tasted like medicine, and in taking it one was "doing something." At the present time, modern medicine has definitive cures for venereal diseases, and the recommendation here would be to avail oneself of such, if any infection is discovered by the reader.

The above fact in mind, it may be of interest to just note what some native Indians did in such cases as discussed by Virginia Scully in her book on Indian herbs. Remember here that what western Indians might have done is quite different from what Indians of the Plains, East, or Northwest might have done.

Anemopsis californica: This is known as yerba mansa, and as a plant of the Southwest, it was the source for a tea made from the whole plant and drunk in quantity for any venereal disease.

Ephedra trifurca and *viridis:* This was known in the West as Mormon tea, and was drunk by the Indians for venereal disease cure. Another species coming from the Far East gives us the drug ephedrine, which has many true medicinal uses.

Lobelia syphilitica: It would be supposed that a plant with such a name would be valuable as a cure for syphilis, and it was so thought to be when it was named by Linnaeus, but is no longer rated to have any value.

Populus (various species): commonly called cottonwood, aspen, or poplar. A concoction made from the bark of this genus was at one time said to be "considered as an unfailing cure for syphilis," a fact now much in doubt.

Salix (various species) : A strong tea made from the inner bark of the willow tree was once thought to be a "perfect cure" for venereal disease.

ODDS AND ENDS
OF HEALTH HINTS

Within the limits of plant medicines, there are a number of miscellaneous plant uses and some little health hints which, while mostly plant oriented, are not easy to include in a large classification.

Taking food plants as an example, it is likely that most readers of this would know that the "hips" or seed pods of almost any rose are very high in vitamin C, actually much higher than oranges. Watercress and parsley both have some valuable chemical constituents, and in addition are valuable as digestants and stimulants to appetite. The tropical papayas, now commonly available in the markets, are excellent as digestants, and the leaves can be used (as done where they grow) as a tenderizer for any meat dish. And for some quick energy there is nothing better than honey, or possibly grape juice, and certainly chocolate and cocoa. For real emergency, brandy is always recommended, and of course, it too comes from grapes. Some health food persons object to the use of coffee and tea, but they are indeed both useful stimulants, and they are both plant products.

There are a few external uses of plants which have not otherwise been covered here, such as the eating of quantities of gelatinous foods as a means of reducing the brittle nature of finger nails. If the skin needs softening, then the combined juice of cucumber and of the shore-gathered Irish moss would be recommended, as would also the juice of the aloes.

Instead of softening, the skin may need stimulation, and here one could rub on leaves of some of the mustards, which are common weeds. An even more stimulating rub would be hot pepper plants.

The conclusion which one might now draw from the listings in this chapter is that the plant world is the source for not only our basic foods but, if we would but study and experiment, a great supply of aids for health and healing.

Yesterday's remedies never really passed completely away. Although packaged botanicals are seldom seen and decoctions, infusions, and tinctures seldom used, drug plants are used as ingredients in nearly half the prescriptions written in the United States. And increasing interest in drug plants is being shown in the medical community.

THE
TASTY HERBS

by Louise Hyde

THREE

To most people just the mention of the word herb cultivates interesting culinary ideas. Herbs lead the way to creative cookery as they culminate the whole process of growing and harvesting herbs. Experimenting with different combinations of herbs can change ordinary cuts of meat, vegetables, or desserts into different and unusual dishes. They can also improve bland recipes for people on restricted diets. Oregano can replace salt, and sweet cicely can replace sugar if restricted diets are required.

Using fresh herbs when they are available for cooking is more preferable, but the dried herbs work nearly as well. The rule of thumb is to use twice the amount of fresh herbs to the dried. Be careful not to overdo either the fresh or the dried until you have tested your family's preference.

When entertaining, be sure to try out a new recipe before serving it to your guests. Sometimes a few more or less sprigs can make a world of difference. Another caution is to limit the number of dishes containing herbs. Two or three unusual flavors are enough for your guests at one meal. Plan your menu with a basic idea in mind and work around this. It is usually easier to decide on the main dish first, then your other foods seem to fall into place.

CULINARY HERBS

A sample of various herbs and some suggestions for their uses can be found in the succeeding paragraphs.

Angelica: This robust and sweet-tasting plant is best known for its use in decoration of cakes and puddings. The stem is candied and used as a confection. Angelica lessens the need for sweetener when making pies or sauces. Rhubarb, angelica, and honey combine to make a tasty sauce. Angelica can also be cooked and eaten as a fresh herb, used for seasoning fish, or made into syrup for pudding and ice cream toppings.

Anise: Anise has the aroma and flavor of licorice. It is used both as a seed and as a leafy herb. The leafy stage is before the seed heads are produced. Chop the leaves and add them to cream sauces, salads, and boiling shell fish. The seed is crushed for flavoring cookies and cakes. The whole seeds are used with sweet pickles, salad dressings, coffee cakes, and soups. Anise oil is used as a base for the licorice flavor that we associate with licorice candy, cough drops, or liqueurs.

Basil: Basil is the "herb of love" and is favored by many. Its sweet flavor and aroma gives it infinite uses, whether for main meals or desserts. Basil is probably best known for its use with tomatoes. It can be sprinkled over sliced tomatoes with an oil and vinegar salad dressing, or used to make homemade tomato or spaghetti sauce. For seasoning pizza, basil rivals oregano for first place. Tossed salads, salad dressings, egg and cheese dishes, vegetable dishes, poultry, and veal, as well as rolls and breads are well seasoned with basil. When baking apples, sprinkle a few leaves over the apples for a delicious flavor.

Bay Leaves: Bay leaves are very spicy and pungent. Usually they are used when cooking meats. Because of their strong flavor only one-half to one leaf is needed for a medium-sized stew. Tongue and corned beef are enhanced when cooked with a bay leaf and a few whole cloves. They can also be added to stews, casseroles, and soup stock.

Borage: Borage is the "herb of courage." It is one of the herbs with a cucumber flavor. The leaves are used in salads to replace fresh cucumbers, in soups, and to enhance the flavor of iced tea and fruit drinks. If the hairy leaves of borage don't appeal to you, peel the larger stalk and cut into chunks for salads. The taste is similar to a cucumber.

Caraway: Most of us are familiar with caraway in the seed form used to flavor many kinds of rye breads, cookies, cakes, and pastries. It is often sprinkled over sauerkraut before it is cooked and can be added to the water before boiling potatoes to be used in making potato salad. Applesauce or cheese combine with caraway seeds to make interesting side dishes.

Steamed comfrey leaves mixed with lemon juice, seasoning, and vegetable oil make a delicious, nutritious summertime treat, providing widely heralded health benefits.

Before roasting a pork loin, rub caraway seeds into the meat on all sides, then sprinkle with salt and pepper — it is delicious.

Caraway seeds add a new dimension to grilled cheese sandwiches. Spread a little mustard on one slice of bread, sprinkle with caraway seeds, add the cheese, top with a slice of bread, and cook. This is company fare.

The green caraway leaves can be added to potato salads, beet salads, cottage or cream cheese, or to soups. The caraway root can be used as a vegetable. It has thick fleshy roots similar to carrots.

Chervil: Chervil is similar to parsley, except that it is sweeter and has a slight anise flavor. It has been called a "gourmet's parsley." Chervil is a prolific grower and can be used with most any dish either as a garnish or as a flavoring. Chervil is especially good with corn or potato soup, salads, salad dressings, chicken, and fish. It is often used in combination with other herbs as it brings out the flavor of these other herbs. Two tablespoons of chervil with one tablespoon of chives added to scalloped potatoes topped with cheese, then baked, is delicious.

Chives: Chives are one of the best known herbs and are a mild onion substitute. Cream cheese and chives as a spread, cottage cheese and chives as a low calorie salad, or chives and sour cream for a topping on baked potatoes are the best known uses. Use one cup of cheese or sour cream to two tablespoons fresh chives. Chives give zest to salads, soups, stews, omelettes, scrambled eggs, hors d'oeuvres, fish sauces, and cooked vegetables.

Garlic chives are a chive with a garlic flavor. They are also called Chinese chives. They can be used the same as ordinary chives. Garlic chives are used in Oriental dishes to give them their characteristic flavor.

Comfrey: Comfrey is the healthful herb. Long known for their healing benefits, comfrey leaves make a good salad, and they can be cooked like spinach. Be sure to use the young, tender leaves for best flavor.

Coriander (Also called Chinese parsley): This herb is used by Orientals instead of parsley. Coriander has a flavor that combines sage and lemon. The leaves contain vitamin C and are good used in curries, soups, and salads. Use them sparingly until you get used to the flavor. Coriander seeds are used as an ingredient in curry powder, pickling spices, and other spice mixtures, as well as to flavor cookies, rolls, sausage, and hot dogs. They are used in soups, vegetable dishes, and over meats before broiling. The whole young plants are used in chutneys, pastries, cakes, cookies, and in making types of tobacco.

Costmary: Costmary leaves have a minty flavor, and the young leaves can be used sparingly in salads. The English call it

Sweet Mary. Years ago, these leaves were used in Bibles or in linens to give a sweet aroma.

Cumin: Hot and pungent is the flavor of cumin. It is probably known best for its use in Mexican-type foods. It is an ingredient in curry and chili powder and is used in meats, pickles, cheese, sausage, and chutney. It can also be used in soups and stews.

Dandelions: Although many of us think of dandelions as a weed to expel from our lawns, their vitamin content makes them a nutritious plant to eat. Before the plant blooms, use the young leaves in salads or cook them up like spinach. The root can be cooked like a vegetable.

Dill: This easily grown annual can be used as dillweed (before the seed heads form) or more commonly as a seed. This latter stage is used when making dill pickles. Relishes, butter and fish sauces, spiced beets, and many other dishes use dill seed.

The lacy green dillweed is usually finely chopped when used. It is especially good when added to scrambled eggs, egg salads, leafy green salads, salad dressings, sauces for seafoods and poultry, or vegetables. Make a cream sauce, add some dillweed, and pour it over boiled or baked potatoes. Dill is an adjunct to tomatoes. A few sprigs sprinkled over sliced tomatoes or a bowl of tomato soup, not only looks but tastes appetizing. It can also be added to cheeses, pot roasts, or sprinkled over lamb chops.

Egyptian Onions: Egyptian onions are also called separators or top onions, for the bulbs form on top of the onion stalk. The flavor is like that of a shallot or mild onion. They may be pickled or used in soups and stews wherever an onion flavor is desired. If the bulbs are planted when they are ripe, the plant can be used as a sprouted scallion.

Fennel: Fennel seeds are used whole or ground to flavor bread, cakes, pastries, soups, stews, sweet pickles, fish, and sauerkraut. Fresh fennel greens are used to flavor fish sauces, chicken, and egg dishes. When cooked with salmon or

Dill seed is a popular condiment, being used to enhance the flavor of pies and pastries, soups and gravies.

mackerel, it has been claimed to help eliminate oiliness.

One variety of fennel, also known as finocchio, grows like a stalk of celery and is eaten raw or boiled as a vegetable.

Fenugreek: Mostly used in tea, fenugreek seeds can be sprouted like bean sprouts and used as a vegetable or a salad. The oil of fenugreek has a maple flavor and can be used for a true maple flavoring in cookies and syrups.

Good King Henry: Good King Henry is a pot herb that is cooked and eaten like spinach. Use the leaves before the plant goes to seed. Wash them and cook in a small amount of water. The leaves can also be used in salads.

Horehound: Horehound is used mostly as a tea. It is used in remedies for sore throats, colds, and coughs. Use the tea to make horehound candy.

Horseradish: Horseradish has a large root with a very pungent flavor. The roots are high in vitamin C. To make horseradish sauce, peel and grind the roots, then mix with vinegar. Horseradish sauce adds a special zip when served with beef.

Add to grated raw beets and sour cream to make a beef relish. It is also good with raw oysters and smoked tongue. A dash on a cracker topped with peanut butter makes an interesting hors d'oeuvre. Horseradish is also used in making cocktail and mustard sauces. In some areas the young spring shoots of horseradish are cooked for greens.

Lamb's Quarter: This weed found in most gardens makes a good spinach substitute. The young tops are pinched off and steamed in a small amount of water. The nutritional value of lamb's quarter is greater than spinach, and the flavor is similar.

Lemon Balm: The lemon-scented leaves of lemon balm impart a lemon-mint flavor to soups, stews, custards, puddings, or cookies. They can also be used in salad dressings and in iced tea and fruit drinks. The leaves are attractive as a garnish.

Lovage: The leaves and stalks of lovage can be used as a celery substitute in many salads. Lovage tastes like celery with an anise flavor. Use the stalks and leaves when making a truly delicious potato salad. In soups and stews it gives added zest. Always dry enough lovage leaves to last through the winter. On a cold day make a cup of bouillon soup, add a few lovage leaves, sprinkle with some grated cheese, and you'll have a gourmet soup.

If lovage goes to seed, use the seeds for making breads, herb butters, chicken salads, meat loaf, and candy.

Jerusalem Artichoke: This fall-harvested tuber grows wild or can be cultivated. The tuber is boiled and eaten like a potato, with butter, salt, and pepper. Eaten raw it is similar to a water chestnut found in Chinese cooking and has the same crunchy flavor.

Marjoram, Sweet: Sometimes sweet marjoram is confused with oregano because of its similarity in flavor and appearance. However, it has a sweeter and milder flavor than oregano. An ordinary vegetable can be given new dimension with marjoram. It is good with beef dishes such as meat loaf, stew, or meat sauce, omelets, scrambled eggs, gravies, sauces, and poultry stuffings. Sprinkle it on green salad, bean dishes, and tomatoes.

Mint: When we think of iced tea, we think of mint, for this is a traditional American beverage ingredient. Orange mint, regular mint, and lemon balm are a good combination for iced teas. Sprinkle chopped mint leaves on peas, carrots, potatoes, and fish. Mint cream sauce has many interesting uses. Leg of lamb with mint sauce is an old favorite. Add a few sprigs to any fruit cup. Mint jelly is easily made too.

Mugwort: Mugwort is used when a fatty piece of meat such as pork or goose is cooked. Rub the meat with the herb, then put some sprigs in the pan. It flavors the meat and makes the fat more digestible.

Nasturtium Leaves: The young nasturtium leaves add a peppery flavor to soups and salads. Dry them for winter use. The young seed pods can also be pickled like capers, and the flowers themselves are interesting when added as a garnish to salads.

Oregano: Oregano is probably the most famous American herb. Its fame is primarily due to pizza pies. Oregano is also known for its use in spaghetti sauce. When making home-made tomato sauce, add fresh basil and oregano sprigs to a large pot of pureed tomatoes.

Oregano is a flavorful addition to beef or lamb stews, gravies, salads, or tomato juice. Zucchini squash sliced into one-half-inch slices, dipped in egg, rolled in a mixture of cracker crumbs, oregano, and salt makes a bland vegetable come alive.

Parsley: Parsley is thought of by many as a sprig with which to garnish foods. Due to the high vitamin C content of this herb, it should be added to foods whenever possible. Sprinkle it over boiled and buttered potatoes, fresh broiled fish, meats, and vegetables. It is also a must for omelets and scrambled eggs.

Parsley is a basic ingredient for *fine herbes*. This is a

blend of herbs, finely chopped, and used to garnish or season a dish. It usually consists of a blend of parsley or chervil, chives, tarragon, basil, and thyme.

Parsley is also used for *bouquet garni*. This means sprigs of fresh herbs that are tied in a bunch or in cheese cloth and immersed in a soup or stew while it is cooking. They may be left for the entire cooking period or just until the desired flavor is obtained. They are then removed from the dish. Parsley, bay leaf, and thyme are basic for bouquet garni, but any other herb may be added.

Another type of parsley is the Hamburg parsley. This has turnip-like roots and is eaten like a vegetable or used in stews.

Rosemary: Rosemary is a very versatile herb. Its fame spreads from breads to meats to jams to desserts. Either rub into or sprinkle lamb, duck, chicken, or pork with rosemary leaves before roasting. They add sweeter flavor to fruit cups, punches, and marinating sauces. Fry small boiled potatoes with the leaves for a tasty and crunchy dish. For some, the flavor may be too strong so use sparingly at first.

Rue: Rue is the herb of grace. It is not widely used as a culinary herb but can be used sparingly in salads or on pumpernickel bread. Spread the bread with butter and sprinkle with a few chopped rue leaves.

Sage: Sage leaves added to poultry stuffing give it its characteristic flavor. Sage is a strong flavored herb—very pungent and aromatic. It is used in sausage, liver, fish, and cheese. If used sparingly, it is good with pickles and onions.

Salad Burnet: Salad burnet is a leafy salad herb with a cucumber flavor. Added to any dish it gives a cucumber taste without the after effects that some suffer from ordinary cucumbers. Add a few leaves to any type of leafy salad, egg salad, or cottage cheese. It can also be used for sauces and soups or in wine and fruit drinks like borage. The young leaves are the most flavorful.

Salvia Dorisiana: Salvia dorisiana is a very aromatic herb that

Rosemary is a versatile culinary herb. It is particularly popular in meat dishes, but is also used in jams, soups, and biscuits.

smells like a combination of pineapple and grapefruit. It is used to rub on fish and beef before cooking.

Savory: Long known to the Germans as Bohnenkraut, savory is to beans as ham is to eggs. There are two types of savory, a summer and a winter savory. Summer savory only grows during the summer months whereas winter savory lasts into the winter. Both savories can be used in hot or cold bean dishes, lentils, meats, or in poultry stuffing. The young shoots are also good in potato salad. Some people find that it helps tenderize the skin of the fava beans.

Skirret: Skirret is in the parsley family. The white root is the part used in cooking. It is smaller than a parsnip, but similar in flavor. In the early spring the roots can be eaten raw, but usually they are cooked and eaten like a carrot.

Sorrel, French: French sorrel is a leafy green herb excellent for soups and salads. The young new leaves are used with lettuce in a salad. The older leaves have a sour flavor and are better used in soup. They can also be used with raisins and honey to make a dessert similar to rhubarb.

Sweet Cicely: Sweet cicely has a sweet, slightly anise flavor. It can be used in cooking to replace some of the sweetener needed. Fruit pies, coffee cakes, cooked fruits, salads, and salad dressings are some examples of where it can be used. It imparts an unusual flavor to fish and carrots. The roots can be eaten raw or boiled. If the plant is allowed to go to seed, the green seeds taste like licorice candy.

Sweet Woodruff: Sweet woodruff is famous for its use with the May Bowl Punch. Steep the leaves and blossoms in one quart of white Rhine wine for a few hours. Add some orange and lemon, strawberries, ice, and more sweet woodruff. Freshly cut sweet woodruff has the aroma of newly mown hay and adds a unique flavor to fresh strawberries.

Tansy: Although tansy is best known for its medicinal value, it is used in small amounts to flavor pancakes, cookies, and puddings.

Tarragon: Tarragon is one of the most widely used herbs. It is best known for use in seafood and chicken specialties. When used with fish it seems to remove most of the fishy taste. Salads made of crab meat, shrimp, lobster, or potatoes, and stuffed mushrooms are all enhanced by tarragon. It is also tasty with leafy salads, most vegetables and makes flavorful cream sauces.

Thyme: The traditional flavor of clam and fish chowders come from thyme. Clam chowder wouldn't be clam chowder without thyme. It is also an ingredient in stuffings for poultry or for breast of lamb. For a variation in flavor use lemon thyme in chicken dressing. It imparts a lemony but traditional thyme flavor. Oregano thyme may be substituted for oregano just as caraway thyme can replace caraway. The upright thymes are best for cooking. Sprinkle them over carrots, beef and lamb stews, and chicken and fish dishes. For lamb shish-kabob, mix some oil, Worcestershire sauce, and thyme, and marinate lamb cubes for a few hours before broiling over the grill. Thyme grape jelly, thyme elderberry jelly, and thyme and apple jelly complement lamb dishes.

FLOWERS
OF INDIVIDUAL HERBS

Not all herbs used for culinary purposes are used for their leaves. The flowers of some play important roles in cooking. Other flowers make pretty decorations for salads and pastries.

Borage: The flowers of borage are a beautiful sky blue color with a star-like shape. These pretty flowers are used for floating on punches or other beverages, adding a slight cucumber flavor to salads, or when candied are nice for decorating cookies or cakes. When used in drinks they enhance the other flavors as well as decorate.

Calendula Flowers: The flowers of this herb are used to color butter, cheese, sauces, soups, and stews. They give the foods a deep yellow color as if many eggs were added. The calendula flowers are a substitute ingredient when true saffron is not available. They are also used in tea for flavor and color.

Chives: The pretty chive flowers lend an onion flavor to salads. Used as a garnish for potato or macaroni salad, they give any meal a festive touch.

Marigolds: These flowers found in many gardens lend a gold color as well as a pungent flavor to rice, soups, and stews.

Nasturtiums: The nasturtium blossoms may be used for a peppery flavor in lettuce salads, or as a garnish for fruit salads. For an unusual spread, mince and blend the flowers with butter.

Rose Petals: Rose petals have long been used for cooking. Rose water, rose syrup, and rose petal jam are familiar to many. The petals can also be used to decorate fruit punches or candied to decorate cakes. Use an old-fashioned moss-type if possible. If these are not available tea roses can be used, however, the white edge of each petal must be removed first or it will make your product bitter.

Safflower: The popularity of this herb is gaining steadily for the fine oil that is produced from the seed head. The flower petals may be substituted for saffron when coloring butter, rice, chicken gravy, or stew.

Saffron Crocus: The stigmas of this fall-blooming crocus are the source of the golden coloring agent commonly used to give the appearance of many eggs as a basic ingredient in the recipe. Saffron is used when flavoring and coloring cheeses, butter, rice, noodles, chicken gravies and soups, cookies, and

There are few things more pleasurable than a mid-day break for a cup of herbal tea. Make a ritual of the break by brewing a teapotful and sharing it with a friend.

pastries. A little bit of saffron goes a long way, so use only very small amounts.

Violets: Violet flowers are used for making violet syrup, jams, and jellies. They are very attractive when candied and used as a condiment or cake decoration.

RECIPES

MEAT MENUS

Spicy Beef Stew

    3 lbs. beef stew meat
      salt and pepper
  ½ cup butter
    2 lbs. onions
  ¾ cup tomato paste
  ⅓ cup red wine
    2 tbsp. red wine vinegar
    1 tsp. honey
    1 clove garlic minced
    1 bay leaf
    1 cinnamon stick
  ½ tsp. whole cloves
  ¼ tsp. cumin
    2 tbsp. raisins

Season meat with salt and pepper. Melt butter, add meat and arrange onions over meat. Mix tomato paste, wine, vinegar, honey, and garlic. Pour over meat and onions. Add rest of ingredients. Cover and simmer 3 hours. *Do not stir.*

Chicken Sesame

    1 frying chicken, cut up
    1 tsp. salt
  ¼ tsp. ground pepper
    1 egg slightly beaten
  ¼ cup whole wheat flour
  ½ cup sesame seeds
  ½ cup butter
  ½ cup bread crumbs

Mix flour, salt, and pepper. Roll chicken in flour, dip in egg, roll in bread crumbs mixed with sesame seeds. Melt butter in fry pan and saute chicken until brown. Cover and simmer 30 mins. or until done. Last 10 mins. remove cover to crisp chicken.

Chicken Rosemary

2 broilers, cut up

¼ cup butter

½ cup minced onion

1 clove garlic, minced

½ cup water

1 chicken bouillon

¼ cup chopped parsley

2 tsp. fresh rosemary

Brown chicken on all sides in butter in skillet. Remove chicken to baking dish. Cook onion and garlic until brown in skillet. Add water and bouillon. Cook and stir until all brown bits in pan dissolved. Add parsley and rosemary. Pour over chicken. Bake 45 min. in 375° oven. Serve over brown rice.

Parsley is a familiar garnish, but its companion here, the leek, is seldom seen in the kitchen. It is, nevertheless, a tasty and useful culinary herb.

Braised Short Ribs

          4 lbs. beef short ribs
       1¼ cup beef stock or broth
          2 tbsp. marjoram
          ⅓ cup whole wheat flour
          3 tbsp. butter
          1 clove garlic, chopped fine
          ¼ cup sherry
            salt and pepper

Brown ribs in shallow pan in oven for 15 min. at 550°. Add broth, cover with foil, and lower oven and cook at 350° for two hours. Brown flour slowly, mix with butter. Remove broth from pan and add to flour mixture. Stir and cook until thick. Add rest of ingredients. Pour over meat and cook 15 min. longer. Serve meat with gravy.

Stuffed Zucchini Squash

          4 or 5 med. zucchini squash about
             6 inches long
            salt
          ¾ tbsp. oil
          ¾ cup chopped onion
          1 clove garlic chopped
          ¼ lb. sweet sausage, casing removed
          ½ lb. ground beef
          ¼ tsp. pepper
          1 tsp. rosemary
          3 slices bread
          ½ cup milk
          3 tbsp. grated cheese
          ¼ cup chopped parsley

Wash zucchini and cut off ends. Cook whole in boiling water

8 min. Drain, cut in half lengthwise, and remove pulp. Cook onion and garlic in oil a few minutes, add sausage, beef, ½ tsp. salt, pepper, and rosemary. Cook 15 min. Break bread in pieces and soak in milk. Add to meat with cheese and zucchini pulp. Place in baking dish, greased. Bake at 325° for 35 min.

Chicken Roll with Sauce

¾ cup sliced mushrooms
¼ cup butter
½ cup chopped chives
¼ cup chopped lovage
2 cups diced cooked chicken or turkey
2 cups mushroom sauce
salt and pepper to taste
biscuit dough, at least 2 cups

In a large skillet, sauté mushrooms in butter. Add chives and lovage and cook 2 min. longer. Remove from heat, add chicken, ½ cup mushroom sauce and salt and pepper if needed. Mix well, chill for one hour. Meanwhile, make biscuit dough. Roll dough until ½ inch thick. Spread chilled mixture over dough and roll up like jelly roll. Seal edges. Cut slits in dough. Place on greased baking sheet and bake 25 min. at 400°. Serve with remaining mushroom sauce, thinning down with milk to desired consistency.

Mushroom Sauce

½ cup sliced mushrooms
4 tbsp. butter
½ cup whole wheat flour
1 cup milk
salt and pepper to taste
2 tbsp. chopped parsley

In a small skillet, sauté mushrooms in butter. Add flour and stir in milk. Cook until thick. Season with salt and pepper to taste. Add parsley just before serving.

Basil is best known as a companion to tomatoes, both in the garden and in the cookpot. Basil is also an excellent condiment to use with soups and stews, salads and vegetable dishes.

VEGETABLE DISHES

Carrots Marinade

6 carrots
1/4 cup oil
1/2 cup basil vinegar
1 1/2 tbsp. honey
1/4 clove garlic, chopped fine
4 tbsp. tarragon, chopped fine

Slice carrots into 3 inch pieces. Cook for 10 min., until just done, yet still firm. Combine in sauce pan oil, basil vinegar, honey, clove garlic, and tarragon. Heat until hot and pour over drained carrots. Let marinate until ready to serve.

Rosemary Potatoes

4 or 5 large boiled potatoes
3 tbsp. butter
2 tsp. rosemary

Leave potatoes whole or slice them into ¼″ slices. Fry in skillet with 3 tbsp. of butter and 2 tsp. of rosemary. Fry until potatoes are brown and crispy.

Harvard Beets

8 to 10 medium-sized beets
2 tbsp. butter
½ cup cider vinegar
1 tbsp. cornstarch
1 tsp. tarragon
¼ cup honey

Gently boil beets until tender. Peel and slice. In a large saucepan, mix rest of ingredients except tarragon and honey. Cook until thick, add tarragon, honey and beets and heat through.

Cucumber in Dill

1 cucumber, unpared and thinly
   sliced
¼ cup cider vinegar
1 tbsp. chopped fresh dillweed
2 tsp. honey
⅛ tsp. salt
   dash pepper

Combine ingredients and refrigerate for a few hours.

Basil Stuffed Tomatoes

2 tbsp. bread crumbs
1 tsp. parmesan cheese grated
1 tsp. butter
2 tsp. fresh chopped basil
4 tomatoes—large

Remove cores and stems from tomatoes leaving hollows in their centers. Mix rest of ingredients. Fill center of each tomato with stuffing. Bake for 45 min. at 350° or until done.

Summer Garden Casserole

1 clove garlic, chopped
2 med. sliced zucchini
1 small eggplant, peeled and sliced
4 med. tomatoes sliced
   salt and pepper
1 tsp. fresh chopped oregano
2 tsp. fresh chopped basil
¼ cup grated parmesan cheese
1 cup grated cheddar cheese
¼ cup bread crumbs
2 tbsp. butter

Combine oregano, basil, garlic, and cheeses. Place layer of zucchini, then tomatoes, then eggplant in large greased casserole. Sprinkle every third layer with cheese and herb mixture. Continue with layers until all ingredients are used up. Mix bread crumbs and butter and sprinkle over casserole. Bake at 350° about 50 mins. or until done.

Stir-Fried Zucchini

1 med. zucchini squash—sliced
1 med. onion—sliced
1 tsp. summer savory
1 tsp. butter

Melt butter in frying pan. Add onions and fry for a few minutes before adding zucchini squash. Cut squash slices in half if they are large. Add savory and stir and fry about 10 minutes or until done.

Note: Keep heat high enough to fry squash without having any liquid form. Do not use lid on pan.

Jiffy Sorrel Soup

good handful of sorrel leaves,
   quartered
2 tbsp. butter
3 med. potatoes, chopped in small
   pieces

1 tsp. salt
    sour cream/chopped chives

Melt butter in pan, add sorrel leaves and diced potatoes. Cook for 5 to 7 minutes, or until leaves are well wilted. Add 6 cups water, bring to slow boil and cook 15 to 20 minutes.

Remove pan from heat and cool slightly. Place mixture in blender and whirl until soup is smooth and creamy.

Reheat soup slowly. Serve hot with dab of sour cream in center; sprinkle with chopped chives.

SALADS AND SALAD DRESSING

Chervil-Tarragon Salad Dressing

6 tbsp. oil
3 tbsp. tarragon vinegar
1 tsp. finely chopped onion
¾ tsp. salt
    pinch black pepper
3 tbsp. chopped fresh chervil

Mix all ingredients and serve over green salad.

Potato Salad

4 whole potatoes
2 tsp. caraway seed
3 tbsp. oil
¼ chopped onion
    salt and pepper
2 tbsp. fresh tarragon
2 tbsp. parsley
1 tbsp. basil
3 tbsp. vinegar
¼ cup salad dressing

Boil potatoes with skins on in water with caraway seeds. When done, peel and cut them in cubes. Marinate in oil, onion, salt, and pepper. Meanwhile chop tarragon and basil. Add to potatoes with vinegar and salad dressing. Mix and serve either warm or chilled.

No-Dressing Tossed Salad

¼ head lettuce
    handful sorrel leaves
1 pepper
1 tomato
2 carrots
2 lovage stalks
¼ tsp. pepper
½ tsp. salt

Chop all ingredients, add salt and pepper. Let set for ½ hour before serving. This salad makes its own salad dressing.

Potato Salad With Lovage

6 or 7 boiled potatoes
2 stalks lovage, sliced and
    diced, leaves and stems
½ onion diced

Salsify is a potherb grown for its root. It is cultivated and cooked like carrots or beets.

1 cup salad dressing
salt and pepper
celery salt

Boil potatoes until done. Cool slightly but while still warm, peel and cut into cubes. Add lovage, onion, and salad dressing. Toss, and add seasonings. Chill before serving. Serves 8 to 10.

SAUCE

Dill Sauce

½ cup shredded swiss cheese
¼ cup salad dressing
½ cup sour cream
1 tsp. dillweed

Cook cheese and salad dressing over low heat until cheese melts. Beat if necessary. Stir in sour cream and dillweed. Heat through. Serve hot over cauliflower, asparagus, broccoli, or carrots.

Mint Sauce

2 tbsp. chopped mint leaves
1 tbsp. vinegar
1 tbsp. honey

Mix and serve over baked lamb.

Horseradish Sauce

½ pt. heavy cream
salt
2 tbsp. horseradish

Whip cream, add sprinkle of salt. Fold in horseradish. Keep refrigerated until use. Use on any type of meat.

DESSERTS

Tansy Cookies

¼ cup honey
½ cup butter
1 egg
2 cups whole wheat flour
¼ tsp. baking soda
¼ tsp. salt
1 tsp. vanilla
1½ tsp. tansy
1 tbsp. yogurt

This flower head is characteristic of the mints, a most versatile group of herbs. The mints have aromatic, cosmetic, and healing uses. In cooking, the mints add a refreshing spark to many dishes.

Beat honey and butter, add eggs then rest of ingredients. Beat until well blended. Roll out to ⅛-inch thickness on floured board. Cut with cookie cutter. Sprinkle cookies with more tansy and bake at 375° for 10 minutes.

Sweet Cicely Coffee Cake

2 cups sweet biscuit dough
1½ cups almond paste
1 large can crushed pineapple
2 tbsp. whole wheat flour
6 tbsp. honey
4 sweet cicely leaves, chopped fine

Roll out biscuit dough on floured surface until about ½-inch thick and oblong in shape. Spread almond paste and crushed pineapple in layers. Sprinkle with 2 tbsp. of flour and drizzle the honey over it. Top with sweet cicely leaves. Fold both sides over filling. Press seams to seal. Bake on lightly-floured cookie sheet for 20 minutes at 350° or until done.

Honey Rhubarb Pie

¼ cup angelica stalk (cut up into small slices)
4 cups rhubarb cut into ½ inch pieces
1½ cups honey
6 tbsp. whole wheat flour
¼ tsp. salt
2 pie crusts
2 tbsp. butter

Mix first five ingredients. Pour into 9 inch pan lined with pie crust. Dot with butter. Seal top crust. Bake at 450° for 10 min. or 350° for 45 to 55 min. or until done.

Anise Bar Cookies

        1 egg
     ½ cup honey
     ½ tsp. salt
        1 cup raw wheat germ
     ½ cup buttermilk
        1 tsp. baking soda
        2 cups whole wheat flour
        3 tbsp. anise seed
     ½ cup pignola nuts

In a large mixing bowl, mix egg, honey, salt, wheat germ, buttermilk and baking soda. Add 1 cup of flour, anise seed and nuts. Mix thoroughly, then add rest of flour. Place in greased pan, shaped long and rounded. Bake at 350° about 30 mins. Remove from oven, cool, and slice. If desired, toast each slice until golden brown for 7 mins.

Blueberry Bars

        1 cup chopped nuts (pecans or
             walnuts)
     ½ cup honey
        2 cups whole wheat flour
     ½ cup butter
        2 cups blueberries
        2 eggs
     ½ tsp. salt
     1½ tsp. cinnamon
        6 tbsp. wheat germ (raw)
        1 tsp. baking soda
        1 cup buttermilk

Sprinkle 9 × 13 greased pan with chopped nuts. Mix honey, flour and butter with fork until crumbly. Pour 2 cups over nuts. Pat smooth. Spread blueberries over this mixture. In a large mixing bowl, beat eggs, salt, cinnamon, wheat germ, soda and buttermilk with left over flour mix. Pour over blueberries and bake at 350° for 35 to 40 mins. or until done. Cool.

Pumpkin Squares

½ cup butter
1½ cups honey
2 cups pumpkin
1 egg
2 cups whole wheat flour
½ cup buttermilk
1 tsp. baking soda
½ tsp. salt
2 tsp. cinnamon
½ tsp. nutmeg
¾ tsp. cloves
½ tsp. allspice
2 cups oats (uncooked)
1 cup dates (quartered)
½ cup nuts

Beat butter, egg, honey, and pumpkin. Add flour, salt, soda, spices and oats. Mix well until blended. Add dates and nuts, mix.

Grease 9 x 9 pan, spread batter evenly. Bake at 350° for 40 mins. or until done.

If desired frost with following icing.

Honey Frosting

½ cup honey
2 egg whites
½ tsp. vanilla

Beat ingredients for about 10 mins. while cooking in the top of a double boiler. Remove from heat, continue to beat until mixture is consistency of frosting.

Safflower is most prized for its oil, which is the highest in polyunsaturates of any available oil.

Poppy Seed Cake

1 cup oil
1 cup honey
3 eggs
3 cups whole wheat flour
¾ cup poppy seeds*
3 tsp. baking soda
1½ cup buttermilk
½ tsp. salt

Mix all ingredients together. Bake at 350° 35 to 40 minutes or until done.

*Caraway or anise seeds can be substituted for the poppy seeds if desired.

Spiced Pear Slices

4 cups pears, peeled and sliced
1½ cups water
5 tbsp. honey
2 sticks cinnamon
1 tbsp. cloves

Mix all together and cook slowly until pears are tender, yet firm. Serve as side dish with meals.

BREAD
Anise and Banana Bread

2 tbsp. butter
¾ cup buttermilk
⅔ cup honey
1 egg
2 bananas
1½ tsp. baking soda
3 cups whole wheat flour
1 tsp. salt
1 cup dates, chopped
1 cup nuts, broken
4 tsp. anise seed

Mix butter, buttermilk, eggs, honey, and bananas together. Add flour, salt, and baking soda. Mix well, then add dates, nuts, and anise seed. Pour into 2 greased loaf pans. Bake 350° for 45-55 mins. or until done.

Caraway Fruit Dessert

1 cup whole wheat flour
2 tbsp. honey
1 egg
2 tbsp. butter
½ cup buttermilk
1 tsp. baking soda
4 cups apples, pears or peaches, sliced
⅓ cup raisins
1 tsp. caraway seed
1 tsp. cinnamon
2 tbsp. honey
¼ cup coconut

In a large mixing bowl, mix first six ingredients together and spread in greased 9 × 9 pan. Spread apples and raisins over this. Sprinkle caraway seed and cinnamon over the apples, then drizzle honey over top. Top with coconut. Bake 1 hour or until fruit is tender at 325°.

JELLIES

Rose Geranium Honey Jelly

2½ cups honey
¾ cup water
6 or 7 rose geranium leaves
½ bottle (3 oz.) fruit pectin
2 tbsp. lemon juice

Combine honey, water, rose geranium leaves and quickly bring to boil. Add pectin, stirring constantly. Bring to full rolling boil. Add lemon juice, remove from heat. Remove leaves from mixture. Place fresh leaf in hot sterile jars and cover with jelly. Seal with parafin and store for a few weeks to allow flavor of leaves to saturate jelly.

Parsley Jelly

3 cups infusion
2½ cups honey
2 tbsp. lemon juice
1 box pectin

Prepare infusion by pouring 3½ cups boiling water over 4 cups of chopped parsley. Let stand 15 min. and strain. Add lemon juice and pectin to infusion. Mix well and bring to hard boil. Stir in honey. Boil at full boil for 1 min., stirring constantly. Remove from heat, skim, and pour into jars. Seal.

Herb Jellies (Sage, Tarragon, Thyme, and Mint)

2 cups infusion
¼ cup vinegar
2½ cups honey
½ bottle fruit pectin

To make infusion pour 2½ cups boiling water over 4 tbsp. dried herbs or 8 tbsp. fresh herbs. Let stand 15 min. Strain; add vinegar and honey. Bring to boil, stirring constantly. Add fruit pectin, and boil hard for 1 min. Remove from heat, skim, and pour in sterile jar containing a sprig of herb you are using.

Sage was originally an important healing plant, but it is now most commonly associated with its culinary uses. A stimulant, sage will perk up any meal, but particularly those with cheese dishes or rich stuffings and meats.

VINEGARS

Herb vinegars are very easy to make. They are also a good way to store some of your herbs for winter use. Fresh herbs make better vinegars, but of course if these are not available, the dried can be used. The flavor and color will not be as true as when using the fresh, but they will still be very tasty.

If the herbs in your garden have been mulched, the foliage will be relatively clean and may not need to be washed. If you do wash the plants, be sure to remove most of the water from the sprigs before making the vinegar. A few good shakes, and then blotting with a towel will accomplish this.

Glass bottles or jars are best when making the vinegar. Use

a non-metal cap in order to avoid a chemical reaction between the vinegar and metal. This reaction could spoil all of your hard work. If a metal cap is used, do not completely fill the bottle. Either the whole sprigs or just the leaves and tips of the herbs can be used. Fill your bottles with these sprigs, cover with vinegar, label, and store in a cool place for at least a month. Check the bottle after a few days to be sure that all of the foliage is covered with the vinegar. Sometimes air is trapped under the foliage. As the herbs settle in the bottles, the sprigs become exposed to the air causing a discoloration of the foliage.

To hasten the herb flavoring, the vinegar can be heated just below the boiling point and poured over the herbs. Care should be taken so that the vinegar is not boiled or it will destroy the acetic acid in the vinegar which is essential to preserve the herb foliage. Heating the vinegar also changes the color of the herbs and causes them to decompose more readily. Thus unless haste is necessary, using the cool vinegar seems to be a more favorable method.

Many gardeners make herb vinegars to enhance their salads. Louise Hyde makes a large quantity of her herb vinegar, then rebottles it, adding a sprig of the herb to each container to enhance the package's appearance. Most any culinary herb can be used. Basil, rosemary, sage, and thyme are among the most popular.

The vinegar can be stored in large bottles. Later when a smaller quantity is needed, it can be divided into smaller bottles and relabeled. If at this time the vinegar seems to be too strong, dilute with plain vinegar before using. A sprig of the herb placed in each bottle enhances its appearance.

There are many different herbs and combinations of herbs that can be used for the herb vinegars. These make excellent salad dressings, marinades, pickling vinegars, and versatile vinegars to use in everyday cooking.

A favorite herb for vinegar is the purple basil. This basil gives the vinegar a rich burgundy color and makes a very impressive gift. With the purple basil add some sweet basil to give it a sweeter flavor. The purple basil is also very good in combination with garlic or tarragon. Basil vinegar is especially flavorful on tomatoes and leafy greens.

Another useful vinegar is made with dill. Either the dillweed (the sprigs before the plant blooms) or the dill seed heads can be used. When the seed heads are used, the vinegar has a pinkish color. This makes a good vinegar for salads and for marinating a combination of sliced tomato, basil, and onion. A dash in tomato juice gives it added zest.

When making hors d'oeuvres, the dillweed from the vinegar adds a flavorful garnish for your open sandwiches. Beets, cabbage, and potato salad are especially tasty when made with dill vinegar.

Tarragon vinegar is a long time favorite. The leaves in the vinegar can be used as the fresh herb. For example, the chopped tarragon leaves add a gourmet touch when added to crab meat, chicken, or turkey salads.

Salad burnet lends a cucumber flavor to the vinegar. When this is used on salads, it gives the cucumber taste without the digestive upset sometimes caused by fresh cucumbers.

Orange mint has a citrus flavor and is excellent where mint can be used. Pick the mint when the blossoms are full and the vinegar will have a pinkish-green color. Orange mint vinegar makes a good base for a dressing used on fruit and fruit salads. Rosemary vinegar can also be used as a fruit complement.

Many other herbs or combinations of herbs can be tried

when making vinegar. Rosemary, sage, thyme, lovage, oregano, marjoram, parsley, or any of the other cooking herbs can be used. Be sure to try out various combinations in small amounts before making large batches. A few sprigs of a strong herb and a handful of a milder herb would make a better vinegar than two very strong herbs which can overpower each other. Spark up your menus with some unusual combinations.

Herb vinegars are used to flavor soups, stews, ground meat dishes, gravies, stuffings for fish and poultry, aspics, fruit and vegetable salads, and for flavorful salad dressings. Inexpensive cuts of meat can be marinated in a combination of your favorite herb vinegar and oil. Many other uses for herb vinegars are sure to be found in your everyday cooking.

BUTTERS

An interesting flair may be added to a meal by using herb butters. These special butters are delicious as a spread on breads, rolls, and biscuits. The herb flavor is enhanced when the butter is spread on the bread, wrapped in aluminum foil, and heated thoroughly. Herb butters are also good on cooked string beans, peas, carrots, tomatoes, asparagus, cabbage, potatoes, or any other vegetables. Before serving cooked vegetables, toss with a compatible herb butter. Broiled fish, steaks, chicken, and chops are given a new flavor when topped with herb butter as they are removed from the broiler. Herb butters can even be used as an ingredient in sauces, casseroles, omelettes, and scrambled eggs.

Herb butters may be made by using either a single herb or a combination of herbs. To make any herb butter, cream ½ cup softened butter with the chopped herb or herbs of your choice. Cover the mixture and allow to mellow approximately two to three hours before using. It will keep several days in the refrigerator. Some suggested combinations are listed below.

Chive Butter
½ cup butter
1 tbsp. chopped chives
1 tbsp. parsley
¼-½ tsp. rosemary

Savory Butter

½ cup butter
1 tsp. savory
1 tsp. dry mustard

Dill and Oregano Butter

½ cup butter
1 tsp. dillweed or dillseed
1 tsp. oregano

Mint Butter

½ cup butter
½ cup mint leaves
2 tbsp. lemon juice

All-Purpose Herb Butter

1 small clove garlic
1 tbsp. dillweed
1 tbsp. tarragon
2 tbsp. chives

Lemon Parsley Butter

½ cup butter
2 tbsp. parsley
1 tsp. chives
½ tsp. lemon juice

Zesty Butter

½ cup butter
1 tbsp. mustard
1 tsp. horseradish
½ tsp. salt
dash of pepper

Tarragon and Thyme Butter

½ cup butter
½ tsp. tarragon
¼ tsp. thyme
3 tbsp. parsley

Sage and Bacon Butter

½ cup butter
4 or 5 strips crumbled bacon
½ tsp. sage

SALTS

Herb salts are a flavorful way of adding both herbs and salt to your meals. They are very easy to make, too. Start with ½ cup of sea salt. Sea salt is very fine and readily blends with your herbs. If using fresh herbs, do not wash unless necessary. If washed be very careful that every drop of moisture is removed from the foliage. Mince the leaves, then crush them with the salt using a mortar and pestle or the base of a heavy jar. An easier method is to put the salt and herbs in the blender and whirl for a few minutes. A very fine end product results.

After crushing, spread the salt on a cookie sheet and dry in a 200° oven for about 40 to 60 minutes, or until the mixture seems dry. Be sure to break up any lumps and stir frequently during drying. When cool, seal in a glass jar.

If you wish to make an herb salt in a hurry you can use dry herbs. Place the herbs and salt in the blender or blend them together by hand. Four or five tablespoons of herbs to about ½ cup of salt works well. Single herbs or combinations can be used. Make sure that the herbs are very fine so that they can be sprinkled through a shaker.

Paprika added to your herb salt, gives a nice red color and enhances the flavor. Use your herb salts to sprinkle in tomato juice, over potatoes or macaroni (plain or in salad form), vegetables, casseroles, or to use as a flavoring in any of your favorite recipes.

TEAS

Unusual teas may be made from various herbs. These teas may be used for beverage or medicinal purposes. If you are not accustomed to drinking herb teas, try using them with one regular tea bag to a pot of tea. This may help make them more palatable for you. Fresh or dried herbs may be used; the dried herbs are more concentrated so use about half the amount as you would for the fresh herbs. Most teas are made by using one teaspoon of the dried herb to one cup of boiling water. Place the herbs in an earthenware or china teapot, fill with boiling water, and allow the tea to steep about five to ten minutes, depending upon whether seeds, roots, or leaves are used. The leaves or seeds may be crushed to obtain more flavor. Teas made from some seeds and roots require boiling for five to ten minutes to extract the full flavor from the herb. Strain the tea before serving. If a sweetener is desired, use honey since it blends better with the herbal teas. Most teas are best served without milk.

Iced herb teas can be made in this same manner, but after straining the tea, chill before serving. As a garnish, use a few fresh sprigs of the herb in each pitcher of iced tea.

Some herb teas are very palatable while others are quite unusual. Some of the most flavorful teas are the mints, scented geraniums, sweet-scented goldenrod, sassafras, pennyroyal, lemon verbena, camomile, rosemary, and catnip. When added to a pot of regular tea a peppermint, rose, or lemon geranium leaf will lend a characteristic flavor. The Pennsylvania Dutch people gather the sweet-scented goldenrod to make a delicious tea with an anise flavor. This is not the goldenrod that is ordinarily found in fields, but a special kind, *Solidago odora*. This tea is also called Blue Mountain Tea.

Combinations of herbs make interesting teas, too. Some herbs make a good base tea while others enhance the flavor. A very unusual tea combination is lemon herb tea.

Lemon Herb Tea

9 tbsp. lemon thyme
3 tbsp. lemon basil
½ tsp. lemon balm
4 tbsp. mild green tea

Anise, caraway, fennel, coriander, and cumin seeds used separately or in combination make refreshing teas. Dill tea is rich in minerals and makes a good after dinner tea.

A relaxing tea is made from sassafras. Use a few pieces of the bark for each quart of water. Let this steep for about five minutes. Sassafras root was originally used for making root beer and this aroma is especially strong as the tea is brewing. Bergamot tea, made from the plant commonly called bee balm, is also called Oswego tea.

Camomile tea, made from the flower heads of the plant, is a good aid to digestion and upset stomachs. It has also been reported to improve one's disposition. Angelica leaf tea is used to stimulate digestion.

Some herbs with lemon fragrances make pleasant tasting teas to be served either hot or cold. Lemon verbena, lemon balm, and lemon grass are three of these. They are tasty used alone, in combination with each other, or with other herbs. They can replace the slice of lemon often served with tea.

Borage leaves, either used for iced or hot tea, are known for giving a "lift" after a hard day. The pretty blue flowers of borage not only add interest to iced tea but also improve the flavor.

A favorite tea of the German people is peppermint tea. This is a relaxing after dinner tea. Other varieties of mint such as ginger, orange, apple, and spearmint may also be used. The herb costmary also has a minty flavor.

Rosemary tea helps cure headaches and colds. Use rosemary alone or in combination with other herbs. It is a very strong tea so use small amounts. Sage produces a full-bodied tea which may be used as a base tea. It is preferred by some to our ordinary Chinese tea. It is useful as a tonic and for colds and fevers. Catnip tea or catnip and fennel tea have long been used to help alleviate colic in babies. It is a pleasant tasting beverage to accompany meals. Comfrey tea, made from the comfrey leaves, is a very nourishing and healthful tea. It is purported to cure most any ailment.

These are just a few of the herb beverage teas. There are many more waiting for you to try. Everyone has his or her own preferences, so be adventurous and discover your own special blends.

LIQUEURS

Liqueurs are cordials, flavored brandies, or flavored gins which are made by mixing distilled spirits with fruit juices or herbs and syrups. The syrup gives the sweetening common to most liqueurs.

When making liqueurs, the alcohol and flavoring ingredients are mixed and allowed to stand at least 24 hours before adding the water syrup. This is to blend the flavor and aroma.

Herb tea can be brewed from individual herbs, or from blends. Some are relaxing, others stimulating. All are pleasurable.

After the syrup is added, age the finished product two weeks or more at room temperature to get a full flavor. If wines are used to make liqueur, use a quality aged wine which has a high acetic content. The high acidity of the wine affects the quality of the end product.

The large commercial producers of liqueurs have their own secret list of herbs and spices which they use to produce special blends. Many of these blends are made with the oils extracted from the herbs and spices. For example, one type of Benedictine is made by blending as many as 15 different oils. This makes an especially tasty blend, but for your own use, crushed leaves or seeds of a specific herb make a very flavorful liqueur. Crush the herb with a mortar and pestle, or place the herb with part of the liquid in the blender. For the syrup needed to add to your liqueur, use equal amounts of honey and water. Boil the water for a few minutes, remove from the heat, then add the honey. The amount of honey syrup added to any liqueur can be varied to suit individual preferences. Three simple liqueur recipes follow:

Aniseed Liqueur

(A licorice flavored cordial)

Crush 3 tbsp. anise seed
Add 1 pint brandy
Let mixture stand 2-3 weeks
  before straining
Add ½ cup honey syrup

Lemon Balm Liqueur

Crush handful of lemon balm leaves
Add 1 pint brandy
Let mixture steep
  24 hours before straining
Add ½ cup honey syrup

Mint Liqueur

Crush 3 tbsp. peppermint leaves or
  3 tbsp. orange mint leaves
Add a few peels of orange rind

Add 1 pint wine or brandy
Let mixture steep 2 or 3
    weeks before straining
Add ½ cup honey syrup

Buffalo grass when added to vodka, gives it a distinctive flavor. Steep one or two blades of dried buffalo grass in the vodka. The Polish call this Zubrowka.

A form of Drambuie can be made with crushed aniseed added to a pint of scotch whiskey. Add three-quarters cup of honey after steeping the seed.

Coriander is used to flavor gin, basil and angelica for chartreuse, and fennel for anethole. Cumin, wild marjoram, peppermint, sage, tarragon, lovage, thyme, vanilla, and angelica seeds are all used as liqueur flavorings.

Mead, a flavorful drink similar to a liqueur, was made by the early settlers in our country and today is still a popular beverage of the Pennsylvania Dutch. It is made by mixing one quart of honey with three quarts of water. A cinnamon stick, anise seed, or fennel seed may be added for extra flavor. Simmer this for about one hour. Cool and add ½ package of yeast. Let this mixture stand until the fermentation stops.

As you become more experienced in making liqueurs, try varying some of these ingredients to make unusual cordials. A few suggested combinations are: rosemary, germander, and lemon verbena; common and Roman wormwood, lavender, and lemon verbena; caraway, mint, and orange peel; sliced orange with fennel seed; and anise seed with lemon peel. Other herbs and spices that make interesting liqueurs are blessed thistle, centaury, angelica root, yarrow, elecampane root, rosemary, clary sage, orris root, Roman wormwood, common wormwood, germander, orange or lemon peel, cinnamon, cloves, cardamon, nutmeg, allspice, mint, or any other aromatic herb that appeals to you.

If you wish to add a finished touch to your liqueurs, coloring with tumeric, saffron, or calendula petals will give them a golden yellow hue. Green herbs lend a pale green color to a cordial with a vodka or white wine base.

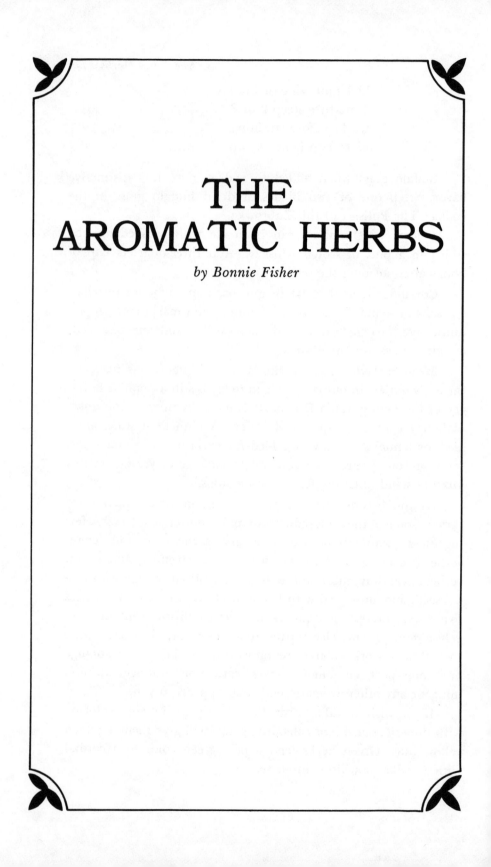

THE AROMATIC HERBS

by Bonnie Fisher

FOUR

The little elderly lady, lacy hanky in hand, faintly smelling of lavender. The richly aromatic garden. The fragrant little pillow quietly scenting all the clothing in the drawer. Silly frilly little girls strewing flower petals and fragrant foliage along a processional aisle.

Aromatic herbs arouse different associations in the minds of different people. I can never shake the association between strewing herbs and the giggly girls, skipping along and skattering the petals from their baskets. It seems so childish and purposeless, yet the tradition has sound roots.

Strewing herbs got its start in the odiferous past, when sanitation was at best rudimentary and aromas of civilization were more on the order of unpleasant odors rather than fragrances. He whose kingly status afforded him the wherewithall had herb-based concoctions with which to mask the odors, concoctions which, on special occasions, included teams of lackeys to spread aromatic herbs on the ground before him. Even *his* dainty step would bruise the herbage, releasing the pleasant fragrance. As society got the hang of controlling odors, the purpose went out of the practice and it evolved into the flower girl image.

Actually, strewing herbs wasn't a practice limited to the rich; any home that had an herb garden could have its floors strewn with herbs. The housewife of old perfumed her home with the scents that today's housewife finds attractive in her home, but today's housewife, more often than not, uses an ersatz fragrance from an aerosol bomb, while the housewife of old used the real thing.

Ancient herbalists were adept at using aromatic herbs to please the olfactory senses, and with a bit of practice, you can too. They brewed sweetly scented soaps, fragrant bathing waters, and aromatic waters used by milady on her face and hair. Floral scented powders and perfume essences were used on the body after bathing. Pomanders, potpourris, and sachets were devised to scent rooms and clothing. The natural aroma of certain herbs was found to be effective in diverting insects. Spicy-scented candles and incenses were an important aspect of ancient rituals. Even the breath was sweetened by herbs.

Montaigne, the great French philosopher, claimed specific essences could make him happy, excited, contemplative, or peaceful. Scented herbs are capable of making one more aware as they are able to stir emotions, bring back memories, and ignite love. By learning which herbs to plant for fragrance and how to use them, you too can enjoy natural scents in your daily life. You will agree it is far more pleasurable to inhale natural and fresh scents rather than contrived chemical scents.

There is, of course, no reason not to use the real thing. Today's herbs are just as fragrant as those of years gone by, and the various means of putting their scents to work in your home are just as simple as they used to be.

You will probably want to start simply, which is why I started with breath sweeteners. There's no easier beginning, even for the most lethargic. Pomanders are put together using ingredients that, for most people, are store-bought, making them just the ticket for folks who have the interest but not the garden. Potpourris, sachets, herbal baths, and aromatic waters can be single-herb products, or they can involve many herbs. Eventually, you'll want—if you find herbal aromatics an engaging hobby—to put herbal oils to use. And you don't have to extract the oils yourself (although you can); a wide variety of such oils is available by mail from a number of botanical supply houses. See the appendix for the names and addresses of several reputable ones. (These suppliers are also sources of exotic herbs you may want to use.)

At some point in your active experience with herbal aromatics, you'll come face-to-face with a need for a fixative. A number of the following pages mention fixatives. A fixative is a plant or animal material used to set and hold the herbal fragrance. Three animal-derived fixatives are ambergris, civet, and musk, and three plant-derived fixatives are orris root, benzoin, and tonka beans. Ambergris is a secretion of the sperm whale, civet is extracted from glands of the African civet cat, and musk was originally taken from the musk deer, a nearly extinct Central Asia native (but today most musk is synthetic). All three substances are unpleasant smelling. But when combined with fragrant herbs, the foul smell of these fixatives is lost and the pleasant scent of the botanicals is amplified, enriched, and set.

The plant-derived fixatives are more commonly used these days. Benzoin is a gum collected from a tree called *Styrax benzoinx*. In Java, Sumatra, and Thailand, these trees are grown commercially for the gum benzoin. Storax, a gum or resin, is also collected in much the same fashion as rubber, permitted to harden, and ground into a powder. Tonka beans are raised in several South American and African countries and in Ceylon.

But the most commonly-used and easily-available fixative is orris root, which is the root of the Florentine iris. The root is dried and stored for at least two years before being ground into powder.

You will never need this information, however, if you don't put herbs and their aromas to work in your home. In the following pages, I'll tell you how, but only you can do it.

BREATH SWEETENERS

Our ancestors didn't place a chemically contrived breath mint into their mouths to cover offensive breath. Instead they relied on sweet tasting and smelling herbs to make their breaths spring fresh.

In early times, one of the most common means of breath purification was to suck on whole cloves. The secret of cloves as a mouth sweetener has been known for over 4,000 years. During the Middle Ages, anise seed was chewed slowly to cover up telltale odors. In the Orient and Europe, cardamon seeds have long been used after eating to cover strong odors. Early American settlers were known to use bits of calamus root, while small pieces of dried orris root were chewed by ladies to make their breath kissing sweet.

To naturally purify your breath, place a piece of nutmeg in your mouth and chew on it, or keep a piece of mace in your mouth for several minutes. Small pieces of angelica root may also

The mints are among the most easily cultivated and useful of the herbs. Their fragrance makes their presence known in the garden, and in the home the minty goodness can perk up meals, baths, and stuffy rooms.

be chewed; legend states that users of angelica root will be blessed with angelic qualities.

Probably the most obvious herbal breath mints are the mints. Eat a leaf or two to take that sour taste from your mouth. Writer and folklorist Gene Logsdon likes to keep a few mint plants between his door and his driveway, just so he can snatch a few leaves when he's in a hurry to get somewhere, but doesn't want to chance offending anyone with stale breath.

The next time you need a breath perk up, turn to your herb garden rather than the medicine cabinet!

POMANDERS

Pomanders are usually associated these days with clove-riddled oranges. The association stems from the fact that today's pomanders are made by pushing whole cloves into a fresh orange, lemon, lime, or apple. But it wasn't always that way.

Historically, pomanders were carried on the person, chiefly to safeguard against infection, disease, and bad luck. That they were pleasantly scented was only an added benefit. And pomanders were originally made of practically everything but oranges and cloves.

In its earliest days, the pomander was called *pomme d' ambre,* French that can literally—though not quite accurately—be translated "apple of amber." More accurately, a *pomme d' ambre* was a ball-shaped aggregation of herbs and spices. It looked like an apple, hence the appellation *"pomme,"* and ambergris, the whale sperm, was the primary fixative, hence the *"d' ambre."* The name pomander also can be applied to the container—many of them intricately constructed and lavishly ornate—the herbal ball was placed in. The pomander was either located somewhere in the home, or worn around the neck or attached to the belt, like a bit of jewelry.

The pomander found its origin, as did many aromatic uses of herbs, in the foul living conditions in medieval society. At the least, the pomander enabled its owner to escape the stenches of rotting garbage and open sewers in the airy pleasantness of garden herbs and exotic spices. The delicate ladies and foppish gentlemen of the aristocracy would daintily wend their way through the bitter realities of the streets, sniffing their pomanders. They believed that their aromatic pomanders not only prevented them from experiencing the unpleasant odors of the streets, but also that the pomanders prevented them from contracting the diseases that were a natural part of the unsanitary conditions. It was this belief, as much as any, that prompted professional men to arm themselves with pomanders: doctors as they made their rounds and lawyers and judges as they tried lower class thugs, thieves, and wretches.

Today's clove and orange contrivance is as far from the original pomander as is the use to which it is put. (In most homes that have them, the pomander is merely an aromatic novelty, though many of the original uses stand the test of legitimacy.) Ancient recipes reveal that wide varieties of fixatives and perfumes were carefully blended. The resinous ingredients—or beeswax or plain soil—served as the basis for the aggregation, with other fragrant materials being added to this cohesive ball. Like most old recipes, included was an assumption that the "cook" had an intangible sense cuing him when enough of each ingredient had been added. The pomander maker added perfumes "to smell," just as a cook will season "to taste."

Today's pomander of cloves and oranges is a far simpler exercise. There are variations, but basically, you push whole cloves—the sort found on the grocer's shelf—into a nice, firm, unbruised orange, lemon, lime, or apple. If desired, the finished product can be rolled in ground spices. In any case, it should be rolled in ground orris root, the fixative, then set aside to air dry for about four weeks.

It sounds simple, and it is, though perhaps a bit tedious. There are a few cautions that can make your number one try a bit more satisfying.

Have a separate bowl for each ingredient: the foundation fruit in one, cloves in another, ground spices and fixative in a third. If you place the uncompleted pomander in the cloves bowl, you will find them getting limp and sticky, and you'll probably have to throw them out. You'll need about a pound of cloves to make pomanders of a dozen oranges. If you choose to dust the pomander with spices, use cinnamon and perhaps a touch of cloves, nutmeg, and ginger

To start, hold the fruit firmly enough to ease the job of pushing the cloves through the skin, but not so firmly that you squeeze out the juices. It's a skill that comes with practice. Scatter the initial cloves over the fruit, filling in open spaces until the fruit is covered with cloves, set head to head. This is the technique least likely to lead to extensive splits of the skin of the fruit. Some practitioners advise using a darning needle or meat skewer to puncture the fruit, while others reject that practice—you'll have to adopt the technique best suited to you. In any case, finish your pomander in one sitting, for overnight drying of the foundation fruit may lessen the quality of the pomander, and a drying period longer than that may prevent you from finishing the pomander at all.

With the fruit covered with cloves, roll it in the spices, dusting it thoroughly. Leave the pomanders in the spice bowl, rolling them around and dusting them about once a day until they are completely dry. The spices will add to the scent and cut down on the shrinkage. But they aren't necessary. Even the fixative isn't necessary, though it will make the fragrance last longer.

When the pomanders are dry they can be put to work in your home (or used as gifts; they'll work in any home, office, shop, even car). You can simply stack them in a bowl. Or puncture each with a big needle, run a string or ribbon through it and hang it up somewhere. Or tie it up with a ribbon. Or wrap it in colorful cloth for fancy netting: just place it on a square of material, gather the corners and tie them up with a ribbon.

Put pomanders in your closets, dresser drawers, blanket chests, and the like to scent your clothes and blankets and to keep the moths away. Insects may hate it, but your nose will love it.

POTPOURRIS AND SACHETS

Since the beginning of civilization, man has been captivated by the scent of aromatic herbs and has sought methods of introducing their fragrance into his home. Greek ladies were known to carry perfumed sachets in their gowns. Roman households boasted large urns of dried aromatic herbs used to perfume the air with summertime fragrance and destroy unpleasant odors. In medieval times and on into the seventeenth and eighteenth centuries, fragrant herbs were used in many ways to mask the odors of the primitive sanitation and to ward off concommitant disease. Even in the lore of early American civilization, one finds herbs being used for aromatic and cosmetic purposes. Indeed many may recall a familiar example of "lavender and old lace."

But with the relatively recent advent of easy to obtain chemical scents, potpourris and sachets lost their popularity. Recently, however, potpourris and sachets have gained in popularity as old recipes are discovered in the attic. Gift stores now display them on their shelves.

There are two ways of enjoying the luxury of potpourris and sachets in your life. You may spend hard-earned money on high-priced potpourri jars and decorative sachet bags or else have the fun of creating your own scents. In a day and age when man is becoming disillusioned with mass production and technology, you can turn back the clock by making blends of herbs that perfume a room or scent your closet. The ingredients for potpourris and sachets may already be growing in your yard or garden. Such aromatic plants as lilac, roses, lavender, sweet peas, mint, rosemary, and thyme are a few of the various makings you can use. And if you don't have any of the above growing in your garden, you can plant and grow them with a minimum of fuss.

Potpourris and sachets are almost identical except that potpourris are composed of coarse broken pieces of herbs, spices, and flowers; whereas sachets are powdered mixtures. Potpourris are kept in pretty glass jars, and whenever a sweet scent is desired, you merely open the lid and allow the fragrance to fill the room. Sachets are decorative small fabric bags utilized to scent a closet, a drawer of clothing, or oftentimes slipped into a purse to perfume its contents.

Here are a few simple rules to follow when concocting your own potpourris and sachets. Cut and collect your herbs on a dry morning after the dew has dried. Collect three to four times the volume you expect to have when finished (drying decreases volume markedly). Cut or pull off flower petals (discarding any browned petals) and lay in a shallow layer on a clean cloth or paper to dry. Dry flowers away from light in an airy place, stirring the petals several times (fast drying helps retain volatile oils). Cut your annual herbs to the ground, perennials about half way down. Take a bunch of herbs, all you can comfortably hold in one hand, and tie securely. Label and hang in a warm, airy, dark location to dry. An attic is ideal. When the herbs are crumbly dry, strip the leaves from the stem. Don't toss the stems on your compost heap. Instead sprinkle them on a wood fire to perfume the air. When drying citrus peel, first scrape off all the fruit pulp from the inner skin, break into small pieces, and allow to dry in

The most fragrant potpourris and sachets get their start in the garden.
As an organic gardener, Bonnie Fisher gets her potpourris and sachets
off to a good, fragrant beginning with natural growing conditions.
The herbs — in this case mint — are harvested just as the sun chases
the dew from their leaves, the time at which the plant's natural oils
are most volatile and thus most fragrant. They are thoroughly dried,
usually by hanging them in bunches in the attic, occasionally in a

moderately heated oven. Then the leaves are stripped from the branches. The branches of many herbs make an aromatic kindling, so Bonnie saves them for that use. The leaves can be stored for future use, or they can be immediately mixed with other botanicals and a fixative.

Most any bowl can be used for the mixing, but never a metal one; Bonnie uses an ordinary china bowl. The ingredients are measured out and dumped in the bowl, stirred with a wooden spoon. If a potpourri is the goal, the hard work is finished; if the goal is a sachet, the hard part is yet to come. In any case, the mixture is put in a tight-sealing container (never a metal one) and shelved for several months. This will blend, mellow, and fix the various scents.

Finally the day comes, and the herbal mixture is ready to put to use. A potpourri need only be transferred to a decorative container. A sachet is created by grinding the herbal mixture to powder, pouring the powder into fabric bags or pillows, and stitching them closed. The potpourri can be used to scent the air in a room, the sachet to lace a drawerful of clothing with its fragrance.

a warm place until brittle. Make sure your ingredients are perfectly dry or else mold will develop and ruin your potpourri.

With the exception of the knife or scissors you clip your herbs with, never expose herbs to metal when drying or preparing. Instead use wood, enamel, or ceramic utensils. Be sure to use botanicals which you know for certain to be free of poisonous herbicides and insecticides. After all you don't want to inhale a lot of poison.

Use a large wooden spoon to stir together all dried ingredients, and blend thoroughly. Measure all ingredients exactly. Pour the completed mixture into a large wide-mouthed jar. Tightly screw the cap on and place the jar in a cool dark place for several months. Under a kitchen sink is a fine place. About once a week, remove the cap, stir the contents with a wooden spoon, and put away again. In several months, your mixture will be ready to make potpourris and sachets.

PUNGENT POTPOURRIS

For potpourris you can search out pretty, old bottles in attics, basements, junk stores, or at auctions or antique stores. Glass food jars may be washed and recycled as potpourri jars. Always make certain your jar is very clean and that it has a tight fitting lid. Now fill your glass bottles, jars, and jugs with a potpourri blend.

For added glamour you may glue bits of colorful yarn, ribbon, sequins, and felt cutouts on the jars and lids. If you're skilled with a paintbrush you may add designs to the jars with acrylic paints. Acrylic paints are fast drying and waterproof when dried.

Besides scenting and beautifying your own abode with your potpourris, they make lovely and longlasting gifts. You may even turn an enjoyable sideline into a small profitable business venture.

SWEET SACHETS

Sachet bags may be made out of any type of pretty fabric. Start collecting pieces and remnants of various multi-colored cloths. Lace, satin, silk, as well as cotton and muslin are appropriate choices. Fringe or frilly lace may be sewn on to make a decorative scented bag. Sequins, stitchery patterns, and small beads may be added. For a quickie sachet, simply place your ground sachet ingredients in a lady's frilly handkerchief, bring the corners up, and tie securely with a piece of velvet ribbon.

Traditionally, sachets are rather small. But fragrant bags needn't be tiny; they can be the size you want them to be. Indeed, in ancient times insomniacs laid their heads on scented pillows, for it was believed—apparently with reason—that such was the cure for their malady. And grandmother sometimes used sparsely-filled bags—more pads than pillows—between blankets in the chest and clothing in the drawer, partly to scent the garments and partly to ward off moths (as we will see later).

For your very first sachet start with a simple one. Collect a small bunch of lavender flowers. Lay the flowers in a single layer to dry. When completely dry, grind the lavender flowers to a fine powder. You can use a mortar and pestle, perhaps a blender, or, if you happen to have one, a flour mill. One lavender plant should produce enough blossoms to fill twelve two-inch square sachets. Place in small cloth bags and sew up the openings. You don't have to age the ingredients; the purpose of aging is to give the scents of the various herbal ingredients time to fuse.

If you are using more than one herb in your sachet, the grinding isn't done until the mixture has been aged. This done, the herbs are ground up, those tiny bags (usually about two or three inches square) are filled, and there you have a sachet.

Now try one of these more involved scent recipes.

THE RECIPES

Keep in mind that the ingredients are the same for both potpourris and sachets, only the consistency of the ingredients is different. For sachets you must crush all flowers to a fine powder and finely grind the spices and citrus peels. Potpourris are made from coarsely broken herbs, spices, and flowers. Some of the following ingredients such as vetiver root (grown in the tropics) and tonka beans will not grow in your garden. Purchase such herbs from a trustworthy herbal, botanical, or pharmaceutical concern. Finally, don't leave out the fixative.

Lemon Verbena

1 qt. lemon verbena leaves
1 C. lemon peel
1 C. violets
2 C. rose geranium
1 oz. clary sage (fixative)

Not only is lemon verbena good to smell, it also flowers beautifully, and its dried leaves make a refreshing tea.

Herb Garden

2 C. thyme
1 C. rosemary
½ C. lavender
1 C. mint
¼ C. tansy
¼ C. clove
½ oz. orris root (fixative)

Citrus Blend

1 C. orange blossoms
½ C. orange peel
½ C. lime peel
1 C. lemon leaf
½ C. lemon peel
1 C. rosemary
½ oz. vetiver root (fixative)

Tangy Orange

2 C. orange peel
1 C. lemon peel
½ C. orange leaves
½ C. lemon leaves
½ oz. cinnamon
½ oz. nutmeg
1 oz. spearmint
1 oz. orris root (fixative)

Sleep Potion

This herbal combination is used to treat insomnia and overcome melancholy.

    3 C. spearmint
    3 C. rose leaves
    1 C. cloves
    1 oz. orris root (fixative)

Love Potion

The combination of violet, orris root, and tonka bean has been used by many a lady to catch her man.

    3 oz. violet
    2 oz. orris root (fixative)
    1 oz. rose leaf
    1 oz. rose petal
    1 oz. tonka bean

All-Blend

    1 C. lavender
    1 C. lilac
    1 C. rose petals
    1 C. sweet pea
    1 C. clove
    1 C. acacia flowers
    2 C. rose leaves
    1 oz. vetiver root (fixative)

Rose-Lilac

    3 C. rose petals
    2 C. lilac
    2 C. marjoram
    1 oz. orris root (fixative)

Lavender-Geranium

    4 C. lavender
    2 C. rose geranium
    2 C. rosemary
    1 oz. orris root (fixative)

Manly Scent

This is a good formula for sachets to place in a man's dresser drawer or closet.

2 C. lemon balm
1 C. thyme
1 C. nutmeg
½ oz. orris root (fixative)

INSECT REPELLENTS FROM THE GARDEN

Great-grandmother was wise in her ways. She knew exactly what green growing things were effective in repelling insects and moths. In her closets and dresser drawers you would find fragrant herbs distasteful to insects which also imparted a sweet aroma to her clothing.

There is no need for you to suffocate both insects and yourself with foul smelling moth balls in your closets or poisonous atomizer sprays intended to be sprayed on you. By all means keep these poisons out of your life, and grow insect repellent plants instead.

To prevent moths from chewing on your clothes, dry some rosemary leaves and sew them up in small decorative cloth bags of any shape you wish. Place several such bags among your clothing in a drawer or closet. A simple method of keeping the herbs in a drawer is to line the bottom of the drawer with paper, sprinkle the herbs on the paper, then cover the works with a thickness of cloth, holding it in place with thumbtacks.

Another moth chaser is a mixture of equal parts of ground camphor wood (from camphor trees native to Formosa) and wormwood placed in bags among your woolens.

An effective moth-chaser that will sweetly perfume your closet is made by mixing equal parts of southernwood, wormwood, and lavender. Sew the dried herbs into cloth pillows and place strategically among your woolen garments.

Try this simple recipe for keeping moths at bay. Into one ounce of melted paraffin, stir 1 T. heliotrope oil, ¼ tsp. berga-

Wormwood (left) and southernwood, two of the many members of the genus Artemisia, *are particularly useful as insect repellents, serving in the garden or, harvested and dried, in the home. Sewn in bags, they may be secreted among the clothing in drawers and chests in lieu of foul-smelling and potentially dangerous moth balls.*

mot oil, and ⅛ tsp. clove oil. Pour the blended mixture into a flat enamel or wooden pan. When cool, cut into small bars and place in your wardrobe to destroy moths.

For a manly scented moth repellent, sew equal parts of cedar wood shavings and ground sassafras root into small cloth pillows and place among sweaters and woolens.

For general moth and insect control in your home, use woodruff which smells pleasantly like vanilla. Mix together vetiver root and crushed bay leaves to repel bugs of all types. For a repellent to freshen your nose while scaring insects away, try this recipe. Combine ¼ C. of each of the following: lemon peel, crushed cloves, lavender, spearmint, and tansy. Place in bags among your clothing, and give the extras to a friend.

A piece of dried calamus root, from the perennial herb more commonly known as sweet-flag, is a good general insect diverter. Place a dried rhizome in each of your dresser drawers. Or sprinkle in several tonka beans. For centuries tonka beans have been worn about the neck as both a good luck and love charm. Patchouli, an herb from the Malay Peninsula, is another effective bug-repellent.

Dry and powder the aromatic flower heads of pyrethrum or feverfew to use as a contact poison for all insects and cold-blooded vertebrates. Pyrethrum is harmless to humans and pets and is a good indoor repellent. However, if you grow pyrethrum in your garden, beneficial pollinating bees will avoid you.

To rid your kitchen of pesty ants, crush some catnip and sprinkle on the ant trails. Ants dislike the smell and will leave your house. To keep flies outside where they belong, combine equal parts of clover flowers, broken bay leaves, crushed cloves, and eucalyptus. Tie this mixture in small mesh bags inside your entrance doors.

Don't let mosquitoes and gnats drive you inside. Make your own insect repellents from herbs which are safe to use. Before encountering those biting insects, apply a little citronella oil to your skin. To extend the oil, add about one-third pure grain alcohol. To attract the man in your life while repelling insects, mix three parts of lavender oil to one part of pure grain alcohol. Dab the mixture on your skin. The distinctive aroma of pennyroyal is also effective in keeping biting insects at their distance. Rub a small amount of pennyroyal on your body as good protection against biting insects.

SCENTS TO PACIFY YOUR PETS

Don't neglect the dog or cat in your life. You can make aromatic pillows for your pets' beds that will keep them free of fleas. Cats are attracted to certain herbs and become playful over simple-to-make catnip toys.

To please the most finicky feline, dry equal parts of camomile flowers and pennyroyal. When crumbly dry, coarsely grind the herbs and fill a fabric pillow. The camomile and pennyroyal will rid your cat of fleas.

To make a flea repellent pillow for your dog, fill a pillow full of rue and place in Fido's bed. Cedar shavings sewn into a dog-size pillow will also keep your pet flea-free.

A few catnip plants will supply your cat with catnip toys all year. When the catnip is dry, strip the leaves from the stems and crumble slightly. Fill small bags (about 1 inch by 2 inches) with the dried herb. The smell of catnip will make Tom a playful kitten again.

Another herb your cat will enjoy is valerian root. Collect, dry, and coarsely grind the herb before filling small toys or pillows for your pet. Bits of felt or pillow ticking will hold up longer than finer fabrics for cat-type toys.

HERBAL BATHS

At the end of a day that for one reason or another was too long, one fills the tub brimful of restfully warm water and climbs in. As the heat and moisture slowly open the pores and float out the dirt, the tensions of the day seep away, relaxing the muscles and the mind. It's a pleasant experience.

But the leisurely bath can be improved upon, and all it takes is a few of the right herbs.

Added to the water, certain herbs can assist in cleansing the body as it soaks, and their fragrance will surely assist the psyche in dispatching those tensions. After that hard day, an herbal bath is a tonic your body needs. Moreover, herbal lore has long attached medicinal values to the herbal bath. There are baths for aching muscles and for stimulating the circulation. Herbal foot baths are reputed to be the cure for any number of ailments. In his book *Of Men and Plants,* Maurice Messegue, a French herbal healer, lists dozens of recipes for foot baths he has demonstrated to be effective against everything from dyspepsia to constipation, and from insomnia to varicose veins.

Many a great beauty of the past has been reputed to have

maintained the loveliness of her skin by bathing in scented waters. Ninon de Lenclos, a famous French beauty, was attractive to young men even when in her seventies. Her secret has been reputed to be the following herbal bath:

> Take a handful of dried lavender flowers, a handful of rosemary leaves, a handful of dried mint, a handful of comfrey roots, and one of thyme. Mix all together loosely in a muslin bag. Place in your tub, pour on enough boiling water to cover and let soak for ten minutes. Then fill up the tub. Rest 15 minutes in the "magic water" and think virtuous thoughts.

Most herbal baths are similarly simple to prepare. You can place the herbs to be used in a pan of water, cover, and boil for about ten minutes. Strain off the herbs and add the decoction to your bath water.

Or you can tie the herbs at the spout so the water washes over the herbs on its way to filling the tub. You can put the herbs in a clean nylon stocking or a cheesecloth bag if you like.

The third possibility is simply stitch up a large muslin "tea bag," which you fill with herbs and hang over the side of the tub in the water. Steep until ready, then hop in.

You'll enjoy your herbal bath more if you first take a quickie soap and water bath or shower. Then relax and soak in the herbal water for 15-20 minutes before patting yourself dry.

The only question remaining at this point is: What herbs should be used? Different herbs have different effects, so your choice should be governed as much by what you wish to accomplish as by what herbs you have available.

If you're interested in merely a sweet scent in your bath water, any one of the dozens of fragrant herbs will do. Lavender is the favorite of many ladies, as it has been for centuries. It's used to scent many commercial bath articles, so why not use your own garden lavender. Moreover, lavender is reputed to be an excellent palliative for nervousness. If you are interested in becoming more loveable, try some lovage. Herbal lore attributes loveability to this herb.

There are a number of recipes that are tonics for the skin. With prolonged usage, comfrey will help regenerate aging skin. Mix equal parts of comfrey, alfalfa, parsley, and orange peel for a rejuvenating bath, or combine ¾ C. jasmine and ¼ C. orange blossoms. This combination smells good, and will help your skin retain its youthful glow. Another bath formula for retaining youthful skin is to combine equal parts of rose petals, orange blossoms, and lavender.

To get pleasant relief from stiff muscles and joints, use a combination of sage leaves and strawberry leaves. Another effective herbal combination to ease aches and pain consists of employing equal parts of agrimony, camomile, and mugwort. For best results, you should massage aching muscles while soaking in the tub. That comforting glow of warmth is a sign that the therapy is working.

An alternative to lavender for tension relief is valerian. One herbal recommends boiling a pound of this herb in water for thirty minutes, then adding the decoction to bath water. Other remedies for tension include the use of a decoction of equal parts of hops and meadowsweet as a rinse during the regular bath, and spiking the bath water with a decoction of a half-pound of calamus roots and leaves.

For the person with circulation problems, an herbal bath may hold some stimulation. A decoction of equal parts of marigold, nettle, and bladderwrack added to the bath is a favorite English recipe. It is said to stimulate circulation and bring a warm glow to the body.

A pleasant smelling herb bath for a man can be made from ½ C. of spearmint combined with ½ C. thyme leaves.

Experiment with various combinations of two or more of the following aromatic herbs to invent your own herbal baths: angelica root, myrtle leaves and flowers, marigolds, lovage root, lemon peel, orange leaves, geranium leaves, rosemary, lavender, pennyroyal, verbena, acacia, sandalwood, cloves, cinnamon, or any other aromatic herbs you have access to.

Indulge yourself in a luxurious herbal bath.

SWEET POWDERS

After partaking of a leisurely herbal bath, indulge your body by smoothing on sweet-scented powders. The ingredients for bath powders are easily found in your garden and kitchen. Make only a small amount so the fragrance is not lost with time.

In a wood mortar, grind to a fine powder 1 oz. rose petals, 1 oz. lavender buds, and 1 oz. orris root. Using a wooden spoon, blend well while adding 2 oz. cornstarch. Store in a powder receptacle. It makes a fine floral scented powder.

For a tangy herbal powder combine ½ oz. powdered clove, ½ oz. powdered sage leaves, 1 oz. powdered orris root. As an extender, blend in 2 oz. arrowroot.

For a spring fresh essence, combine 1 oz. violet, 1 oz. lilac blossoms, and 1 oz. of orris root all of which have been ground into a very fine powder. Add 2 oz. cornstarch, blending thoroughly. Pat on your body with a soft powder puff and feel great!

AROMATIC WATERS

After a long day refresh your weary mind and body with aromatic waters. After rinsing or washing your face, splash some on your face and neck for a fragrant lift. Aromatic waters are pure waters that have been blended with fragrant herbs and are used as skin toners and tonics, body washes, or hair rinses. Sweet smelling waters may be stored simply in decorative glass bottles in the bathroom or boudoir. You can be sure your home-brewed cosmetic waters are free of all harmful ingredients. The combinations below are all good enough to even drink as tea.

Never use water containing chlorine or fluoride when concocting aromatic waters. Use pure spring water free of all chemicals. If you're one of the lucky few that have their own pure spring water use that, or else purchase a bottle at the health food store. Distilled water or rain water may also be used. Mix your aromatic waters in glass or ceramic containers, never metal ones.

Mint water is used to refresh and stimulate your skin. Puree fresh spearmint leaves with cold water in an electric blender. Dab on your face and neck. Dried mint may also be used: add 1 C. of dried, crushed mint to a pint of pure water in a quart glass jar with a tight fitting lid. Put this glass jar in a convenient place and shake once or twice daily for two weeks. Strain and store in small glass vials with tight fitting lids.

To make old-time rose water, gather rose petals early in the morning, place them in an enamel pot, just cover with water and slowly bring the mixture to a boil. Simmer for several minutes and strain. Rose water makes an excellent hair rinse, especially for oily hair. Also use as a rinse on oily skin. Rose water is often used to flavor foods in many countries. In India it is used to flavor sherbet, ice cream, and cakes; Arabs use it as a glaze for roasting fowl; Turks use it much as we do catsup.

Another sweet water helpful in correcting oily skin and hair is lemon water. Use fresh or dried lemon leaves and prepare as you would rose water.

Orange leaves and blossoms, clover, and acacia flowers also make aromatic waters which are effective in correcting dry skin. Drop the freshly collected botanicals into an enamel pan, barely cover with water, bring to a full boil and simmer for two minutes. Strain and use. Store extra water in glass jugs with tight sealing lids to protect the aroma. Camomile water helps firm skin tissue, keeps the skin youthful, and perks you up. Add 1½ C. camomile to one pint of water, allow to age for two weeks shaking twice daily. Strain and bottle. Blondes will find camomile water to be a good hair rinse.

Herb vinegars, the same ones you use in cooking, are helpful to both dry and oily complexions and act to refine the skin pores. Vinegar tightens skin pores and reestablishes the skins natural acid balance. Refer to the recipes for making herb vinegars that appear in Chapter Three. Start with either apple cider vinegar made from organically grown whole apples or white wine vinegar. Add one cup of petals or leaves for each pint of vinegar and place on a sunny window-sill in a tightly sealed glass bottle. Shake vigorously daily for two to three weeks. Strain and rebottle.

Such pungent herbs as sweet basil, thyme, sage, rosemary, dill, or marjoram may be aged in vinegar and used either as a facial rinse or in your cooking. For a more delicate floral fragrance, you may select lavender, violet petals, roses, carnation, lemon verbena, honeysuckle, sweet pea, or lilac, or experiment with your own combinations of two or more scents to create exciting new aromatic surprises. For a citrus aromatic vinegar, add

Rose water is easily made, and works wonders when dabbed on oily skin. Simply cover rose petals with water, bring the mixture to a boil, then cool and strain.

½ C. of grated orange peel, ½ C. orange leaves, and ½ C. orange flowers to one quart of warm vinegar. Place in a glass jar and shake daily for almost three weeks. Strain and use as an astringent or hair rinse.

EXOTIC HERB OILS

Using herb oils is using the very essence of the herbs from your garden. The more you use herbs for aromatic and cosmetic purposes, the more likely you are to find a situation where only an oil will do. It is at that point that you will get into a most delightful aspect of herbal aromatics.

Herb oils are most commonly extracted by distillation. But this is a process that is beyond the scope of most individuals. Given a bit of patience, however, you can extract oils from herbs. (If you haven't the patience, or if there's some other reason that prevents you from extracting the oils of your herbs, you can purchase a wide variety of herb oils from those botanical suppliers I mentioned earlier.)

If there is only one oil you choose to brew, by all means make it attar of roses. Attar (or otto) of roses sells in the vicinity of $150 per ounce! This fine-quality oil takes over 200 pounds of roses to produce a mere ounce. To make attar of roses, fill a large clean ceramic crock with rose petals. Now lightly press the rose petals down and cover them with pure spring water or rain water. Place the crock outside where it will receive a full day's sun. Watch the surface of the water for scum to form (this will take four to seven days). This scum is the attar of roses and should be oily with a yellowish color. With a small piece of cotton absorb the oil and squeeze it into a small vessel. Remove the rose oil daily. If rain threatens, cover the crock so the roses aren't flooded and your precious oil lost.

A faster method of extracting attar of roses is to place two pounds of freshly picked rose petals on a cloth tied around the edge of a large enamel pan filled with hot water. Keep the water hot on the stove and place a dish of cold water upon the petals. Keep changing the pan of water on top to keep it cool. Soak up the rose oil with cotton and place in glass bottles.

Pure herbal oils may be kept for a long period of time if stored properly. Once the oil is extracted, tie several pieces of cheesecloth over the bottle and allow any water to evaporate that may be mixed with your oil (several days should do). Next sterilize a one ounce or less amber- or green-colored bottle with a tight fitting lid. Carefully pour your exotic oil into this small vessel for storage.

Oils can be extracted from practically all botanicals using this technique. Happily, not all herbs are as parsimonious with their oils as roses. You'll use far fewer blossoms and leaves of other botanicals to collect similar quantities of oil—take heart!

You may make oils from the following flowers: lilac, geranium, honeysuckle, lavender, lemon blossoms, orange blossoms, violets, lemon verbena, acacia, sweet pea, and other sweetly scented flowers. Collect only top quality floral petals early in the morning. Place the petals in a clean ceramic crock and just cover with rain or spring water. Place the crock in a sunny location and watch for the filmy scum to appear (this is the oil). Once the oil begins to collect, carefully absorb it into a small ball of cotton and squeeze the oil into a small jar. Store in tiny colored glass vials.

For herbal scented oils select such aromatic botanicals as mint, rosemary, sage, marjoram, basil, dill, or thyme. Cut only select quality leaves and proceed as you do with floral oils or attar of roses.

You may also extract the essential oils of fragrant woods such as cedarwood, sandalwood, rosewood; the sweet essence of roots such as sassafras, orris, calamus; and the aromatic oils of barks such as cinnamon. First reduce the wood, root, or bark to shavings using a wood plane for thick tough roots and wood, a garden shredder, or electric blender. To extract the oils merely follow one of the recommended methods for creating attar of roses.

To make oil of roses, sometimes called rose composition oil, collect a half-pound of rose buds. Use a mortar and pestle to crush them fine, place them in an earthenware crock, and add a quart of olive oil. Place the crock in a sunny location for three

You can make your own attar of roses, the fabulously expensive oil. Make sure you use the most fragrant varieties of roses. Submerse them in water and, after several days, carefully collect the oil that forms on the surface with a cotton ball.

to four weeks stirring daily. At the end of this period, heat the roses and oil in an enamel bowl until warm, force the warmed mixture through a fine sieve or use a blender. Filter through four layers of cheesecloth before storage in two-ounce size (or less) dark glass bottles.

Once you've collected herb oils, you'll never lack ideas for using them. The remaining portions of this chapter will get you started.

PERFUME ESSENCES

Perfumes have been made for over 20,000 years since man first learned to extract fragrance from aromatic plants. When kings and queens reigned in every European country, members of the court each had their own "secret" essence. Perfumes are made from aromatic roots, woods, flowers, seeds, and leaves. In the fourteenth century, alcohol was first used as a carrier for perfume. Herbal fixatives are used to prevent the volatile botanical essences from evaporating.

The nice thing about homemade perfumes is that the ingredients will all be natural with no artificial chemicals. You don't have to rely on a chemist's test tube to make you smell good. If you grow, collect, and brew your own perfume concoctions, you'll also save the expense of high-priced perfumes.

Perhaps the easiest way to make an herbal perfume is to pack fragrant botanicals — leaves, blossoms, shavings — with sweet-oil soaked cotton in a glass jar with a tight fitting lid. Sweet oil is a highly refined olive oil and is available in many drug stores. Just stuff some cotton in your jar, pour on just enough oil to saturate the cotton, then add the blossoms or leaves or shavings and cap the jar. Put it in the sun for the day. Next day, change the botanicals. And the next day and the next. Eventually the cotton will be as saturated with the scent as it is with the oil. At that point you merely squeeze the oil into a vial and you have your perfume. As a cautionary procedure, refrigerate the oil to prevent it from going rancid.

Other perfumes can be made by combining herb oils, aromatic waters, and other fragrant ingredients. Directions for making both herb oils and aromatic waters have previously been given. Just follow the recipes below to more herb-based aromatic delights.

Scent of Roses

1 C. 75% alcohol
¼ C. rose water
1 T. rosemary oil

2 T. rose oil

1 T. storax oil (fixative)

Combine ingredients in a glass bottle. Shake well and wait four weeks before using.

Herb #4 Scent

1 C. 75% alcohol

1 tsp. basil oil

1 tsp. sage oil

1 tsp. dill oil

1 T. sandlewood oil (fixative)

Combine and store three weeks, shaking often, before using.

Lavender Cologne

1 pint 75% alcohol

½ C. lavender water

2 T. lavender oil

1 T. storax oil (fixative)

Combine and enjoy after several weeks.

Lemon Perfume

1 C. 75% alcohol

2 T. lemon oil

1 T. citronella oil

1 T. lemon verbena oil

1 T. sandlewood oil (fixative)

Place ingredients in a glass bottle, shake well. It gets stronger with age.

Spicy Essence

1 C. 75% alcohol

1 T. clove oil

2 T. cinnamon oil

¼ C. ground orris root (fixative)

Combine above ingredients in a tight sealing glass vial. Set aside for two months. Filter and store in sterile glass perfume bottles.

SOAPSWEETLY SCENTED

Most people believe soap making to be a difficult task and view it as something they wouldn't attempt. Actually, making your own scented soaps is simple and very inexpensive—with the added bonus of knowing just what ingredients are in your soap. No chemical dyes, hardening agents, chemical additives, alcohol, or fillers in your homemade soap! Homemade soap can be cooked in small amounts in city apartments or in large amounts in country iron kettles.

It is believed that soap was accidently discovered over 3,000 years ago in Rome. It has been deliberately made ever since. The Pakistanis made soap from silkworms, while the American Indians made soap from desert plants. The two essential ingredients for soap are fat and lye, both of which are easy to obtain. Here are some general rules that must be followed for successful soap: 1. Never use aluminum utensils; instead use enamel or iron (lye reacts with aluminum). 2. Use only clean fat or lard. 3. Never allow aging soap to get in a cold draft as it turns hard and flinty. 4. Pour soap into molds of about 1½ inches (too thin a soap will curl when drying; soap too thick is difficult to hold). 5. Aging improves soap.

To render fat, fill a large pan with several inches of hot water and add the finely cut fat. Cook over a medium heat stirring occasionally until the fat is all melted. Strain the melted mixture to remove all impurities. Allow to cool, then lift off lard (from swine) or tallow (from cows).

Dr. Maggie's Old-Fashioned Lye Soap

This recipe comes from Dr. Margaret Ballard, a retired doctor and professor of medicine. Every summer she attends mountain festivals where she charms old and young alike attired in her "mountaineer" dress as she demonstrates soapmaking in her large iron kettle. She instructed me in the art of soap making in her kitchen. The batch of soap we started before dinner was finished after dinner.

4 lbs. grease (country lard preferred)
1 can lye (13 oz.)
¼ lb. Borax
2 oz. rosin
2 gal. water

1. *Heat water in a large enamel or iron kettle.*
2. *Add lard and stir until dissolved.*
3. *Sprinkle in lye a little at a time stirring constantly with a wooden spoon.*
4. *Gradually stir in the rosin and borax.*
5. *Bring to a slow boil and allow to simmer until the soap "flakes off" the wooden spoon.*
6. *Stir often while "cooking."*
7. *Pour into 2-inch deep greased enamel or glass pans and cool overnight.*
8. *The next day cut into cakes, but do not remove from the pans for two days.*
9. *Place on waxed paper and allow to dry for three to six weeks before using.*

Basic Soap

1. *Heat 6 lbs. of lard or tallow to 120°-130° in an enamel kettle.*
2. *In a separate enamel pan stir together 13 oz. of lye and 5 C. of cold water and heat to 90°-95°.*
3. *Slowly pour the lye solution into the melted fat stirring with a wooden spoon.*
4. *Simmer and stir until thick enough to hold its shape (around 30 minutes).*
5. *Pour to a depth of 1 to 1½ inches in greased glass or enamel pans.*
6. *Cool overnight.*
7. *Cut into bars and remove from pan after several days.*
8. *Allow to age two weeks before using.*

SCENTING YOUR SOAPS

Just before pouring your soap into molds, add any of the following oils for a sweet smelling aroma: lavender, citronella, rose, rose geranium, rosemary, cloves, cinnamon, sassafras, lemon

White sage (Artemisia ludoviciana) *is an American member of the genus* Artemisia *and a native of the western states. Though generally used as an ornamental — it has unusual gray foliage, often with a hint of blue or yellow — it shares many of the useful characteristics of the artemisias.*

grass, or lemon. To the Basic Soap recipe add 2 T. of one of the above oils; to Dr. Maggie's recipe add ¼ C.

Citronella oil will leave you smelling like a lemon while making your skin lustrous. Besides smelling delicious, lavender oil is also good for acne. Olive oil is a good addition if your skin is dry; sandalwood oil is an effective astringent and disinfectant. Oils that work as deodorant aids are thyme oil and patchouli oil. Other oils and combinations you may experiment with are palm, mace, peach kernel, and sage.

To naturally color your soap, add the juice of fresh strawberries. Strawberry soap is a wonderful complexion soap. To make your soap lather, add soap bark herb (contains saponin which creates a lather when it comes in contact with water).

To make a good shaving soap fill a glass soap mug with finished soap and add ¼ tsp. of sage oil or clove oil or else add 1 T. of powdered sage leaf or powdered clove. Allow to cure one week before using.

To really pamper yourself, use a luffa sponge as you bathe with your scented soap. The luffa, or sponge gourd, is the skeleton of the Japanese Bottle Luffa *(Cylindrica)*. When dry the luffa is flat; when placed in water it inflates into a luxurious bathing sponge. Save a spot in your herb garden for a few Cylindrica seeds to make into long-lasting sponges.

ROSE BEADS

The rose, aristocrat of the flower kingdom, is a most versatile plant. Not only is the rose acclaimed for its fragrance and beauty, it is also cultivated for its "hips" which are rich in natural vitamin C and are brewed into rose hips tea and natural vitamin C supplements. Rose petals are also used in jelly, may be candied, or made into rose water. Rose leaves are ingredients for potpourris and sachets.

Rose beads, made from rose petals, are a fun way to enjoy the delightful aroma of roses all year round. Rose beads have been made and worn by countless women over the centuries, and their fragrance must have played a part in many a romance.

If you have access to any of the old-time perfume roses, such as Damask or Cabbage Rose, by all means use them in preference to newer varieties of roses. Deeper-colored roses are more fragrant than the lighter ones. However, any variety of rose may be used. Collect your roses early in the morning on a dry day. Pull the petals off and, using a mortar, crush very fine. Then spread the finely mashed petals on a piece of waxed paper to partially dry. Return the petals to the mortar and add a small amount of water to create a fine paste. Dip your fingers into rose oil (see the section on oils) and then proceed to roll the petal paste into small beads. Ebony colored beads may be made by crushing the roses in an iron mortar or iron pot (the roses are oxidized by the iron, turning them black).

The rose is the basis for some of the most exquisite and desired essences in the world.

When still wet, carefully poke a needle through the centers of the beads to make a hole for threading later. Lay the finished beads to dry on clean waxed paper turning several times so they dry evenly. When thoroughly dried (it will take two to three days), polish them with a soft cloth.

Now that all of your pretty sweet-smelling beads are made, you can decide how to use them. Rose Beads may be strung on thin nylon cord (for durability) of varying lengths to be used as a scented necklace. Several threaded strands may be made into a belt. Buy yourself an inexpensive pair of earring findings and design your own dangling scented earrings. The very ambitious may even attempt a room divider or screen made out of multi-colored rose beads.

When your beads begin to lose their sweet smell, merely dip them in rose oil and allow to dry. This way your handcrafted rose beads will always smell of summer delights.

FRAGRANT INCENSE

Incense has been used for centuries as a part of various pagan and religious rituals. In recent years the burning of incense has become increasingly popular as a method of perfuming a room. Intricate incense burners and many aromas of incense are available in gift stores. Incense is easily made and becomes more fragrant if aged several months before use.

Here is a recipe for frankincense incense. Combine and mix together well 2 T. powdered frankincense, 1 T. powdered orris root, and 1 tsp. powdered clove. Stir 1 T. of oil of lemon through the mixture. Place in a cool dark area for two to three months. To use, sprinkle a little on some burning charcoal.

For a light floral incense, combine 2 T. ground rose petals, 2 T. ground lavender, and 1 T. powdered vetiver. In another small bowl mix ½ tsp. oil of lemon and ½ tsp. oil of lavender. Blend the oils through the dry mixture. Store several months before using, again by sprinkling on a piece of burning charcoal.

A spicy incense may be concocted by mixing together 2 T. ground cinnamon, 2 T. ground cloves, 1 T. ground cascarilla, and 1 T. powdered orris root. Stir in 1 T. oil of cloves. Sprinkle on smouldering charcoal after aging.

CANDLE CRAFTING

During the last few years there has been a revival in the age-old craft of candle making. Hobby shops feature candle making supplies and candle shops have sprung up everywhere. You need not rush out to buy a lot of fancy candle-making equipment. Your kitchen will provide almost everything you need with a little help from your herb garden plus some ordinary paraffin from the grocery store (the same kind used in canning) and a length of candle wicking from the hobby store.

To get down to the business of candles, first collect all of the materials you'll need. Plenty of paraffin, candle wicking, an old double boiler to melt the wax in (or a big tin can and a saucepan), and molds. Molds are fun to locate with many being in your kitchen, attic, or basement. Waxed milk cartons are a perfect mold, as are used plastic bottles of all shapes and sizes; glass bottles that food or drink was packaged in add variety to your candle shapes. For the scent you'll need aromatic herb oils or powdered herbs.

Cut your paraffin into pieces and place in the top of a double boiler to melt. Don't use a good cooking utensil as it will be ruined. If you don't have an old double boiler, make an imitation by melting the wax in a large size tin can placed in a pan of boiling water (never melt wax directly over a flame). Scent your wax with additions of clove oil, mint oil, rose oil, sage oil, lavender oil, lemon oil, or other aromatic herb oils. Various combinations of fragrant oils are often pleasing. Or you may add powdered aromatic herbs to the melted wax. Use a mortar and pestle to powder your dried herbs. After warming the mold, insert a length of wicking to the bottom of the mold allowing for about one inch extra above the top of the mold. If you have trouble with your wick moving, tie on a small weight (nut or screw) before dropping the wick into the mold. For colored candles melt a piece of wax crayon in the paraffin. Now slowly pour the scented wax into your slightly warmed molds. As the wax cools, a depression will form in the center of the candle. Refill this depression with hot wax until the mold is filled and level.

Allow your candles to thoroughly dry before removing from their molds. Tear away waxed cardboard molds, molds with tapered tops such as glass catsup bottles and plastic soap bottles will have to be cut off (for glass employ a glass cutter). Glass, plastic, and metal molds with straight sides may be briefly placed in very hot water to enable the candle to slip out of its mold.

For a finer quality of candle, add one part pure beeswax to one part of paraffin, melt and pour into molds. You may also make candles out of beeswax with no paraffin added.

Turn out the lights, light your candle, and enjoy the beauty and aroma of your candle crafting!

The possibilities for making practical use of the aromatic qualities of herbs are virtually unending. You are limited only by your time, interest, and imagination. Even if you have time for nothing more, a walk through a garden of fragrant herbs is a refreshing experience. And once taken, it may compel you to make some time for aromatics.

The aromatic qualities of herbs can be captured and used in so many ways, yet the most natural, and perhaps the most satisfying, is the aromatic garden, which captivates with its potpourri of fragrances, all inviting the visitor to stop and sniff.

THE
COLORFUL HERBS

by Barbara Foust

FIVE

I can rarely resist the siren call of a yarn shop—even though the walls of my house almost bulge with uncounted skeins of the woolly stuff. All those textures! All those colors! I have a friend who owns such a shop, and we share the same excitement over the visual and tactile joy of wool and color. These yarns, to me, have a life and character quite special. They remind me of homespun, vegetable dyed yarns—to me the most beautiful of all woolen yarns.

And best of all, subtle, glowing, infinitely varied colors are quite easily available for the making. If your definition of a truly satisfying hobby is like mine—one which involves you in constant adventures, chances to learn, even chances to travel (which costs relatively little), and which produces a unique and practical product—then consider vegetable dyeing.

Vegetable dyeing is a strange phrase which to some people seems to conjure up remarkable transformations from palid shapes to *red* beets, *orange* carrots, *purple* cabbage. Not so at all. It means the use of naturally occurring substances for dyeing.

This includes both animal, mineral, and vegetable.

The "animal" dyes include, for example, cochineal, the dried bodies of an insect which grows on cacti and is raised as a crop and imported as a very beautiful, very versatile, but also very expensive dye which yields pinks, reds, and purples.

The "mineral" dyes include rust (iron oxide), a very permanent one indeed, and the variety of earth color which the American Indians have been able to transfer from their radiant mesas to wool.

The "vegetable" dyes do sometimes include edible vegetables, but also the great sweep of growing plant materials—leaf, bark, root, nut, fruit, berry, and flower seed.

I admit that a dictionary would define herb as "a plant the stem of which dies down to the ground after flowering in contrast to the trees and shrubs that have woody stems," but, taking my rationale from several fine herbals I know, I shall insist, here-

Barbara Foust grows some plants expressly for her dyepot, but most of her colors are derived from wild herbs she gathers from the woods and fields surrounding her rural home.

with, on my own definition: "that class of plants, some portion of which has been used for medicine, perfume, flavor, or color."

I am assuming you are going to find vegetable colors as evocative, lively, and beautiful as I do, but perhaps you are devoted to commercial dyes or the process of dyeing sounds rather involved and/or messy. Why bother?

I agree. Synthetic dyes are inexpensive. Synthetic dyes are easy to use—quick and relatively (some very) permanent. Synthetic dyes come in a wide range of colors. With careful mixing, an infinite range is possible. Quantity is unlimited. With care, they dye evenly in any degree of depth desired. I also agree vegetable dyes are a lot of trouble—picking (sometimes drying), soaking, washing, mordanting, and dyeing, sometimes with less than satisfactory results.

So why bother?

For the fun of discovery every step of the way, the hunt for dye plants, the identification. The experiments with age, growing habits, season, part of plant, mordants, heat, timing.

Synthetic dyes are pure colors. They do not readily sit beside each other harmoniously. Vegetable dyes are impure. Because each color contains elements of many other colors, the skeins harmonize with each other. It is almost impossible to find a "clash" of colors.

Vegetable dyes have a very special life — a subtle character all their own. They blend happily with other earthy handicrafts such as wood and pottery. Vegetable dyes, when they fade eventually, will fade to a softer tone of their original color, still keeping their original identity (witness old coverlets and tapestries). (You *know* what terrible things can happen to synthetic dyes—fading to sometimes different and ugly colors.) Vegetable dyeing puts one in touch with a fascinating world of history.

Vegetable dyeing can even lead to dye gardens. If you are so inclined, it can open a world of horticulture to you, can turn you into an amateur botanist, can lead you far afield to other climates and cultures, and can make you feel at home in any part of the world.

And then there is the sheer joy of helping in the transformation of one natural product into something else quite different and beautiful, and also natural. There is a satisfaction here that is rarely found in the slick plastic, synthetic world we often are forced to live in.

And it's even useful, though really it doesn't have to be. It pleases the soul just to see and handle the rainbow of colored wools, to know that you had a part in the magic of their creation.

GETTING STARTED

Have I convinced you that it is worth some time and mess? I hope so. There is no need to rush in full tilt—small skeins dye just as readily as large ones. Consider the start as experiments. Four ounces of yarn made up into, perhaps, two dozen small skeins can open a whole world of pleasure.

You will need:

1. Woolen yarn, undyed. I prefer it to be unbleached, too. We have our own wool spun commercially. But many dyers get good results with the cheapest of white or off-white yarn from

the "Five and Ten." "Fisherman's Knit" is lovely. The most beautiful of vegetable dyed yarns is homespun, either dyed "in the wool" (before spinning) or "yarn dyed" (after spinning). It has a dimension and character unbeatable in machine-spun yarn. All you need are carders, a hand spindle, and a bit of spinning technique.

2. Cotton thread (crochet thread or butcher's twine is fine) for tying skeins so they may be boiled, yet still be recoverable as skeins.

3. Mild soap or dish detergent for washing the skeins free of all grease, dirt, or chemicals that might repel dyes.

4. Lots of water, preferably soft. Our ancestors would have used rainwater. Lacking a rainbarrel, you may need a softener like Calgonite or a bit of vinegar, if your water is "hard." The minerals in the water can affect the clarity of the dye.

5. Some sort of stove. Dyeing outdoors can be lovely, but a modern kitchen range gives you great control over the speed and degree of heat. My family is very tolerant, as long as I assure them that my dye pots are *not* part of an important meal.

6. Pots, as non-reactive as possible. Never, never aluminum. Never iron, either, unless you want your colors to be deliberately gray. Brass and copper are near the bottom of the list. Stainless steel is perfect. A lot of my work is done in Revere Ware. Unchipped enamel is just as good, and much cheaper. (When chipped, the iron in the pot can work into the dye and dull it. Pyrex would be fine. A canner can hold enough water (4½-5 gallons) to handle a pound of wool at a time.

I really must tell you right here and now that I have often dyed in cook pots and my family is marvelously healthy. But, some chemicals you will use are poisonous. Some plants

The array of dyeing equipment shown here can be acquired from second-hand or variety stores. The supplies are available by mail from a number of firms. These items, plus the skill, imagination, and patience of the dyer are all that's needed to imbue wool with herbal colors.

you may use can cause adverse reactions. *Therefore, it is best to have dye pots entirely separate from cook pots.* Potassium dichromate and oxalic acid are considered poisonous. Avoid inhaling fumes and keep food away from all utensils used with them.

Actually it becomes fun, once you are more involved, to find really cheap, used utensils which can be used exclusively for dyeing at flea markets and outworn shops. It is amazing and somewhat sad how little some people value really fine tools as soon as they have lost a handle, a knob or a lid or received a cruel dent. One of the nicest presents I ever received was a five-gallon stainless steel milk kettle my daughter found for me in a junk shop.

7. Something with which to stir and lift the yarn in the dye pot. Glass rods are ideal, but expensive and rare. Smooth sticks of your own devising or hardwood dowels are just fine, as long as colors do not bleed from pot to pot.

8. A sieve, cheesecloth, or collander (always listed, but by me seldom used).

9. Mordants, properly jarred and labelled—a whole section on this is coming up.

10. Measuring spoons and utensils—glass or stainless or unchipped enamel best—but here plastic is a possibility.

11. A thermometer (maybe later, but not at the start).

12. A scale, if you need to measure things. For small amounts of chemicals, a letter scale will do.

13. Notebook, tags, and a file box.

14. Containers or sink for washing/rinsing.

15. Storage space for wool, utensils, and dye plants.

16. A good, basic library (starting here) and working on, as you get more excited, into botany, dyeing, herbals—perhaps even chemistry and history.

17. If you're very neat or have sensitive skin, you may want rubber gloves. Most of us settle for just looking grubby about the nails.

18. Last, but so important—a tolerant family. In time, they may even be enthusiastic.

TYING

Start with a well-tied skein which can literally boil (simmer) for hours and still come out as a recoverable skein. If you begin with small skeins, you'll need only two ties. If large, perhaps four. Here is where we use the strong crochet cotton (you might even use a variety of permanent colors as a code to indicate mordant, or year, or special place). It is tied around the yarn in a figure eight fashion, tight enough so the wool does not move too much beneath; loose enough so the dye may flow beneath the ties. You can tell just what the proper snugness will be.

You'll be well-advised to take the trouble to tie the two ends of the skein together, then incorporate the tag ends from this knot into a skein tie. This way you'll always be able to locate the ends at once, for taking a sample or winding into a ball. On a big skein, this eliminates a considerable aggravation, later.

WASHING

And now, even though it looks clean and new, wash the skein(s) on the chance that there may be traces of dirt, oil, or chemicals that would repel the dye. (If you dye "in the wool," it must first be opened with cards and then all the natural oils and yoke must be scoured out so that the dye will be even. After dyeing and before spinning you will replace this with a water-soluble oil.) (If your skeins are all the same size—perhaps wound around a book—they'll be a lot prettier to look at later when they're ready for display.)

Lots of books call for a mild soap for washing. If you don't have ideal conditions, this can be difficult to rinse thoroughly. Therefore, I like a mild dishwashing detergent which is far easier to rinse. After a thorough set of rinses we can talk of mordanting. Either squeeze the skein gently and hang to dry in the shade, or leave it soaking in clear lukewarm water for a while.

Because wool is microscopically scaly, it will twist into yarn. Because of microscopic air spaces, it will hold heat, even when wet. In the presence of heat, water, and pressure, it will shrink and stick together or "felt"—a fine property if you want pretty

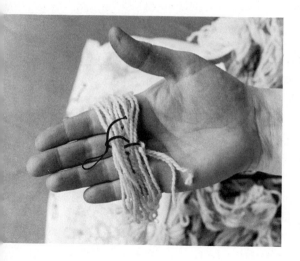

Using cotton crocheting cord strung in a figure-eight loop, loosely tie together small skeins of woolen yarn for the dye process.

Christmas decorations, but a curse if you want soft, pliable yarn.

Surely the question I am most asked when demonstrating is, "Why can you boil wool that way, and nothing happens, but I can't even wash a sweater without ruining it?" Well, wool *does* shrink at every step of the process, but you aim to have it controlled. Wool can literally be boiled for hours and still emerge with life, but two things you can never do to wool without insulting it are (1) agitate and (2) change the temperature too fast.

Never stir the dye pot—poke. Lift and turn gently. Always have plenty of water around the yarn so the yarn swims and dives freely, without help. *Never agitate wool.*

When you are ready to put wool into a boiling dye pot, either cool down the dye pot to the temperature of the wet wool, or bring the rinse water with its wool slowly up to the temperature of the dye pot, and then transfer it. On rinsing reverse the process. Hot, then cooler and cooler rinses. Or cool the dye pot (best). Or lift the wool and air cool it to the rinse temperature. *Never shock wool by fast temperature changes.*

Once you have these two rules etched on your brain, you can amaze your friends by "boiling" wool with impunity.

(If you've been thinking that I have been concentrating solely on wool, you're right. Wool is by far the easiest of the natural fibers to dye. But cotton, linen, and silk can be vegetable dyed. The color range is not as wide, the mordant process is different and more complicated, but there are books to tell you how, if you're really ambitious.)

Remember, the washed and well-rinsed wool was either gently dried or left to soak. Now we can talk of mordanting—the last step before the real fun.

MORDANTING

Most vegetable dyes need some sort of chemical assistance to be permanent. Otherwise they fade soon, take up little dye, or "bleed."

In earlier days, they used what was handy to assist the wool to hold dye: lye made from hardwood ashes (the American Indians still use either this or a lump of alum found in the desert), any naturally occurring tannin such as sumach or oak galls, salt, and for our early settlers (and still preferred by some Irish and Scottish cottage dyers) chamber lye (just stale human urine). In fact, this was what early commercial dyers largely depended on. Not only did it "set" the colors, but (so they say) it leaves the yarn soft and shiny, too.

But there are obvious and not so obvious drawbacks to most of the early methods. Some added an unwanted tan color to the wool. Some were only half-safe.

Now we have available metallic salts which add little or no color to the wool, are easily measured, and give dependable results. These salts have an affinity for both the dye and the dye-stuff. And it is this property of "fixing" which is the definition of mordant.

The one you will use most often is alum, not the pickle-pucker variety but potassium alum (potassium aluminum sulphate or potash alum). It is usually used with cream of tartar (tartaric acid) to brighten colors. Four ounces of alum (3 for fine wool) and 1 ounce cream of tartar to 1 pound of wool (or for 4 ounces of yarn [1 skein]—1 ounce alum, ½ ounce cream of tartar).

Translated to *very* rough measurements (using powdered rather than lump alum) :

⅔ C. alum and ¼ C. cream of tartar for 1 lb. wool (or 2 slightly rounded tablespoons alum and 2 slightly rounded teaspoons tartar for 4 ounces of wool.)

If you're lucky enough to have a scale, you can control the weight factor to a fine tolerance. But it will be possible to get satisfactory results (at least to start) with a rough approximation of weights, I'm quite sure.

Mordanting with alum is usually done before the dyeing, but mordanting can be done before, during, sometimes even after the dye process. To mordant *before* means the skeins may be dried and stored away (all labelled, please) so that when you find a dye plant, all you need do is soak and rinse the premordanted wool thoroughly to have it ready to dye.

Back to the mordant pot. Add the chemicals to the warm water (1 + gal. for 4 oz., 4½-5 gal. for 1 lb.), stir until it is dissolved, add the wool (heated to mordant pot temperature), *slowly* bring it to a simmer (190° approx.), then hold at that temperature and water level for an hour. Turn off the heat, and let it sit until morning. If you've put in enough water, the wool will be able to move freely with the need of only an occasional poke or gentle lift and turn from you. Now the mordanted wool can be wrapped in a towel and used in a dye pot soon (with only a rinse) or dried, stored, then soaked and rinsed much later.

Before I mention other mordants, I beg you to tag your nicely mordanted wool. Dates can be helpful, too. You think you will remember which was mordanted, which only tied and readied for mordanting. But sometimes you won't. This goes double for dye lots. Even sketchy notes and simple tags will save you great frustrations.

You will be able to dye lots and lots without feeling the need for any other mordant but alum. But eventually you will be bitten by the urge to experiment more widely. Your next step will probably be chrome (potassium dichromate).

The process here is much the same as with alum, but chrome is *poisonous* and light-sensitive, so you keep the light from the pot (with a lid) while mordanting. And keep the mordanted skeins in the dark, too. Chrome adds color to the yarn (yellowish-green) but allows a large, new dimension to your experiments. For example, coreopsis with alum yields a bright yellow; with chrome a gorgeous brick-red. The contrasts are not usually so dramatic or desirable, but you'll probably want to try chrome sooner or later. The amount for 1 lb. is small—½ oz., (for 4 oz. —⅛ oz.). In rough measure, 2 tsp. for 1 lb. (or ½ tsp. for 4 ozs.). It is best not to store chrome mordanted wool, but to use it at once. Uneven dyeing is a consequence of storage.

With both alum and chrome you can dye for years without wanting more. If ever you want to gray or "sadden" a color, at the end of the dye process, lift the wool out of the pot, add a *very* little ferrous sulfate (iron) about 2 tsp. for a whole pound of wool (or ½ tsp. for 4 ozs.) or less, stir to dissolve. Return wool. Then, as soon as the color is changed, rinse *very* carefully. Iron tends to make wool harsh. It also tends to make dye pots hard to use for any other mordant.

There are times when you will want stannous chloride (tin) to sharpen reds and yellows. This tends to make wool brittle. Use even less of it than you would of iron. Use it as you do iron, but always with cream of tartar or oxalic acid. Be sure to rinse in soapy water.

Only occasionally you will see copper sulfate (copper) called for in a recipe (to develop greens).

Besides the mordants, you can either acidify or alkalize the dye pot, often affecting the color greatly, say from red to blue. (The most easily available acid is vinegar [acetic acid]; the most easily available base is ammonia [sodium hydroxide], the clear kind, not the sudsy variety.)

So, here we have alum, ammonia, chrome, copper, cream of tartar, iron, tin, and vinegar which can be used alone or in combination with any dye bath. The mathematical possibilities are impressive!

It probably doesn't need to be said, but still, the more careful the mordanting, the more likely the dyeing will be as even and permanent as it can be.

There are a few vegetable dyes which carry their own mordant (often in the form of a tannin) with them. These are known as "substantive." They'll need no chemical help from you. Tea, sumach, and black walnut are among the very few in this category. A mordant would only be used to alter the color (to perhaps a yellower or greener shade).

The dye process is begun by weighing out the mordant chemical and the wool (left). The wool is soaked in clean water (below), and the chemicals added to water in the mordanting pot. The wool is gently transferred to the mordant pot, slowly heated and simmered, then cooled.

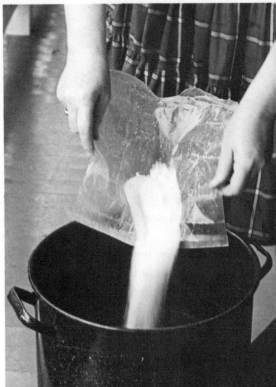

DYEING

At last, we can talk about the actual dyeing. We have narrowed this dye chapter to the use of plants. When you consider that a plant is a living thing, that its internal chemistry changes from minute to minute and depends on so many factors like season, soil conditions, moisture availability, proportions of sunlight and shade, and variety within species, it is no wonder at all that a recipe I'd give you is almost sure to bring different results for you than for me. Consider the variables in the dye process itself: 1. the plant species with all the aforementioned variables, 2. fresh, dry, from what part of the plant picked, 3. length of time between picking and dyeing, 4. mordanting, 5. length and heat of soaking, 6. length and heat of brewing, 7. type and twist of wool, 8. time and heat of wool in dye pot, 9. additional chemicals, 10. method of rinsing, and 11. type of drying. With these in mind, perhaps you will forgive dye recipes that disappoint you, but will be thrilled as you gain control of these variables.

Again, I suggest good record-keeping. You can have fun without it, but you do forget. I prefer a card file. Others a notebook. A card bearing a notation on each of the above variables might read as follows:

Variable	Entry
code	73-12c
(a)	Lily-of-the-Valley *(Convallaria majalis)*
(b)	dried leaves picked NE side of house 9/72
(c,e)	3/73 shredded 1 qt. leaves, soaked overnight in 1 gal. H_2O.
(d,f,h,j)	Simmered 2 hrs. Chrome mordanted. Wool entered. Simmered 30 min. Rinsed. Washed in warm soap.
(k)	Rinsed. Dried in shade.
Note	Note: Try fresh leaves in May. Try with Cu added.

A sample of the dyed wool (g) would be attached to a corner of the card.

A code number is helpful. I try to tag it with the year, the number of the project in that year, and a code letter for the mordant (a is for alum, c is for chrome). On one side of the tag attached to the wool would be lily-of-the valley, on the other

Barbara Foust records information about each dyeing on an index card and attaches a bit of the end product to the card.

73-12c. I am sure you will work out your own system. But at least tag it with the plant material. When dyeing with ripe material, I would include an *exact* date, for even a day can make a large difference in further experimentation.

Many dye plants work as well dried as fresh. Some (like goldenrod) do not. They tend to give brighter colors when fresh. A freezer is the place to store plants and dye baths for further use, if the season overwhelms you.

Flowers are best gathered *just* as they open (that is, in preference to full-bloom). Plants are best young and healthy. Leaves are used as they are ready to mature. Roots are best collected in the fall. Bark is best taken in the spring; second best, in the autumn. Berries just when ripe are best. Lichens are best collected when easiest to take, in winter, or with the rains of early fall when they are swollen. Flowers should not have too much heat applied too long. Plant material must be dried very carefully to avoid mold and mildew, which would make it worthless for dye.

I know how tempting a stand of dye plants can be, whether

in a neighbor's garden or deep in the woods, but please, please, I beg you to pick selectively, leaving many plants for renewal, never downing a tree for a part of it. For example, once I picked all the flower heads from a patch of day lilies (they don't give you orange). This is a common plant hereabouts, and I thought we'd never notice the loss. But it was two years before the patch bloomed again. Perhaps I was the only one who missed that splash of color along the road, but it accused me of greed each time I passed. Our plants are too dear a gift for us to devastate *any* patch of them *any*where.

INTO THE POT

Ready for the dye pot? We will begin with tearing, chopping, and pounding the dye material into small pieces. If it is bark root or nut, this sometimes takes considerable time and muscle. Then our finely-divided dye plant is put to soak in tepid water, at least overnight. Tough, fibrous plant materials may need to soak several days. Now slowly raise the temperature of the dye pot to extract a lot of color. Too much heat may be harmful, so don't just turn up the heat and let it boil furiously. (A pinch of alum when the water boils may help the color flow). When the dye pot is simmering, you can turn your attention to the mordanted wool by "wetting it out" for perhaps an hour in lukewarm (95°F) water. For an even dye, you want the wool wet through and through, not just on the surface. Gentle squeezing and turning — "opening" and "working" the wool — help the water penetrate the strands.

At this point, with a strongly colored ooze, most other dye instructions will tell you to strain out the dye material and discard it. Too many times, as a beginner, I threw out the dye plant only to find shortly that with more soaking or simmering, perhaps with repeated coolings and simmerings, I could extract more color. I've even been known to scrape the discarded materials off the ground to reboil them. Now I break all rules and almost never strain out the dyestuff. The books say this may make uneven dyes. I may have had extraordinary luck, but this has not happened yet. If you wish to be neat and strain out the dye material, perhaps you'd want to save it to boil in another pot. If much color results, you can add it to the dye pot. But this takes impractical extras: a pot, water, space, and heat. You can tie the dye stuff in cheesecloth, to be removed before the wool is entered.

The only time I have regretted *not* straining was a bath of dried marigold flower heads. I had removed the calyxes, exposing the seeds. The sharp seeds pierced the wool. While most dye materials rinse off easily or are removed with a few flicks of the wrist, these seeds have persisted to this day, even after much picking. It makes for most interesting-looking skeins, but ones I would not care to wear.

If you do leave dye plants in and do not have plenty of

After the dye plant has brewed in water sufficiently, strain off the plant materials . . .

and gently place the soaked and mordanted wool in the dye liquid.

water, you can expect the wool to dye unevenly. Some of the handsomest yarn I've known was dyed by my daughter and her husband in an early attempt to dye lots of wool in too small a pot. Wool, black walnuts, and water all crowded together made a variegated yarn which is full of life and character—one of those fortunate mistakes you can hope for sometimes.

With a likely looking ooze, you are ready to introduce the wetted wool. Back to the don't-change-temperatures-too-fast rule. Best to cool down the ooze.

It took me a long time to appreciate that adding water to a dye pot does not dilute the dye. There is so much color in a pot. Adding more water does not take away color. It just spreads it out. No matter how dilute, the same amount of color will still be there and available to the wool. So keep plenty of water in the dye pot, adding it as needed, but not with any shock to the wool, please.

Temperatures equalized, the mordanted wool joins the ooze, and now you're entitled to a bit of hovering, an occasional gentle lift, just to see how things are going. Wet colors always look darker than dry ones. To get the best idea of how the yarn is taking up the color, what shade is coming, lift a bit of yarn just clear of the water. Let it cool just enough so you can pinch it to extract all the water possible. *Now* you have an idea of what's really happening. Keep the wool beneath the water's surface. Keep the water level up. Keep "working" the wool, moving it about very gently, occasionally, all with an aim to an *even* dye.

When you really feel your yarn has captured the depth of color you want, it can either be moved from the pot into hot rinse water, or (the method I prefer) left in the dye pot to cool. Sometimes, however, quite a bit more color is taken up as it cools. If perhaps it still is not the depth of color you'd hoped for, successive simmerings and coolings may very well help.

Rinsing is, of course, always done with minimal temperature shock. Ammonia in the rinse water often brightens flower colors. Most dyers like to dry their skeins in the sun, feeling this adds to the brightness, too. If you wish to block the skeins, a weighted device at one end will straighten the fibers nicely.

Back to the dye pot. Most dyes, even when they've given up a lot of color to the wool, will still have color left in them. This, too, can be extracted with a new skein of yarn. "Exhausting" the pot or "dyeing till clear" is fun. The first skein will take up the most dye. The second less. The third even less, and on and on till there is no color left at all. You will end up with 2, 3, 4 or more skeins, all the same shade, but various gradations of intensity, a very desirable product, especially if you'd like to use the wool to weave, embroider, or knit true-to-life patterns of flower, leaf, bird or sky.

Of course all the wool that must match for one project must be dyed all at once in one pot. Don't ever hope to dye an identical color in a subsequent pot. You may end up with much less or often much better than you hoped for, but never, never the same. But then, commercial dyers, with all the control they have of every step of the process can't make exact matches, either. So there is no need to apologize for our limitations.

First a general rule. To dye 1 lb. (4 ozs.) of wool it takes approximately

1 Lb.	4 Oz.
1 peck of chopped bark	(2 quarts)
¾ peck of chopped drive leaved	(6 cups)
1 peck of hulls	(2 quarts)
1½ qt. dried or ⎱ flowers	(1½ cups)
1½ pecks fresh ⎰	(3 quarts)

There is a wide variance of the amount of dye in each plant (lots in coreopsis, little in sunflower petals) so the rule has to be very general.

STEP-BY-STEP

We're ready now to go step by step through a dye recipe. Here is a good one to start with:

Onion skins *(Allium cepa):* By using the dry papery outer skins you won't get the rich brown put on Easter eggs, but from alum-mordanted wool you can get burnt-orange, from chrome-mordanted wool, brass. Both are fairly permanent colors. It takes quite a few, so go begging at your grocers if you're impatient

The principals of herbal dyeing are wool, water, and one of the colorful herbs. You soak the herb, then the wool, in water.

to start, or (as I do) save every jot and browbeat relatives (my sister actually volunteered). For one pound of wool, you'll need 10 ounces (for 4 ounces of wool 2½ ozs.). Translated into rough but perhaps more practical measurement, the lesser amount (for 4 oz. of wool) is about ¾ quart tamped down *solidly* (so you see the need for cooperative friends and relatives).

The dry husks can now be put to soak and boiled for half an hour. I prefer to soak them overnight in lukewarm water then simmer until I've a nice deep (and yes, smelly) ooze. Here standard recipes say strain the husks out. I don't.

The mordanted wool, I hope, has been soaking in warm water for perhaps an hour. You've squeezed and turned it occasionally.

The dye pot (with or without skins) is brought up to the required volume—4½ to 5 gal. for 1 lb. (1 + gal. for 4 oz.) by the addition of cool water. If your mordanted wool rinse water and the dye pot temperatures are equal, you can transfer the wetted wool to the dye pot. Otherwise, either cool the dye pot further, or heat the wetted wool pot. Then transfer the wool. (It is easier on the wool if you squeeze out the water before putting it into the dye pot. The weight of the water on the wool puts a strain on the fibers when you lift it.)

Your dye pot is boiled or simmered for half an hour (or more). If you want the deepest color possible, you can cool the wool in the dye pot and air-dry it and repeat the heating, cooling, air-dry process several times.

But if you're happy with the color, the yarn can be removed from the dye pot (hot pot to hot rinse water or cool pot to cool rinse water), thoroughly rinsed, then dried. If you didn't strain out the skins, most will float off in the rinse water. The rest will flick out in the drying. No smell remains in the finished yarn.

Aren't you proud of yourself! Go ahead and admire. Lucky is the dyer who has at least one friend or relative genuinely enthusiastic about the process. Not everyone, I suspect, delights in having newly-dyed skeins waved joyously before their eyes.

Before you start knitting, weaving, embroidering, plaiting, hooking, or in any way *using* your beautiful new wool colors, I think you'll want to prove to yourself that the colors are as good and permanent as they ought to be (you'll surely not want to use any that will fade away at once).

So plan to devise some way to test carefully identified samples. A file card will do nicely. When all the snippets of wool are lined up along one edge, then cover parts of all of them. Use the folded-over edge of the same card, or clamp it firmly between two strips of wood. Then hang the samples in a sunny window, or if you've been clever enough to devise a way to protect the identification from the weather, hang your device out in the wind, rain, sun, and snow for a few weeks. Perhaps you'll want to check it each week and add an "x" if it remains unfaded. By the time you've exposed it to the full sunlight for a month, you'll have a very good idea of how it will look in your fine handiwork in a few years.

Expose a length of the finished, dyed wool to bright sunlight for several weeks while shielding another length of the same piece to determine the color's permanence.

Once you're "hooked" on dyeing, I suspect you'll try dyeing everything in sight at the earliest possible moment. (An insipid yellow-green in endless variety is easy.) Soon you'll yearn for certain colors; then the entire spectrum. You'll start collecting dye books (fortunately they're quite inexpensive—I know of none over $10, and two of the best are under $2), then bigger and better dye pots, an accurate scale, thermometer, and imported exotic dyes. Then you'll start looking up other dyers and exchange ideas and recipes. In the process you may start a dye garden. You may learn to spin so you, too, can dye in the wool and create a rainbow in a skein of yarn.

Now, of course, you want to go on beyond onion skins. Or perhaps you'd first prefer to play some more with onion skins. Try various varieties. Try a pot of red onion skins (you'll be surprised!). Try dyeing with the whole onion. Try dyeing with just onion sprouts. See whether fermenting the skins first makes a desirable change (it may not, but sometimes it makes a huge and wonderful difference).

Then there is a chance to try out all those various mordants, acids, bases, salt.

No, of course you can't do it all (unless you're an onion grower knee deep in skins), but in every recipe, keep in mind the possibilities and carefully record, noting possibilities for future recipes, control of variables, thoughts about what might have gone wrong. Refer to previously related recipes.

MORE RECIPES

Black Walnut *(Juglans nigra)*—There is dye in all parts of the tree. It is most concentrated in the hulls (which you surely know if you've even cracked any). Other nut hulls contain dye, but not as generously as black walnut. And requiring no mordant, to boot. The trick is to produce the desired depth of color. This always involves soaking, the longer the better. The addition of mordants will alter the color (variations on basic brown). For deep, blacky shades, you can boil in an iron kettle (the kettle itself acting as a mordant, which is why we avoid iron kettles for most dyes). Old timers put the hulls in cold water, lidded the pot, and fermented it to get deep dark shades. Once you have a good ooze, you can dye *lots* of wool in it, but do not boil the wool too long, for it tends to make the wool harsh.

Sumac *(Rhus):* I hope you know that the sumacs with the red berries are non-poisonous. (Beware the white-berried varieties.) The berries and the leaves dye without mordant needed and will give you grey and brown respectively, altered by various mordants.

Goldenrod *(Solidago):* This has beautiful golden yellow shades that have a good permanence. Use the formula for proportions with the fresh opening tops. You'll like all the shades, but some of them can be dyed in indigo to get a good green or top-dyed with madder to give brick or rosy brown shades.

St. John's Wort *(Hypericum perforatum):* Yellow with alum. (The leaves yield a green.)

Scotch Broom *(Cytisus scorparius):* Yellows with alum and chrome. This is a good one to top-dye with indigo for a good green.

Safflower *(Carthamus tinctorius):* The tinctorius in a botanical name always signals lots of dye available. This one, too, yields yellows.

The leaves and flowers of goldenrod yield beautiful gold and yellow colors in the dyepot.

Coreopsis *(Coreopsis tinctoria):* There is "tinctoria" again. And this plant, if no other, will put chrome in your repertoire. With alum you get a nice yellow, but with chrome a beautiful permanent burnt-orange. Tin and cream of tartar give a very bright yellow.

Remember to rinse all flower colors in warm, soapy water.

Eventually you'll read many recipes for flower colors. Good luck to you. I have had disappointing results with forsythia, hollyhocks, lady's bedstraw, and harebells. I have yet to try asters, begonia, buttercups, calla lily, camellia, carnation, cinerarias, blue columbine, orange and pink cosmos, flowering crab, cyclamen, daffodils, dahlia, delphinium, dianthus, gallardia, geranium, gerbera, gladioli, iris, lupin, Maltese cross, marguerite, monkshood, mullein pinks, pansies, peonies, periwinkle, rose rugosa, snapdragon, spiderwort, tulips, or zinnias though they are all listed as possibilities, mostly because I've never had enough for my greedy dyepot. But I am at work on remedies and have plans for bigger and bigger gardens featuring more and more dye plants. And I do covet others' gardens quite unashamedly. Sometimes people take pity.

Flower dyes have on occasion given me some delightful surprises. I have gotten lovely greens from a decidedly orange ooze made from orange chrysanthemum petals. I have gotten lavender wool from the bright petals of Oriental poppies, and once from a deep royal-purple ooze of wild violet petals what emerged was a clear, icy green. It won't happen quite that way for you, but I wish I could be peeking over your shoulder as you finally lift the wool from your dye pot. I'd almost always be delighted, and never bored.

The list of dyes from leaves is a long one. These are a lot more reliable, if less exciting—all tending to the yellows and browns.

Privet (picked in the fall)—golds and yellows; lily-of-the-valley, with chrome gives one shade in the fall, another in the spring; lombardy poplar, lime yellow with alum, golden-brown with chrome; blackberry (young shoots) with alum yields grey (a late addition of iron deepens it); peach leaves (and bark) with alum yield a gold. Tobacco (the best reason I know for buying a pack of cigarettes!) gives a nice brown.

Because of the scarcity of good, natural sources for blue dyes (and by top-dyeing with yellow to get greens or over reds to get purples), indigo *(Indigofera tinctoria)* is absolutely essential for blues. It is a very lovely, very permanent dye (it's the blue in old coverlets, jeans, African tie-dyes), but since it is insoluble in water, it belongs to a different category of dyes, vat dyes. The dye powder is extracted from the leaves of the indigo plant, a complicated process in itself. Although indigo was once grown as a staple crop as far north as South Carolina in colonial days, it eventually could not compete with rice and cotton. Indian indigo is better and cheaper. Now it is made synthetically.

The insoluable indigo, to be usable, must be put into a soluable form. In this state it is put into the fibers, then the dye is oxidized and the color develops. The methods for performing this magic are many, from fermentation in urine to balancing caustic soda and hydrosulfite solutions.

One can now buy a soluable form of indigo which gives fine and easy results — no mordanting either (unless you plan to top-dye with another color which would need it). If you wish to do it the "old way," dye books can give you quite a choice of procedures.

Woad, also extracted from leaves and *the* important dye of the Middle Ages should also be mentioned, but I do not recommend it for beginners. Its extraction, in the words of a British dyer, is "a bit of a fiddle."

By now I'm certain you have the feeling that your repertoire will soon be top-heavy with the yellow-green range. It will, indeed, if you are limited to neighboring fields, but don't sneer. Even when you get what seems to be an indifferent, perhaps even undesirable color, you'll find it has its own place and beauty when set with its fellows. When made up in a rug, tapestry, or needle project, you will have an enviable range of colors for foliage and flowers.

I have had much fun doing a "noxious weed" series of skeins —ragweed, purslane, amarynth, cocklebur, Queen Anne's lace, yarrow, black-eyed Susan, and so on. Some of the colors are surprisingly beautiful. Some indifferent. Taken as a whole, they are lovely. And, oh, the fun of plucking them, root and all, from a place I preferred them not to be and seeing them turn into color. I read that a good black dye may be gotten from poison ivy. Here, my enthusiasm wavers.

Among the fruit and berries, most yield the pink-lavender-grey range (but some are fugitive). Try sarsaparilla, blueberry, blackberry, grape, privet, horsebriar, mulberry, wild spikenard, cherries, cranberries, sumac, elderberries, barberry, naked viburnum, various varieties of evergreen cones (chopped and soaked), and pokeberries.

This last item, pokeberries, is an interesting one. We know the American Indians used it for war paint, the settlers for ink. It gives beautiful oozes from reddish orange through reddish purple, but has stubbornly refused to give an even, permanent dye to wool. It faded, even in the absence of light.

Rather recently someone found that after mordanting 1 lb. of wool in ½ gal. of vinegar, dyeing in the berries, then boiling the wool in another ½ gallon of vinegar, a much more even and permanent dye could be made. But still not a quality suitable

To many gardeners, purslane is a noxious weed. To some gourmets, it is a salad herb. But to the curious herbal dyer, purslane is a potential dye plant.

for heirloom handicrafts (and that's what we want, isn't it).

Another source of dye is lichens. These are the crusty plants which grow fast to rocks and trees. They account for many of the Irish and Scottish tweed colors. With the proper method of extraction, there is a range of colors from pinks through plums to lively golds and browns. Finding an adequate source and identifying them is the trick. If you're interested, look up *Lichens for Vegetable Dyeing* by Eileen M. Bolton (Charles T. Branford Co.).

If you find a generous source of lichens, to test the color potential, put a small sample in a small capped jar of ammonia water. In a few days, color will develop.

Roots: Roots used for dyeing include madder, *(Rubia tinctorum),* the red of Colonial coverlets. It is possible to grow it in the United States, but the best grades were imported. This is one dye that prefers "hard" water, a minimum of heat. (The more heat, the more browny-yellow the dye.)

I am given to understand that there are many other madder-family plants (goosegrass, lady's bedstraw, viper's bugloss) with a reddish color in their roots, none, of course, as bright as madder.

Sassafras Root Bark *(Sassafras albidum)*, 12 ounces for 1 lb. wool (3 oz. for 4 oz. wool), with alum yields brown, with chrome yields rose-brown.

Dock roots *(Rumex obtusifolius)*, ½ lb. of the root for 1 lb. wool, plus alum yields a dark yellow. Cedar *(Juniperus virginiana)* root yields purple.

Nuts: Besides black walnut, try other nut hulls and acorns (horse chestnut plus chrome gives a nice gold).

Barks: Most of the color in barks is in the inner layer. Try sassafras, white oak (for chartreuse, boil in an iron kettle, no mordant), maple, hickory, apple, alder, cherry, plum, madrona, and willow.

I don't want to throw in a note of discouragement, but I'm afraid you'll be disappointed with either the color (or lack of it) or fastness of beets, turmeric, barberry root, and many berries and flowers. Just experiment with small quantities of yarn. Who knows, *you* may be the one to discover new ways to extract colors and make them permanent.

With increased leisure time, more and more people are turning to the systematic and scientific pursuit of vegetable dyes. Every day, it seems, new color possibilities are found in herbs.

Nobody ever used to consider common milkweed *(Asclepias syriaca)* a dye plant, perhaps because its sticky white juice made it seem impractical for wool dyeing, but thanks to a dye workshop and follow-up experiments with both milkweed and bitterweed *(Helenium amarum)*, experiments made them yield a large range of colors from clear ice-green to oranges, some completely unique.

But you needn't be a scientist to experiment. One lady I heard of extracted a different shade for every month of the year from rhododendron leaves!

Milkweed is more familiar as a wild herbal plant than as a dye plant, but it will yield some unique colors.

I've never heard of any one comparing the dyes made from the barks of different varieties of apples, or perhaps various kinds of pine, spruce, or balsam cones. The range would be subtle but probably infinite. Perhaps some day *I'll* do it. Or you?

For my last birthday, my son and husband felled three trees and built me a large outdoors tripod from which I can hang an old brass kettle.

Perhaps the time has come when I shall actually find out whether the chamber lye really does set colors well and also leaves the wool soft and shiny. Perhaps I shall try to dye with woad, whose fermentation so offended the nose of Queen Elizabeth I that she outlawed even the sowing of the plant within five miles of her residence. Or perhaps I shall just enjoy two great pleasures simultaneously—dyeing and being outdoors. And to you all I wish the same—Happy dyeing!

Dye Plant	Part	Mordant	Pink	Orange	Yellow	Green	Blue	Tan-Brown	Lavender-Purple	Grey-Black
Agrimony Agrimonia eupatoria	leaves and stalks	a or c			x					
Bayberry Myrica pensylvanica	leaves	a								x
Bearberry Arctostaphlos uva-ursi	leaves	a								x
	berries	a					x			
Blackberry Rubus, var. sp.	young shoots	a								x
Black Oak Quercus velutina	fresh inner bark	a or c			x					
Black Walnut Juglans nigra	nuts or hulls	no						x		
Blueberry Vaccinium, var. sp.	fruit	a					x		x	
Bloodroot Sanguinaria canadensis	root	a		x						
Buffalo Berry Shepherdia argene	fruit	no	x							
Buckwheat Fagopyrum esculentum	stalks fermented 5 days	a					x			

Name	Part used	Mordant						
Cedar (red) Juniperus virginiana	root	a	x					
Camomile Anthemis tinctoria	flower	a				x		
Cochineal—an insect; not an herb, but a natural dye	dried insect	var.	x			x		x
Coffee Coffea arabica	green beans	a		x				
Coreopsis Coreopsis tinctoria	flower	tin				x		
		c					x	
Dahlia Dahlia, var. sp.	flower yellow best	c				x	x	
Dock Rumex obtusifolius	root	a				x		
Dyer's Broom Genista tinctoria	flowering tops					- x		
Elderberry Sambucus nigra	fruits	var.	x		x			
Goldenrod Solidago, var. sp.	flowers and plants	a or c	x			x		

Plant	Part	Mordant						
Grape Vitis, var. sp.	fruits	a					x	x
Indigo Indigofera tinctoria	fermented leaves	no					x	
Lady's Bedstraw Galium verum	roots or tops	a or c a or c	x		x			
Lily-of-the-Valley Convallaria majalis	spring leaves fall leaves	c			x	x		
Madder Rubia tinctorium	root	a or c	x					
Marigold Tagetes, var. sp.	flower	a c			x			
Mulberry Morus, var. sp.	fruit	var.					x	x
Onion Allium cepa	dry husks	a c		x	x			
Orchil Lichens	plant	var.	x					x
Pokeweed Phytolacca decandra	fruit fruit	vinegar a and cold water fermented	x	x				x

Plant	Part used	var.							
Safflower Carthamus tinctorius	flowers		x	x	x				
St. John's Wort Hypericum perforatum	flowers	a	x		x				
		tin	x						
Scotch Broom Cytisus scoparius	flowering tops	a or c			x				
Sumac Rhus glabra	leaves and shoots	no				x			
Tea Thea sinensis	leaves	a or c				x			
White Birch Betula alba	leaves	a			x	x			
	inner bark	no							
		a			x				
		iron							x
Zinnia Zinnia elegans	flowers, any color	a			x				

Do not let the chart limit you. It only suggests possibilities and some of the more predictable results.

a = alum and cream of tartar

c = chrome

CULTIVATING THE HERBS

by Heinz Grotzke

SIX

Herbs have been companions of man for many, many centuries. You have seen the many uses to which herbs can be put, accompanying and serving man through his life. Our interest in and intensive work with these loyal companions is nothing but a continued comradeship between two beings from different realms of life.

The mutual relationship in many cases is quite an intimate one, and if for some reason ever broken, it will find means and ways of re-establishing itself. My own experience could be a good example. Herb plants thrive not only outside in the garden, but year after year they reveal their undefinable ability to grow to one's heart. The variety of fragrances, the display of brilliant colors, the pride of their majestic growth, the surrounding liveliness of humming insects, all these imponderables and more make lasting impressions upon the soul of the observant grower. The beginning herb grower might not yet know that there is such a mood that might be called homesickness for herbs, though it only means his work has not immersed him into the subject as deeply as is possible. Just wait and read on.

From early childhood, herbs were my personal companions, whether they appeared as home-remedies and taste improvers or as preferred fodder for chickens, geese, and rabbits. Who could deny the iron strength of nettle, what could surpass the proven healing powers of sweet flag, or how could you please the animals more convincingly than giving them a handful of dandelion leaves? Can there be a better way to improve the taste of boiled flounder than finely chopped rue? Who knows all the names, and who can describe all the fragrances of herbs to one who never made their acquaintance? It is an impossible task. The reliable advice to an interested person remains the suggestion to grow them himself and travel the road of herbal delights and experience the seasonal changes of growth and aromatic intensities first hand. The following pages are meant to be an aid for just such undertaking.

CLASSIFICATION OF HERBS

For many years we as growers and sellers of live herb plants and seeds have classified herbs as follows:

Tender Annuals
(for example, basil, marjoram, borage, nasturtium)
Hardy Annuals
(for example, camomile, heart's ease)
Biennials
(for example, clary sage, angelica, mullein)
Tender Perennials
(for example, rosemary, curry plant)
Hardy Perennials
(for example, lavender, sage, hyssop, chives)

The *annuals* have to be seeded each year unless conditions are favorable enough in the garden to seed themselves. The *biennials* also should be seeded each year so that, for example, a mullein will be in flower each year. These plants form leaves only the first year and flower the following year. The *perennials* last for many years with proper care and can be started from either seed or a purchased plant which over the years can be divided or used for cuttings. Placing the herbs in the garden should take into consideration these differences of above mentioned categories. Perennials quite often are planted as the framework of a garden around which the annuals are grouped.

CLIMATIC REQUIREMENTS

Often, when the question of physical requirements for herbs is brought up, people are consciously unable to distinguish between herbs on one hand and other plants like vegetables and fruits on the other. Herbs throughout the centuries have remained "simple" plants, fully expressing their characteristic individualities simply because man has left them alone and did

Mutual friends are developed early. The love of herbs is an affair oft begun in childhood contacts. And that love of herbs is reflected in the care they are given in their first days in the garden.

not subject them to rigorous selection and breeding programs. Unlike vegetables they have not been bred for quantitative growth, hybridization is nearly absent, and attempts of genetic change through atomic radiation are unknown to me. A visitor from the Egypt of 3000 years ago would still recognize a coriander plant growing today in our garden.

The ability of herb plants to hold and reproduce the original characteristics over thousands of years helps us today in answering questions of physical requirements for these plants. The first step is to find the natural habitat or environment of the specific herb. The more the climate in which we grow it resembles that of its home region, the more ideal are the climatic conditions. Since in general most herbs originate from the areas around the Mediterranean and north, we are safe to assume that a similar climate would make our herb plants feel at home and grow without much trouble. So the great majority of herbs prefer a climate with a great amount of sunshine, low humidity, seasonal changes, and an even distribution of an average amount of rainfall.

SOIL REQUIREMENTS

The above approach also works in determining the preferable soil requirements for herbs. We know that the soils to be found around the Mediterranean are not the most fertile and productive. Herbs are modest creatures, quite often pioneering plants which make use of the smallest amounts of nutrients a soil can offer and still thrive well and look healthy. Lavender, for example, or camomile and thyme are able to flourish where other plants would make a very poor showing. Though there are exceptions to this rule, I do not hesitate to say that the majority of herbs feel comfortable in a well-drained soil of sandy, even gravelly, structure. This does not mean, however, that they would not do well on other soils, but drainage remains always an important factor. Herbs like peppermint, tarragon, lovage, and others have to be excluded from this generalization because they want to scoop from full barrels. For the purpose of a home gardener every type of soil can actually be prepared without great effort to accommodate any herb that he or she desires to grow.

SOIL PREPARATION

Obviously, different herbs prefer different types of soil and soil conditions and consequently need specific soil preparation. So particulars are discussed with individual herbs in Appendix A. There are, however, some initial requirements for successful herb growing that apply to all herb plants.

DRAINAGE

Drainage is a term in farming and gardening describing the ability of a soil to handle the water from rainfall or irrigation. The ideal type of soil is expected to absorb any normal amount of rainfall within a reasonably short time without leaving excessive water for run-off. A soil which is able to meet these expectations is said to have good drainage. A soil having problems ingesting all water from rainfall, and thereby causing run-off, is said to have poor drainage.

The reasons for poor drainage are varied. It can be a sign of low organic matter content because the organic matter, primarily in the form of humus, can absorb a great amount of water. The home gardener could do worse than to add a high amount of manure compost over a period of years until the organic matter content has been improved sufficiently.

Some gardening areas never seem to produce impressive growth. Drainage is poor; the rain runs off, and during a dry period the soil becomes a dry powder. Plants even begin to wilt unless artificially watered. Closer investigation will usually reveal a rock formation or layers of shale or rock a foot or more below the topsoil. The water-holding capacity of this type of soil is rather limited, and plant roots are confined to the few inches of top soil. Here improvement will be achieved by breaking up the subsoil, removing the rock materials, and replacing them with topsoil. Should this be too cumbersome or expensive, the only other solution would be to start a garden in a more ideal location.

Another reason for poor drainage could be a so-called hardpan caused by excessive application of chemical fertilizer over an extended period of time. The water-soluble salts are taken into solution by the rain water and leached into the subsoil where they combine with other elements, often iron, and form a rocklike layer that separates the topsoil from the subsoil. Neither water nor plant roots can penetrate the hardpan within a reasonable time. During winter months this can cause herbs to frost-heave, during summer months to drown if the water stands too long on top of the soil. An organic grower should not have to face this problem unless he acquires property with soils that were mistreated by the previous owner. The first correction is of course to omit water-soluable chemical fertilizers and replace them with organic substances and compost. The hardpan itself has to be broken up by mechanical or biological means, the first being double-spading or subsoiling, the other planting of plant varieties with long tap roots which are able to penetrate the hardpan. After the seasonal growth these tap roots decompose, thereby creating channels into the subsoil which can be utilized by successive crops. Pioneering plants of the herb group able to correct the situation would be alfalfa, fennel, root parsley, lovage, false indigo, angelica, and horseradish.

In preparing an area for herbs, another requirement should be kept in mind as an important part of soil preparation. Quite a number of herb seeds are small and slow to germinate, while another group of herbs, especially all the thymes, grow closely to the ground and hardly reach a height of more than two inches. For both groups it is mandatory to grow them in soil that is as weed-free as possible and where quack-grass is entirely absent. If the future herb garden harbors this nuisance grass, and some of the best soils sometimes do, there is no other choice but to get the spading fork and rid the soil of the white, vigorously running roots by shaking them out of their element. While doing so, there is no reason to become annoyed at this strong weed. It not only is an indicator of good soil, but is by tradition considered an herb. The white roots may be washed, cut into pieces, dried, and used one teaspoonful per cup as an herb tea. The task thus could be an introduction to herbology.

The other weeds should be discouraged by an early working of the soil. Prior to planting the soil can be hoed, raked, rototilled, or cultivated at weekly intervals, thus preventing the sprouting weed seeds from getting established. Plowing or spading the garden in late fall aids in weed control and prepares a fine seed bed for spring planting. The pulverizing power of the frost works to benefit the fine seeds of thyme, marjoram, and others which can be seeded outside if the soil preparation allows it.

The same line of thought applies to rocks. For ease of gardening, especially rototilling and seeding, all stones larger than a small egg should be picked up and deposited into a "stone savings box" for future needs. Whatever stones pass through the spaces of a rake may be considered harmless.

FERTILIZERS

The section on fertilizer for herbs can be kept brief simply because herbs have kept their natural taste for manures and composts and never gain in herbal qualities if treated with water-soluble chemical fertilizers. The amounts of concentrations of essential oils in most herbs determine the quality. The formation of these oils is not so much dependent upon the earth but more

For those herbs that are encouraged by a well-fertilized soil, the best fertilizers are natural ones. Dried manure (left) and seaweed and kelp mixtures are good, and they are common commercial varieties.

so on cosmic factors of light and warmth intensities. All animal manures, used as fertilizing agents, support rather than inhibit the gradual build-up of oils and other ingredients in the herb plants. The most ideal manure in my experience is sheep manure, with cattle manure closely following. Remember that all fertilizers, above all artificial nitrogen, which stimulate and bring about a quantitative growth do so by making intense use of water. The plants are encouraged to absorb an optimum of watery solutions causing the plants to become larger and heavier. An herb grower however does not really want this because he has to dry the herbs after harvesting which means he has to pay to get rid of the water. And what remains after drying is actually his crop. Granted that herbs are also used fresh and at times sold fresh. Even then a quality difference will be found in fragrance and taste. In summary, let us repeat that herbs thrive best on manures and composts.

COMPOST

Everybody knows what compost is, and organic growers certainly have made one. Composting is a controlled decomposition of organic materials. It is usually done above ground and is used to preserve and stabilize plant nutrients. In addition, composting breeds beneficial soil microbes which, after reaching the garden with the scattered compost, continue their activity of digesting and converting crop residues in the soil itself.

Herb plants respond quite well to fertilization with compost; in fact, long experience has shown that compost is the ideal fertilizing agent for all herbs, though the stage of breakdown in the compost pile at time of application can vary with the specific plants. For the home gardener and all-purpose use, the compost should be made from a variety of materials (manures, leaves, weeds, kitchen garbage) and should be well decomposed at the time of application. In northern climates it takes about a year to finish a compost, including two turnings. Less time is required in warmer areas. Detailed information on composting can be found in *The Complete Book of Composting,* available from Rodale Books.

Compost is the very heart of the organic method and the base for your herb garden. In its many forms and variations, compost is a substance which gives fertility to soil and thus productivity to plants. If you are a successful compost maker, chances are you are a successful organic gardener and will be a successful herb grower.

From every corner of your home and garden come materials for the compost heap. Every shred of organic matter on your place — leaves, vegetable wastes, weeds, garden harvest leavings, manure from whatever animals you have — can go into the compost pile. You build it, turn it a few times and forget it. One day you walk back to the compost pile and spade it over. It crumbles apart — a rich, humusy, dark-looking substance usually full of earthworms. Smell it. All that waste and rot has turned magically into the sweetest smelling stuff in the world. The end product has become fertilizer for the next growing season.

The compost pile is the beginning and the end of your operation. What happens is that by properly building your pile, you start a ferment in the pile that within two weeks creates up to 160 degrees of heat. This heat kills disease organisms and weed seeds. It comes from the furious action of billions of soil bacteria upon the undigested matter in the pile.

The first step in actually making compost is gathering your materials. A ratio of five parts vegetable matter to one part nitrogenous animal matter such as manure is ideal. Don't forget natural fertilizers

such as rock phosphate, cottonseed meal, and bone meal. Prepare the ground by spading, exposing soil bacteria to the bottom of the pile. Getting enough air into the pile is essential, and composting proceeds faster when more compostable surface is exposed, so shredding is the best technique we know to get the pile cooking. You can use a shredder or a rotary power mower to reduce stalky, twiggy materials to green confetti.

Now start building layers: First a "hot" layer of manure and garbage, about an inch or two thick; then a foot or so of green

matter; then sprinkle on your granite dust, rock phosphate, or other trace additives; top this with an inch of soil, then start layering the same way over again until the pile reaches five feet. It can be as small as three feet and still work. If you insert poles during the layering, you can remove them when the pile is completed to create air spaces. Cover the whole thing with dirt or straw, then water. The pile should be watered frequently, as the heat of decomposition dries it and stops the action after a few days. Tread carefully, though, for too much water will drown the pile's inner fire. The secret is to keep it moist, but not soaked. As decay commences, the right consistency is warm, moist, and crumbly. Turn the pile twice within the first two weeks and you'll have compost before you know it. The turning gets air to all parts of the pile and brings slower-decaying surface materials to the hot center of the pile. Turn once a month, thereafter. Your compost, though, should be finished not long after 14 days with all the shredding, turning, and watering. How long you let it cook depends on how fast you want compost.

You can't apply too much of this fertilizer and soil conditioner to your herb garden. The fall, after harvest, and the spring, before planting, are the best times to work compost into the soil. It can't "burn" plants, and the thicker you spread it, the more humusy, moist, and nutritious your soil will be — and that goes for the things you grow in that soil, too. Remember, there's no one way to make it . . . it makes itself. Just do it and it'll work out.

Apply compost in spring, after spading or plowing the ground. It should be worked into the soil by cultivation, hoeing, or rototilling within a day. If planting does not immediately follow, it is advisable to rototill or work the soil once more before setting out the herbs, thereby destroying young weeds that have germinated in the meantime and at the same time helping to distribute the compost more uniformly throughout the soil.

MULCHING

There is no question that herbs should be mulched. The first and foremost reason is to keep the leaves of the herb plants clean in case of heavy rains. Parsley and oregano, for example, grow so low that whole plants can be blown over in a strong storm and pushed into the soil. A mulch prevents this from happening. The rain and soil stay separated and cannot hurt the herb plants.

Another main reason for mulching, of course, is weed control. In stands of vegetables or flowers, weeds can become a real nuisance, as many gardeners will readily admit; in herbs, however, weeds are unthinkable because they generally are much higher and faster growing than the low herb plants and actually would choke the herbs out if not controlled. Herbs need sun and light and moving air around them, all things that weeds selfishly would deny them. Mulching becomes a tool of the gardener to *deny the weeds* the conditions which would allow them to germinate and grow without an effort. The most effective way is to cover the soil with several inches of mulch material soon after planting. The young weed plants then grow into the mulch trying to get their heads on top of it, where the light is, but most get exhausted before they reach the sunlight. A few super-toughies might conquer and defeat the mulch barrier, though they rarely escape the eye and action of the waiting gardener, who can easily pluck them from the moist, friable soil.

A final benefit of mulching worth mentioning is its ability to preserve soil moisture. Evaporation from the soil is extremely low because the mulch material is shading the soil continuously. Furthermore the impact of the falling rain or irrigation water is

Mulch is a layer of material, preferably organic material, placed on the soil surface. Mulch acts in several ways. It fills a role as protector of the topsoil, conserver of moisture, guardian against weather extremes, and comfortable, bruise-saving cushioner under ripening produce. On top of all that, mulch boosts soil fertility — it adds organic materials by decomposing gradually into the earth's top layer and stimulating helpful microorganisms.

When you set out to mulch a home garden of any considerable size, there are three factors to be considered: (1) how the material will affect the plants most intimately concerned, (2) how the com-

pleted mulch will look, and (3) how easily and inexpensively the mulch may be obtained. Organic gardeners like their mulch of old plant matter. Such mulches have a plus — they decompose into the essential life-giving elements of a rich, dark humus.

Plants themselves literally demand to be mulched because that's the way they've been able to survive repeated disasters through the ages. Spontaneous mulching has been going on for a long time — millions of years — by the time man first began to raise a few favored crops about 15,000 years ago. As the leaves fall to the forest floor, forming the basis of nature's mulch protection, they also decompose into a compost that makes up a rich soil-rebuilding program of nature. Out in the open fields, dead tops and foliage of the annual plants fall over to cover the ground and protect it from the rigors of winter. This fact is important: composting and mulching go hand-in-hand and are, in many instances inseparable. Remember that in dealing with your soil. The aim is to build and maintain nature's complete soil pattern as far as possible. Mulching alone, as a mechanical ministration, cannot offset completely the shortage of fertility in the soil. Conversely, building up the fertility can be all the more reason for mulching also, a combination with doubled benefits because of the more efficient use of both the soil and the mulch that covers it.

It's pretty apparent that you're missing out on a lot of good gardening if you don't mulch — and mulch with whatever is cheap and handy. Leaves contain twice as much plant food as barnyard manure — pound for pound. Buckwheat hulls are fine, but so is hay. Sawdust will keep the weeds down and the soil moist, but be sure you add some form of nitrogen if you're going to raise a crop right away. Try leaves, straw, hay, grass clippings, weeds, crop residues. Remember that the more humus you get into your soil, the better the herbs you'll grow.

broken by the mulch, and the water gently led to the soil, where shallow roots can immediately receive it.

As far as materials for mulching go, each herb grower has his own favorites, partly chosen on the basis of availability. Among the most popular herb mulches for home garden use are cocoa hulls, freshly cut grass, chopped hay, chopped straw, chopped seaweeds.

Cocoa hulls are the most ideal, because they are dark brown in color, keep little water for themselves and are high in nitrogen. A mulch material influences soil temperature to a great degree by shading the soil and keeping it cooler than it would be without a mulch. However, a dark mulch material, like the cocoa hulls, absorbs rather than reflects the sun's warmth, and in a way resembles soil in this respect, or, if the soil is of sandy texture and light color, even tops it. Herb plants like a warm soil, especially thymes and rosemary, which fact should be kept in mind when selecting a mulch material.

The other above mentioned materials are well known to the organic grower and are generally easier to get. They are handled the same way they would be for vegetables, except the thickness of application should be less for herbs. Chopped material is preferred because it settles better, looks neater, and is less prone to interfere with harvesting. Mulching is, of course, a whole subject in itself. *The Organic Way to Mulching* (Rodale Press, 1971) is an excellent reference.

PLANT PROPAGATION

After all above preparations and considerations are completed, the next step for the practical herb grower is planting. Like all other plants, herbs can be propagated from seeds, cuttings, divisions, and to a lesser degree, layering. The following chart might help to classify them at a glance by listing only the most successful or possible method of propagation.

HERBS

From Seeds	From Cuttings	From Divisions
Basil—all var.	Cottage Pink	Chives
*Marjoram	Curry Plant	Tarragon
Dill	Lavender	Lovage
Savory	Santolina	Beebalm
Chervil	Oregano	Peppermint
*Thyme	Pennyroyal	Hyssop
*Oregano	Peppermint	Lemon Balm
Parsley	Pineapple Sage	Sweet Woodruff
Sage	Purple Sage	Horseradish
*Camomile	Rosemary	Yarrow
Fennel	Lemon Thyme	Nettle
Coriander	Southernwood	Spearmint
Anise	Spearmint	Roman Camomile
Borage	Tarragon	Lady's Mantle
Salad Burnet	Tri-Color Sage	Mugwort
Caraway	Winter Savory	Welch Onion
*Catnip		Oriental Garlic
*Korean Mint		Tansy
Oriental Garlic		
Pot Marigold		
Sorrel		
Garden Cress		

*These seeds should be started indoors, all others do well if seeded directly where they are meant to grow.

HERBS FROM SEEDS

Although it was rather difficult to find a satisfactory assortment of herb seeds a few years ago, the increased interest of gardeners in herbs persuaded many established seed houses to enlarge their listings. Commercial herb growers especially offer a wide variety of herb seeds. Herb seeds are bought by the package. An average package of herb seeds — with a few exceptions like Egyptian onions, bay laurel, and sweet cicely—will have enough seeds in it to get up to 100 plants. And since most perennial herbs should have a minimum growing area of one square foot, it is easy to see how far a few seeds can go. In general, gardeners tend to overbuy seeds, especially herb seeds, unless it is explained in simple terms what to expect from one package alone. It's wiser to purchase new seed each year rather than to test the viability of the previous year's seed. Re-seeding always means an unfortunate delay, particularly so with herb plants because they need all the time they can get to show satisfactory growth.

To start herb seed indoors is easier than you think. There are just a few rules to follow and steps to take. Above all, the herb gardener should stay cool and not get overly excited if the sun through its mere presence seems to predict an early spring. Herbs to be started indoors for later transplanting are best started from seed no earlier than March; otherwise they will get too spindly, weak, or fall prey to insects and diseases. Each variety should be seeded in a separate container to allow for the varying length of time each variety needs to germinate. Garden cress, for example, germinates within 48 hours, while lavender might take three weeks. The choice of container is a personal one; but the chosen container should make it possible to plant the seeds in rows rather than scattering them over the whole surface area. This is, of course, suggested for a reason.

Anyone who has started plants from seeds indoors has probably experienced the decimation of his young sprouts, which suddenly mold away soon after germination. This is called damping-off and is caused by an organism which can come from the rooting medium, from an unclean container, or even from the air. To avoid this problem, the modern commercial florist or greenhouse grower either steams his soil or treats it with some kind of fungicide. Until recently the favorites were mercury compounds, which were sold as liquid solutions, diluted by the florist and then used to saturate the soil.

The organic grower employs other means, one of which is the planting of seeds in rows. Contact between seeds is thereby kept at a minimum, and a pocket of damping-off can be isolated or even removed.

Of course, to see an epidemic break out among the seeds, they must be visible. Seeds are sown in rows *without* covering them; the seeds remain exposed to the air. The rows should be at least one inch apart and about 1/4 inch deep, the growing medium itself one inch below the rim of the container. After the seeds have been thinly sown in the row or rows, they are watered with a fine mist of water, the container covered with two sheets

of newspaper, then placed in a warm area, preferably 70 degrees or a little warmer. From then on, the seeds need misting with water about three times a day. If damping-off is feared or noticed, the misting should be done with a thin tea of camomile, which will help control the disease.

First choice for a growing medium should be finely milled sphagnum moss straight or mixed with crushed granite. Substitutes would be Jiffy-mix with or without crushed granite, or finely screened, aged compost mixed with equal parts crushed granite. Bear in mind that seeds started indoors do best in a growing medium which in itself has hardly any plant nutrients.

Once the seeds develop their first seed leaves, which in most cases should happen in 7-10 days, they need to be transplanted either into 2¼ inch pots, one to a pot, or into flats with a minimum spacing of 1¼ inches. At this stage the little plant should have a single root, which may be tipped for easier transplanting. Set the plant itself into the soil deeper than it grew in the seed flat. Side-root formation is thereby stimulated. The soil into which these little plants are set can be a regular potting soil or at least a richer medium than that of the seed flat.

After four weeks the plants will be ready for transplanting into three inch pots and from there, after another three to four weeks, may be planted outside any time depending on variety and weather.

HERBS FROM CUTTINGS

A large variety of herb plants has to be propagated from stem cuttings because either the plants do not form seeds or the seeds do not come true to variety. In addition, in our above chart a few herbs have been included which could be started from seed,

The most common propagation technique is to start plants from seed. The seeds of many plants may be sown directly in the garden, but some must be started indoors. These are seeded in flats filled with a sterile planting medium. As the seedlings develop their first leaves, they should be transferred to small pots. Peat pots can run into a bit of money, but when the herbs have achieved sufficient size and hardiness to be transplanted into the garden, one merely plants pot and all. The pot will rot away; the plant hopefully will flourish.

but for the limited need of the home gardener the propagation from cuttings is probably somewhat easier and faster. These are oregano, rosemary, lavender, cottage pink, pennyroyal, and winter savory.

The rooting medium for cuttings can be a variety of substances, again the question of choice is an individual one. For the beginner a mixture of equal parts of milled sphagnum moss, crushed granite, and finely screened aged compost or humus is suggested. Some cuttings, especially the soft cuttings of pennyroyal, also do quite well in the fairly recently offered Jiffy-7 growing pellets which upon addition of water expand into little pot-like objects held together by polyethylene netting. This netting is the real disadvantage as it does not disintegrate in the soil, and thus must be removed by hand.

A cutting is actually a term used for the sprig which is cut off the tip of a branch, and for our purpose should be about three inches long. Starting at the bottom, the leaves are removed with a sharp knife to within $1\frac{1}{2}$ inches from the top. This then is the prepared cutting ready for the final cut and planting.

The final cut of the prepared cutting should be made with a sharp knife by cutting, not pressing, with a downward stroke through the stem at a slight angle. Having done this, the gardener should have about one inch of bare stem left. This finished cutting is planted into the well-packed growing medium which could have been placed in $2\frac{1}{4}$ inch pots, a flat, or a special growing area for cuttings. A uniform soil temperature of at least 65°F. should be maintained and the cuttings misted several times daily to prevent wilting. After about three weeks they should have formed enough roots to be transplanted into individual pots or shifted from the $2\frac{1}{4}$ inch pots to three inch pots. Planting the herbs outside is determined again by variety and weather conditions.

As was the case with mulching, many more details could be mentioned in regard to cuttings, more than the scope of this book allows.

One of the easiest and most effective methods of propagating plants
is by cuttings. Cuttings are parts of plants — leaves, stems, roots —
cut from a parent plant and inserted in water, sand, soil, peat moss,
or some other medium where they form roots and become new plants.
Plants identical to the parents are reproduced, making cuttings an
excellent method for propagating unique varieties developed through
hybridization or mutation. With a sharp knife, carefully trim the
lower leaves from a stem (left), then sever the stem (right) and insert
it in a rooting medium (below).

HERBS FROM DIVISIONS

Dividing older plants as a means of propagation and also rejuvenation is an old practice which also can be made use of in the case of herbs. It of course works only if the herb grower already has an old plant. Dividing plants is the easiest way of plant propagation and the most foolproof one, mainly because it is done right in the garden within a relatively short time. In general, spring is the best time of year for division. The individual plant is dug, the soil shaken off, and the clump either pulled apart (chives, oriental garlic), cut into sections (hyssop, woodruff, tansy), or carefully separated (lady's mantle, all mints, roman camomile). Each section of plant with a good amount of roots is then treated and planted as an individual plant. Sometimes one clump will give up to a dozen new plants.

HERBS
FROM COMMERCIAL GROWERS

The beginning herb gardener cannot avoid purchasing a variety of plants from a commercial herb garden, especially those that cannot be started from seed, like tarragon and santolina, or others which are rather hard to grow from seeds, like rosemary, oregano, and lavender. Also space in the house might be a limiting factor, or time to tend them seven days a week. Fortunately during the past few years small local herb gardens have sprung up all over the country and will be able to supply at least the more common varieties of herb plants. A few growers also ship herb plants to people who have no access to nearby herb gardens. The best and safest time to plant all varieties outdoors is May or early June, with the exception of a few hardy plants which may be planted in April or even earlier.

Customers of local herb gardens have the real advantage to ask the grower to dig plants in the field in April, carry them straight home, and plant them there. These plants will need the least care because their growth would be in harmony with the season and accustomed to the weather.

Root division is a method of multiplying the number of plants by splitting mature plants into two or more smaller plants. Of course not all herbs

lend themselves to division, but chives, for example, do. Simply grasp a bundle of stalks in each hand and pull them apart. Or, using a sharp knife, cut a large plant clump into several smaller ones.

INSECTS AND DISEASES

Up to this point insects were only mentioned as being necessary for pollination, and this is actually their main function in herb growing. All individual species of herb plants still have strong genetic resistance to insects; the less the variety has been tampered with, the less prone it is to insect attack.

In my experience it is only basil which in some years becomes host to Japanese beetles in our area, the juicy lettuce leaf variety being most favored by them. The timing of their attack, however, coincides generally with the beginning flowering of basil, the stage in which basil should be harvested anyway. For some strange reason, the Japanese beetles would never stay on the remaining lower leaves of the basil after harvest, but would simply vanish. It is true, we have had in some years such heavy infestation that the basil would have been stripped over a weekend if no measures of control were taken. The safest and most efficient control I found was to flame the Japanese beetles off with a burning propane torch early in the morning while the dew is still on the plants. The beetles are very sensitive to fire and drop off the leaves in an instant with burned antennae, wings, and even chewing apparatuses. The plants will show no harm if the handling is done right, especially fast enough.

Of the other insects, aphids could possibly attack camomile or sometimes dill, though by observation, I noticed that only a small percentage of individual plants are attacked. I never attempted to control aphids outside. It seemed that each time aphids tried to get established, the population of ladybugs somehow exploded and cleaned up and ate up the entire aphid colony. I bypass plants that still show aphids at time of harvest.

In growing herbs for culinary or beverage purposes, it should be remembered that *any* substance which would cause a residue on the leaves, will alter the flavor of the finished product and diminish the purity. So keep away from even rotenone or pyrethrum.

The above applies in a similar way to the treatment of plant diseases which are rare to begin with, in organic herb growing that is. Timely harvest is very important in order to avoid over-aging of leaves. As the leaves grow older, they show less resistance to disease and occasionally become host to mildew, especially if cloudy moist weather persists for more than three days. For a small area it is preventive disease control to pick up yellow leaves from the ground after harvest or cover them with an inch of good compost. Furthermore, it is important to plant sun-loving herbs actually in a sunny spot, and, above all, keep good drainage in mind.

INDOOR CULTURE

There's no need to forego the companionship of fresh herbs once winter sets in. Many herbs can be brought indoors, and with proper care, survive the winter months easily. Proper care merely means providing enough light and moisture, a good climate—not too hot or cold, with a daily breath of fresh air—and room for growth.

August is not too early to begin selecting the plants you want to move indoors. Some you may select because you want a fresh supply all winter; this will undoubtedly be the most compelling reason. If your area has severe winters, you may select some tender perennials to protect them. Still others may be selected simply for companionship.

The basic step is to assure yourself that you have a window that gets sufficient light. While direct sunlight is to be most prized, it isn't absolutely necessary, and some herbs don't like direct sunlight anyway. But most herbs do like direct sun, and the window that gets at least five hours of direct sun each day is the best for your indoor herb garden.

Your next task is to select containers. All sorts of pots are available, in plastic, clay, and terra-cotta. Redwood and cedar boxes of many sizes and configurations can also be bought (or made). You'll have only to suit yourself, so long as you provide enough room for the roots of your herbs. The common rule of thumb is to use a pot with a diameter of one-third to one-half the ultimate height of the plant.

Any good organic potting medium will serve. You can use the mixtures of milled sphagnum moss, ground granite, and finely

Late summer is the time to pot herbs you want to winter indoors. A simple potting mixture is made by combining ordinary top soil with peat (above), various rock powders (above left) and gravel (left). Cover the drainage holes in your pots with small stones, then a layer of the potting mixture.

Carefully arrange the roots of the herb in the pot, making sure you don't try to put too big`a plant in too little a pot (right). Cover the roots with potting mixture, tamping it firmly. Finally, give the newly potted plant a thorough soaking.

screened compost mentioned earlier in this chapter. Just remember that not all herbs desire fertile soil, and conduct your potting accordingly.

Herbs can be simply transplanted from the garden to the pot, or they can be started from a cutting or from seed. Probably the most foolproof technique is to transplant a healthy plant from the garden.

Select a proper-size pot. The drain-hole in the bottom should be covered by stones, a bit of broken crockery, or a layer of sphagnum moss to prevent the soil from blocking the drainage area. Partially fill the pot with potting soil. Hold the plant in position, with the roots spread naturally. Add more potting soil, tamping it firmly with the fingers. When you are finished, the surface of the soil should be about a half-inch below the rim in small pots, and about an inch from the rim in large (six inches in diameter and up) pots. If you put too much soil in the pot, your herbs won't get enough moisture when you water; too little soil and your herbs may drown.

When the plant is in the pot, thoroughly water it and leave it outside for several days, permitting it to establish itself. Do move the potted plant indoors before the first frost. Avoid any sudden temperature changes.

Once indoors, the potted herb should be, of course, kept in that sunny spot you've selected. Once a day, give the herb a breath of fresh air by opening a window or door in an adjoining room. Don't shock your herb with a cold draft. The herbs like a temperature of 50 to 70 degrees. Never let it get above 75 degrees. Herbs also like a fairly high humidity, and since most home heating systems tend to provide dry heat, you'll do well to frequently water the plants and spray their foliage. These humidity measures will keep the herbs healthy and pest-free. Should pests invade, you can hand-pick the pests or spray them with soapy water. An occasional taste of a weak manure tea will keep the herbs well-nourished.

With the herbs established in your home, adding their fragrance and color to your living environment, don't fail to add them to your meals too. Their foliage will only be fresh and ever-burgeoning if you keep cutting and trimming.

HARVEST AND STORAGE

Don't wait until the last days of summer to think about how you are going to preserve your herbs. Not only will you work yourself into a dither trying to get them all dried or frozen before the first killing frost, but you'll have missed the prime harvesting time for most herbs. A little planning and thought at the season's beginning will enable you to make the best use of your herbs.

There are several ways to preserve herbs, but you'll want to take into account what you want to use them for and when they'll be ready for harvest. Most herbs you'll want to dry; but some you'll freeze or refrigerate. And if you move your favorite culinary herbs to the windowsill in winter, you'll use them fresh all year.

Most herbs for culinary use are ready to harvest just before the flowers appear on the plant. At this time, the plant contains the most oils and therefore the greatest flavor and fragrance. A good example of this is the nasturtium. Before the plant blooms, the leaves of the nasturtiums are a storehouse of vitamin C. The leaves should be cut at this time since the vitamin C diminishes as the plant blooms.

The herbs for drying should be harvested early in the season so that successive cuttings can be made. Harvesting perennial herbs late in the season not only causes a lessening of flavor, but the possibility of plant loss as well. Plants need the chance for regrowth in order to survive the winter. Another caution is to not cut annuals such as basil and borage too closely to the ground. This lower foliage is necessary for continued plant growth. At the end of the growing season for annuals, the entire plant can be harvested

The best time of day to harvest herbs is in the early morning, just as the sun dries the dew from the leaves, since the oils are the strongest in the plants at this time. A chemical change takes place in the plants as the sun becomes more intense and the oils diminish. It is best to do this harvesting on a good clear day.

As soon as the herbs have been cut, waste no time in getting them ready for drying. If the foliage is dirty, wash the leaves, then shake off the excess water. If the plants have been mulched, it is not usually necessary to wash the plants before drying. This is especially important for basil which bruises easily from too

Air drying of herbs is most common, even on a large scale, as above. The screen rack at left is excellent for small-scale use. But hanging bunches of herbs around the kitchen as at right is satisfactory, fragrant, and picturesque.

much handling. The tops and leaves can be picked off the heavier-stemmed herbs such as lovage and basil. The reason for removing the leaves from the stems is to shorten the drying time—thus getting better flavor and color. For herbs like parsley, leave most of the stems on until after drying.

DRYING

Probably the most commonly mentioned method of drying herbs is the most picturesque. The mention of herb drying inevitably conjures up visions of crispy-dry bunches of herbs hanging from some convenient nail.

To dry herbs this way, one simply gathers the herbs and ties them in small bunches. These bunches are then hung in a warm, dark place for about two weeks until they are dry. One drawback to this method is that the herbs sometimes get dusty. Each bunch of herbs can be put in a paper bag, then hung up to dry, but this variation extends the drying time by several weeks.

This latter variation is good, however, for drying seed heads, such as fennel, coriander, dill, cumin, caraway, and anise. Care must be taken to avoid shattering the heads and scattering the

seeds everyplace but where you want them. The care begins with the harvest. The seed heads should be gathered in the early stages of ripening, just as the seeds turn from green to grey or brown. It should be done in the morning, just as the dew leaves the plants. Maneuver the seed heads into a large paper bag or paper-lined basket, then clip the stems. When tying the stems, be sure to tie them into the neck of the sack so that they hang freely. Make certain that the seeds are perfectly dry before storing them since it takes seed longer to dry than foliage; give them two to three weeks.

Another variation on the air drying theme is to disassemble the herb plants and spread the parts on screens to dry. You can use a window screen or one constructed especially for the task. Prop it up in some way to permit the air to freely circulate through the screen. Place it neither in the direct sun nor in some damp spot.

The fastest drying method is oven drying. The oven temperature should be 150° or lower. Herbs are placed on sheets of brown paper. The paper should have slits cut in it to allow for the passage of air. The oven door is left ajar to allow the moisture to escape. With this method it takes from three to six hours to dry the foliage. After a few hours the leaves can be easily removed from the stems, then dried further if necessary to ensure complete drying before storing. Basil and chervil are very sensitive to heat and a temperature of about 90° F is best to dry these to retain their color and prevent browning.

In storing the herbs dried by either of these two methods, an airtight container such as a glass jar should be used. The herb must be thoroughly dry before sealing in your jars. Check after a few hours and then again after a few days to make sure that there is no moisture present on the inside of the bottle. The moisture indicates that there is still water present in the herb. If not dry,

The herbal experience is rooted in the garden. No one knows herbs as well as the person who raises them, or enjoys them as much. By all means get to know herbs by growing them, in a garden or in a few pots by your sunniest window.

remove from the bottle and re-dry. The herb should crumble easily and be crispy when it is dry.

Leave the herb foliage whole when storing. The flavor is retained longer when whole leaves are stored. Crumble the leaves as you use them. Keep the dried herbs in a dark place to preserve the natural color. Sunlight will fade the leaves and destroy some of the flavor. Label all containers before storage to alleviate later confusion.

FREEZING

Freezing is a very simple way to store the culinary herbs for winter use. Gather the herbs at the specific times previously mentioned for drying, wash them if necessary, shake dry, and then place in plastic boxes or bags, properly labeled. Place these immediately in the freezer. The herbs can be chopped or left whole.

The herbs can also be blanched before freezing, although it is not necessary.

Do not defrost the frozen herbs before using. If the recipe calls for minced herbs, it is easier to chop them while they are still frozen, since they break apart so readily. Chives, sorrel, parsley, dill, oregano, sweet marjoram, lovage, tarragon, and mint leaves freeze well.

Another method to freeze herbs is to place the chopped herbs into ice cube trays filled with water. After freezing, place the cubes in a plastic bag, label, and store in the freezer. When needed just pop an ice cube with herbs into soup, stew, or casserole.

FRESH STORAGE

When storing the fresh herbs in the refrigerator, harvest them as usual, place in plastic bags or special crisper boxes, and refrigerate. Herb foliage lasts longer if washed just prior to use rather than before it is stored. This method is especially suitable in the late fall, just before frost. This way fresh herbs are available for Thanksgiving and sometimes even for Christmas.

Herbs can be your year round companions. Get to know them; use them for their fragrance, their color and their flavor. Travel the road to herbal delights in your own garden and home.

THE
COMPANIONABLE
HERBS

by William H. Hylton

SEVEN

Up to this point, we've dealt largely with the traditional uses of herbs. We've talked about all the qualities that make them herbs and companions. Yet we haven't mentioned the companionship most herbs provide for the other plants in your garden.

Herbs have special qualities that make them your botanical garden aides, just as they work for you in your medicine chest, in your kitchen, and throughout your home. We're talking, of course, about the role of herbs in companion planting, and beyond that, about how herbs can work for you to improve your garden.

In the next, and final chapter, you'll learn how to put herbs to work to decorate your home landscape, how they can, of themselves, constitute an exciting, challenging, and beautiful garden. But herbs can improve your existing or planned flower or vegetable garden in a number of ways. That is what this chapter is about.

Using herbs and plants to repel or destroy insect pests seems to be part of nature's design. The conscious use of nature's design is largely based in folklore, since no one has yet sufficiently documented and stringently tested this part of the design to suit the scientists and academicians in the field.

The practical uses of herbs in the garden have generally been passed orally from gardener to gardener or through channels supported by people who put more stock in practical results and common sense than in scientific certification. The existing body of knowledge is an accumulation of observations and happy accidents, such as that of Mrs. Marion Wilbur, the author of the landscaping chapter.

"Our family drinks a lot of herb teas," she says, "and I started putting the used tea leaves on a potted pothos plant in the kitchen window, thinking it would act as a good mulch. Before long there was a noticeable difference in the plant's appearance. Lots of new growth appeared, with a marked increase in leaf size.

The foliage shone as if freshly waxed and polished. The tiny insects which occasionally crawled around on the soil disappeared."

Intrigued by these changes, Mrs. Wilbur began to treat some of her other houseplants to the herb tea mulch—with the same good results. Then one of her diffenbachia plants became infested with mealybugs. If soil insects were repelled by the herb mulch, she thought, perhaps an herb spray would be effective for those on the foliage.

She blended together some of the strong herbs noted for their insect-repellent qualities:

> 4 parts American wormwood
> 4 parts desert sage
> 2 parts erigeron
> 2 parts eucalyptus
> 2 parts silky wormwood
> 1 part yerba santa
> 1 part wild buckwheat

Next, she put a tablespoonful of the mixed herbs into a pint of hot water and let them simmer for about 15 minutes. After cooling and straining, she sprayed the mealybugs with this brew. The residue of tea leaves was used as a mulch.

"It worked!" she says. "A few days later there was not a sign of mealybugs on my plants, nor of any other pest."

Encouraged by success, she applied her new technique to another gardening problem. "I had tried to start some flower seeds in little flats in my dining-room window, but as the seedlings began to sprout, all but a stubborn few were eliminated by fungus, damping-off, and pests," she explained. "I planted another tray of seeds, and immediately watered them with the herb brew. There was no fungus, no damping-off, no pests. As the seedlings grew, I watered them about once a week with a weak solution of the brew. They grew sturdy and showed no signs of any disease or insect infestation."

Carrying her little experiment one step further, Mrs. Wilbur tried using the herbs directly in the planting medium. The dried herb mixture was placed in a pan and scalded with boiling water.

Not all tiny winged creatures are garden pests. Many herbs hold a special attraction for bees, who perform a natural service by spreading pollen from plant to plant.

Excess water was squeezed out (saved for later use) and the moistened herbs were mixed with the regular planting medium—one-third herbs and two-thirds soil mix. The seeds were then sown in this mixture. They sprouted much sooner than those in the straight mix, and every seed produced a healthy plant. "I never saw so many stout, healthy seedlings from one packet," she says.

She began to wonder where she was going to put them all, and what the sow bugs, always one of her big problems when setting young plants out in the garden, would do to them. Bravely she took the small flat of seedlings and set them outdoors in an area where the sow bugs were very active. Although the bugs were all around, they avoided the seed flat. Not even the tender seedlings could lure them into the flat. Evidently they just didn't like the herbs.

Since then, Mrs. Wilbur has used the herb brew extensively

in her gardening, both indoor and outdoor. When transplanting seedlings or rooted cuttings, she waters them well with the herb brew. There is never any wilting or other sign of transplanting shock. When insect infestations occur, she sprays the infested plant with the brew and invariably, within a day or even hours, no pests remain.

USING PLANTS FOR PEST CONTROL

Since hearing this tale, I've done quite a bit of research and some experimenting of my own, and I've found there are many ways herbs can benefit your garden, particularly, but not only, your vegetable garden. Many of you are undoubtedly acquainted with "companion planting," and you know that herbs figure prominently in that body of garden lore. Yet it's often believed that companion planting is only a method of pest control. It *is* that, but it's more than that, as we'll subsequently see. Of course, the wide regard for companion planting, particularly of herbs and vegetables, is not without foundation. Herbs do, I discovered, help control insects. Many of these herbal insect controls are rooted in the folklore of plants, for, after all, pests are nothing new.

Most gardeners aren't primarily concerned about pests. "The main thing on my mind while I'm tending the garden," says Ruth Tirrell, a New England herb fancier, "is good fertile soil. That's what I work for first." Then she tries to give each plant its own needs and the proper culture. Grow each one the way it should be grown, she contends. It *does* matter, and the results are healthier plants.

Just the same, pests do sometimes appear, so one can't be too nonchalant. That implies carelessness. "Like every gardener, I have some pests," says Miss Tirrell. "I don't get panicky. But I don't 'do nothing.' A possible pest becomes a real menace when it is present in such numbers that it destroys the usefulness of a crop, or merely spoils the appearance of a plant."

Organic gardeners try to keep that from happening by using harmless methods of pest control. And using plants to help control insects and other plant pests is a fundamental part of the lore of organic gardening.

There are several ways in which plants figure in pest control. Some plants — a few relatively exotic varieties — consume bugs outright. Others simply repel bugs. Still others are attractive to bugs, enticing them to one spot for easy hand-picking. These practical qualities of the plants can be applied in the garden in a variety of ways. The most familiar is by interplanting, commonly known as companion planting. Mrs. Wilbur's experience involved two other methods—making sprays and mulches of the specially-endowed plants. In addition, there are variations on these two methods.

The key to the success of the method is to use the right plant. Plants that help control pests tend to have a common characteristic—a strong scent—and this strong scent is the key to their effectiveness. Most repellents do not actually "repel" insects so much as they mask, absorb, or deodorize the attracting scent of the plants being protected. Plants that repel insects usually have a strong, sharp taste as well, but it's the potent smell that confuses the pests, thus protecting companion crops that might otherwise be subject to attack.

Herbs are such plants. I have seldom seen insect pests swarming over an herb (though bees do), and I can't recall the last time I saw a pest nibbling on its strong-smelling, strong-tasting leaves.

PLANTS THAT TRAP INSECTS

Now of course, as with all rules, there is an exception, and it is those exotic plants which trap and actually consume bugs. Many of these plants can be classified as herbs, since herbal lore attributes to them some use that would qualify them as an herb. The varieties listed below can thus be called herbs, though they might not commonly be thought of as such.

These insectivorous plants, so called because they "eat" insects, have long been a subject of curiosity because of their odd forms and their unusual methods of obtaining at least a portion of their nutritional requirements. Such curiosity, more than the effect they might have on the insect population of your garden, might spur you to spot one or several of them here and there in your garden.

The pitcher plants induce insects to enter the tubular leaves, then drown them in a digestive juice secreted at the bottom. The best known of these is *Darlingtonia californica,* often raised in the hot house, and found in swampy, humid areas of California and southern Oregon. It has tubular leaves with an arched hood; the flowers grow on two foot stems and are yellowish to brownish red, about one inch across and bloom from May to July. *Sarracenia purpurea* is a native of cold mountain areas from the East Coast to the Rocky Mountains. It has leaves as long as ten inches with purple-greenish flowers, two inches across, and can be easily grown in bog gardens. *S. drummondi* is a southern species up to four feet tall with trumpet-shaped petals. Several other interesting varieties need to be grown in the hothouse. The pitcher plants can be cultivated in pots of sandy muck, covered with sphagnum, in full sunlight and plenty of moisture. They can be grown from seed.

Bladderwort *(Urticularia),* an aquatic plant used in pools and aquaria, has floating, bladder-like leaves which have valve-like openings that trap small insects.

Sundew *(Drosera)* are native, swamp loving plants with clusters of white, pink, or red flowers. The leaves are in rosettes and are covered with glistening sticky hairs in which insects become entangled. The sticky secretion then turns acid and digests the insect. The smallest of the insect eating plants, sundew is about the size of a silver dollar. Some varieties are grown in the greenhouse in mucky soil and full sun. They are propagated by seed, division, and cuttings. The Venus fly trap is of this family—its leaves are two-hinged blades, with sensitive hairs, that close when touched, thus entrapping the insect.

Butterwort *(Pinguicula)* are small, stemless herbs with sticky leaves which attract insects that adhere to its surface. Varieties with yellow, purple, or white flowers can be grown on rocks in the bog garden or moist parts of rock gardens. They are increased by seeds and offsets.

The venus fly trap, a curious plant that does have herbal virtues, can do a small part to eliminate some plant pests. This ant, and any curious creature who ventures into the fly trap's jaws, triggers the botanical systems that close the jaws and begin the digestive process. The plant does eat bugs.

Silene, catchfly, or campion are members of the pink family, with a glue-like substance on the stem which catches flies. They are grown from seed, divisions, or cuttings. Alpine catchfly, four to six inches with white flowers, is suited for rock gardens or edge of borders. Royal catchfly grows to four feet with panicles of deep scarlet flowers, fine for naturalizing in the wild garden. Sleepy catchfly, open only in bright sunshine, has its flowers closed most of the day.

COMPANION PLANTING

Companion planting is a traditional gardening practice. Very little is actually known about it, and many gardeners tend to view it as a mixture of witchcraft and wishful thinking. But some very good gardeners swear by it, and generations of folks close to the earth have noticed that certain plants seem to grow best when planted with certain others.

For the uninitiated, companion planting is the practice in gardening of locating plants that "like" each other in close proximity, while locating those plants that "dislike" each other far apart. The idea is to capitalize on plant symbioses to bolster plant health, control insects, and boost yields.

Herbs are key figures in any companion-planted garden, for just as they are worthy companions for the medicine man, the cook, and the homemaker, herbs are worthy companions for other plants. This is not to say that herbs appear in every beneficial companionship, but a companion garden without herbs isn't qualified for the name. To understand why, let's take a good look at what is known and what is not known about companion planting.

There is no explanation given for much of the information on companion plants. "Carrots and dill dislike each other" is the usual explanation. No one knows why tomatoes, asparagus, and parsley are supposed to make a companionate threesome. But the value of some types of companionate planting can be explained, as Richard Merrill of New Alchemy Institute West did in *Organic Gardening and Farming* (April, 1972).

> In wildlife communities there is a wide variety of plants growing together in the same area that form a natural plant association. These plants are able to co-exist because they complement each other's requirements, provide direct benefits to each other or make demands on the environment at different times. Some live in shade while others thrive in direct sunlight; some have shallow roots, while others penetrate deeply; some serve as food for predators that feed on pests of other plants; some grow quickly, seed out and die before making room for slower growing forms. All available space is used at all times by an array of differently adapted plants.

Similarly, people have learned through years of observation that different types of cultivated plants, growing close together in the garden, have certain beneficial effects upon one another. The nature of the relationships, however, may be different than those in more natural situations. This point is implied by George Scott in his concise book, *Plant Symbiosis*. Scott lists several requirements that make a plant relationship truly symbiotic, most of which reflect the fact that the plants have actually evolved together for mutual benefit. The association may be a permanent feature of the life cycle of the plants (as with the mycorrhizal root fungi and their hosts), or may result in a direct exchange of chemicals, change in morphology, etc. In considering "symbiosis" between cultivated plants, remember that most cultigens have evolved separately in different corners of the earth and have only been thrust together recently by man's activities. There are numerous exceptions, of course, but the majority of beneficial associations between garden plants are more helpful than necessary for survival. For clarity, then, the term "companion plants," rather than symbiosis, seems appropriate.

The most complete book on the subject is *Companion Plants and How to Use Them* by Helen Philbrick and Richard Gregg. Although admittedly only a primer, the book is invaluable as a compilation of formal experiments and casual observations, and contains enough information for a lifetime of study and experiments on the subject.

Many of these experiments are being conducted informally in backyard gardens throughout the country. These are the experiments which contribute to the lore of companion planting. But they don't necessarily satisfy the scientific community.

"We sense companion planting works, that it exists . . . but we have no proof," says Professor C. H. Muller of the Department of Biological Sciences at the University of California at Santa Barbara.

His attitude sums up the scientific community's views of companion planting. Very little, if any, formal research is being done on the phenomenon. Yet no one denies that companion planting exists, and many call for hard research on the subject.

There is some scientific evidence for companion planting's value. Men are now working in related fields, especially the area of allelochemics, which is the study of plant excretions on one another. And the Bio-Dynamic Association has done some remarkable work on companions by making circular paper chromatograms.

"The study of companion planting has been largely the trials and errors of individual gardeners up to this point," Dr. Muller says. "While scientists have studied the allelochemic effects of weeds and trees and grasses, we have neglected it when dealing with food plants. Maybe this is because the negative effects are easier to measure than stimulation."

Allelochemical effects may be a clue to why companion planting works. If plants excrete substances that hinder germination, help dissolve soil so roots can push through and perform other functions, it is reasonable to assume that other plants can enhance the growth of certain plants nearby.

The late Dr. Ehrenfried E. Pfeiffer of the Bio-Dynamic Association and his associate, Erica Sabarth, conducted extensive tests on companion plants using paper chromatography, which is a relatively simple method of measuring the biological value of any product. Plant solutions are placed in a shallow dish, pass up through a special wick, and precipitate out in a circular pattern on suitable filter paper treated with a photo-reactive substance. The resulting colors and patterns give a "picture" of a single substance or substances in combination. The color variations and the overall pattern show not only the quantity of chemicals involved, but the quality of a plant or plants as a whole. The results are amazing.

Companion planters believe that cucumbers like beans and that beans dislike fennel. Extracts from these plants were mixed and chromatograms made on them individually and in combination. The cucumbers, beans, and fennel alone each yielded a chromatogram of fine detail, good shape, and color. When the companions—the beans and cucumbers—were tested, the resulting composite chromatogram showed an enhancement of the features of both. The peculiar bean design was still there, and so was the peculiar cucumber design, but both were enhanced, made stronger and more viable. But when the beans and fennel were tested together, the resulting chromatogram was muddy, dull, ill-defined.

Though these Bio-Dynamic researchers don't say why companion planting works, they do give credence to those who believe that it *does work*. The why's are still a mystery. But one thing is sure: everything is interrelated in nature.

The possible combinations of plants helping one another are quite numerous, and the obvious kinds of mixed cultures —intercropping and rotations—are undoubtedly familiar. Intercropping involves planting certain combinations: fast- and slow-growing plants, shallow- and deep-rooted ones, tall crops and shade crops, vine and supporting plants, and so forth. The most obvious benefit of such combinations is the saving of space, but there are others. Rotation simply involves planting certain plants in a particular sequence, the idea being that the initial plant in the rotation leaves behind beneficial conditions for the plants that follow. The use of nitrogen-fixing legumes is the most familiar.

Recent work has shown that during times of the year when pests are in short supply, insect parasites may subsist on honeydew and pollen from certain available flowers. This is an example of a third way in which plants help each other: providing food for natural enemies of plant pests. Along these lines, other workers at Berkeley have shown the effectiveness of artificial food sprays in increasing the birth rates of some parasites. Although very little is known about this subject, the possibility that flowers of various plants may serve other than esthetic purposes in the garden is intriguing.

Plants have evolved a vast array of defenses against their pests. The most important, however, are a great variety of poisonous or repelling compounds deposited in the plant tissue. Of course, these poisons are often bred *out* of crops so the food will be safe and palatable. As a result, cultivated plants tend to be susceptible to attack by plant-feeding animals. There are two ways to combat this in the garden: by using resistant varieties, or by interplanting with other species of plants which have retained their repelling compounds.

Aromatic plants play an important role in determining the presence of certain insects. It is well-established that insects are attracted or turned away from plants more by their odor than anything else. The scent is due to certain essential oils excreted as waste products from the plant. The corn earworm moth and the European corn borer, for example, are attracted to the odor of corn plants. Some caterpillars seem to be attracted to the strong odor of mustard oils common to members of the cabbage family.

Other plants, especially aromatic herbs and pyrethrum flowers, may repel insects by their odor. Early repellents of mosquitoes, for instance, were oil of citronella, eucalyptus, pennyroyal, rose geranium, cedarwood, thyme, cassia, and anise. Scattered throughout organic literature are numerous references to plant repellents. Some are old-time remedies, while others are the more recent results of rigorous experiments.

When planting a companion garden, it's good to get the companions right next to each other. One way is to plant zig-zag rows, with the zigs and zags of the beets and onions tucked into one another. Another method is to use the techniques of intercropping, and plant several companions in the same row. You'll find that your companionate garden breaks down into loosely defined "sections." The corn, squash, cucumbers, and pumpkins might be in one section. The strawberries, spinach, and beans might be in another. Paths are best made between these sections, rather than between companions. Borders of wormwood, yarrow, and marigolds might be planted. Sprinkle these and the other insect-repelling herbs and flowers among the vegetables, checking the chart to make sure you're not near a foe instead of a friend. If you plant fennel at all, plant it away from the garden; it seems to be low man in the garden's pecking order.

Make up your own companionate garden by using the charts which accompany this chapter. Just remember that while your cucumbers like your peas, and your peas like your beans, and your beans like your potatoes, your potatoes just don't like cucumbers.

Mint, like the curly variety at far right, is a deterrent to the white cabbage moth in the garden and a tasty condiment after the harvest. Horseradish should be planted with the potatoes to deter the potato bug and to produce a healthy crop of roots to be made into horseradish sauce at season's end.

A Companionate Herb.

A list of herbs, their companions, their us

HERB	COMPANIONS AND EFFECTS
Basil	*Companion to tomatoes; dislikes rue intensely. Improves growth and flavor. Repels flies and mosquitoes.*
Beebalm	*Companion to tomatoes; improves growth and flavor.*
Borage	*Companion to tomatoes, squash and strawberries; deters tomato worm; improves growth and flavor.*
Caraway	*Plant here and there; loosens soil.*
Catnip	*Plant in borders; deters flea beetle.*
Camomile	*Companion to cabbages and onions; improves growth and flavor.*
Chervil	*Companion to radishes; improves growth and flavor.*
Chives	*Companion to carrots; improves growth and flavor.*
Dead nettle	*Companion to potatoes; deters potato bug; improves growth and flavor.*
Dill	*Companion to cabbage; dislikes carrots; improves growth and health of cabbage.*
Fennel	*Plant away from gardens. Most plants dislike it.*
Garlic	*Plant near roses and raspberries; deters Japanese beetle; improves growth and health.*
Horseradish	*Plant at corners of potato patch to deter potato bug.*
Hyssop	*Deters cabbage moth; companion to cabbage and grapes. Keep away from radishes.*
Lamb's-Quarters	*This edible weed should be allowed to grow in moderate amounts in the garden, especially in corn.*
Lovage	*Improves flavor and health of plants if planted here and there.*
Marigold	*The workhorse of the pest deterrents. Plant throughout garden, it discourages Mexican bean beetles, nematodes, and other insects.*
Mint	*Companion to cabbage and tomatoes; improves health and flavor; deters white cabbage moth.*
Marjoram	*Here and there in garden; improves flavors.*

Nasturtium	*Companion to radishes, cabbage, and curcurbits; plant under fruit trees. Deters aphids, squash bugs, striped pumpkin beetles. Improves growth and flavor.*
Pot Marigold	*Companion to tomatoes, but plant elsewhere in garden, too. Deters asparagus bettle, tomato worm, and general garden pests.*
Purslane	*This edible weed makes good ground cover in the corn.*
Pigweed	*One of the best weeds for pumping nutrients from the subsoil, it is especially beneficial to potatoes, onions, and corn. Keep weeds thinned.*
Peppermint	*Planted among cabbages, it repels the white cabbage butterfly.*
Rosemary	*Companion to cabbage, bean, carrots, and sage; deters cabbage moth, bean beetles, and carrot fly.*
Rue	*Keep it far away from sweet basil; plant near roses and raspberries; deters Japanese beetle.*
Sage	*Plant with rosemary, cabbage, and carrots; keep away from cucumbers. Deters cabbage moth, carrot fly.*
Southernwood	*Plant here and there in garden; companion to cabbage; improves growth and flavor; deters cabbage moth.*
Sowthistle	*This weed in moderate amounts can help tomatoes, onions, and corn.*
Summer Savory	*Plant with beans and onions; improves growth and flavor. Deters bean beetles.*
Tansy	*Plant under fruit trees; companion to roses and raspberries. Deters flying insects, Japanese beetles, striped cucumber beetles, squash bugs, ants.*
Tarragon	*Good throughout garden.*
Thyme	*Here and there in garden. It deters cabbage worm.*
Wormwood	*As a border, it keeps animals from the garden.*
Yarrow	*Plant along borders, paths, near aromatic herbs; enhances essential oil production.*

This information was collected from many sources, most notably the Bio-Dynamic Association and the Herb Society of America.

Many herbs are worthy companions in the vegetable garden. Borage (above) is not only beautiful, it deters the tomato horn worm and improves the growth and flavor of neighboring tomatoes, squash, and strawberries. Dill is a companion for cabbage, improving its growth and flavor.

"Always in cases of plant friendship it was found that not only do they grow better but they are also less affected by pests and diseases than when grown alone or with hostile plants," says Spencer Cheshire, an organic gardener who publishes "The Land Bulletin" from the Land Fellowship in Smithville, Ontario. "This is an indication as to the true nature of pests and diseases. They do not strike at, but are invited by, organisms living with less than optimal vitality and under stress."

In a statement on recent tests of companionate planting at the Rodale Experimental Farm in Emmaus, Pa., Kenneth Polscer said that "the protection offered by companion planting is usually not 100 percent effective in keeping plants insect-free. The degree of protection, however variable, was sufficient to cause insect damage to be well below that considered acceptable by most gardeners."

This protection may be due to the increased vigor and thriftiness of vegetables growing near their friends. If stress is reduced, vitality can soar. Insects pass them by, looking for weak or sick plants, fulfilling their role as censors.

Add to a good program of companionate vegetables a number of aromatic herbs, flowers and even weeds, and your garden will mimic Nature's mixed crops.

As to the value of weeds in the garden, there are theories and there are theories. The most common is that weeds rob the soil of nutrients needed by the crops, and so the garden soil either remains bare between rows or is covered with mulch. A garden overrun with weeds is no garden at all, but the wise use of weeds can prove invaluable.

Weeds can pump subsurface minerals and nutrients to the surface. They can act as a ground cover and green mulch. Their roots open up areas of the subsoil most vegetables can't penetrate.

"One woman showed me some Bermuda onions she had harvested from a jungle of weeds," says conservationist Joseph A. Cocannouer in his book in praise of weeds, *Weeds: Guardians of the Soil.* "Every onion was a picture of perfection. 'I thought the onions in that part of my garden were gone,' she told me. She then showed me the onions she'd harvested from her cultivated rows. 'After all my work—look at the difference! And they're keeping better, too. Not a one of my weed onions is rotting!'

"The clean land onions were a little more than half the size of the weed-patch onions. I was a bit surprised there, because her weeds were growing entirely too thick. However, onions collect their food materials in the shallow surface of the ground, except where there are weed roots to open up the lower soil. As it happened, this woman's weeds were deep divers. While they seemed too thick to feed very deep, they still fed deep enough to provide the onions with a larger-than-usual feeding zone."

The type of weed has a lot to do with its effect on the garden. Cocannouer recommends letting the deep divers grow in not too thick profusion amongst the vegetables. These include giant ragweed, annual smartweed, dead nettle, sow thistle, ground cherry, burdock, pokeweed, mullein, annual black nightshade, lamb's quarters, pigweed, purslane, and others. And of course, though Cocannouer refers to them as weeds, the herbalist would find some herbal use for many of them. Burdock, dead nettle, purslane, mullein, lamb's quarters, and many many other "weeds" figure prominently in herbal folklore. Such plants weren't cultivated for the herbal qualities, however, since the herbalist could easily collect them from the wild. Nevertheless, those plants more commonly thought of as herbs also deserve to be in a companion garden.

"The presence of companion herbs is thought to improve the growth and flavor of the vegetables and also to deter garden pests," says the Herb Society of America in a release they titled, "Try Herbs Instead of Sprays." Catnip, they say, deters flea beetles, mint drives away the white cabbage butterfly, garlic can turn away the Japanese beetle, and so on.

But let's look at yarrow. Here is an herb steeped in lore, as well as hot water by those who know the brisk light tea made from its leaves. Yarrow increases the aromatic quality of all herbs —and it's the aromatic, essential oils that deter insects. Yarrow is thus the herb's herb. "Yarrow has a definite effect on the quality of neighboring plants," say the authors of *Companion Plants,* "increasing not so much their size as their resistance to adverse conditions and thereby improving their health." And resistance to insects, too.

A study carried out by G. Mahlke in Halle in 1953 showed that when yarrow is grown with perennial rye grass, yarrow cuts down on the protein content of the grass. This can be explained by the competition for nitrogen by the plants. But yarrow also increases the fiber content of the grass. When a mixture of the two plants was analyzed, it was found that it yielded about the same amount of carbohydrate as the grass, but 40 per cent more protein than the grass alone (due to the high protein content of yarrow).

A wide variety of herbs belongs in every organic garden. It's only been since the Renaissance that flower, herb, and vegetable gardens have been generally separated. Before that, everything grew together, and we can believe they all grew well.

REPELLENT HERBS

The largest group of herbs fall into the category of insect repellent plants, and, as noted, they repel the bugs through a variety of means. The second group of herbs are those which attract insects. Then there are herbs which can be used in crop rotations. Finally, there are herbs which can be made into pest-fighting sprays and dusts. Some herbs fall into more than one category.

Garlic

If I were limited to one pest repellent, it would be garlic, because I really think it's the most valuable one. It takes up little room, yet it is most powerful. It's easy to grow and has a multitude of uses in cooking. Its one disadvantage is its spindly appearance. However, when planted amongst the raspberry canes, about the grapevines, and close to the vegetables, it just doesn't show. When it might, one of the other *Alliums,* such as chives, Oriental garlic, or Egyptian onions, can be used. They aren't as powerful as garlic in repelling pests, but they *are* more attractive.

Plant cloves of garlic near fruit trees, cabbages, berry canes, or any other susceptible crop to keep away aphids or Japanese beetles. Some gardeners plant it with beans—a clove in each hill of pole beans or a row of garlic between two rows of bush beans. A thin, upright plant, garlic takes up little room so you can't plant too much anywhere.

A pound of bulbs doesn't go very far, so garlic may seem relatively costly, but it is more than worth the cost. One-quarter pound of garlic bulbs, separated into cloves and set thickly in early spring here and there among your plants, will keep out Japanese beetles the following summer. (Tansy might do it too, but it takes up more room.) The garlic seems to create an immune area.

For year-round protection, so that the grubs won't live and hatch out in the mulch under the berry bushes or in the sod nearby, leave the garlic in the ground. There it will multiply, each clove planted developing into a full bulb of many cloves.

Some can be harvested in midsummer. It's so good home-grown that it's hard not to. What's left in the ground generally is quite hardy, living on safely through quite severe winters. Tender shoots push up early in spring and even during winter thaws.

Does garlic taint the flavor of the raspberries, grapes, or other crops it's planted near? Apparently not. It doesn't taint the taste of fruit, though it might taint root crops. The pungent bulbs are below the ground, and there is no noticeable odor in the garden. Thus, while most herbs scent the garden, the most powerful pest control herb doesn't.

Marigolds

Probably the most popular plant for companion planting is the marigold, but only the variety known as pot marigold *(Calendula officinalis)* is an herb. Pot marigold has strong-tasting and smelling flowers. It repels the asparagus beetle, and it does to some degree discourage nematodes. Dwarf French marigolds *(Tagetes patula)* and African marigolds *(T. erecta)*—again, neither is an herb—are highly regarded as natural nematocides.

Basil

Some herbs have an affinity for specific crops. Basil, for instance, is reported to protect tomatoes "almost as if giving them a wrap-around shield."

Each year Ruth Tirrell plants about a dozen basil plants parallel to her tomato patch of about three to four dozen plants. "Except for a defoliated branch or two, my tomato plants simply do not have pests or disease," Miss Tirrell says. Yet her plants occupy the some space year after year, and their debris stays on the site over winter as part of the mulch, returning to the soil what had been taken from it.

Varieties of basil range in height from one to two and a half feet, much smaller than most tomatoes, and are not appropriate

Dwarf French marigolds and African marigolds are among the most popular companion plants, valued as deterrents to nematodes. Their herbal qualifications are questionable, however.

to grow in the midst of a tomato jungle. But basil might enclose a tomato planting. Both are tender annuals and like a warm, rich environment.

Another benefit is that the tomato tastes best as it grows best, accompanied by basil. The "royal herb," as the French call it, also lends a marvelous flavor to other foods — potato, rice, spaghetti, and eggs — so even if it did not have the power to keep pests away, many people would want to grow it.

Basil is famous as a fly-repellent, too. It can be potted up for the house or terrace, or grown in a border near an outdoor picnic area.

Savory

The herb savory, especially the annual summer savory, protects beans of all kinds. It's not as easy to grow as basil—the very fine seeds may germinate poorly—and it is regarded as not quite as effective a pest-chaser. Mexican bean beetles are often a most troublesome insect, and savory can help keep them under control.

Start the fine savory seed in a flat. Later, as you plant your beans, space the young seedlings at intervals along the furrows in place of bean plants. The mature savory plant is slightly shorter than bush beans. Of course, in addition to interplanting summer savory, go over the bean bushes regularly, wiping off any of the eggs or fuzzy yellow larvae that appear on the undersides of the leaves. Later, clean up any of the beetles that might appear. It helps, too, to make small successive sowings of quick-growing beans, each in a different location. Probably this combination of controls will get rid of any bean beetles.

Those who use this system contend that even if the savory didn't play a part, they'd grow it anyway, for the "bean herb," so-called in Germany, seasons so many bean dishes very well.

The Mints

The mints keep pests from the cabbage family. Spearmint is what most people grow, but there are many others. Some of the best are: peppermint, apple mint (woolly leaves), lemon or orange mint, and pineapple mint (more delicate in scent and flavor, so probably not such an effective pest repellent, but very pretty with gray and white leaves). European pennyroyal *(Mentha pulegium)* is a creeping herb with long flower stalks. Insects dislike its "peppermint" fragrance.

Mints are hardy perennials. Most have vigorous growth and spreading habits. A few rooted runners set near cabbage or broccoli should be enough to repel pests. Or grow a single large plant like Brussels sprouts in the vicinity (not too close) of an established clump of spearmint. One gardener I know tried this latter approach. Despite unfavorable growing conditions that year—a severe summer drought occurred—no pests came near the Brussels sprouts, whereas a half-dozen purple cauliflowers in another part of the garden, not near to mints (or any strong-smelling plant), were attacked by aphids. Apparently the spearmint protected the sprouts. You can also plant mint near the barn and henhouse door or foundation. Flies don't like mint, nor do rats.

Tansy

Tansy is a tall, hardy perennial that reaches four feet or more in height. It's coarsely handsome, with jagged leaves and clusters of yellow-orange, button-like flowers which dry dark-gold and are attractive in winter bouquets. The old herbals always mention tansy. The leaves were once used and still are, though rarely, in England and New England to brew tea and to flavor pudding and a special pancake. Because the scent of tansy is a sentimental reminder of her grandfather's farm, one gardener planted a bit of it in the center of her black raspberry patch. Tansy is a rampant spreader; raspberries spread readily, too, and hold their own. "Japanese beetles don't come near the black raspberries," she reports. "To some extent, they've fed on the red raspberries at the other end of the garden. Both varieties grow in a favorable environment and bear good crops." It *is* possible that the black raspberries are more resistant than the red. But the tansy appears to be a factor. Supporting this is the fact that Tanacetin Oil, which is distilled from tansy, has been used as a fly and insect repellent. Another known merit of tansy is that it discourages ants, which, of course, encourages aphids. Tansy planted at the back door will keep ants and flies from the house. The dried

Tansy is a handsome border plant and an insect repellent too.

leaves of tansy sprinkled about—in cellar or attic—are a harmless indoor "insecticide." So it's worth experimenting.

Such an experiment might be to plant tansy in your flower bed, since flowers have pests, too. Try planting tansy in the background of the border.

Rue

Rue is a hardy perennial about two feet in height, very attractive to look at, and very offensive to pests. Rue has powerful properties and very bitter, blue-green leaves. Start rue from seed or make new plants from root divisions. Rue spreads readily and will help dispel insect troublemakers among vegetables, flowers, shrubs, or fruits. (Note: Don't confuse rue, the bitter herb, with the common wildflower of the crowfoot family, meadow-rue, which has white or purplish blossoms. They're not related.)

Thyme

The thymes comprise many varieties, from low ground covers to shrubby plants a foot or more high. This fragrant family attracts bees (thyme honey is greatly prized) and is effective as a pest repellent, although probably not so much so as rue. (It is probably more useful in the kitchen, though, seasoning fish, meats, stuffings, vegetables. Lemon thyme also flavors fruit juices.)

Borage

A two- to three-foot annual, borage grows from seed sown in spring, self-sows the same season and usually for years thereafter, and flowers continuously up to frost with bright-blue or pink blossoms. Pests keep out of its way, and—just as important for the garden's welfare—borage attracts bees in great masses. Ruth Tirrell reports that the fruit-set on her tomatoes and winter squash was exceptionally good the summer she planted borage nearby. It also benefits strawberries.

Some Others

The castor bean plant *(Ricinus communis)* is known to protect vine crops from pests. Because of its size (eight to twelve feet) the castor bean is more suitable for field pantings of squashes and similar plants than a small garden. Children should be warned, however, not to eat the toxic seeds.

Sage *(Salvia officinalis),* the perennial herb commonly used for poultry seasoning, is about two to three feet in height, has pebbly-green leaves, and purplish-blue flower spikes in spring. It's a handsome plant that is visible in winter, and chases many troublesome insects, particularly from vine crops and the cabbage family.

Coriander and anise, a pair of annual herbs, have a reputation for repelling aphids. These herbs seem immune themselves, and no pests seem to bother plants nearby.

Several other pest-chasing herbs deserve to be briefly mentioned: (1) Oregano is especially effective near vine crops (cucumber, melon, etc.). Where winters are cold, treat it as an annual. Oregano makes a good ground cover for steep banks. (2) Lavender has a strong, cool, clean, small, and pretty, soft-gray foliage. It reaches one and a half feet in height and grows well among stones. It is not reliably hardy, however. Up to now, I've kept mine potted in the cellar. This winter, I've taken the risk

Pyrethrum flowers are decorative as well as useful. They are pretty to the gardener, deadly to the insect invader. They can be planted next to plants you want to protect, or ground into an insecticidal dust that is harmless to humans and animals.

and mulched. (3) Santolina or lavender cotton is not related to true lavender above but with similar clean, aromatic smell. Foliage is silvery and in one variety, greenish in color. It's a good edging plant. (4) Lemon balm, though it gets weedy if not cut back often, grows to two feet. Mulched, balm survives cold winters. (5) Beebalm or bergamot, not to be confused with lemon balm or lemon bergamot, is a handsome plant, three to four feet in height, with large scarlet flowers and a fine fragrance. (6) American pennyroyal is strongly aromatic like the European or true pennyroyal. It makes good tea. Leaves were used in early America as an insecticide. Sow the seed and grow as an annual.

Many flowers regarded as merely "pretty" have valuable pest-repellent qualities. Almost without exception, these flowers are strong-smelling, not sweet like the rose or violet. Although their strong smell is still agreeable to humans, insects find them overpowering and generally keep out of their range—by about three feet. Nearby fruit and vegetable crops that might be subject to attack by pests, are thus protected. It is true that some of these flowers in certain environments may have pests of their own—chrysanthemums, for instance. But none *encourages* the common pests of vegetable crops into their vicinity.

Pyrethrum, often called painted ladies or painted daisies, is a perennial related to the chrysanthemum, but a more effective pest-repellent. It has big daisy-like flowers of various colors. One variety, golden feather *(Pyrethrum aureum)* is grown for its chartreuse foliage; the clusters of small white "daisies" can be kept sheared, if desired. Golden feather makes a good edging (eight to ten inches) for a path in the vegetable garden. No pest will come near it. One gardener reports having sown seed a few years back and now having dozens of plants that must regularly be divided and reset.

An insecticide of the same name is made from the dried flowers of pyrethrums. If you want to bother, a homemade spray can be prepared from the ground flowers mixed with water. Pyrethrum is toxic to many soft-bodied pests, but not to plants. In my opinion, its presence here and there in the garden is enough.

Feverfew *(Chrysanthemum parthenium)*, sometimes also called pyrethrum, seems absolutely bug-proof, keeping pests from plants close by. My wife grows feverfew in a border near her roses, but it would do as much good near vegetables. Feverfew grows about one and one-half feet tall, has yellow-green ferny foliage, masses of small, white, daisy-like flowers, and self-sows readily.

ATTRACTANT HERBS

Some mention should be made of "lure" plants or "catch crops" which attract pests to themselves and away from more valuable plants. Many of these plants are herbs. And they all play a part of successful companion planting. The idea is to plant a most attractive—but expendable—plant near another that, for one reason or another, you want to protect. The plant pests congregate on the "lure," making extermination a simple task. But remember: the point of the "lure" plant is lost if you neglect to gather and destroy the plant pests it attracts.

In this group we find the white geranium *(Pelargonium)*

Feverfew is another attractive herb that the garden pests avoid. It is a hardy perennial, surviving the coldest winters and the closest prunings. It can be grown in full sun or in the shade of other plants.

which attracts Japanese beetles, who are said to die upon eating it. Hyssop, planted near cabbages, will attract the cabbage worm butterflies. Planted near grapevines, it will increase yields of grapes. Nasturtiums attract aphids and squash bugs. Scotch broom *(Cytisus scoparius)* also attracts aphids.

This can all get a little confusing, so *Organic Gardening and Farming's* helpful "Companionate Herbal" has been included in this chapter. In checking this chart and planning your companionate garden, bear in mind that there are some antagonistic combinations you should avoid. (1) Basil and Rue do not get along. (2) Camomile *(Matricaria chamomilla)* in large quantities may be detrimental to the growth of wheat and onions. In very small amounts it is helpful. When grown near mint, it will have a higher content of volatile oils, while the mint is reduced in volatile oils. (3) Dandelion can inhibit growth and height of neighboring plants and also cause early maturing of fruits or flowers. (4) Dill, allowed to bloom, can reduce carrot crop. (5)

Fennel inhibits growth of caraway, beans, tomatoes, and kohlrabi. Wormwood and coriander inhibit germination and growth of fennel. (6) Garlic, onions, and shallots will stunt peas and beans. (7) Hyssop should not be planted too closely to radishes. (8) Wormwood can inhibit growth of some plants in the garden, including fennel, sage, caraway, and anise and should not be placed where very young plants or seedlings are growing.

HERBAL CROP ROTATIONS

Including herbs in crop rotation is another way you will find them beneficial in your garden. Where unhealthy or problem soils exist, they can be conditioned or corrected with plants and herbs. Plant the soil-benefitting plant, then cut and compost it, or plow it under before planting the garden.

Calendulas and marigolds can be allowed to naturalize for an attractive as well as practical conditioner. Soapwort and other saponin-rich plants, including primrose, pokeweed, and mullein, make the soil environment favorable to plants that follow.

Nasturtium is a pot herb which does double-duty in the vegetable garden. Its leaves and flowers are tasty salad ingredients. And it attracts aphids and some other garden pests, making hand-picking a one stop chore.

Legumes increase available nitrogen, and many have herbal uses. In this group are alfalfa, clover, peanuts, false indigo, and lupins. The lupins improve sandy soils. Some plants add humus, loosen heavy clay soils, and make them friable. These include camomile, soybeans, stinging nettles, caraway, flax, and buckwheat. Buckwheat will also choke out weeds and eradicate them and add large quantities of calcium to poor soils. Scotch broom also supplies calcium.

Dandelion will attract earthworms, create a humus where it grows, and contribute a wealth of minerals and nutrients to the compost heap. Valerian also is attractive to the earthworms and stimulates the phosphorus activity in the soil area. A spray of its juice improves the health and resistance of other growing plants.

Mustard, radish, and turnip are considered "antiseptic" crops and, when turned under, are said to improve the soil and rid it of harmful organisms.

AFTER THE HARVEST

Even after you've harvested your pest-repelling herbs, you can put them to work in your garden. In some cases, sprinkling the dried and crushed herbs in the crop rows will be of some benefit, while in others, a simply made spray will help.

Powdered, dried pyrethrum flowers can be dusted on plants, or used on pets and poultry for fleas, lice, and other parasites. Oak leaves, oak bark, dry wormwood and rosemary leaves, and stinging nettle can be sprinkled around to repel snails and slugs. Dried tansy and southernwood leaves will drive away ants. A mixture of aromatic herbs can also be very successful. The basic ingredients include American wormwood (sagebrush), white sage *(Salvia apiana)*, button sage *(S. mellifera)*, eucalyptus, silk, wormwood, wild buckwheat, yerba santa, nettles, and tansy, or as many of these as are available. Catnip, rosemary, feverfew, and rue can be added. The dried, chopped-up herbs can be sprinkled around problem areas. You may find it more effective to scald the herbs with boiling water before using as this will help release the volatile oils. The dampened herb mixture can also be added to the planting mix when potting plants. Excess water is drained off, and can be diluted to water or spray on plants and seedlings. This combination is effective for repelling or eliminating aphids, mealy bugs, ants, and sowbugs. Plants are healthier and sturdier and damp-off problems are eliminated.

The debris of herbs has value too. Many herbs, like the mints, for instance, are rank-growing and must be kept within bounds. What you root out or cut down can be laid under crops that seem likely prey for pests. The coarse growth of Egyptian onions, which should be cut down in summer after the top bulbs have ripened, makes excellent mulch.

SPRAYS

Mrs. Wilbur's initial spray concoction was a pretty complex mixture, but even simple sprays can be very effective. Plain garlic makes a spray that even has the scientific community interested.

As outlined earlier, making a spray usually involves concocting a strong herb tea. Place the herbs in a pot, cover with water, and bring to a boil. Remove from fire, cover, and let steep until cool. Dilute with three to four parts of water, and strain before using.

Thyme can be made into a spray for flies. Rosemary and catnip teas are effective as general insect sprays. Garlic, onions, chives, and cayenne peppers are made into sprays to control caterpillars and tomato and cabbage worms. A combination of several aromatic insect repelling herbs can be concocted that will be beneficial to growth and protect from pests. These may include tansy, eucalyptus, southernwood, wormwoods, and sage, particularly *Salvia apiana* and *S. mellifera*.

Camomile (*Matricaria chamomilla*), as noted previously, is helpful in combatting damp-off and other diseases. Soak the dried blossoms in cold water for several days, and spray or water seedlings and plants with the resulting brew.

Pyrethrum and feverfew flower heads can be dried, powdered and mixed with water and soapsuds (to make the solution stick to the foliage) to make a spray for a large variety of insect pests on plants.

Horsetail *(Equisetum arvense)* can be dried and cut. About one and one-half ounces can be boiled in one gallon of water for 15 to 20 minutes. Cool and strain. The decoction is an effective spray for fungus and mildew on roses, vegetables, grapes, and fruit trees. Horsetail and stinging nettle teas combined are effective as a spray for peach leaf curl.

Stinging nettle, rich in vitamins, minerals, and iron, is very helpful in promoting plant growth, strengthening, and protecting them. A fermented brew is prepared by cutting the nettles and covering them with water. Then leave this mixture to decompose for several weeks—the plants will be completely digested. This is then used as a spray.

Old-time gardeners swore by flowers belonging to the daisy family, like mums, calendulas, marigolds, and the painted daisies to rid their gardens of pests. They grew these flowers with their vegetables, among other cutting flowers, and even used the "grind and spray" method.

By this method, the blossoming plants were picked and then ground with the plant juices saved. Water was added, the amount depending on the gardener's own experiences; the mixture was sprayed on infested plants as needed. Favorite targets were cabbage worms, asparagus beetles, and ordinary flies.

Onion was another common plant used years ago for protection, and many of today's gardeners still use it. Some even combine it with the "grind and spray" technique. For example, Betty Marble of Brigham City, Utah, tried starting delphiniums from seed, but when they were about two inches high, the red spider took the life right out of them. She solved the problem this way:

> I clipped off two handfuls of chives and put them in the blender with two cups of water. I had pure green liquid in about one minute, strained it, and added another quart of water.
>
> I put the mixture on each delphinium leaf, top and bottom, and could see the improvement in a very short time. The tiny plants came right back to life. As the new leaves appeared, I sprayed those as well, using a plastic squeeze bottle with a pointed top. There was no sign of the red spider mites after this treatment.

A similar spray, and one of the best of all, is made with garlic.

Companion Plants says that a tea made of garlic is effective against brown rot in stone fruit and in controlling severe diseases of potatoes and tomatoes. Over the years, many organic gardeners have used a garlic spray to control insect pests.

Now the garlic spray is receiving the attention it deserves. David Greenstock, a vice-president and researcher with the Henry Doubleday Research Association, an English organization, has issued "Garlic as an Insecticide," a report on his work. Greenstock recommends the following recipe for a garlic spray:

> Take three ounces of chopped garlic bulbs and let them soak in about two teaspoonfuls (50 cc.) of mineral oil (toilet paraffin) for 24 hours. Then slowly add a pint of water in which ¼ ounce of oil-based soap (Palmolive is a good one) has been dissolved, and stir well. Strain the liquid through fine gauze, and store it in a china or glass container because it reacts with metals.
>
> Try it against your worst pests, starting with a dilution of one part to 20 parts of water, then going down to 1-100, so you use as little as possible. . . .

In his report on Greenstock's report, Lawrence Hills suggested the garlic spray could be "the new insect control the whole world needs." His article in *Organic Gardening and Farming* (September 1972) stated:

> Greenstock's report describes a number of solvents and emulsifiers for garlic, including some that will keep the substance active on the leaves for up to 30 days. Others enable weak solutions to be watered on the land to kill underground pests. . . . The emulsions were highly effective against cabbage white and ermine moth caterpillars, scoring 98 per cent kills, and without passing any undesirable flavor to the crop, for the insecticidal principle has nothing to do with the smell, which is gone in four days.
>
> In a laboratory experiment, the garlic solution killed 87 percent of the pea weevils. . . . At the same time, it spared the Colorado beetle, however, and this quality of hitting weevils and missing beetles appears to be near to that of nicotine, which is harmless to ladybirds and their larvae. But there is scope for a great deal of research to find the emulsifiers and solution strengths that will be safe for as many of our friends as possible.
>
> By feeding it to chickens, mice, and rabbits, Greenstock has established that all the garlic sprays are harmless to birds, livestock and wild life. In fact, they improved the health of the experimental animals

One of the most effective and safest garden sprays is made from garlic. There are a number of ways to make your own garlic spray, but a simple technique is to blend several garlic cloves with water (above). The best cloves to use are those that were grown organically. Pour the garlic puree through several layers of cheesecloth to strain it, then pour into a spraygun. The spray has been demonstrated to have an astonishing effectiveness against a wide variety of plant pests. Happily, it is non-toxic and won't harm curious youngsters or pets.

compared with the non-garlic-receiving controls, and an accidental outbreak of myxamatosis in the rabbits showed they had gained greater resistance.

The qualities of garlic that Greenstock has uncovered might surprise people not familiar with herbs and herb lore, but its effectiveness as a pest spray and a repellent companion plant has been presaged by the lore that has surrounded it for centuries. Horace called it "more poisonous than hemlock," Homer said "yellow garlic" saved Ulysses from being changed by Circe into a pig, and a European superstition suggested that a runner could prevent competitors from getting in front of him by eating garlic. And even the lore of companion planting, a relatively recent body of knowledge, presages the discovery of garlic's insecticidal qualities.

As we have seen, of course, garlic isn't the only herb with such qualities. And such qualities, when added to all the other, more traditional, qualities of herbs can mean only that you have more reason than ever to raise herbs in your garden.

LANDSCAPING WITH HERBS

by Marion Wilbur

EIGHT

Many people have a very limited concept of herbs as landscaping plants. They picture herbs as belonging on the windowsill in pots or in some corner of the vegetable garden. There are some, of course, who recall the intricate, formal gardens of days past, gardens duplicated here and there in the United States, usually at some historic landmark. But most people fail to appreciate herbs for themselves.

The problem with such a limited concept is that it robs one of the pleasure and beauty of herbs in the landscape.

There are many trees and shrubs used by landscape gardeners today which are not generally thought of as herbs; however, herbs they are. They have been recognized and used as such for centuries, by both ancient and modern herbalists.

Herbs are generally very easily grown and require less watering and attention than most other plants. The natural, internal chemistry that produces volatile and aromatic oils, resins, and tannins also renders them relatively immune to insect attack, and provides protection for other plants in the vicinity. Use of chemical fertilizers and sprays can upset this chemical balance and destroy those qualities for which they are valued.

The added pleasure of the fragrance they provide must not be overlooked. The hovering sweetness of lavender seems to float over and around other scents in the garden. Rosemary's spicy aroma makes the air fresh and clean. Few things are more delightful than a creeping thyme trodden upon, or the fresh, cooling fragrance of mint or lemon balm brushed against in passing.

Herbs found their way into gardens in the first place because of their useful qualities. The medieval housewife often had a semi-wild kitchen or medicinal garden beside the door. The landed gentry had the stiffly formal gardens many people associate with herbs. However, the herbalist often gathered his medicinal plants from the wild. The point of this chapter is not to delineate a history of the traditional formal herb garden or to tell you what

An herb garden is a personal thing. It can be a small oasis, such as this small circular garden of low-growing varieties, or it can be extensive and elaborate. It can be stiffly formal, or it can be as wild and unkempt as nature.

others have done, but rather to demonstrate to you that your home can be landscaped in a variety of ways—formal, informal, wild—using herbs and only herbs. You can, in other words, have a unique herbal landscape. (And if you want traditional forms, there's supplemental material on that.)

The herb garden can be formal or informal, contemporary or naturalistic; it may be on level ground or a hilly terrain, large or small, but the basic principles of garden design should be observed in order to achieve the desired effect.

The garden must be in harmony with the architecture. In planning a garden, the first consideration must be the house itself. There must be a one-ness with the dwelling, from which the garden design must proceed. A layout or plan should be made designating the features or divisions that may be required.

Foundation planting designates the material required or desired to cover foundations and footings where needed, and to frame the building, tie it in to the site, and make it an intrinsic part of the landscape. Generally, the outside corners of the structure form the starting point. The foundation planting should never be made in straight rows along the foundation, but should form a triangular or curving line, with the wider part at the outside narrowing toward the entry or walkway. Taller shrubs are used in the corner itself, and against this would be placed

An herb garden can dominate the landscape. Herbs come in striking variety, with low, crawling plants as well as towering shrubs and even trees. Herbs can be found to complement the most impressive buildings and the most humble cottages.

lower shrubs with even smaller ones here and there to bring the mass toward the ground as it moves outward from the building. The natural irregularity, varying shapes and masses of the shrubs will overcome any tendency toward a stiff, regular descent and will be suggestive of a natural thicket, terminating at the edge of a lawn or ground cover area.

The garden area may incorporate a terrace or other level space to unite house and garden, an expanse of lawn, or ground cover, with beds or borders for the planting of a flat terrain, or a series of multi-level terraces and slopes on a hilly plot.

Contrast is an important element in garden design. It may be achieved through size — size of divisions and material used, through use of color, light, and shadow. Proportion, mass, and perspective are just as important in a harmonious and beautiful garden design as they are in a painting on canvas.

Every garden has a mood, either by design or by accident. Be it ever so subtle, an emotional response is evoked by the vista presented the viewer. The formal garden presents a mood of stately dignity—an expanse of low growing plants or lawn, framed with a precise hedge, bordered by tall trees or shrubs arranged in perfect symmetry and balance. The beautiful geometric patterns of Renaissance herb gardens are a classic example of formality in garden design.

Gracefully drooping willow boughs reflected in a quiet pool, surrounded by a delicate green carpeting of sweet woodruff, create a mood of quiet tranquility. This is a very different herb garden.

An entry screen with wood panels, offset and alternated with vertically slatted sections, forms a backdrop for a rectangular bed of white crushed rock. The slender, angular stems of a night blooming cereus reach across the dark wood screen. A large succulent *Aloe vera* plant, set to one side, occupies the foreground. Sharp contrasts in form and color, balance of mass and structure, create an arrangement of functional beauty, well suited to the contemporary setting. And this too is an herb garden.

Flowering herbs in a sunny border, with their bright splashes of color, create a mood of gaiety, while the deep shaded greenery, with sounds of water spilling over rocks can provide the peace and coolness of the deep forest within the garden boundary. And a boundary there must be, whether wall, fence, or dense planting. Whether large or small, there can really be no garden in the true sense until the garden limits are defined. The word garden means a place apart, protected or enclosed. Rather than a separation, the boundary should be considered a union between home, earth, and sky. The treasures of the garden are displayed against a background of lifting growth, carrying the vision skyward.

You may want to landscape your entire home with herbs, or you may wish to only plant herbs in a selected area of the home site. There are several elements to the whole herbal landscaping project. One should consider the borders, the ground cover, and the trees and shrubs; you may begin your landscaping experience with any one or all of these elements. Too, you must decide, before you go too far, whether you want an overall design that is formal or informal, contemporary or traditional. You may even want to consider a rock garden or a wild garden.

In the pages which follow, you'll find information on each of the landscape elements and on creating a design suited to you and your home. Hopefully, your eyes will be opened to some new and exciting ways in which herbs can complement your home.

THE PERENNIAL BORDER

The herbaceous bed or border is a flexible feature and can be used to beautify a variety of areas in the garden — a space between hedges and lawn, a corner between garage and wall, or any other location that would benefit by a decorative planting.

For an attractive border, flowering from spring through fall, materials should be carefully planned. Consideration must be given to decorative effect, size, habit, color, texture, blossoming season, and fragrance. Hardiness and adaptability to soil conditions are important. Plants requiring moist shade cannot be planted alongside those sun loving varieties if they are to thrive.

Taller plants should be placed to the back, the dwarfs in the foreground, and the intermediate ones distributed throughout the rest of the area. Arrange for interesting contrasts in foliage

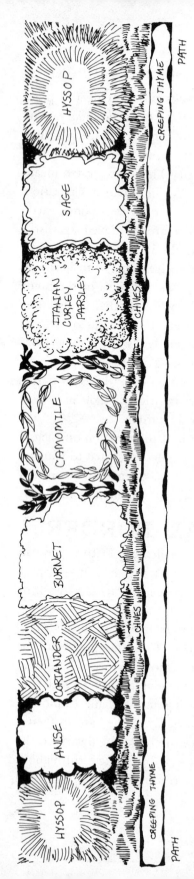
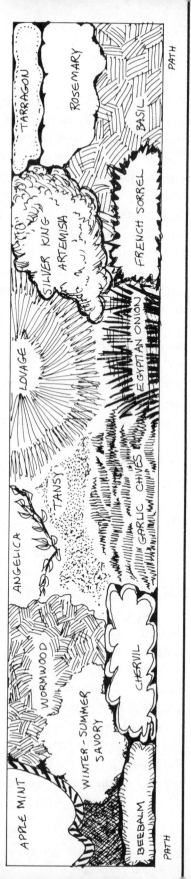

The border border garden is the perfect starting point for anyone interested in herbs. Relatively few homes are without some spot suitable for a border garden. An herb garden can be an unusual, beautiful, but utilitarian foundation planting, a striking perimeter for any size backyard, or a useful border for walks and drives. Because the border garden is generally small, it is a good beginner's garden. Its limited scale makes it easy to start and to maintain. The garden should be in a sunny spot. Soil fertility and drainage should be good, though a lack of fertility or good drainage doesn't present insurmountable problems.

It's best to sketch a plan of your garden and select the herbs you would like to include. Then determine the best means of propagating them and make arrangements to get the necessary seeds, cuttings, or plants. In planning the garden, remember to put the sun-lovers in the sun, the tall wallflowers in the background, the creepers in the foreground. Remember too that some herbs, like the mints, will take over garden if given the chance, so don't give it to them.

Perhaps the best overall approach is to start with small block plots for individual herbs (top), setting the whole off with a low-growing "sill" planting. As you get to know the herbal characters, you can plan more elaborate borders. While the border gardens depicted here are all decorative, all are populated with culinary herbs, making them suitable kitchen gardens too.

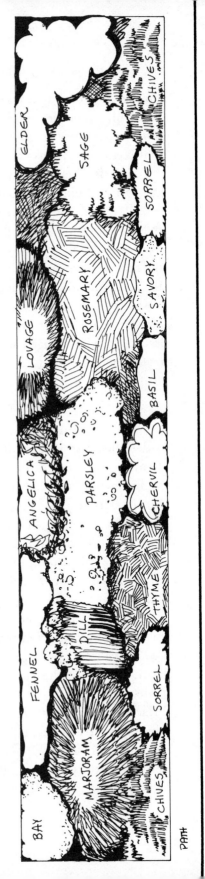

and pleasing combinations of color. Intersperse the insect repelling plants in the border to give protection to the others, and by all means have a few fragrant ones within easy reach for a pinch of their scented leaves as you go by.

Here is where we find many of the old favorite herbs of long ago—tall mullein in purple, red or yellow, veronica in shades of pink, lavender, or blue; red valerian or brilliant monarda with its long season of scarlet flowers; tall clumps of white, daisy like feverfew; and in yellows we have ferny tansy with little button like flowers, rue with its blue-green foliage, daisy flowered arnica, silvery cinquefoil, and adonis. And no herb garden could be complete without lavender.

An edging may be desired, especially in the more formal designs. Silvery fringed wormwood and dark opal basil are good for foliage contrast. Germander can be clipped into a neat hedge. Neat patches of fragrant thymes are always welcome.

CULTURE AND CARE

The perennial border or bed has been called the "lazy man's garden" because if carefully prepared, it requires a minimum of attention for a beautiful display. Perennials can be expected to last for many years, and the bed should be well prepared prior to planting. If drainage could be a problem, the area should be dug out and a layer of coarse gravel and sand should be placed at least two feet below the soil surface. The planting soil must contain a good amount of humus, well rotted manure, and about ten pounds of bone meal for every 100 square feet, all thoroughly mixed.

A well-prepared bed, well mulched requires a minimum amount of watering and weeding. Proper watering is important. Too much water will produce leggy plants, lacking aroma and flavor. Spraying the surface is not desirable as it will have a tendency to bring roots upward and keep them close to the surface, where they can easily dry out. Watering must be thorough to reach deeper roots. Give the plants enough water to make it stand in puddles on the surface, then don't water again until it is really needed. With a deeply developed root system, plants can stand long dry periods without suffering any damage.

Morning watering is best, especially during warm, close weather, since damp foliage overnight may encourage and spread fungus diseases. A mulch over winter is usually adequate protection, and for lusty spring growth, a top dressing of compost is beneficial.

GROUND COVERS

The use of ground covers provides many interesting possibilities in creating pleasant little garden scenes within the landscape design. They can be used to define various areas by contrast of form and color. A ground cover may be the best solution for an area too small for the lawn mower, or too shaded for a satisfactory lawn. Ground covers are used to beautifully cover dry banks or steep slopes and help prevent erosion.

Camomile can replace grass and will take mowing. Creeping myrtle *(Vinca minor)*, a broadleaf evergreen, does very well in shaded areas, and sweet woodruff also likes shade. Ground ivy

A shade loving plant, sweet woodruff is an excellent ground cover for sites protected from the sun's light and heat by trees. Its curious pinwheels of leaves and its pretty little flowers lend interesting shapes and textures to densely planned areas.

(Nepeta hederacea), related to catnip, is a hardy perennial that rapidly forms an attractive mat in either shade or open situations. Low growing thymes and veronica can be used to advantage in small areas. Ajuga, available in several colors of foliage, thrives in shade or sun and is well suited near rockery. The woodland garden might have wild ginger or a trailing arbutus spreading under the trees.

For hilly banks, slopes, and other large or dry areas, prostrate rosemary, uva-ursi, or low growing junipers can be planted with advantage.

Pennyroyal and fringed wormwood can be used along borders while creeping thyme and corsican mint will fill in the crevices in the walkways.

An herbal ground cover can be found to suit most any situation or location.

TREES AND SHRUBS

Trees and shrubs are divided into two main types, the deciduous and the evergreens. Deciduous trees and shrubs lose their foliage in the fall. Many leaves go through a brilliant change in coloring before dropping to the ground. Deciduous trees and shrubs can easily be transplanted in their dormant season without taking soil with the roots. Bare root plants can be obtained in nurseries, usually from January until about March. The roots are generally wrapped with peat moss, or shavings and kept damp until planted. Many of the ornamentals and most fruit bearing trees are in this classification.

Evergreens hold their foliage from season to season. The leaves are shed eventually and replaced by new ones, but so gradually that the loss is not noticed. The evergreens are classified as conifers and broad leaf. Conifers include some of the most valuable plants used in landscape work, and are used for windbreaks, boundaries, backgrounds, as specimens and hedges. Arborvitae, pine, juniper, hemlock, cedar, and cypress are in this class, and some of their varieties at least, have been used for their medicinal virtues. They vary in form from dwarf trailing groundcovers to tall towering pines. Conifers serve as a quiet green

Trees and shrubs can serve as the primary elements in a formal doorway planting. The key elements here are the lollipop-like clipped bay trees, the juniper at their bases, the feathery arborvitae and the taller and slightly more rotund English holly. Twin hedges of rosemary and grey santolina line off the beds from the lawn.

frame in the garden design to set off contrasting texture of deciduous trees and shrubs and bright coloring of smaller annuals and perennials.

Conifers require very little pruning, except in situations where they are used as formal hedges. If the soil is properly prepared when they are planted, very little care is required, perhaps an occasional application of compost, well-rotted manure or bone meal. Many are well adapted to poor, sandy soil. They are best moved in early spring before new growth starts, or early fall after new growth has ripened. Care must be taken to prevent injury to the roots, and plants obtained from nurseries will be in containers or balled and burlapped.

Broad leaved evergreens also vary greatly in size and form. They will range from a bay tree reaching a height of 80 feet or more down through the shrubs of varying sizes to the low ground covers, like the pink trailing arbutus and running myrtle. They vary greatly in their requirements, and the soil should be carefully prepared and a suitable location selected before planting.

After plants have become established, the soil around them should be disturbed as little as possible. Keep well mulched, and an occasional top dressing of compost and well-rotted manure is beneficial.

SELECTION: Trees

Because of their size and permanent nature, trees and large shrubs should be the first materials selected for the garden plan. Trees play an important role by providing shade, cooling comfort and are a background and frame material. Flowering trees provide beauty and pleasure with their color and fragrance, and the fruits of some varieties are an added attraction. The sounds of leaves rustling in the breeze, birds singing in the branches, provide still another form of garden pleasure.

It is most important that selections be made carefully, to insure their suitability to the site and purpose. Trees generally are not readily transplanted from one spot to another.

In a new planting, it may be very desirable to select one or two of the rapid growing species to provide quick shade or screening. Chinese sumac, the decorative castor bean, or some of the fast growing poplars might be considered.

In a very wet or moist area, willows or the alder will thrive, improving the drainage and eventually eliminating undesirable swamp vegetation, while the birch, fringe-tree, or sweet bay can add their beauty to the lawn area.

SELECTION: Shrubs

Shrubs are selected for placement in borders, background, and foundation plantings. Size, form, and texture must be considered in relation to placement. An occasional needle-leaved evergreen in a shrub border can provide a pleasing accent, but a series of accents is not a desirable arrangement. Sun-loving varieties, such as the junipers, rosemary, cassias, should not be placed where shading of larger varieties would be detrimental.

Low, muggy spots, areas where drip from overhang causes dampness should be reserved for plants that will thrive or at least tolerate these conditions. An alder, blueberry elder, wintergreen, witch hazel, or creeping barberry might be placed in such an area. Scotch broom, poinciana, manzanita, and sumac prefer dry, sunny locations.

Plants of questionable hardiness can be given winter protection in cold areas to help them survive. Planting in more sheltered areas, winter mulching, and a healthy, thriving growth are all helpful to increase winter hardiness.

When young shrubs are set out, ample space should be provided for their ultimate growth. These gaps can be filled in with perennial plants, which can be relocated when maturing growth begins crowding them. Some of the taller artemesias, with their silvery foliage can serve this purpose and add color contrast as well. Ferny-leaved tansy, feverfew, and southernwood blend into the greenery. The tall, fast growing *Salvia leucophilla* spreads from the root. It will quickly screen a fence or boundary with its purple chenille-like flowering stalks while the young shrubs are maturing.

PLANTING AND CARE

Plants may be purchased from nurseries in containers, balled and burlapped or bare-root. Container plants can be set out at any time. Transplants should always be protected against wind and sun for a period of time. Bare-root plants should be kept moist until they are put in the ground. Roots and soil of burlapped plants should also be kept moist. These are best planted during the dormant period.

Dig a hole large enough for the roots to spread out without bending or crowding. Check the drainage. To do this, fill the hole with water. If it seeps out fairly fast, drainage is good. If it remains for any length of time, steps will have to be taken to improve the drainage. Dig much deeper, removing sub-soil and replacing it with sharp sand or gravel. In any case, prepare the planting soil according to the needs of the individual plant. Organic materials, compost leaf mold, and well-rotted manure should be mixed into the soil at the bottom of the hole. Chemical fertilizers should never be used on herbs or natives. Add sand or humus, according to the type of soil. It is better and easier to

Any gardener who is a real gardener in every sense of the word derives true enjoyment from his plants and finds caring for them neither exacting nor tedious. For this person, having an attractive, year-round garden is the zenith of gardening joy. True, any nature lover receives an exciting lift of spirit upon sighting the first sprout of spring, but he or she also experiences the autumnal gloom. So a year-round garden is a comfort.

In the middle south and southern regions of the country, it is naturally easier to cultivate herbs that are too tender for northern climes. But there are herbs aplenty for the northern gardener, even wintertime varieties, the evergreen herbs.

The following suggested varieties have beauty months on end and are edible or fragrant too. In the gray group are woolly betony or lamb's ears, lavender cotton, English or French thyme, lavender, southernwood and other artemisias, rue, horehound, and sage. The herbs which give greenery to the winter scene are on a par with the gray types. Beginning with edging material, the gardener has the creeping thymes and bedstraw. Other evergreen herbs include burnet, germander, green santolina, hyssop, and rosemary.

If the garden calls for a picturesque combination of the gray and the green herbs, both will give effectiveness with the varied shades and textures of the foliage. Herbs that have enduring qualities as well as the ability to bolster the appearance of the general scheme may be placed to fit the plan of the terrain. As no herb gardens are ever alike, individual tastes have free play.

Use winter herbs for rock gardens or on difficult slopes, especially if the terrace is in full view of a window. When somber skies prevail, the scenery will be enhanced and enjoyed from indoors. In good weather, the stimulating effects of a stroll in the evergreen garden will add an extra measure of returns. Do not overlook the possibilities of the doorstep form of planting. The vision of verdant herbs along the walkway and by the front steps gives a homey and sincere touch. They will present a heartwarming welcome to friends and visitors as they approach the house. Likewise, rear steps down an embankment afford fine landscaping effects for a planting of herbs.

Whether you are a northerner or a southerner, don't overlook the landscaping potential of the evergreen herbs.

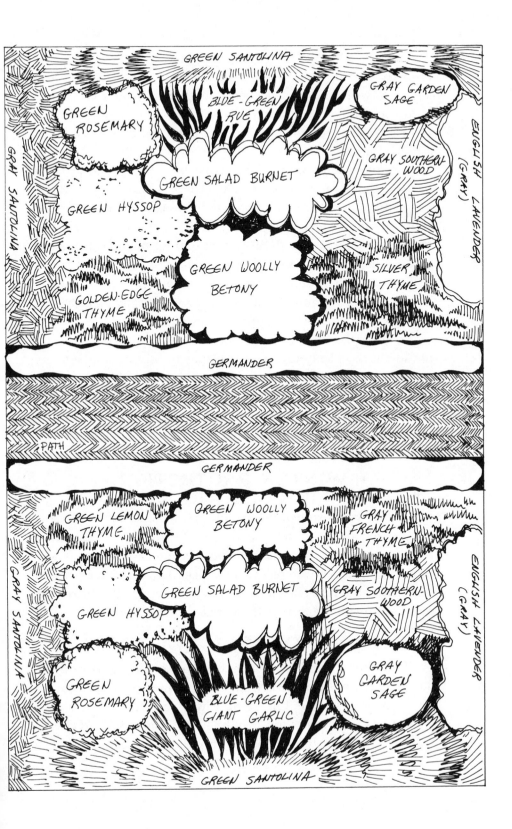

properly prepare soil before planting than to try to correct it later. A wise old gardener once told me, "You can have a beautiful garden if you put a two-bit plant into a ten dollar hole —but only disappointment when you put a ten dollar plant into a two-bit hole."

Set the tree or shrub at the same level that it was growing before. Burlap need not be removed or loosened—it will rot away quickly. Fill around roots with prepared soil until it is about three-quarters full. Flood with water to settle any air pockets, then fill level with the surface of the ground. A depression may be made in the soil in a ring at the outer edge to help hold water, but it should drain away from the trunk or stem. Thoroughly saturate the soil, then provide temporary shading or shelter for the newly transplanted material.

During the first growing season, water with extra care. Do not allow the plants to dry out during the spring and summer growing season. Less watering is required in early fall to help harden the plants for winter. Unless there is ample rainfall, resume watering from October until the ground freezes in cold areas. Evergreens should not go into a winter with dry soil around the roots.

WINTER PROTECTION IN COLD AREAS

Newly transplanted, very young trees and shrubs, and those of questionable hardiness, need special protection from frost. Smaller plants can be packed or heavily mulched with hay and leaves. Branches of evergreens can be placed around larger shrubs, and tied at the top, tent fashion. Lath frames or burlap barriers can also provide protection from cold winter winds.

THE FORMAL GARDEN

The formal garden, whether large or small, begins with the design which must proceed from the dwelling. The doorway or walk-way will set the line from which the design must flow. Almost any geometric form may be used. It may be a square or rectangle, divided by a cross of walks which may or may not

*Formal need not mean elaborate. Four brick-outlined beds surround-
ing a fancy sundial make this garden at once simple, attractive, and
formal.*

have a central feature, such as a sundial, fountain, or statuary
where they cross. The four lesser squares or rectangles can be
broken into smaller parts, separated by smaller walks.

A circular pattern may be used with walks radiating from
the center like spokes of a wheel. Designs may be adapted from
some of the early medieval gardens where the geometrics used
formed a knot design as the focal point of the pattern.

For the formal garden, symmetry and perfect balance are
essential. Elements of equal size and weight balance each other.
They must be neat, trimmed, and precise. Plants are grown
within the beds formed by the walks. Lower growing plants are
placed adjacent to the central walk, with taller varieties radiating
outward. The varied symmetrical forms of coniferous evergreens
make them adaptable to the formal garden, as backgrounds,
borders, and accents. Shrubs and plants with irregular growth
habits will need pruning or symmetrical arrangement when used
in formal groupings.

One of the most curious garden forms is the labyrinth or maze. Plantings are arranged as hedges to create a long, winding path or passage. Perhaps the simplest form would be a spiral from the outer perimeter of the garden to the exact center, but of course the design is never that pure. The idea is to offer the opportunity for a long, interesting stroll in a limited area. The form had its greatest popularity in the fifteenth and sixteenth centuries, but the form does survive.

There is some question as to the difference between labyrinths and mazes. One authority says that the maze is a low planting, while the labyrinth is a tall planting, taller than a man. But another says that the maze forces the stroller to make choices at intersections and risk cul-de-sacs, while the labyrinth offers no choice, just a single route. Whether or not the latter distinction was recognized by the early landscape designers is questionable, since both of the old designs above were labelled labyrinths though only the one on the left is a labyrinth.

There is no question, however, that the labyrinthine form was not strictly a garden form, or that, in its garden form, it was not strictly an herb garden. But the most interesting of these gardens always included some herbs and often were strictly herbal plantings.

The variety of texture, mass, and color available in herbs create interesting contrasts and give definition to the overall design. These elements must also be considered in producing the symmetry and balance required. The formal garden is usually bordered by a trimmed hedge. Individual beds may be defined by neatly trimmed, low growing plants.

HERBS FOR THE FORMAL GARDEN

The choice of plant material is governed by individual taste or preference, climate, and availability. However, to be proper and correct, the essential materials for the traditional formal herb garden must include the great herbs, as they were called. These are basil, pot and sweet marjoram, balm, bergamot, mint, sage, hyssop, rue, spike vervain, lovage, and lavender.

For year-round beauty, the perennial herbs must form the framework of the garden, allowing areas for the annuals desired to be planted in their season. Plan carefully the arrangement of plant materials according to size, texture or mass, and color. Arrange foliage colors to provide interesting contrasts, silver-gray against reds or bronze, dark greens to accent varigated or golden-green colors.

Some of the low-growing plants with silver or gray foliage that may be used are woolly thyme, betony or lambs ears, dittany-of-Crete, and antennaria. All of these are woolly, silver-gray. The low growing artemesias, fringed, or silky wormwood, and silver mound are feathery, grey-green; santolinas have finely divided foliage, coarser than the artemesias. Dwarf sage and French thyme are also low growing, with gray-green foliage. Among the taller plants of this coloring, we find the lavenders, Roman wormwood, mugwort, horehound, sage, and marjoram.

Deep greens can be found in winter savory, English thyme, white yarrow, green santolina, germander, and rosemary. Rue has a definite blue-green coloring.

For shades of red or bronze, use bronze ajuga, a low growing ground cover, purple or dark opal basil for a medium height, and bronze fennel for tall, background effect.

Varigated leaves can be found among the scented geraniums.

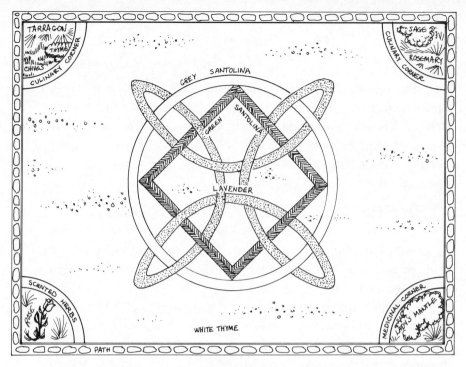

The knot garden is ornamental and nothing else. It is an old European garden form which achieved its high point in sixteenth century England. The idea is to arrange textures and colors of foliage in a manner that produces the appearance of cords looping over and under one another. It is probably no surprise that the only plants used are herbs. Today, the knot garden is largely a curiosity, being cultivated in botanic gardens and the private gardens of herb lovers.

Oddly enough, the knot garden got its start as a curiosity for the rich and the royal. During medieval times, the garden was utilitarian and generally looked it. The beauty of the garden was a function of the plants, not the form. But as the Renaissance swept Europe, it touched and shaped landscape architecture as it did other facets of life. The French especially developed palatial estates with elaborate and ornate gardens. The first knot garden was undoubted designed by an enterprising (and creative) landscaper in the hire of a gentleman seeking to outdo his peers. A notable quality of the new garden form

was that it was viewed to its best advantage from an overlook, such as a terrace or second-floor window.

The knot form spread, evolved, and became more elaborate. There was the open knot, a loosely stitched creation with floral herbs spotted in the open loops. There was the closed knot, a winter as well as summer garden tightly formed of evergreen herbs. As the form reached its zenith, the typical knot gardens were plotted in groups of four, either marking the corners of a larger and more varied garden, or forming the quarters of a larger square. Each knot garden itself was square, and each was different.

Many herb gardeners today regard the knot garden as more trouble and work than it is worth. It is strictly ornamental; it is time-consuming to design, plot, and plant; it must be pruned regularly. But other herb gardeners find the unique beauty justifies the bother. Even in a contemporary setting, the knot garden is in harmony. And it is always a focal point.

If you believe the experience will be rewarding, try a knot garden, such as the one plotted at left. A sixteenth century design, it is woven of only three different herbs, lavender and green and gray santolinas. Corner plantings have scented, culinary, and medicinal plantings.' Having succeeded with a simple knot, you might be tempted to try the four-knot grouping below, or one of your own design.

In designing and plotting a knot garden, it is vital to plan every sweep to scale, coloring in each different herb so you see the over-and-under effects. Plotting the design on graph paper and on a corresponding grid on the planting site will ease the task of tracing the design (using sand or lime) for actual planting. All the tips, reminders, and cautions of herb gardening apply; and you should set out plants, rather than trying to start a knot from seeds. Suggested plants include those noted above, as well as germander, hyssop, Roman wormwood, winter savory, and boxwood. The low hedges of herbs should be trimmed regularly, rather than sharply pruned occasionally, for it is the appearance that counts. And when properly planned and maintained, the knot garden will have the most striking appearance of any herb plots.

Dwarf varigated sage leaves are grey-green and white with accents of purple. Varigated mint leaves are green and yellow, with a reddish stem; pineapple mint, green edged with white. Golden thyme has gold tinged leaves in winter and spring; silver thyme leaves are green, edged in silvery white. Both of these are low, upright thymes. Golden lemon thyme is a creeper with golden green leaves. Most of the other culinary herbs are in the medium green color ranges.

Plants that lend themselves to clipping into hedges include germander, gray and green santolina, hyssop, lavender, and southernwood. By careful selection the garden can be as colorful and harmoniously designed as a Persian carpet.

CONTEMPORARY GARDEN DESIGN

For a house of contemporary style, garden designs often feature paved areas and patterns with distinct angles and curves, worked out by use of beds containing plants and various combinations of crushed rock, bark, and pavings. Plantings are based on tone, texture, and form of the plants. The object of interest or specimen plant is placed off-center, balanced by a larger area of subdued importance. Within the boundaries of the garden may be divisions, perhaps only one or two, or several. These functional divisions are planned and arranged, somewhat like the rooms of the dwelling, into areas for the various activities needed or desired by the occupants. Each is a separate area, yet together they form a harmonious unit, without pettiness or a sense of clutter.

Areas for outdoor living and dining flow out from the dwelling, becoming an integral part of the house itself. Shade here might be provided by the wide branching sweet birch or

This landscape plan of contemporary design uses only plants with traditional herbal virtues. Included are some of the more commonplace herbs like lavender, rosemary, and thyme, as well as some of the plants that are not commonly considered herbs, like the carob and linden trees and horsetail.

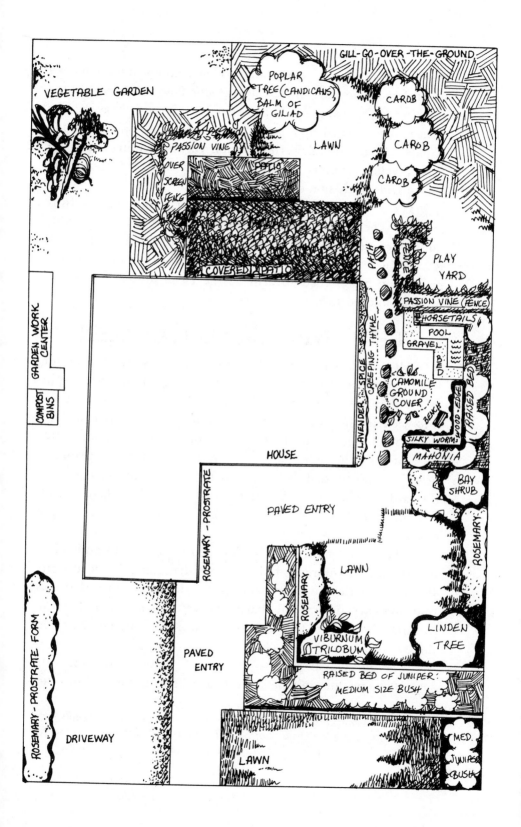

slippery elm. Ground covers of varying textures and colors can set off larger plantings. Bronze ajuga, blue flowering vinca, or the creeping thymes and mints are effective. Service areas can be attractively screened by a group of fast growing poplars, broom, or elder. The exotic flowering passion vine or twining hops with papery yellow clusters on attractive wood framed supports can also provide a division or screen.

The possibilities of the garden's area should be carefully studied. The enthusiastic desire for as many varieties as possible can sometimes result in overcrowding and a cluttered effect. Reasonable restraint, discrimination, and a sense of scale and proportion are needed to achieve the clean, quiet, functional, beauty required by contemporary design.

THE INFORMAL GARDEN

All things that are found in formal gardens are suitable for use in informal design, the difference being in the manner in which they are arranged. Rather than the symmetrical relationship seen in the formal plan, the informal garden is casual in effect, yet by no means does it come into existence accidentally, without planning, but it must be carefully ordered and planned, bringing into mutual relationship the various characteristics of the garden situation. It does not imply a naturalistic handling of existing materials in the sense of unkempt wilderness or jungle conditions.

The formal garden can be designed with compass and ruler, but the art in informal design is one that conceals the design. It requires strict discipline applied in such a manner that the resulting effect is graceful charm and ease. It might be likened to milady's coiffeur—they fussed and worked with her hair for three hours, so it would look casual!

The individual peculiarity of each garden situation will suggest the manner in which it can best be incorporated into the

The informal landscape design is more relaxed, less structured. This landscape plan uses both traditional and unusual herbs to surround the home with fragrant, beautiful, and useful greenery.

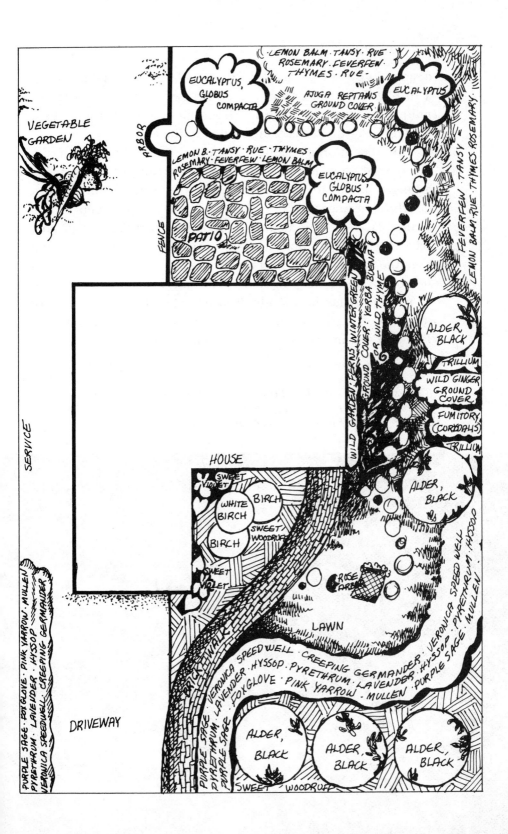

design. Existing trees and shrubs, irregularities in land contours, a rock wall, or rustic fence can all be used to create a design of unique beauty. The transition from house to garden must be a uniting link—all elements are related to the whole.

In the informal garden, there exists the intrigue of the unexpected — delightful, apparently unplanned features, so arranged as not to be evident until arrived at. It might be a delightful arrangement of rockery with tiny creepers, delightfully scented lavenders and delicate blossoms, or perhaps a small pool reflecting light airy branches, with bright green arbutus trailing over the banks, accented by a clump of tall, reed-like equisetum nearby. A small stepping-stone path may lead to a wild garden of natural plants in a shady, wooded area. The lazy melaleuca might be sheltering a patch of low growing wild ginger or ferny fumitory within the curve of its reclining trunk.

This side-yard garden represents well the qualities of the informal herb garden. The plantings are harmoniously arranged without being rigidly structured. It is a pleasant retreat.

Straight rows of border plants, precise beds, and trimmed hedges have no place here. Arrangement of plant material must allow for the natural plant forms to complement and contrast each other into satisfying combinations; light airy growth contrasted by darker masses, low growing plants accented by a few flowering spikes.

More freedom in selection of plants is permitted in the informal garden. It is possible to develop the entire garden around certain kinds of plants—not necessarily to the exclusion of all others, but rather in a manner that will emphasize the importance of the chosen ones.

Although less maintenance is required for trees and shrubs than in the formal arrangement, removal of dead and unruly growth, pulling of weeds, thinning and replanting of perennials, as in any garden, are definite requirements. Order and discipline are just as important as in the formal garden; the significant difference is that they are not so apparent.

ROCK GARDENS

Rock gardens are primarily used for the growing of alpines and other small plants and herbs which cannot be properly grown in the herbaceous border. It is important, therefore, to create the growing conditions required in a pleasing and natural arrangement. As with other features, the rock garden must be an integral part of the landscape, in harmony with the surroundings. A rock pile, or collection of geological specimens can be the result if the arrangement is not made to look convincingly natural. An examination of natural outcroppings will be time well spent before starting the project.

A naturally uneven, rocky terrain creates a natural setting for a rock garden. Slopes and banks are ideal for arrangements of rocks and plants. A terraced rock garden, between two levels can be most attractive. Rocks and rock loving plants blend and contrast each other in a beautiful, natural way, each emphasizing the best qualities of the other.

A pathway leading to informal stone steps, up and over a sloping bank, can be a perfect setting for clusters of small plants

Rocks and herbs go together, whether as a consequence of naturally rocky terrain or of the gardener's contrivance.

set among rocks on either side. A group of spring blooming primroses, graceful sprays of Oriental chives with white, star-like flowers, patches of quaint Johnny-jump-ups, make a colorful picture among the rockery. A dwarf sage or clumps of dark green savory can contrast with silvery silky wormwood drooping over a step. Creeping mats of thyme and corsican mint planted in crevices and between the stepping stones give off their delightful scents underfoot, while the fragrance of lavender pervades the air. Small evergreens can be placed at the sides and top, or a slim birch set to cast its scattered shade over the rockery.

ROCK GARDENS
IN THE FORMAL LANDSCAPE

Generally, most rock gardens are considered informal or naturalistic in design. With careful planning and arrangement, they can, however, be included in the formal landscape. The outer edge of a small lawn area, with a background or boundary planting of shrubs and trees, could be an appropriate location.

A low semi-circular formation of rocks can be arranged, and

back of this a small deciduous tree to cast light shadows over the rockery. Perhaps a tree-form hawthorn or dainty jujube would be used here. A group of nicely spaced, low-growing junipers frame the crescent of rocks. Well-chosen alpines and rock plants are set neatly among the rocks with a mat of bronze ajuga within the semi-circle contrasting the green lawn, to complete the scene. Careful placement and balance is needed to produce an arrangement that will be in harmony with the rest of the garden design.

BUILDING THE ROCK GARDEN

An exposure sloping or open to the east is most desirable; however, others can be utilized if proper shading can be provided to protect plants from the direct rays of the afternoon sun. Background trees should not create dense shade.

Good drainage is one condition that rock plants invariably demand. It is not too difficult to provide moisture when they are dry, but if drainage is poor and a period of wet weather occurs, nothing can be done and some of the choicest plants can rot away overnight. The area selected for the rock garden should be dug out a foot or more. This should be half-filled with broken stone, bricks, or gravel. Add a layer of sand and gravel and wash in with the hose.

Rocks on a slope should slant in and down to prevent loosening and to direct moisture toward the roots. On steeper slopes sink in an occasional flat rock in a vertical position with only the top edges showing, to check washing. Dense, creeping plants, such as thyme, will also help check erosion.

Whether rocks are collected or purchased, the same general type should be used in one garden. Most rocks found in the prevailing area can be used. As they are native to the environment they will always look as if they "belong." Worn, weathered rocks have a natural appearance and irregular, angular forms are preferred to round boulders. Color, texture, size, and shape are carefully considered to determine their placement. In natural formations, rocks are submerged—only a portion being above ground. Too many little rocks can be a detraction. For walks or paths, flat stepping stones sunk flush with ground level are the most attractive.

A mixture of good loam, compost, and sand, with the addition of some limestone chips, will meet the soil requirements for most plants. The needs of each plant should be carefully checked before planting and those with the same soil requirements should be planted in the same area. It is possible to intermix the plants, the acid-loving among those requiring limy soil, if you want to take the time to prepare each rock pocket individually before setting in the plant. A large number of rock plants send down deep roots and a good depth of soil, at least a foot, should be provided.

A great many beautiful and interesting plants can be obtained which grow easily in rocky surroundings. The ideal plant should be a hardy perennial, of neat habit and small stature. It should be easily grown, but should not be a rampant spreader and should be free flowering. Others may be included for their beautiful foliage, fragrance, or exceptional blossoms.

A terraced rock garden can be constructed quite simply. A layer of soil is placed over the drainage material and soaked in. Next place an irregular rim of rocks around the edge, some flush with the ground, others above it. Fill the enclosure with soil and again thoroughly soak in with the hose. This soaking-in prevents air pockets and reduces settling, which, occurring later, might mar the finished garden. Another terrace is constructed on the plateau thus formed and again watered in, and this process continues for the desired height. Irregularity in width and height is important for a natural effect. Rocks must all be firmly set so they do not move if stepped on.

The best time to plant is in early spring when frosts are past or early autumn. Rock garden plants are not generally suited to straight-row plantings or geometric patterns. Slow growing varieties are set in groups while one or two of the spreading type are sufficient in each spot. Place trailing plants where they can droop gracefully over the rock. Tiny little beauties should be placed where they will not be overshadowed by lustier plants. Don't crowd plants; give them room to grow and develop and for air to circulate around them.

When the plants have been set in place, cover the soil around them with a mulch of fine gravel or stone chips. This gives a well-groomed look, ties plants and rock into a harmonious unit, and serves a functional purpose as well.

Maintenance of a rock garden is easier than that of an ordinary herbaceous garden. However, it must be kept free of weeds and watered when necessary. Some plants need to be cut back after flowering. Tender plants may need winter protection in cold areas. Hay or evergreen branches make a satisfactory covering. An annual top dressing of compost in the spring will insure fresh nourishment for spring growth.

THE WILD GARDEN

Suitable materials for a wild garden are dependent upon the area in which the garden is located. In its truest sense, it is a collection of ecologically correct plants, native to the area. A wild garden of cacti and desert plants would not be appropriate for the seashore, nor would a collection of bog plants be suited to the prairie.

In planning a wild garden, a study should be made of the plants in their natural state, observing their locations and choice of companions, in order to create a similar environment in the garden. In many areas where forest conditions still prevail, or at least once existed, a wild garden can be worked out which will appear as a piece of untouched woodland. Whether it occupies a large area, or just a tiny planting at the foot of an evergreen, it must not look planted, but rather as if it had been there all along. And to look natural, it must be planned that way.

Good drainage is important and must be checked and attended to at the outset. Woodland plants require soil very rich in humus. Large amounts of compost, leaf-mold, and aged manure are needed. Proper shade must be provided, whether it be the dense shade of evergreens, or light airy midsummer shade of a deciduous tree. Plants should be set out in colonies—groups of one species growing together. Colors and varieties should not be mixed. A natural, harmonious arrangement that provides interest and accent is accomplished through careful planning and design.

During the first season, adequate water and winter protection are required. Once established, woodland plants require very little attention and care.

OBTAINING PLANT MATERIAL
FOR THE GARDEN

Many herbs and native plants can be purchased at nurseries. In most areas, there is at least one grower who specializes in collecting and propagating the natives that can be adapted to the garden environment. Your local nursery may be able to direct you to one. Be sure to have the proper botanical name for the plant you desire. A request for stagbrush, or cramp bark might result in a blank stare, but if you ask to see the viburnums, a group of plants would probably be presented for your selection. There may be several common names for one plant, and several different plants may have the same or very similar common names, but there is one proper botanical name for each plant. Seeds may be available from various specialty seed suppliers by mail. Check catalogs that are available from different parts of the country.

Arboretums, botanic gardens, and wild life preserves have many outstanding collections of native shrubs, trees, and wildflowers, either in a natural setting or landscaped, where the plants can be seen, and often indicating where they may be located. Books, pamphlets, and leaflets on native plants can be studied to help identify plants when they are found in the woods. The Department of Agriculture in many states publishes well illustrated leaflets, showing growth, habit or form, leaf, root, flower, and seed. These can be of great assistance in identifying various native plants. There are books in public libraries covering the same subject. Frequently, long-time residents of an area are very knowledgeable of the local flora and can be very helpful.

Collecting wild plant material can become a fascinating

This simple garden is a good design for the beginner. The plot is relatively small, but includes plants which are both useful and pretty, and is suitable for a spot with full sun.

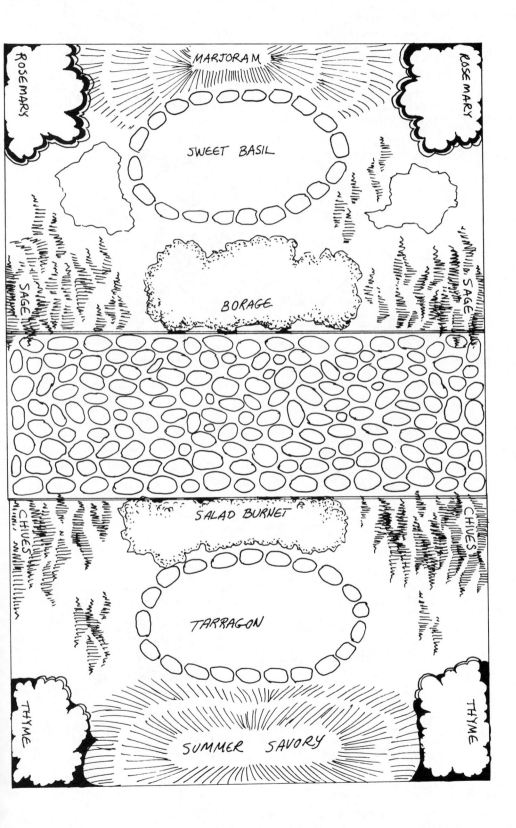

The circular herb garden is a popular traditional form. For a small garden, an old wagon-wheel can be used to delineate the beds. A larger garden could have gravel paths segmenting it and leading to a central statue or sundial.

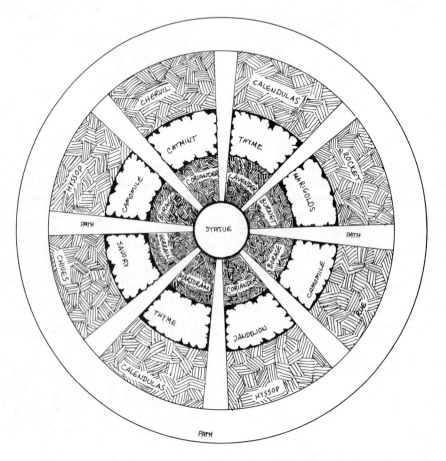

hobby. A few basic preparations can turn an ordinary trip into an interesting adventure. A supply of small sandwich bags, staples, notebook, pencil, and clippers are the supplies required. When an interesting plant is encountered on a country roadside, or nearby wood, a few notes or sketches should be made in the

A kitchen garden includes only herbs of culinary value. The plot sketch opposite provides space for a variety of fragrant, lovely, and useful herbs in easily maintained rectangular beds.

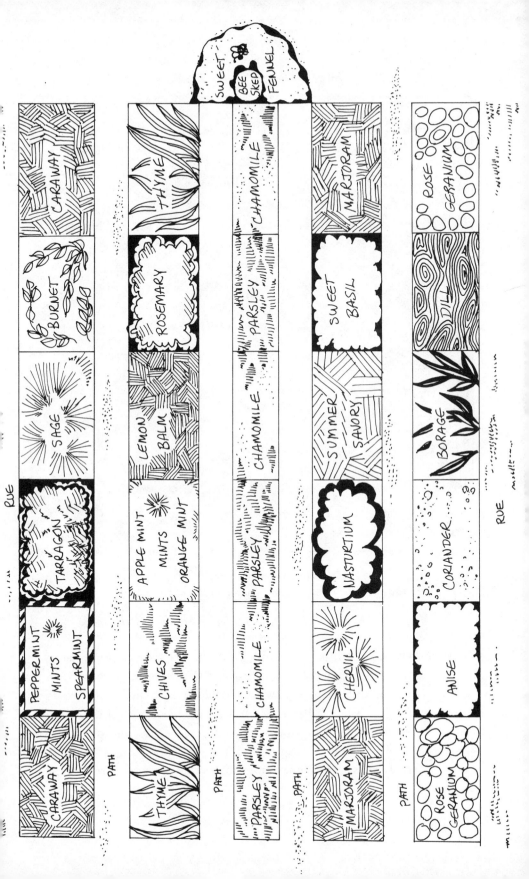

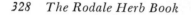

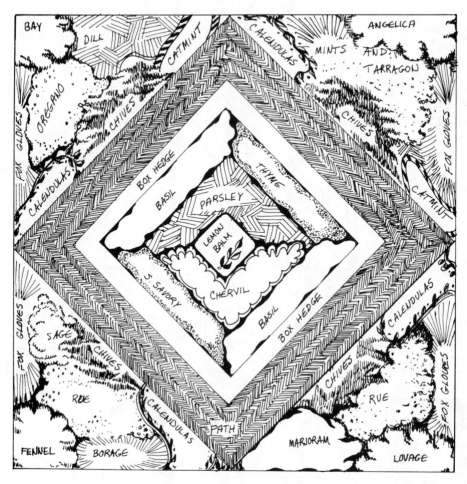

Many a city dweller believes his or her tiny backyard unsuited to any but the most simple garden. But a plot only ten to fifteen feet on a side is sufficient space for this richly varied herb garden. The herbs included are beautiful, and they serve many uses in the home.

notebook. Include date and location, brief description, height, coloring, and outstanding features. Observe the area to decide on its suitability for the garden. Does it seek sun or shade? Is it located on a dry hillside, or in a moist, woodsy location? These items should also be noted in your book. Into one of the little bags, place a leaf or twig, blossom or seed pod, then staple to the page of notes. Sometimes more than one trip is required for positive identification. We may want to see the bloom or seed before we can be certain of the species. The notes and specimen can then be compared to descriptive literature or actual plants displayed in the botanic gardens, or may be taken to the arboretum for identification.

Once identified, we need to know how the plant is propagated, whether cuttings can be taken in spring or fall, or is it easier to plant the seeds. A few of the woodland plants can be transplanted into the garden, but in most cases digging up the plant is not advised. It is most unlikely that the transplant would be successful. Moreover, many wild plants are protected by law and their removal is prohibited. Seeds may be gathered, or cuttings taken at the proper season, without injury to the wild life, and even in protected areas permission may usually be obtained to gather seeds.

It is best to get plants by seeds, cuttings, or division of the wild plant. As a point of ecology and conservation, the wild life is being increased and by starting this way the plants are accustomed to the environment and conditions you have provided from their infancy and do not have difficult adjustments to make. Starting plants from seed, from cuttings, or by division is covered in Chapter Six, but some hints on gathering and using wild seed may be in order.

GROWING FROM SEED

Growing native shrubs and trees from seed may require persistance and patience. Some require very long periods for germination. Most varieties are very rugged and can last for long periods of time, as in an extended drought, lying dormant until conditions are just right for their germination. Through observation, persistance, and sometimes chance, man has discovered some of the secrets of the seeds, and recorded his findings and results for posterity.

There are a few varieties of wild flowers that were thought lost or extinct for many years, only to reappear after fire had burned over the area. Fire was required to break their dormancy. The beautiful matilija poppy is an example of this. To germin-

Herbs come in all shapes and sizes. They serve in low borders (bottom left), but provide bushy masses too (top left). Some can be immobilized in one spot, while others, spread far and wide. And what is more striking than a graceful, potbound rosemary bush (right)?

ate these seeds, the flat is covered with straw and burned, then watered.

Some varieties of seeds require freezing to break their dormancy. If one does not wish to leave them out all winter, or the climate is not cold enough, they can be dropped into water in the ice cube tray, frozen, then stored in the freezer for the required period of time, which is usually much shorter than a winter season.

Seeds vary in the amount of time required for germination —it may be three weeks or three years. Some require warmth, others prefer cool temperatures. Some need light, others prefer darkness. Many require a period of dormancy or "after-ripening" before planting. Relatively few seeds will sprout as soon as mature. Most of them require a period of rest or dormancy, which varies in length with different plants. These are thought to be necessary for certain changes related to the ripening of the foods stored in the seed.

A few methods of shortening the dormancy are commonly used, combining moisture and heat, moisture and freezing. Stratification is an important and long practiced method used to break down the hard shells and hasten germination. This process of stratification may require freezing, or warmth, dependent on the individual species. Most varieties are stratified, or stored in moist sand for several months, at about 40 degrees. Some are subjected to alternate freezing and thawing throughout the winter. Some seeds need to be very fresh, others will germinate after being stored ten years or more. Seeds harvested during muggy weather are usually less viable than those gathered under dry conditions.

Fleshy seeds are usually planted as soon as they ripen, whereas hardcoated seeds may need to be gently cracked or nicked to hasten the process. Most winged seeds (such as conifers) need to be stratified in moist sand all winter at 35 or 40 degrees and are planted in the spring. (Remove the wings first.) Fine seeds, harvested in the fall are stored cool and dry until spring. These are generalizations, and where specific instructions are not available, can serve as guidelines for the types of seeds being sown. When in doubt, it is a good idea to plant the seeds in several different ways. Whatever the type of seed being used, one rule is rigid — the medium must never be allowed to dry out from time of sowing through germination and up to time of transplanting.

A general method that has been successful with many seed varieties is to fill flats about two-thirds full of prepared soil, cover the surface with screened sphagnum. Sow the seed on the moss, water with a fine spray, then cover the surface with a piece of coarse moist cloth, such as burlap. When seeds start to sprout, remove cloth covering.

THE END
AND THE BEGINNING

The formal tour of our herb garden is all but completed. There are still individual herbs to meet, books about herbs to discover, and places to visit or write for herb products. But the story has been told. Hopefully, you'll stop by this vista again and again, for the herbal landscape is one that seldom tires or bores.

While this seemingly is the end, it is really only the beginning, for the simplest herbal garden and the most elaborate

This is the beginning. Whether your interest is color, fragrance, health, or taste, the herbs to fulfill it have the same beginning. For your herbal experience to be complete, you must start at the beginning too.

herbal landscape, the most casual acquaintance with herbs and the deepest, fondest love of them all begin at the same place. One can purchase a packet of powder that once was a living plant, and one can use it to alleviate or remedy some personal ailment, or to enhance the flavor of a favorite dish, or to color a pound of wool, or for any of the myriad of uses that herbs have. But the beginning is the plant, and the beginning has been experienced by some other. Herbs are, after all, plants first and foremost.

The herbal landscape is the beginning. Whether contrived or discovered, the herbal landscape should be experienced, and not simply through the pages of a book. If you have the space, do plant an herb garden, even if one of only a few common varieties and of limited space. Put a pot of herbs in your sunniest window. And if you haven't the space, visit an herb garden, public or private, for business or pleasure.

Then use your herbs for their fragrance, their taste, their color, or for themselves. Enjoy them, but put them to work. Beginning is the hardest part, but it is only as difficult as planting a seed.

APPENDICES

An Herbal Encyclopedia

A Glossary

A Bibliography

A List of Sources

AN HERBAL ENCYCLOPEDIA

ACONITE

Monkshood, Wolfbane
Aconitum napellus, Linn.
Ranunculaceae

Aconite is a lovely plant for the garden, but also a dangerous one, for it is a deadly poison. It has some medicinal value, but an inaccurate dose can kill, so it is not for experiments.

A hardy perennial, aconite will top four feet in height, making it a suitable plant for the back row of a border. Its flowers have a curious shape, which earned the plant the nickname monkshood during the Middle Ages, and are quite pretty in cut flower arrangements. The common variety produces blue flowers, but others produce white and mauve.

Root division is the most practical method of propagation for aconite, though it reportedly can be grown from seed. The plant takes two to three years to flower if started from seed. Root division procedure is out of the ordinary, for aconite is not an ordinary plant. Each year, the roots develop small "daughter" roots, then die off. It is these daughter roots that are replanted to propagate the plant. In the autumn of every third or fourth year, aconite should be dug up and divided.

Aconite likes rich, somewhat moist soil. Use lots of well-rotted manure and compost. The location should be partially shady. The individual plants should be about 18 inches from their neighbors.

Aconite is chiefly a garden plant, though it has been cultivated for its medicinal properties. The dried root has the effect of a sedative or depressant, and has been used to reduce pain and fever. Doses must always be small and carefully controlled, since it is a poison.

Historically, it is aconite's poisonous properties which stand out. It has been called wolf's bane or wolfbane because it was supposed to have been used to poison arrows used in hunting wolves. The generic name is said to be derived from *akontion,* a dart, because it was used to poison arrows. To be fair, it has also been suggested that *Aconitum* is derived from *akone,* cliffy or rocky, because the plant is oftimes found in rocky areas. The old herbalists list the poisonous nature of aconite, most noting its usefulness against venomous creatures, and Gerard pointing out its power was "so forceable that the herb only thrown before the scorpion or any other venomous beast, causeth them to be without force or strength to hurt, insomuch that they cannot move or stirre untill the herbe be taken away." And stories of aconite poisonings, deliberate and accidental, abound.

Aconite has had widespread use. The Europeans knew and used it. The Chinese also used it, and it remains one of the principal drug plants used in Chinese medicine today. In America, the Indians discovered the beneficial and dangerous properties of the herb and used it in early phases of pneumonia and in erysipelas and rheumatism.

ADDER'S TONGUE
Dog-Tooth Violet
Erythronium, various species
Liliaceae

A large species of bulbous herbs of the lily family, this herb is native to many parts of the country. It has two leathery basal leaves, often richly mottled, and miniature flowers nodding from the top of a central stem in very early spring. It usually is about six inches high, and is particularly effective in the rock garden or naturalized in the wild garden in masses. Adder's tongue likes fairly shaded places and a light soil, full of humus. It is increased by seed and some varieties spread by underground rootstalks. The best time for transplanting is when leaves die away after flowering. Bulbs should be planted at least three inches deep.

Erythronium americanum (trout lily), best known in the east, it has richly mottled leaves and yellow flowers with recurved petals. *E. californicum* has cream colored flowers and is easily naturalized. *E. giganteum* or *watsonii* is one of the most beautiful varieties and has mottled brown and green leaves and creamy flowers with a touch of maroon at the base. *E. hendersonii* has mottled leaves and recurved purple flowers, and *E. dens-canis* (dog tooth violet) is the Eurasian form with green leaves splotched with red and rose or purple flowers.

The leaves and bulb are used medicinally. Fresh root simmered in milk is used as a poultice for scrofulus ulcers and tumors; the dried root is nutritive. It is listed as emetic, emollient, and antiscorbutic.

AGRIMONY
Church Steeples, Cocklebur
Agrimonia eupatoria, Linn.
Rosaceae

Agrimony is a yellow-flowered, spiky plant that grows between one and three feet in height. It has few branches. The flowers blossom profusely along the stem. The leaves are narrow and about five inches long with saw-tooth edges. The whole plant is deep green and is covered with soft hairs.

Agrimonia eupatoria is a European native, but it has been spread widely in the United States. The plant is listed in early American herbals as *Agrimonia gryposepala*. The plant is good as a rock garden plant or in a wildflower border. It is easily started from seed, and once established, it will self-seed. It thrives in a dry, lightly shaded location, though some direct sunlight won't hurt it.

The old herbalists always listed agrimony as an astringent, tonic, and diuretic, and had especial regard for it as a jaundice remedy; Dioscorides called it "A remedy for them that have bad livers." Agrimony was also regarded as a remedy for skin blemishes and diseases. Infusions of the plant are still valued for sore throats: mix an ounce of the dried plant with one pint of boiling water, sweeten with honey, and drink a half cup as frequently as you like.

The plant is also a valuable dye plant, generally yielding a yellow color, with plants gathered in September giving a light hue, and those gathered later in the year yielding a darker color.

ALDER

Common Alder, English Alder
Alnus glutinosa, Gaertn.
Betulaceae

Members of the birch family, alders grow in cool, moist, even wet soils. They can be used effectively along garden boundaries, in groups, and combine well with birch and hazelnuts. Along streams or ponds, the dense root system will help retain the banks and drain wet soil. Alder logs can be used to build walks or retaining edges in wet soil as they will not decay easily, even when continuously wet.

They are decorative with attractive foliage and flowers. The green hanging catkins blossom early in spring; pistillate catkins are woody, resembling small pine cones. Some alders will reach a height of 70 feet. Propagation is by seeds gathered in fall and kept dry, then sowed in moist shady soil in spring. The shrubby varieties grow from hardwood cuttings and suckers.

The bark and berries are cathartic, similar to cascara in action. The astringent bark, prepared as a decoction, is used for gargle for sore throat, to induce circulation, check diarrhea, and for eye drops. Leaves are glutenous and used to cure inflammation. Fresh leaves applied to the bare feet, are said to be excellent for burning and aching feet, also used as a foot bath when brewed as a strong tea.

The bark and cones were used for tanning leather and a yellow-brown dye was made from bark peeled in the spring.

Leaves, with morning dew on them can be placed where fleas are a problem. They will gather the fleas and can then be quickly disposed of. It has also been reported that insects are repelled by freshly picked leaves.

ANGELICA

Garden Angelica
Angelica archangelica, Linn.
Umbelliferae

Angelica is a veritable giant in the herb world. The towering plant is widely travelled and has a background rich in herbal lore. Use has been made of leaves, stems, roots, and seeds in cooking and in medicine.

Believed to be a native of Syria, angelica has spread across the world, growing particularly abundantly in Iceland and Lapland. It likes cool, moist places. Angelica is neither a true annual nor a true perennial. It dies off after flowering, but since the plants often take more than two years to achieve the bloom of maturity, they aren't really *bi*ennials. The gardener can play on this quality of angelica and maintain the plant as a perennial simply by pruning the flower stalks and preventing the setting of seeds. Thus the gardener will be able to develop and maintain the plant as a seven to eight-foot member of the garden, but thus too will the gardener miss out on the spectacular yellow-green or white-green blossoms.

These blossoms make their appearance early in May, and by July the plant goes to seed. It is the date of blooming that has, in some quarters, been regarded as the source of the plant's name. The day of Michael the Archangel used to be May 8, and angelica blooms on that date; hence *Angelica archangelica.* There is more of angelica in the folklore, such as the legend that an archangel revealed in a vision that angelica would cure the plague. In time, angelica came to be regarded as a simply angelic plant, and was known widely as "The Root of the Holy Ghost."

But the history of the plant is rooted in prehistoric times and even the passage of centuries couldn't shake the associations between angelica and pagan beliefs from the Christian mind. It is altogether possible, then, that the plant acquired its angelic stature in the folklore because of the pagan's regard for the plant as an infallible guard against witches and evil spirits and their spells and enchantments. Peasants tied angelica leaves around the necks of the children to protect them from harm, and even the name was supposed to be helpful in a jam.

An interesting story repeated in a number of herb books supports the antiquity of angelica's lore. It is alleged that it is the custom in the lake district of what was once Latvia for country peasants to take part in an annual procession, carrying angelica stems to sell in the towns. Part of the procession is the chanting of a chorus with words so old that no one knows what they mean. The ritual is simply an early-summer custom and the words of the chorus have been passed from generation to generation. Certainly the rite is pre-Christian.

Just as certainly, the country folk had good reason for dealing in angelica beyond the religious or superstitious significance of the plant. The good reason was undoubtedly the taste, for angelica is a culinary herb of no small repute. Perhaps best known are the confections made of the angelica stems, by combining them with an incredible amount of sugar. You are undoubtedly better off trying angelica in some other dish. The stems, for example, may be cut and prepared like asparagus. The leaves, fresh or dried, may be added to soups and stews. Use about a half tablespoon of the leaves to a quantity that will serve four, adding it in the last minutes of cooking.

Angelica is most used in the countries where it is most abundant. In Iceland, both the stems and roots are eaten raw, with butter. The Norwegians make a bread of the roots. In the multinational region known as Lapland, the stalks are regarded as a delicacy. A popular tea, tasting much like China tea, is infused from fresh or dried leaves.

Angelica has long had commercial value as a flavoring in wines and liqueurs, and occasionally as an ingredient in perfumes. The entire plant is aromatic, including the root, but the aroma of the plant has little to do with its aromatic use. Rather, the fresh root, when cut, will weep a resinous gum much like the fixative benzoin. The gum is in fact used as a substitute for benzoin in perfumes. Not all of the commercial uses of angelica are obvious. Some suspect, for example, that certain Rhine wines owe their fine flavor to the secret use of angelica. French absinthe has as an ingredient a blend of herbs, including angelica and wormwood. Both seeds and roots are used in chartreuse, the seeds help flavor gin and vermouth, and the leaves are used in preparing bitters.

You can brew your own bitters by combining one ounce of dried angelica, one ounce of dried holy thistle and a half-ounce of dried hops, infusing the herbs in three pints of boiling water, and straining them off after the brew has cooled. A wineglass of the bitters taken before meals is supposed to be a good appetizer.

It should be clear that not all of these uses are strictly culinary. The bitters obviously are a tonic. Eating angelica stalks is said to relieve flatulence and soothe "a feeble stomach." It is true with angelica as with other herbs that the medicinal and the culinary overlap. Just as angelica has some fairly broad culinary applications, it also has some broad medicinal applications. It is said to possess carminative, stimulant, diaphoretic, tonic, and expectorant properties. It is supposed to be good for colds, coughs, pleurisy, flatulence, colic, rheumatism, and urinary troubles. (It should be noted that angelica has a tendency to increase the sugar in the urine, so those with a tendency to diabetes should avoid it.)

The old herbalists expressed a high regard for the herb in their writings. Parkinson wrote that it "is of especial use . . . in swounings . . . tremblings and passions of the heart,. to expell any windy or noysome vapours from it. The green stalkes or the young rootes being preserved or candied are very effectual to comfort and warm a cold and weake stomacke; and in the time of infection is of excellent good use to preserve the spirits and heart from infection." He wrote that it would sweeten the breath. Moreover, he claimed that taking dried, powdered root in wine or other drink would "abate the rage of lust in young persons."

Culpeper too viewed angelica as "of admirable use." He enumerated the various uses and included some no one else had (or has). He said angelica's juices, if dropped into the eyes or ears, would remedy dimness of sight and deafness. It would work similarly for toothaches. Powdered root, mixed with a

Angelica

little pitch and "laid on the biting of mad dogs or any other venomous creature, doth wonderfully help." So too with open wounds; it "doth cleanse and cause them to heal quickly."

According to Culpeper, angelica "is an herb of Leo; let it be gathered when he is there, the Moon applying to his good aspect; let it be gathered either in his hour or in the hour of Jupiter: let Sol be angular: observe the like in gathering the herbs of other planets, and you may happen to do wonders. In all epidemical diseases caused by Saturn, that is as good a preservative as grows."

You can make a good tonic simply by infusing angelica leaves. This is a stimulating and aromatic tea, and if you only take it several days in succession, you will experience the beneficial effect.

An infusion made by pouring a pint of boiling water on an ounce of the bruised root, when taken in two tablespoon doses three to four times daily, is said to relieve flatulence. It is also a bronchial tonic and an emmenagogue.

Another bronchial tonic from an old herbal is made by

boiling a handful of angelica root in a quart of water for three hours, straining off the fluid and adding sufficient honey to make a syrup. Two tablespoons should be taken at night and several times during the day.

And here's an herbal curiosity: tuck a couple fingers full of ground angelica between lip and gum or in the cheek. Swallow the juice. It's reputed to be an excellent stomach tonic and remedy for the nervousness that comes from too much smoking.

Angelica's size keeps it outdoors, but if you have the space, it is a nice garden plant, for itself and for the uses to which it can be put. Only the first seeds need be purchased, for the plant self-sows readily. Indeed, the seeds should be gathered soon after formation, in early July, if they are going to be gathered at all, for they easily fall to the ground and germinate. The seeds themselves are fairly large and coated with a straw-like substance.

The seed germinates in light in 21 to 28 days at a 70° F temperature. Because it germinates in light, the seed must not be covered; rather it should be pressed lightly into the soil and kept moist until germination is evident. The seeds do lose vitality rapidly, so the best time for sowing is in late July or early August, right after harvesting. The seed will remain viable for at most two years.

For best results, the seeds should be started indoors. Transplant them at the appropriate time to a spot with very rich, moist soil, preferably with some shade. Angelica doesn't mind being cultivated under trees at all. The best alternative to starting them indoors is to start them outdoors in their favorite sort of place. In any case, fertilization should be high, using well-rotted manure and compost. Mulching is many times suggested because the habitat of best growth is such that weeds can easily start underneath the angelica unless it is mulched (or planted so thickly that no weeds can come up).

Harvesting of angelica varies in accordance with the part being harvested. The leaves can be harvested at any time of the year at which they are large enough to handle, and can be continued from that point on to the end of the growing season. The seeds should be harvested as they turn from green to yellow.

Since they fall easily upon ripening (denoted by the change in color), it is best to be prompt and to lean the seed heads into a bag or lined basket so they will drop into the container when clipped from the plant without loss of seeds. The stem should be cut in June or early July. The root should be dug up in the autumn of the plant's first year.

Drying is simple. For best drying the angelica leaves should be chopped, then scattered on screens or on paper for drying in the shade. The seeds can be cured in the sun until dry. The root tends to be thick and juicy, so incisions made in the thickest segments of the roots will speed the drying process.

There are two other angelicas, American angelica or masterwort (*Angelica atropurpurea*) and wild angelica (*A. sylvestris*). American angelica is similar in most respects to *A. archangelica* and has been used as a substitute. But the root is lighter and less branched and has a burning acridity when fresh (though not after having been dried). The plant's aromatic quality is tempered. Wild angelica has been used as a dye plant, yielding a yellow color.

ANISE

Aniseed
Pimpinella anisum, Linn.
Umbelliferae

If a better mouse trap is ever developed, it just may use anise as the bait. Most people don't think of anise in terms of its popularity with mice, but in the sixteenth century, anise found wide application as a mouse-trap bait. According to several old herbals, the mice found it irresistable. Of course, many humans find anise irresistable too, for it has a wide variety of applications in cooking and medicine.

Anise is an annual which grows from 18 to 24 inches in height. The first leaves to develop are fairly large and wide, while the secondary leaves are feather-like. It is these secondary leaves which prompted the ascription of the generic name *Pimpinella* to anise. *Pimpinella* is said to be derived from *dipinella* or twice-pinnate (pinnate meaning feather-like). By midsummer, two-inch clusters of tiny yellow-white flowers appear, followed in late summer by the gray-brown seeds for which the plant is generally cultivated. Each plant will have one to six umbrella-like clusters bearing six to ten seeds each.

The seeds are the most useful part of the plant, though the leaves can be used in cooking. The so-called aniseed is actually the fruit of the plant, and the seed is actually contained within the eighth-inch long, crescent-shaped ribbed kernel. Usually a bit of the stem clings to the fruit after harvesting. The aniseed is easily dried by spreading it on paper or cloth in the sun or half-shade, or indoors by placing it in a moderate heat. Once dried, they store well in tightly sealed containers.

The taste of the aniseed is sweet and spicy. Indeed, it is one of the four great hot seeds. It has a wholly agreeable aroma. These characteristics of the seed are those which have dictated its use: it has contributed its licorice-like flavor to cakes, soups, beverages, and medicines, and its aroma to all these and sachets and potpourris besides. It has been valued as a diuretic, carminative, aphrodisiac, and a remedy for halitosis.

Gerard reported that "the seed wasteth and consumeth winde, and is good against belchings, and upbraidings of the stomacke, allayeth gripings of the belly, provoketh urine gently, maketh abundance of milke, and stirreth up bodily lust. . . . Being chewed it maketh the breath sweet and is good for them that are short-winded, and quencheth thirst, and therefore it is fit for such as have the dropsie: it helpeth the yeoxing or hicket (hiccups), both when it is drunken or eaten dry; the smel thereof doth also prevail very much. The same being dried by the fire and taken with honey clenseth the brest very much from fleg-maticke superfluities; and if it be eaten with bitter almonds it doth helpe the old cough. It is to be given to young children and infants to eat which are like to have the falling sickness (epilepsy) or to such as have it by patrimonie or succession. It takes away the Squinancie or Quincie (a swelling in the throat) being gargled with honey, vinegar, and a little Hyssop gently boiled together."

The virtues enumerated by Gerard had been recognized for centuries. The plant is indigenous to Egypt, Greece, and Asia Minor, and the peoples of those countries were making use of it long before Christ. In the sixth century B.C., Pythagoras listed anise for epilepsy, suggesting that merely holding an anise plant would ward off epileptic attack. Hippocrates, a century later, recommended anise for coughs. Pliny the Elder noted that anise "has the effect of sweetening the breath and removing all bad odors from the mouth, if chewed in the morning." He also said, "This plant imparts a youthful look to the features, and if suspended to the pillow, so as to be smelt by a person when asleep, it will prevent disagreeable dreams." The Romans cultivated anise on a large scale for these virtues and its uses in flavoring foods and in perfumes.

A most prominent bit of culinary lore from anise's past ties it to the tradition of the wedding cake. The Romans liked to finish off a big meal with a cake called *mustacae,* which was simply a mixture of meal and a number of savory seeds, including anise. The intension of the *mustacae* was to ease digestion and prevent flatulence. Since it was a custom to conclude really big feasts, like a wedding feast with a serving of *mustacae,* many lorists view *mustacae* as the forerunner of today's wedding cake.

Perhaps a better measure of the value of anise to the Romans was the fact that it — along with cummin and other spices and savory seeds — was a negotiable commodity used to pay taxes. "Woe unto you, scribes and Pharisees," said Jesus in Matthew 23:23, "hypocrites! for ye pay tithe of Mint and Anise and Cummin, and have omitted the weightier matters of the law." A famous herbal quotation, but unfortunately a mistranslation in the eyes of some scholars, who contend that the original Greek was *anethon* or dill *(Antheum graveolus* to some botanists, *Peucedanum graveolens* to others), not anise.

Halfway around the globe, the Chinese too put anise to good use (although there is some confusion among anise, star anise, and fennel in the orient; the star anise [*Illicium anisatum* or *Illicium verum*] has properties very similar to anise and the two are virtually interchangeable). The Chinese use the seed as a

Anise

condiment and believe it to be carminative, diuretic, and tonic in value.

None of these properties have been diminished with the passage of time, of course. Anise still enjoys a reputation as a cough remedy. Anise tea is also helpful in cases of infantile catarrh. Pour half a pint of boiling water on two teaspoons of bruised aniseed. Sweetened, this should be frequently given in one to three teaspoon doses.

Anise is a stimulating condiment. It can perk up the taste of many a soup. Just add a few seeds to the liquid. Or try substituting aniseed for the cinnamon or nutmeg you add to applesauce. Mix a teaspoon of aniseed with a cup of cheese spread and smear on crackers for an interesting party or evening snack. Aniseed can also be added to most any basic recipe for breads, cakes, or cookies. The stomach-warming seeds will brighten up most any baked good.

All this ignores the uses to which anise leaves may be put, largely because the seeds have the tradition and the reputation. But the leaves will add a fine aromatic taste to salads and dishes such as carrots if they are finely chopped and sprinkled sparingly over the food. A tea can be made from the leaves, and it is reputed excellent for colds.

Moreover, anise is a lovely garden plant. It is easily grown, though the seed needs 70° F warmth for germination and the plant similar warmth for the fruit — "seeds" — to ripen. A cool, damp summer can prevent you from getting a crop. It is, however, a short season plant, and if you plant in May, the anise will probably clear the garden by August.

Since its long tap root makes transplanting a risky proposition, anise should be seeded wherever it is to grow. The seed should be sown in rows, rather than broadcast, to ease the task of weeding, which will be necessary in the early weeks of growth. Cover the seeds with an eighth to a quarter-inch of soil. The seeds should sprout in four to six days. Again, germination takes warmth, so don't plant too early in the year.

Anise is modest in its demands, and in fact doesn't like too much fertilization. It is best grown in annual rotations, following such herbs as basil. Mulching may not be necessary, for anise's growing season is short and it grows tall enough to keep its leaves and flowers out of the dirt.

As the seeds ripen, turning from green to gray-brown, harvest them. The best time is in the morning while the dew is still on them. As with other umbelliferous plants, clip the seed clusters into a bag or container of some kind so the seeds are not scattered and lost. The leaves can be gathered discreetly throughout the growing season.

ARBUTUS, TRAILING

Ground Laurel, Winter Pink, Mayflower
Epigaea repens, Linn.
Ericaceae

One of our choicest native wildflowers, trailing arbutus is a flat evergreen creeper with hairy stems and bright green oval leaves. In early spring it has white or pink fragrant flowers. It requires moist, humusy, acid soil. It is propagated by divisions and layers, but best plants are obtained from seeds, which should be planted as soon as ripe in a mixture of peat moss and sand and covered with a shaded pane of glass. Seedlings emerge in about four weeks.

Known as an astringent, trailing arbutus has the effect of contracting and hardening tissues and deterring secretions by the mucus membranes. It has been used generally in urinary disorders, but it is said to be particularly useful in cases of kidney stones.

It is commonly suggested that an infusion be made by adding one ounce of the leaves to a pint of boiling water and that it be taken freely several times a day.

ARBORVITAE

White Cedar
Thuja occidentalis, Linn.
Pinaceae

A native of the United States and Canada, this handsome evergreen ornamental is well known and extensively used in garden plans. Although a slow grower, it can reach 60 feet, retaining its dense, pyramidal form. It is a hardy evergreen of the pine family with dense, scale-like foliage, waxy to the touch, and fragrant. It does best in a cool location in moist, sandy loam. In a dry situation, it will suffer from both heat and cold.

The arborvitaes are used for foundation planting, as screens, and to shelter more tender plants. They are frequently selected for hedge plantings because their slow growth and compact form requires less trimming. Most nurseries stock several varieties.

The leaves and tops are used for chronic cough, fever, and gout. An infusion made of one ounce of the tender leaves to a pint of boiling water may be taken a tablespoon at a time as a diuretic, emmenagogue, and uterine stimulant. Applied externally, it is said to remove warts and fungoid growths. As a counter-irritant, it is useful for relief of muscular aches and pains. A salve for external application can be made by boiling a quantity of the leaves in lard.

Most of these uses of arborvitae were discovered by the

American Indians and passed along to the white settlers. For many years, arborvitae leaves and twigs were officially accepted drug botanicals used for stimulant, diuretic, emmenagogue, and irritant purposes. Later, these plant parts were superseded by the distilled oil in the official pharmacopoeia, the oil being used as a heart and uterine stimulant, as well as a general stimulant, irritant, and antiseptic. The oil has also been used as an aromatic ingredient in soap liniment.

Arborvitae oil may be home distilled and used as an insect repellent. The odor of the essential oil is pungent, almost overpowering. It is matched by a strong bitter taste. Taken in excess, the oil can produce unpleasant results; it was officially listed as an abortifacient and convulsant in overdose.

ARNICA

Mountain Tobacco
Arnica montana, Linn.
Compositae

Arnica is an herb noted chiefly for its medicinal properties. A popular folk remedy, it is seldom used internally, though it has stimulant and diuretic properties, since it is something of an irritant to the stomach and cases of fatal poisoning are on record. It is most used externally on wounds, bruises, and swellings.

Arnica has slightly hairy basal leaves and a long stalk, one to two feet tall with large heads of yellow ray and disk flowers. There are three to four of these daisy-like flowers in a cluster.

It is easily grown in any good garden soil. Arnica spreads rapidly by division and is very effective in the woodland garden, border, or rock garden. It can also be grown from seed, which should be sown in a cold frame in early spring. The flowers are collected and dried as they bloom, and the roots may be dried in autumn.

Arnica montana is a European native, but there are a number of species which are American natives: *A. fulgens, A. sororia, A. cordifolia* and others. These species were widely used by the American Indians who were said to apply an arnica-based salve to stiffened muscles and an arnica tincture to open wounds and gashes. Both of these uses were taught to the white settlers. The salve made by the early colonists consisted of an ounce of lard that had been heated for a brief time with an ounce of arnica flowers. The tincture was made by steeping two heaping tea-spoons of arnica flowers in a pint of boiling water, applying the preparation after it had cooled.

In addition to the uses the Indians had for the tincture, it is said to be helpful when painted on unbroken chilblains, sprains, wounds, and bruises. Repeated applications, however, may produce inflammations. The salve may be similarly used. A slightly different salve is made by mixing equal parts of vaseline or mineral oil and powdered arnica. Adding a half-ounce of the tincture to a hot water foot-bath is said to provide relief for tender feet.

The European variety remained the official drug plant until shortly after World War II, when the American species listed above joined *A. montana* in the *National Formulary*. Pharmaceutical preparations of arnica have been used orally, intravenously, and externally.

BARBERRY

Oregon Grape, Mountain Grape
Berberis aquifolium, Pursh.
Berberidaceae

An erect, quickly growing shrub, barberry tops six to ten feet in height and has holly-like leaves, fragrant yellow flowers in racemes, followed by drooping clusters of red berries. There are about 175 different species in the genus *Berberis,* and they are considered among the most useful and ornamental shrubs of good growth habit. The many evergreen varieties are not entirely hardy in the north, but will survive given a sheltered position.

All are lovely garden shrubs, many with bronze-crimson autumn leaves. Barberry is easily grown and adapted to various soils and situations. They grow well under trees, especially in moist soils. Propagation is by seeds, cuttings, suckers, and layers. Growing from seed may produce interesting results and some very beautiful forms have originated in this way. True reproductions can be obtained only by vegetative means.

The wood is a beautiful yellow color, used frequently to make crucifixes. An excellent wine and jelly is made from the fruit. Berries, boiled in soup, add flavor. The bark and roots are used for yellow dye.

Berberis aquifolium is an American native, known as Oregon grape, found usually on the mountain ranges of the Pacific coast area. The Indians there made a decoction of the roots which they took for general debility or to create an appetite. Such uses were picked up by the settlers and the use of roots as a bitter tonic was introduced into American medicine during the late 1800s and was listed in official pharmacopoeias until almost 1950. A variety known as American barberry, *B. canadensis,* had some medical use, as did the European variety, *B. vulgaris.*

While the bark of the root was the source of the official drug berberis, the berries, leaves, and bark have also been used. The leaves were chewed for acne. Some Indians used the roots and bark for ulcers, as a tonic, for heartburn, and for rheumatism. A root decoction was used for cough, kidney and liver ailments, and as a wash for cuts and bruises. Commonly, herbals list barberry as an astringent bitter, a tonic, and a stomach aid when administered in small doses. Large doses have a cathartic effect, causing watery diarrhea and abdominal pain.

For the gardener, there are a number of interesting varieties suitable for propagation.

B. repens, creeping barberry, has bluish green leaves, with three to seven leaflets and crawls low over the ground.

B. nervosa, a free suckering dwarf variety, has large lustrous leaves of 11 to 19 leaflets.

B. bealei or japonica is not as hardy as the others and grows up to 12 feet high.

They are very effective in shrubbery borders, grown in masses under trees. They are available at many nurseries.

BASIL

Sweet Basil, Common Basil, Garden Basil
Ocimum basilicum, Linn.
Labiatae

Probably nowhere else in the herb world is there a plant with such a split personality as basil (rhymes with "dazzle").

Basil, although a favorite culinary herb in today's kitchens, stands in the midst of a centuries-old controversy that, on one hand, attributes awful and evil powers to it and, on the other, holds it an object of sacred worship.

"This is the herb that all the authors are together by the ears about, and rail at one another, like lawyers," wrote the old master herbalist, Culpeper.

While acknowledging that several ancient Greek physicians "hold it not fittingly to be taken inwardly" and another "rails at it with downright Billingsgate rhetoric," Culpeper also reported that other ancient herbal masters defended its salutary effects on health.

Culpeper himself reserved judgment on basil's virtues although his writings on basil are tinged with dread. Being one who always sought to divine an herb's astrological character, Culpeper examined basil and found it to be "an herb of Mars and under the Scorpion, and therefore called basilicon, it is no marvel if it carry a virulent quality with it.

"Being applied to the place bitten by venomous beasts, or stung by a wasp or hornet, it speedily draws the poison to it. Every like draws its like," Culpeper said.

He added that a French physician "affirms of his own knowledge that an acquaintance of his, by common smelling to it, had a scorpion bred in his brain.

"Something is the matter; this herb and Rue will never grow together, no, nor near one another; and we know Rue is as great an enemy to poison as any that grows."

Culpeper typified one Western attitude toward basil. Many European herbalists said basil had an affinity for poison, that scorpions were drawn to it and even bred mysteriously by it.

Early Greek and Roman physicians believed that basil would thrive only if it were sown amid vile shouts and curses. That tradition gave rise to the contemporary French idiom *semer le basilic* — "sowing the basil" — for raving.

The Eastern sentiment toward basil, though, is one of unequivocal reverence. In its native India, the herb is hailed as a protector. Sprigs of the Indian variety, *Ocimum sanctum,* are placed on the breasts of the dead to protect them from other-worldly evil. Pots of the herb are grown in temples, and it is believed that a home built where basil flourishes will be safe from all harm.

O. sanctum, incidentally, is chiefly a decorative plant, with little medicinal or culinary use, and it is nearly impossible to cultivate well in the United States.

However, it would be unfair to say that Westerners have heaped only scorn on basil through the centuries. There are pleasant European associations with it, too.

In Italy, for example, basil is a sign of courtship. A beau can guarantee the love of his lady by offering her a sprig of basil; a pot of basil on the balcony is a tacit sign that the lady within is ready to receive her suitor.

And despite the rancorous French idom spawned by basil, the French name for it is *herbe royale* — the royal herb.

One of England's great romantics, Percy Bysshe Shelley, hailed basil as a symbol of love itself. He wrote:

> Madonna, wherefore hast thou sent to me
> Sweet basil and mignonette?
> Embleming love and health, which never yet
> In the same wreath might be.

Western ambivalence toward basil seems to be crystallized in the old herbalists' belief that it's useful both as an aphrodisiac and an abortifacient.

"It expelleth both birth and after-birth," advised the wary Culpeper. "As it helps the deficiency of Venus in one kind, so it spoils all her actions in another.

"I dare write no more of it."

Whatever basil's true mystical nature, it is one of the most widely known and used herbs in modern cookery. It exists in a bewildering profusion of varieties, the most common of which is sweet basil or garden basil.

A similar dwarf bush that rarely exceeds six inches in growth is *O. minimum.* More suitable for indoors cultivation because of its size, *O. minimum* in Tudor times was a common favor bestowed by English farmers on their guests.

O. basilicum, enshrined in the works of such diverse authors as Boccaccio, Keats, Shelley, and Drayton, is an annual that needs insect pollination for seed formation. Leaves are egg-shaped to oval, curled inward along the spine as if they had turned their backs to the world, and depending on soil fertility are yellow-green to dark green. White flowers form in whorls around the end of each stem. Seeds are very small. On contact with water, they develop a greyish gelatin around them through which sprouts appear after four or five days at 70° F. Only the leaves are used for seasoning.

Start basil from seeds each year, since the herb is very sensitive to frost. As soon as that danger has passed, seed in rows not more than a quarter-inch deep. Or, if basil is started indoors, transplant the young shoots only after the danger of overnight frost has passed. Keep them 12 inches apart.

Because basil likes a rich, weed-free, and well aerated soil, its bed should be cultivated thoroughly and treated with well-rotted manure or manure compost before planting. After sprouts appear, mulching with cocoa hulls or other suitable cover will hold soil warmth and moisture and will discourage weeds. If basil's leaves curl downward during a dry spell, sprinkle the plant with temperate water.

Basil grows best if it's harvested before the stems go to flower. The first cutting takes the main stem—a ridged and hairy growth—out from the top, although it should let stand at least one node with two young shoots intact.

The remaining growth will branch out to be ready for another trimming in two or three weeks. Harvesting can continue until the first frost, which will turn the leaves dark and halt all growth.

Basil

To prepare the leaves for storage, pinch them off at the stem and dry them in a well ventilated shady area. If they aren't dry within three days, finish the process in a low oven or leaves will turn brown and black.

Suburban gardeners might take a hint from an ancient Chinese herbal that recommends the extensive planting of basil in backyard gardens to keep down the malodors of fertilizer.

Peptic, aromatic, and carminative properties are ascribed to it, and traditionally it has been used as a treatment for mild nervous disorders such as headaches and nausea. The golden-yellow oil of basil seems to have little use except as an ingredient of perfumes.

In the kitchen, basil imparts a delicious clove-like flavor to bland vegetables and soups, salad dressings, and egg dishes. For an interesting sandwich spread, add chopped basil to creamery butter. Use basil on broiled tomatoes and even in onion dishes. The French find it indispensible in turtle soup, and also use it widely in ragouts and sauces.

Basil also can be preserved for winter use by soaking a few fresh leaves in vinegar. Fill a pint jar one-third with basil leaves, then pour white vinegar over it, close the jar and let it stand in the sun for three weeks. Or macerate a double handful of fresh leaves in a two-gallon crock of ceramic or stainless steel, then add a gallon of white or malt vinegar. Bringing the mixture to a boil will shave one week off the steeping time.

Fresh basil leaves can be boiled and eaten, spinach-style, as an aromatic vegetable dish, and basil tea is an enjoyable refreshment that some hold to be a good tonic against the effects of rheumatism.

BAY

Sweet Bay, Laurel, True Laurel
Laurus nobilis, Linn.
Lauraceae

Nothing is too much trouble to keep a bay tree alive, well, and in your herb collection, some herb lovers will tell you. A storied medicinal and culinary herb, the bay tree is probably most familiar as a plant grown for its looks, usually in big wooden tubs. It indeed is worth a special place in the landscape design.

Left in its natural form, it is a lovely evergreen aromatic shrub, with elliptical, shiny, dark green leaves. Flowers are inconspicuous, greenish-yellow in small umbels in the axils of stems, followed by dark purple berries. It can be grown as a single-trunk tree by pruning side growth and suckers as they appear. It is slow growing, and when pruned and shaped as a tub-planted showpiece, the bay seldom exceeds ten feet in height. But in the south and in Mediterranean areas the bay tree has topped 60 feet in height. The bay is, however, very frustrating to grow from seed and even using cuttings, the most popular method of propagation, will try one's patience.

"Theoretically," reports one herb grower, "it can be started from either seed or cuttings, but in our experience we have planted seeds almost every year and were never able to germinate one. For some reason they always mold." The seeds are about

Bay

the size of a pea and have a dark brown color. They are said to germinate at a temperature of 75 degrees within four weeks. The most reliable starting technique is to use a cutting, selecting a fresh, green stem. One should use standard practices, but exercise a bit more patience, since the cutting may take as long as six months to root. As a permanent growing medium, a moderate soil with good drainage will do. Bay does like the sun. (This fact makes it difficult to maintain as a houseplant; it does much better in a greenhouse, apparently requiring top sun.) It also needs protection from freezing temperatures and icy winds.

Bay leaves can be picked and dried the year round. The leaves have a delightful fragrance and are commonly used as seasoning for soups, stews, meat and fish, puddings and custards, and other foods.

The leaves are used to drive away fleas and lice, and placed in cannisters will prevent moths and bugs in flour and cereals. The tree is pest and disease resistant and will protect other plants in the area from insect pests.

The leaves and berries have been used in medicine, both having excitant and narcotic properties. The leaves were regarded as diaphoretic and, in large doses, as emetic, generally being infused and administered as a tea. The berries served many of the same purposes. An oil can be distilled from the leaves and berries and is used externally on sprains and bruises. It has also been dropped into the ears to relieve pain.

The old herbalists saw bay as a virtuous tree. "They serve both for pleasure and profit, both for ornament and use, both for honest civil uses and for physic, yea both for the sick and for the sound, both for the living and the dead," wrote Parkinson. Galen, the Greek physician, was quoted as recommending the leaves, berries and bark as a diuretic and for liver ailments. And Culpeper wrote:

> The berries are very effectual against all poisons of venomous creatures, and the sting of wasps and bees, as also against the pestilence, or other infectious diseases, and therefore put into sundry treacles for that purposes. . . . A bath of a decoction of the leaves and berries, is singular good for women to sit in that are troubled with the mother, or the diseases thereof, or the stoppings of their courses, or for the diseases of the bladder, pains in the bowels by wind and stopping of urine. A decoction likewise of equal parts of bay berries, cumin-seed, hyssop, origanum, and euphorbium, with some honey, and the head bathed therewith, doth wonderfully help distillations and rheums, and settleth the palate of the mouth into its place.

Culpeper also wrote of some of the superstitions surrounding bay. "It is a tree of the Sun, and under the celestial sign Leo, and resisteth witchcraft very potently, as also all the evils old Saturn can do the body of man. . . ." Any time protection was needed, bay was bound to turn up. Always it was a part of weddings and funerals. " 'Tis thought the King is dead: we will not stay, the Bay trees in our country are all wither'd," wrote Shakespeare in *Richard II*.

The Greeks too had a superstitious regard for bay. They dedicated the tree to Apollo, and as such viewed it as emblematic of the sun god's powers. It provided protection against evil and guarded man's social well-being. Moreover, it was related to cultural activities: music and song, poetry and drama. The Greeks also related bay with prophecies; the Delphic priestesses, oracles of Apollo, held bay leaves between their lips as they made their prophecies. It is supposed that they were drugged with bay as a part of the ritual.

Still another famous use of bay developed from the Apollonian symbol the tree was. Victors, heroes, and artistic figures were given the laurels, crowns of bay. It is suggested that this practice gave rise to the term baccalaureate, derived from *bacca-laureus* or laurel-berry, associated with academics.

"Neither witch nor devil, nor thunder or lightning will hurt a man in a place where a Bay Tree is," said Culpeper. He may have overstated the case, but protective or not, the bay tree is worth the effort it takes to have, if only for its culinary and visual appeal.

BAYBERRY

Wax Myrtle, Candleberry
Myrica cerifera, Linn.
Myricaceae

Recognized as a most useful medicinal plant, the wax myrtle is a large evergreen shrub or small tree, widely distributed in temperate regions. One or two varieties are hardy in cold climates. They are used in the garden for their attractive aromatic foliage and decorative fruits. Flowers appear in May before leaves are fully opened. The height varies from two to 12 feet, dependent on variety and location.

Bayberry needs a lime-free soil. Some species grow in poor, sandy soil, but most prefer a moist, peaty situation. Leaf mold added to the soil is also beneficial. It is propagated by seed, layers, and suckers.

Wax of the berries is used to make fragrant candles. To obtain the wax, boil the berries in water. The wax floats to the surface and can be removed when hardened.

The bark and roots are used medicinally as an astringent, tonic, and a stimulant. Leaves are aromatic and a stimulant. A tea is used as an excellent gargle for sore throats, catarrh, and jaundice. The bark is used for diarrhea and dysentery; a decoction is made and injected as an enema. This is also used as a wash or poultice for sores, boils, and carbuncles, or the powdered bark may be directly applied to wounds.

The root bark is the official medicinal part. Roots are collected in late fall, the bark is stripped off, dried, then pulverized. It should be stored in dark, sealed containers. Its astringent properties are liberated in water; alcohol is used to extract the stimulating properties.

BEDSTRAW, LADY'S

Cleaver's Vine, Maid's Hair, Cheese Rennet
Galium verum, Linn.
Rubiaceae

A good rock and bank plant, lady's bedstraw has leaves from one to two inches long in rings of six around a squarish stem, and abundant clusters of small yellow flowers. Native plants grow in moist thickets and banks of streams and flower from June to September.

Bedstraw is most easily established through the use of root divisions. Obtain a first plant, or several plants, and each spring after the plant has taken hold, divide the roots. A spreading plant, it will crowd out weeds. It does well in full sun or partial shade. It is not particular as to soil, but does require a well-drained location.

The name was derived from the practice of stuffing mattresses with the mown bedstraw. (This would suggest that the plant can be cut back sharply, and indeed it can; bedstraw may be cut before or after blooming.) Christian legend has it that it was used to provide a bed for the Christ child in the manger in Bethlehem.

In any case, the herb was used in the days of King Henry VII as a hair dye, hence the nickname maid's hair. Gerard said that "the people of Thuscane do use it to turne their milkes and cheese, which they make of sheepes and goates milke, might be the sweeter and more pleasant to taste. The people of Cheshire especially about Nantwich, where the best cheese is made, do use it in their rennet, esteeming greatly of that cheese above other made without it." Hence the nickname cheese rennet.

In America, the Indians used it as a healing agent for burns and wounds. The Elizabethan herbalists suggested bedstraw for nosebleeds, for internal bleeding, and for anointing the feet of weary travelers. There is later mention of bedstraw as a remedy for kidney stone and urinary diseases.

A relative of madder, a famous dye plant, bedstraw does yield a dye, though relatively large quantities of it are required. The leaves and stems yield a yellow color, while the roots yield a red color.

BEEBALM

Bergamot, Oswego Tea
Monarda didyma, Linn.
Labiatae

Beebalm is a part of America's history. An American perennial, it is the source of a tea which was a popular substitute for the imported variety amongst the mid-Atlantic patriots in the wake of the Boston Tea Party. That period was probably the best in beebalm's history, though it retains its mystique, thanks, perhaps, to a striking appearance and the richly American nickname, Oswego tea.

The plant features a fairly tall, very erect leafy stalk topped by a fuzzy flower cluster, brilliant scarlet in color. At least two of the plant's nicknames are derived from the showy flower. Both bees and hummingbirds are much attracted by the blossoms, hence the name beebalm. The brilliancy of the scarlet has earned the appellations scarlet monarda and red bergamot. The leaves are dark green, growing four to six inches long. It has a dense, rather shallow root system, with many runners, making root division a most reliable method of plant propagation.

Beebalm is a native of the Oswego, New York, area, and some herb books suggest it attracted the name Oswego tea from the town. It is far more likely, however, that both the town and the tea acquired the name Oswego from the Indians inhabiting the

Beebalm

area, who had it first. The Indians passed their knowledge of the plant to the newcomers, and one, a John Bartram of Philadelphia, reportedly sent seeds to England in the mid-1700s. From England, beebalm traveled to the Continent, where it is still cultivated, generally under the names gold melissa and Indian nettle.

Among the foremost growers of beebalm in the United States were the Shakers, who had a settlement near Oswego, New York. The Shakers were among America's great herbalists; they valued beebalm not only for its tea and its other culinary uses, but also for its medicinal virtues. An infusion of beebalm is good for colds and sore throats. Further values classify it as a stimulant, carminative and rubefacient. But the leaves can also be used to flavor apple jelly, fruit cups, and salads.

The entire plant emits a strong fragrance similar to citrus, but most like that of the tropical tree, orange bergamot, hence the nickname bergamot. The fragrance contributes to its value as a garden plant, and, moreover, makes it suitable for use in potpourris and other scented mixtures.

The most reliable way to start beebalm is to buy a plant. Plants from seed are very seldom uniform, since beebalm easily cross-pollinates with wild bergamot. The hills surrounding a Shaker settlement outside Pittsfield, Massachusetts, are rife with bergamot, wild and domestic, testimony to both the wandering quality of the plant and its proclivity for cross-pollination. The plant does set seeds, of course, and they are light brown ovals which germinate in about two weeks in diffused light. The viability of the seed falls sharply after the second year.

Aside from the questionable uniformity, starting beebalm from seed is vexsome because of the long-term nature of the process. It takes at least a year for the seedlings to establish themselves, so little or no harvest can be expected that first year. Transplanting beebalm, on the other hand, is very successful any time of the year except late fall. Once a planting of beebalm is established, it should be divided every third year, or, because of its rapid spreading, it is apt to die out. The roots are easily pulled apart by hand. The center roots should be thrown out, and only the outer roots replanted.

Fertility, and especially the moisture-holding capacity, of the soil should be high. A sunny location and free exposure are a further guarantee of healthful growth. Weeding is mainly hand labor, since the shallow spreading of beebalm makes hoeing or cultivation impossible. Spacing of clumps should have a minimum distance of two feet. In late fall the entire area with beebalm ought to receive a one inch covering of compost which acts as a winter protection and source of nutrients for the following year.

All herbs for tea can be used fresh and cut freely as needed, and beebalm is no exception. But beebalm needs a severe pruning, as much as to within an inch of the ground, as soon as the lower leaves show signs of yellowing. The flowers will have barely formed at this stage. There are other harvesting variations. One can increase the size of the second year bloom by sharply cutting back the plant before it blooms in its first year. Cutting back the stalk immediately after it blooms will generally promote a second, early autumn bloom. And one can harvest twice: once just before the plant flowers and again after it flowers; the teas made from the two harvests will differ, and some growers sell the two harvests as two different teas.

The best quality tea material is achieved if the leaves are stripped off the square, hollow stems and dried in warm shade within two or three days. A longer drying period might discolor the leaves, producing an inferior type product. When necessary, the leaves should be finished off with artificial heat.

BIRCH

Betula, various species
Betulaceae

Various species of birch can be used effectively in the garden landscape plan. They will add a distinctive charm in the dormant season with their delicate branches and conspicuous barks. They blend well into a naturalistic or woodland type of planting, or near a rocky pool where the autumn gold of the leaves reflects in the water.

Young birches have dark bark and do not develop the characteristic color until they are several years old. The white birch grows to 60 feet, has drooping branches and white bark that peels easily. The branches produce catkins containing both male and female flowers.

Sweet or cherry birch is wide branching with a high head, making good shade but allowing for sun and air underneath. The bark is dark, clean and smooth, similar to cherry.

Several varieties have orange or reddish bark, and a very hardy dwarf species lies flat against the ground. A very slow grower, it is suitable for cool rockery.

Most birches thrive in moist, sandy loam. They are propagated by seed sown or stratified in sandy soil, also by green wood cuttings under glass.

Beer is often made from the sap of sweet birch. A type of oil of wintergreen is distilled from the inner bark and twigs. It is also used for remedies to purify the blood, rheumatism, and to expel worms. Applied externally it is beneficial for boils and sores.

Bark and stems of European or white birch is bitter and astringent. These are distilled into birch tar oil which was used to prepare Russian leather, as an insect repellent, and as an ointment. Juice extracted from the leaves was used for kidney and bladder stones and as a mouth wash. Birches improve soil, restore fertility to barren soil, and planted near the compost area, encourage fermentation. Leaves should be added to the compost.

BLOODROOT

Puccoon, Indian Plant, Red Root
Sanguinaria canadensis, Linn.
Papaveraceae

A smooth perennial of the poppy family, bloodroot grows throughout the United States in rich, moist, shaded woods and thickets and is easily transplanted into the wild garden. It may be propagated by seed or division. Each bud of the prominent rootstalk produces a single large, lobed, leaf, about six inches high. It has white flowers with golden centers and blooms from April to June.

One of the earliest reported uses of bloodroot, or puccoon, as it was then commonly known, was as a dye. John Smith reported in 1612 that "Pocones is a small roote that groweth in the mountaines, which being dryed and beate in powder turneth red: and this they use for swellings, aches, annointing their joints, painting their heads and garments . . . and at night where his lodging is appointed, they set a woman fresh painted red with Pocones and oile, to be his bedfellow."

In medicine, bloodroot has been used as a stimulant, expectorant, emetic, tonic, and alterative. Although all parts of the plant have been used, the rhizome and roots were the official drug portion. These should be collected in the early spring, carefully dried, then ground into a powder. In a dose of one-twentieth of a grain (a grain is 0.002083 ounces), bloodroot is a gastric and intestinal stimulant. In a slightly larger, one-twelfth of a grain dose, it is an expectorant, reportedly having been used with some success in cases of bleeding lungs, pneumonia, chronic bronchitis, whooping cough, croup, colds, sore throat, and like ailments. Doses any larger will produce emetic effects.

One of the early experiments with bloodroot as an emetic was performed in 1803 by William Downey, who was studying medicine at the University of Pennsylvania. Downey reported that he dissolved powdered root in water and served eight grains of the preparation to an aid who had eaten breakfast four hours before. "In fifteen minutes a slight nausea came on with a burning at the stomach," Downey reported; "forty, he complained of a head-ach [sic], the nausea, at intervals, much more violent; sixty, he was vomited twice, the motions were pretty strong." The cautions surrounding care in doses is clear.

The drug was usually administered in several-drop dosages of a tincture. One Indian folk medicine guide recommended a tincture made by filling a pint bottle half-full with finely mashed root and adding equal parts of alcohol and water until full. The recommended dosage ranged from one to seven drops every three to four hours.

Bloodroot also had external medicinal use. It was reported effective in cases of ringworm, running sores, and other wounds. A recommended ointment was made by mixing an ounce of the powdered root in three ounces of lard, bringing the mixture to a boil, simmering briefly, then straining.

BLUE FLAG

Poison Flag, Flag Lily
Iris versicolor, Linn.
Iridaceae

Blue flag was among the most popular Indian remedies. It is a native American, both beautiful and potentially poisonous.

It is an iris similar in foliage appearance to the sweet flag, *Acorus calamus*. Unfortunately for some, it has quite different properties and if mistakenly used internally as one might sweet flag, the results can be disastrous. Blue flag grows erect, reaching three feet in height, and has narrow, sword-shaped leaves and, from May through July, violet blue flowers streaked with yellow, green, and white. It prefers wet, swampy locations and is found in such spots from Canada to Florida and west to Arkansas.

The flowers do yield a blue infusion which can substitute for litmus paper in testing for acids and alkalies, but it is the root which has been most widely used. When fresh, the root has a slight odor and a pungent, acrid, and nauseous taste, a natural warning of the actively poisonous nature of the fresh root. Although the Indians had some uses for the fresh root, it was usually collected in autumn and dried.

Listed throughout most of the nineteenth century in official pharmacopoeias, blue flag was recognized for its qualities as a cathartic, emetic, and diuretic. It has also seen use as an alterative and purgative. In folk medicine, it has been used for skin diseases, liver ailments, blood impurities, syphilis, and rheumatism.

A simple home medicine may be made by infusing a teaspoonful of the dried and powdered root in a pint of boiling water. The infusion should be taken cold in two or three tablespoon doses six times daily. An alcoholic tincture is made by dissolving an ounce of the root powder in a pint of alcohol. Recommended dosages of the tincture range from ten to twenty-five drops in a half-cup of water, three times daily.

BONESET

Thoroughwort, Feverwort, Indian Sage
Eupatorium perfoliatum, Linn.
Compositae

Boneset was one of early America's foremost medical plants, a popular panacea of extraordinary powers. Today, it is chiefly regarded as a weed with an interesting past.

An American variety of the extensive *Eupatorium* genus, boneset was first used by the Indians, who passed along their high esteem for the plant to the white settlers. It was in wide popular use for perhaps a century before earning a mention in the medical literature. Once recognized, however, the plant moved to the forefront, being mentioned in virtually every work on

American materia medica produced during the eighteenth and nineteenth centuries. In addition, it was recognized as an official drug plant in the pharmacopoeias for 130 years.

The botanical name, *Eupatorium,* was selected to connote Mithridates Eupator, a king of Pontus about 115 B.C., who supposedly discovered an antidote to poison among the species of this particular genus. When taken captive by his enemies, he preferred death to captivity, but had to have a slave stab him, for he had so thoroughly fortified himself against poisoning. The genus includes some 400 species, quite a number of which are reputed to have medicinal virtues. Boneset and Joe-pye weed are among the latter species.

Boneset was never used as an antidote to poison, but it was a very popular antidote for colds and fevers. The American Indians were the first to so use it. The Iroquois and the Mohegans used it for colds and fever, while the Menominees used it for fevers. The Alabamas used it for the relief of stomach-aches, and the Creeks for general body pain. By the time Dr. Benjamin Barton wrote in his *Materia Medica of the United States* that "this medicine is used by our Indians in intermittent fevers," it was in common use and was so thoroughly associated with the Indians that it was known as Indian sage.

Throughout the nineteenth century, boneset remained a common remedy for fevers, particularly the variety called breakbone fevers. The name boneset is derived for the popular conception of the plant's efficacy in such cases. During the Civil War, boneset was recommended as a febrifuge medicine for the Confederate troops. A boneset infusion, said one doctor, "drank hot during the cold stage of fever, and cold as a tonic and antiperiodic, is thought by many physicians to be even superior to the Dogwood, Willow, or Poplar, as a substitute for quinine. It is quite sufficient in the management of malarial fever that will prevail among our troops during the summer, and if it does not supply entirely the place of quinine, will certainly lessen the need for its use."

A contemporary herbal reports boneset to be a tonic stimulant, which promotes digestion and strengthens and restores "the tone of the system." It lists it as a sudorific, alterative, antiseptic, cathartic, emetic, febrifuge, corroborant, diuretic, astringent, and deobstruent. Boneset was said to be used for rheumatism, typhoid fever, pneumonia, catarrh, dropsy, flu, dyspepsia, jaundice, and, of course, colds and fevers.

The portions of the plants used were the leaves and flowers. Commonly an infusion is made by combining an ounce of the dried herb with a pint of boiling water and administered in wineglassful doses. One Indian folk medicine guide recommended tablespoon doses of the cold tea be given every three or four hours as a tonic, and doses of two to three ounces of the hot tea for colds and fevers. Larger doses produce an emetic effect. A salve for external application may be made by combining equal parts of the powdered herb and vaseline.

The plant is usually found in swamps, marshes, and other low, wet spots near streams throughout the eastern half of America, north to Canada, south to Florida, and west to Texas and Nebraska. An erect plant, it grows to three or four feet, topped by clusters of small white tubular flowers, which usually appear from July through September. The leaves are somewhat hairy and grow opposite each other in such a way that opposites appear to be joined and perforated by the stem. It is this unique arrangement that prompted the species name *perfoliatum*.

BORAGE

Borago officinalis, Linn.

Boraginaceae

Borage is such a cheerful plant to have in your garden or potted by a sunny window that it isn't surprising to learn that it was prescribed four hundred years ago for melancholy. It is, moreover, inextricably aligned with courage in the minds of herbalists everywhere, to the point that it is the inevitable introduction to the herb. There is no break with tradition here.

In the garden, borage is almost constantly in bloom, almost constantly surrounded by interested bees, who alone can pollinate it, hence the moniker "bee bread." It grows quite rapidly, spreading over a fairly broad area, and self-seeding proficiently.

It is classified as a hardy annual. It grows about 12 to 18 inches tall, but it isn't an erect plant, and a single healthy plant will spread over a four-square-foot area, covering it with hairy stems and leaves, brightening it with strikingly blue star-shaped flowers. Occasionally, a borage plant will bear both blue and pink flowers; the capacity to bear more than one color of flower at a time is characteristic of plants of the Boraginaceae family, of which borage is, of course, the namesake.

There is some controversy over the source of the borage name. Some say the Latin *Borago* is a corruption of *corago,* from *cor,* the heart, and *ago,* I bring, an obvious reference to the long-standing association between the plant and the effect. Others point out that a connection is apparent between the plant's name, its hairy appearance, and the low Latin term for a flock of wool, *burra,* and its derivatives, *borra* (Italian) and *bourra* (French), both of which mean much the same thing. Still a third opinion suggested that a derivation stems from the apparent connection between the Celtic term, *barrach,* which means "a man of courage," and the herb's character. The range of speculation is interesting, if inconclusive.

Not in contention is the history of the plant as a source of emotional strength and courage. The Welsh named it *Llanwenlys* or herb of gladness. Sir Francis Bacon noted that "the leaf of Burrage hath an excellent spirit to repress the fuliginous vapour of dusky melancholie."

Even earlier writers viewed borage in the same general terms. Dioscorides declared borage to be the nepenthe of Homer, the legendary tonic which brought absolute forgetfulness; ". . . if wife and children, father and mother, brother and sister, and all thy dearest friends shouldst die before thy face, thou couldst not grieve, or shed a tear for them." Pliny echoed Dioscorides' assertion, and it has been re-echoed throughout herbal literature. John Gerard recorded in his herbal centuries later:

> Pliny calls it Euphrosinum, because it maketh a man merry and joyfull: which thing also the old verse concerning Borage doth testifie:
>
> | *Ego Borago* | I, Borage |
> | *Gaudia semper ago.* | Bring alwaies courage. |
>
> Those of our time do use the flowers in sallads to exhilerate and

Borage

make the mind glad. There be also many things made of these used everywhere for the comfort of the heart, for the driving away of sorrow and increasing the joy of the mind, . . . The leaves and floures of Borage put into wine make men and women glad and merry and drive away all sadnesse, dulnesse and melancholy, as Dioscorides and Pliny affirme. Syrup made of the floures of Borage comforteth the heart, purgeth melancholy and quieteth the phrenticke and lunaticke person. The leaves eaten raw ingender good bloud, especially in those that have been lately sicke.

Borage is believed to have originated in Aleppo, a city in northwestern Syria. An independent plant, it spread throughout Europe, and it remains a fairly common wild plant on the Continent. And it remains, too, a difficult plant to keep strictly to the garden.

As noted by Gerard, borage is a salad herb and was widely cultivated as a potherb. The young leaves are excellent in salads, as the taste of borage is suggestive of cucumbers. The leaves may also be cooked and served as one would spinach. The leaves should be boiled with only a little water, then chopped finely and served with butter. The flowers are edible, as Gerard said, and their brilliant color makes them particularly decorative in the salad bowl. The flowers are oftimes served candied. Dip them in egg white, then sugar, and dry.

One of the oldest uses of borage blossoms is as a flavor-enhancing decoration in beverages. The Greeks and Romans floated the blossoms in their wine cups, but you can add them to cider, punch, lemonade, or other beverages. The leaves can be used to make their own beverage. Steeped in boiling water, borage makes a tea that stimulates the circulation and soothes the throat. The tea may be served hot or cold.

Culpeper contended in his day that borage was chiefly used fresh, "yet the ashes thereof boiled in mead or honied water, is available against the inflammations and ulcers in the mouth or throat, to gargle it therewith . . ." ". . . the dried herb is never used, but the green," he maintained. Today, though, borage is dried, chiefly for use in making tea. The leaves gathered for this purpose must be selected carefully, after the dew is off the plants, then chopped and dried in an even heat. The dried herb must be stored in tightly sealed containers, for it absorbs moisture readily.

While Culpeper and other early herbalists emphasized the cheering, stimulating effects of borage, it is also listed in herbals as a diuretic, demulcent, and emollient. Because of saline constituents, borage is an effective diuretic and has been used to carry off feverish catarrhs. A drink suggested for fever sufferers is made by pouring a pint of boiling water over a sliced lemon and a half-dozen sprigs of borage. The brew is cooled, strained, and served freely. Another suggested infusion is made of an ounce of leaves to a pint of boiling water. This tea is given in wineglassful doses. Externally, a poultice of borage leaves has been applied to inflamed swellings.

The gardener will find borage quite easy to cultivate. If he or she has strawberries, the borage plant will make an excellent companion. The two plants are said to be mutually beneficial, if the borage is kept to a relatively small proportion. Borage is also said to strengthen the resistance to insects and disease of any plants neighboring it.

Borage can be started from seed either indoors or in the garden. Whether seeded directly or transplanted, the plant should be given sufficient garden space to develop properly. It should be about two feet from any neighbors. Once established, borage will self-seed, and offspring may well sprout around the parent plant before the growing season is through. Although borage is relatively hardy, it shouldn't be seeded or set outdoors until the danger of frost is past.

Borage requires a fairly rich soil. A manure compost is the best fertilizer. The soil should be loose, well aerated, and hoed regularly to eliminate weedy competition. A mulch is a good idea, for borage likes a moist environment.

Borage is a nice plant to maintain in an indoor garden. It will easily survive a pot-bound existence, given sufficient root space, a fertile potting medium, sunlight, and moisture. It has been said that a garden without borage is like a heart without courage. The same might be true for your windowsill. But if nothing else, the potted borage will cheer your home and put a little spark in your diet.

BROOM

Scotch Broom
Cytisus scoparius, Linn.
Leguminosae

This attractive, evergreen shrub of the pea family, a native of Europe, Asia, and Africa, has become naturalized in some parts of North America. It has bright green, almost leafless stems with yellow pea-like flowers in June. The height ranges from three to ten feet and can be trimmed back after flowering for a more compact shape.

Broom requires full exposure to sun and wind, prefers poor soil with perfect drainage. It is useful for planting on dry, gravelly banks and can also be used in borders, background plantings, or standing alone as an attractive point-of-interest shrub. The bright green stems and yellow flowers make a good display.

Small plants are easier to establish than large ones. They are easily started and grow quickly from seed, but may be propagated by cuttings or layers. There are several species of *Cytisus*, some grown as greenhouse plants.

Fresh green tops are picked just before flowering. It contains an active principal — sparteine sulphate, which is used as a cardiac depressant to quiet an overactive heart. The plant is rich in potash and has been used for many ailments including dropsy, toothache, problems of spleen, kidneys, and bladder. It makes a good ointment for lice or vermin.

Like nasturtium, it may be used as a bait plant for aphids, attracting them away from other plants, yet seemingly suffering no ill effects from their presence. One of the legumes, it also increases available nitrogen in soil, benefiting plants growing around it, and is a collector of calcium.

BUGLE

Ajuga, various species
Labiatae

A low, creeping or spreading perennial, *Ajuga* blooms generally in May and June and again in fall. It is rather coarse, has opposite oblong leaves on squarish stems with flowers in dense whorls in terminal spikes.

It is easily grown in ordinary garden soil, sun or shade, and can be propagated by seed and division. It is a popular ground cover, for edgings, and in rock gardens. Several popular varieties may be found in most nurseries.

Ajuga genevensis (Geneva bugle) is a taller species with light green, oval, toothed leaves and blue flowers. It is used as a ground cover in shady places.

A. reptans (common bugle) is a prostrate variety whose stems root as they creep. The flowers are pale blue or purplish. Other species include: *A. reptans* var. *atropurpurea* (bronze ajuga) which has blue flowers and bronze leaves; var. *multicolor* with red, brown, and yellow foliage; var. *rubra*, which has dark purple foliage with pink flowers; and var. *varigata* with leaves splotched and bordered with cream and blue flowers.

A. pyramidalis has blue flowers, slightly larger than others, stays neat and small, and is less likely to spread.

This herb has several medicinal applications. The bruised leaves may be applied as a poultice for cuts and wounds or bruises. It is also made into an ointment. Decoction of leaves and flowers is used for cough remedy and also for "hangovers." It is recognized as a bitter, astringent, and aromatic.

BURDOCK

Great Burdock, Burrs, Beggar's Buttons
Arctium lappa, Linn.
Compositae

Burdock is a weed quite popular with wild food foragers and has a notable past as a medicinal plant. It is a tall, large-leaved plant commonly found in waste places, and it is well-known for its autumnal propensity for attaching burrs to all who brush by. It is certainly a plant to know, but few find it really worth cultivating.

A European native, burdock was naturalized in this country with the first foreign travellers. It was already known and widely used in the Old World. Parkinson reported it a helpful remedy for venomous bites. Culpeper said the leaves were "cooling and moderately drying, whereby good for old ulcers and sores." The seed, he continued, "being drunk in wine 40 days together doth wonderfully help the sciatica. . . . The root may be preserved with sugar for consumption, stone, and the lax. The seed is much commended to break the stone." Such commendations notwithstanding, burdock was never accorded listing in the European pharmacopoeias of the seventeenth and eighteenth centuries.

The white settler in America, however, passed their knowledge of its usefulness to the Indians. And the plant eventually did appear in American pharmacopoeias, being listed for use as a diuretic and diaphoretic.

Most herbals list those effects, add alterative, and report that burdock is one of the best blood purifiers.

The dried root is the most commonly used plant part, though the leaves and seeds (properly called the fruits) are also useful medicinally. The dried root must be dug in the autumn of the plant's first year; a plant without a flower stalk is such a plant.

Generally, the roots are difficult to excavate, a post-hole digger or slender spade being helpful in the task. The roots may extend twelve inches or more and be an inch in diameter, about a quarter of which is usually a grey-brown bark with a remainder being the whitish pith. The leaves should be collected when they are still young, the seeds as they ripen.

The common prescription is a decoction of the dried root. Add an ounce of the root to a pint and a half of water, boil down to a pint, and take in wineglassful doses three or four times daily. This same decoction has been used as a wash for ulcers and scaly skin disorders. In any case, the use of the decoction must be continued over a relatively long time for it to be effectual.

An infusion of the leaves is said to be useful as a stomachic. The leaves have also been used as a poultice for bruises, swellings, and tumors. A tincture of the seeds is of service as a remedy for certain skin diseases.

The wild food forager relishes burdock for its root particularly, but also for its leaves and stem. The Japanese, who cultivate burdock to some extent, consider it a source of strength and endurance, and something of an aphrodisiac as well. The first-year roots should be peeled, sliced crosswise, cooked for about thirty minutes in water to which a bit of soda has been added, then cooked another ten minutes or so in a very little water. For the best eating, the roots should be gathered in June or early July. The flower stalks should be gathered just as the flowers are forming. These should be carefully peeled of the bitter rind and cooked as you would the roots, using two waters with a bit of soda in the first. The young leaves so cooked are a serviceable green vegetable.

A beverage may be made of fresh burdock roots. Combine a quart each of burdock, wild sarsaparilla, and spikenard roots, cleaned, sliced lengthwise, and cut in half, and boil them in six quarts of water. Boil until but two quarts remain, then cool and strain the fluid. Add a pint of molasses or a half-pound of sugar and sufficient yeast to generate fermentation. The bitters may be drunk as soon as fermentation begins, but it is best to wait three or four more days. The beverage is said to be "a good article for cleansing and purifying the blood."

Burdock is a quick-growing biennial with large, wavy, egg-shaped leaves, and, in its second year, with globular purple (and very occasionally white) flowers. The flowers appear on a stalk which reaches three and sometimes four feet in height. They are followed by the burs, which have been a distinguishing characteristic of the plant throughout its history. Its botanical name *Arctium lappa* is derived from the Greek, *arktos*, for "a bear," an allusion to the roughness of the burs, and from a word meaning "to seize." The burs have prompted a number of nicknames over the years and earned a place in the literature of William Shakespeare. "How full of briers is this working-day world!" exclaims Rosalind in *As You Like It*. And Celia responds: "They are but burs, cousin, thrown upon thee in holiday foolery. If we walk not in the trodden paths, our very petticoats will catch them." And so they will even today.

CAJEPUT

Punk Tree, White Tea Tree
Melaleuca leucadendra, Linn.
Myrtaceae

Australian natives of the myrtle family (related to bottle-brush bush), cajeput are grown in warmer parts of this country as lawn and street trees. Small, leathery leaves, dense spikes or heads of conspicuous flowers in colors from white to red, and its pleasing growth habit makes it a very ornamental landscape tree. The crooked trunk will often recline, or twist along the ground before finally assuming an upright position. They are able to withstand drought, salt-water, and wind and used frequently in areas near the seashore. Thick, spongy bark, useful for many purposes, peels in thin layers.

It is propagated by cuttings of ripened wood and from seed. It will self-seed occasionally, and seedlings will grow into nice sized trees within a few years.

Oil distilled from fresh leaves and twigs (oil cajeput) is a stimulant, antispasmodic and diaphoretic, highly esteemed for internal and external pain, as a lotion for rheumatism, neuralgia, sprains, bruises, and for toothache.

It is insect resistant and seems to have a protective influence on the plants growing around it.

CALAMUS

Sweet Flag, Sweet Sedge
Acorus calamus, Linn.
Araceae

Calamus resembles the cattail or the iris, but it is allied actually to the jack-in-the-pulpit and skunk cabbage. The sword-shaped leaves are sheathed about the stalk at their base, and arise erect, though falling at the ends, being about three feet long. A flower stalk projects at a slight angle from the axils of the outer leaves. The entire plant has a spicy, lemon fragrance.

Marshes, low meadows, and the waterside are the favorite habitat of calamus. It is easily grown in any spot, so long as the moisture is abundant. The clumps of plants or the rhizome, or rootstock, is divided in early spring or autumn, and the divisions are set about a foot apart and covered well.

The aroma of the plant is the basis for its long history in herb lore. The foliage was widely used as a strewing herb, as the aroma released under the bruising footstep could mask that of unwashed bodies. The lower stem and rhizome can be dried, cut into pieces, and used to scent drawers, closets, and chests.

The rhizome is collected in the early spring or late autumn of its second or third year, dried, and powdered. The scent is sweetly aromatic, but the taste is somewhat bitter and quite pungent. The dried root powder is infused one ounce to a pint of water, then taken in wineglass doses for fevers and dyspepsia. The dried root may be chewed to ease digestion and to clear the voice. In cooking, the calamus root is sometimes used as a substitute for ginger, cinnamon, or nutmeg because of its spicy nature. Commercially, the rhizome has found its way into hair and tooth powders and beverages, including beer, bitters, tonics, liqueurs, and cordials.

CALENDULA
Pot Marigold, Marigold
Calendula officinalis, Linn.
Compositae

Originally from southern Europe, the calendula or pot marigold is a hardy annual plant of the Compositae family. It has light greenish yellow leaves and forms flowers in different shades of yellow and orange. The history of this herb is filled with poetry and symbolism, most of which has been in reaction to and appreciation of an unusual behavior characteristic which has fascinated poets and prose writers alike. At dawn, the moist blossom opens and rises with the sun, creating the poetic image of the awakening of a "weeping" flower. Its golden orange color brightens the day until sunset when the early-to-bed marigold closes for the evening. The plant has become immortal, because of this sensitivity to the sun.

Of all the allusions made to the marigold in literature, the most beautiful may be John Keats' poem "I stood tiptoe upon a little hill" (London 1817):

> Open fresh your round of starry folds,
> Ye ardent marigolds!
> Dry up the moisture from your golden lids,
> For great Apollo bids
> That in these days your praises should be sung
> On many harps which he has lately strung;
> And when again your dewiness he kisses
> Tell him I have you in my world of blisses!
> So haply when I rove in some far vale
> His mighty voice may come upon gale.

It was the Romans who recorded that the marigold was usually in bloom on the first day, or *calends,* of every month. From this observation, the Latin generic name *Calendula* and the common Italian name *fiore d'ogni* were given to the herb.

Calendula

Because of the flower's sensitivity to the sun, it was also appropriate in some writings and reports to call the plant *solsequia* or *solis sponsa*. Nevertheless, the Anglo Saxons perceived the lovely golden plant from another perspective and labeled it *merso-meargealla,* or marsh marigold, the obvious precursor of its familiar name today. In medieval England, a popular religious legend described the Virgin as being accustomed to wearing golden blossoms which the monks of the period decided should be named in her honor; from that association of the golden herb with the Virgin Mary, old poets began calling the herb "Mary Gowles" and "Mary Golde." Years later in Shakespeare's *Cymbeline,* the marigold flowers were referred to as the "winking Marybuds."

The Latin specific name *officinalis* was the standard term applied to herbs with official medicinal qualities. According to Fuller, the medicinal powers of the marigold were familiar to all: "We all know the many and sovereign virtues in your leaves, the Herbe Generalle in all pottage," (Antheologie, 1655). In *Maison*

Rustique, or the Countrie Farme (1699), Stevens listed some of the body pains and problems which marigold was considered effective in healing: headache, jaundice, red eyes, toothache, and ague.

The seventeenth century herbalist, Culpeper, had some other suggested uses for the marigold:

> They strengthen the heart exceedingly, and are very expulsive, and a little less effectual in the smallpox and measles than saffron. The juice of Marigold leaves mixed with vinegar, and any hot swelling bathed with it, instantly gives ease, and assuages it. The flowers, either green or dried, are much used in possets, broths, and drink, as a comforter of the heart and spirits, and to expel any malignant or pestilential quality which might annoy them.

To provide aid to an ailing heart or any kind of fever, Culpeper recommended placing a "plaister" made from a mixture of powdered dried flowers and lard, turpentine, and rosin on the breast of the ailing. From Stevens, we get another formula, this time using marigold flowers for a cure of plague or pestilence; he writes that a "conserve made of the flowers and sugar, taken in the morning fasting, cureth the trembling of the harte, and is also given in the time of plague or pestilence." Generally only the deep-orange marigold was expected to fulfill any healing obligations.

These early herbalists had in accordance with certain religious and astrological principles, a very specific and mystifying set of instructions for picking the beautiful marigold flower. To preserve the virtue of the herb, which Culpeper said was commanded by Leo, one famous herbalist recorded that it must be gathered only when the moon is in the sign of the Virgin; picking it during the rise of Jupiter will result in its loss of all virtue. The person assigned to the gathering of the plant must be free of deadly sin and must remember to say three *Pater Nosters* and three *Aves*. Once gathered and worn by someone, the marigold plant can give that person the power to perceive and recognize anyone who has robbed him or her. Moreover, it will strengthen the eyes of anyone who so much as looks at it.

In more modern times, calendula has been used primarily as a local remedy with a stimulant and diaphoretic effect. Chinese herbals list the common marigold as a remedy for persistent bleeding piles. It can provide local relief and prevent suppuration when taken internally or applied externally and has been known to be helpful in the treatment of chronic ulcer and varicose veins. During the American Civil War and the First World War, the marigold flowers were used as a hemostatic. Even today calendula ointment serves as a dressing for small wounds. For relief from the pain of a wasp or bee sting, one might try rubbing a marigold flower on the affected part. Sprains and cuts can be much less painful if a lotion made from the marigold flowers is applied to them. When a fever attacks, an infusion of freshly gathered blossoms will encourage perspiration and expel any collected mucus or suppuration. The stinging effect of the plant has also been proven to be effective in removing warts.

The culinary uses of the marigold herb are primarily in salads and dried in broths and soups. The taste of the leaves is at first pasty and sweet and then quite salty. The strong-tasting juice which can be extracted from the leaves has been effective as a remedy for constipation. Although Gerard once said, "No broth is well made without dried marigold blossom in cooking" when he wrote in his essay on "Christ's Hospital" (1823) about "boiled beef on Thursday, with detestable marigold petals floating in the pail to poison the broth."

The seeds of the marigold plant are unusual in shape and formation. Light yellow in color with at least a half dozen shapes ranging from a winged seed to a curled seed, the calendula seed holds its germination for only a year; thus, fresh seeds are needed for each planting.

Sometime in April or May, when the sun is shining, the seeds can be planted. The soil temperature should be at least 60°F for the seeds to germinate well. Although the plants need to be kept free of weeds and thinned out to nine or ten inches apart, there is not much more cultivation necessary in the care of marigolds. The different varieties offered by seedsmen usually represent various forms of double or single flower plants with color ranging from yellow to deep orange, the latter color marigold being excellent for herb teas. If the soil is fairly rich, the flowers will begin to appear anytime from June to August. If you are interested in retaining a healthy flowering until early October, the phosphate content of your soil will be important. Although Calendula may survive the first frost, the harder frost of 25° F will damage it.

As far as harvesting is concerned, most people are interested in the marigold flower which on sunny days can be pinched off the stem. Each petal of the harvested flower head is pulled out by hand, leaving the green center of the flower. Because the only part of this plant generally used in food and medicine is the flower petal, it is considered to be a very expensive herb. In order to produce a cheaper quality medicinal or cooking herb, some growers harvest the flower head and dry the whole head. After shredding and grinding it, they offer the petals mixed with the green flower center which is of course an impure product. The petals should be dried in the shade on paper rather than on screens, since once they are dried they have a tendency to hold tight to the screen, making it difficult to remove them. They should also be kept from touching one another, since this can lead to discoloration. Because the marigold petals are so hydroscopic, they should be stored in a moisture-proof container to preserve color and flavor ordinarily lost in humid conditions.

CAMOMILE, ROMAN
Anthemis nobilis, Linn.

CAMOMILE, GERMAN
Matricaria chamomilla, Linn.
Compositae

Camomile is an herb with a split personality, chiefly because it is really two plants though most people think of it as a single plant. The trouble is that German camomile and Roman camomile are two distinct plants with similar characteristics, but people familiar with one tend to think of it as the only camomile. Sometimes they simply remain ignorant of the other plant; other times they are aware of it but choose to ignore it; and still other times they resort to the ploy of denigrating the other plant, attempting to disprove its legitimacy as a camomile. (Variations of spelling add to the confusion; camomile is often spelled chamomile, but either spelling is correct.)

The camomiles are perhaps best known for their apple-like fragrance and flavor, qualities which always come as a surprise to the uninitiated, for neither camomile has any visual resemblance to an apple or apple tree. The apple-like qualities, however, have been strong enough throughout man's acquaintance to have earned the plants the name camomile, which is derived from the Greek *kamai* (on the ground) and *melon* (apple) for ground apple.

Although the plants are generically different, their common characteristics are sufficient to confuse them in the minds of many. Both have daisy-like blossoms, the apple-like fragrance, and foliage that could be characterized as feathery. Moreover, the genus *Matricaria* is not as clearcut as some botanists would like it to be, being difficult to distinguish from *Anthemis* and *Chrysanthemum,* and perhaps from *Pyrethrum.* Nevertheless, there are some distinguishing characteristics.

Anthemis nobilis is a low-growing perennial, seldom topping more than nine inches in height. It has finely divided leaves. The flowers have a large, solid central disk of a deep yellow color and creamy rays. The variety of best medicinal value has double flowers, but there is a variety with single flowers. The entire herb is strongly scented.

Matricaria chamomilla is an annual with fine-cut foliage (though somewhat more coarse than *A. nobilis)* and a single daisy-like flower with a yellow, hollow disk and white rays. The flowers are smaller than those of *A. nobilis* and less strongly scented. The plant is erect, growing two to three feet tall. The plant has medicinal properties similar to those of *A. nobilis,* but as in the matter of scent, they are of a lesser quality.

The most obvious difference between the two plants on paper, then, is that one is an annual, the other a perennial. Such information isn't particularly useful for making identifications, however. Perhaps the most useful and pronounced distinction is the stature: *A. nobilis* is nearly prostrate, while *M. chamomilla* is erect. The flower sizes are different, and the flower structure is different, one having a solid disk, the other a hollow disk.

These differences haven't been sufficient to prevent some confuting of the two plants throughout history. In general, the Germanic peoples have considered *M. chamomilla* to be *the* camomile, hence the name German camomile, while the English-speaking peoples have considered *A. nobilis* to be *the* camomile. But the uses, at least, are so similar that confusion is bound to develop when camomile is spoken of.

Of course, the dogmatism of some herbalists contributes further to the confusion and leads to denigration. In English herbals, *M. chamomilla* is oftimes labelled a weed, but the name-calling cuts both ways. A gardening book of Germanic orientation notes, for example, "The more commonly found Camomile called Mayweed and others of the genus *Anthemis* often become obnoxious weeds; they are not cultivated as a rule."

The truth of the matter is that both plants are cultivated, but both escape cultivation at every opportunity and are occasionally found in the wild and the untended places of Europe and the United States. As to which plant is the true camomile, one might speculate that *A. nobilis* is the true camomile and that Linnaeus, who classified and named both plants, chose the specific name *chamomilla* for German camomile simply because it closely resembled the plant commonly called camomile, *A. nobilis*.

Both German and Roman camomiles have been held in considerable esteem as medicinal herbs. Both are particularly useful as tonics, being taken in the form of an infusion of the blossoms. The usual infusion is made of a half to a full ounce of the dried blossoms and a pint of boiling water.

Roman camomile is said to have, in addition to its tonic effect, stomachic, anodyne, and antispasmodic properties. The plant has also been used in instances where a diuretic or diaphoretic effect was desired. An infusion of an ounce of the blossoms to a pint of boiling water is said to have a "wonderfully soothing, sedative, and absolutely harmless effect," and has been used to calm the nerves, remedy delirium tremens, and prevent nightmares.

Equal amounts of camomile flowers and poppy-heads were combined and crushed to produce a poultice or fomentation for external swellings, inflammations, and the like. Muslin bags were filled with the flowers, boiled, then applied to the painful spot. Infusing the two kinds of flowers—a half-ounce of each to a pint of boiling water—yields a liquid that has been used as a facial wash to sooth neuralgia and toothaches.

Roman camomile was held in esteem throughout history for these medicinal qualities. The Egyptians consecrated it to their gods. The Romans didn't go that far, but they did make extensive use of it for its medicinal properties. Throughout the Middle Ages, it was so widely used that when, as civilization moved into a new age, Culpeper began his record of plant medicines, he didn't bother to describe the plant, saying, "it is so well known every where that it is but lost time and labour to describe it." He remarked on its history: "Nechessor saith the Egyptians dedicated it to the Sun, because it cured agues, and they were like enough to do it, for they were the arrantest apes in their religion I ever read of." And he included a lengthy list of the reputed virtues of the herb.

Gerard and Parkinson generally echoed Culpeper's view of camomile. And Turner wrote:

> It hath floures wonderfully shynynge yellow and resemblynge the appell of an eye . . . the herbe may be called in English, golden floure. It will restore a man to hys color shortly yf a man after the longe use of the bathe drynke of it after he is come forthe oute of the bathe. This herb is scarce in Germany but in England it is so plenteous that it growth not only in gardynes but also VIII mile above London, it groweth in the wylde felde, in Rychmonde grene, in Brantfurde grene. . . . Thys herbe was consecrated by the wyse men of Egypt unto the Sonne and was rekened to be the only remedy of all agues.

Turner's remark that camomile was little seen in Germany doesn't make clear whether the German's regard for German camomile was the cause or the effect. But the fact remains that to the German herbalist, German camomile was the true camomile. Heinz Grotzke, one such herbalist, traces the origins of German camomile to southern Europe and the Near East, noting that "the Germanic tribes considered the camomile sacred in ancient

Roman Camomile

times and dedicated it to their sun god Baldur because to them the camomile's yellow center and white petals around it seemed to convey sun forces." Dioscorides and Pliny recommended a camomile poultice or bath as the cure for headaches and illnesses affecting the liver, kidneys, and bladder.

The English herbalists were not so kind toward German camomile. Culpeper called it "a hateful weed," mollifying that a bit by adding that "it possess virtues that may recompense all the damage it can do among the corn." Of those virtues he merely reported: "These have the virtues of the flowers of camomile, but with more cordial warmth. For those who have cold and weak stomachs, scarcely any thing equals them. They are best taken by way of infusion like tea."

(Curiously enough, Culpeper refers to German camomile as feverfew and labels it both *M. chamomilla* and *Pyrethrum chamomilla*. Parkinson, for his part, likened camomile to feverfew too. Feverfew's botanical name is *Chrysanthemum parthenium*, but it has been called *P. parthenium* and *M. parthenium*. All of this

German Camomile

serves to point up the relatively unclear distinctions among the members of the genera *Matricaria, Chrysanthemum,* and *Pyrethrum).*

A more contemporary English herbalist, Maude Grieve, commented in her herbal that German camomile "is not ranked among the true Chamomiles by botanists. . . ." She, too, acknowledges the value of the herb, however, listing its medicinal properties as carminative, sedative, and tonic. As with most herbals, the uses listed in Grieve's book are very similar to those listed for Roman camomile.

Both camomiles, of course, have served in more than a healing capacity. Camomile tea, made from either herb, is a soothing beverage at any time, and it has some other uses too. It is an excellent rinse for blonde hair. It is reputed to be an excellent insect repellent; sponge it over the body, leaving it to dry on, and no insects will bite you. In addition, immersing a cut of meat in camomile tea, as was done in the days before refrigeration, eliminates or masks the odor of the meat slowly turning bad. In Spain, where the camomiles are called manza-nilla, the flowers are used to flavor the finest dry sherries.

Either camomile is an excellent addition to the garden, but German camomile especially can serve the gardener in more than an ornamental capacity. The versatile camomile tea is reputed to be an excellent greenhouse spray, serving to stem or prevent a number of plant diseases, particularly damping-off. Followers of the bio-dynamic method have long used camomile tea—a strong tea allowed to brew a day or more—to spray on flats of seedlings to protect them from damping-off.

Bio-dynamic gardeners also use German camomile as a principal ingredient in their special compost preparation, a powder which is mixed with water, then poured over the compost heap just after it is constructed. The reason for this is "a very mysterious affinity" which existed "between camomile and cal-cium in nature," in the words of Heinz Grotzke. Since they regard calcium as vital to plant health, the bio-dynamic gardeners are particularly interested in this herb which, they say, "guides the calcium formative forces in the breakdown of the raw materials" in the compost heap.

For the companion planter, roman camomile is said to be a generally beneficial herb, it too serving in more than an orna-mental capacity. "Nothing contributes so much to the health of a garden as a number of chamomile herbs dispersed about it," notes one turn-of-the-century English herbal. "Singularly enough, if another plant is drooping and apparently dying, in nine cases out of ten it will recover if you place a herb of chamomile near it." This quality earned the herb the nickname physician's plant.

Roman camomile can be cultivated in a number of ways. It can be propagated from seed, but the plants often turn out to be the less desirable single-flowered variety. The seeds should be sown after the last danger of frost has passed, should you choose to start from seed.

A more reliable method of getting the variety you want is to purchase a plant (or several plants) and increase it by runners or root division. In some moist climates, it can be planted as an aromatic lawn. This has been done in England, but the American climate is not always conducive to it. The spreading nature of the herb together with its hardiness makes it possible. The plants are set about six inches apart and watered regularly until they fill the gaps amongst them. The first and second cuttings should be done with hand shears, but thereafter, the roots having established themselves, the camomile lawn may be mowed with a lawnmower, the blades being set fairly high. The herb should be mowed regularly, to prevent blooming.

German camomile, being an annual, has to be started from seed. The camomile seeds are very tiny and of unstable viability. They have a germination rate of about 70 percent the first year and rapidly lose viability thereafter, unless they are planted and subjected to freezes and thaws, which helps to maintain the viability for three years or longer. Camomile seed is one of the rare seeds that needs light for germination.

The most practical and successful method of starting the plants is to broadcast the seeds in early August, pack the soil lightly, and water until the little plants can be seen. By early September the plants will have developed enough to transplant them, if so desired, to the location where they are supposed to grow. No winter cover is needed as the plants are extremely hardy.

The seeds may also be started indoors in March and transplanted outside when large enough to handle, after they gradually were hardened off, meaning exposing them to cold temperatures over a period of time, and not suddenly. Or they may be seeded directly in the garden after the danger of frost has passed. They should be sown in rows rather than broadcast, however.

There are several other members of the *Anthemis* genus which have the appearance and some of the characteristics of the camomiles, making them worthy of note here. *A. arvensis* is a wild plant generally called corn camomile. In France it was considered an excellent febrifuge. *A. tinctoria* is the yellow or ox-eye camomile, which also is a wild plant. As its specific name implies, it yields a yellow dye. *A. cotula* and *M. inodora* are wild camomiles which are also known as mayweeds.

A. coluta is known as stinking camomile, foetid camomile,

stinking mayweed, dog fennel, and a wide variety of other names, all of which indicate in one or another way that it is not a plant you love to have around. It has an unpleasant smell, and it has a reputation of blistering the hand that touches it. But it shares the medicinal properties of the more well-known camomiles.

M. inodora is known as the scentless mayweed and corn feverfew. Although it shares the medicinal properties of the camomiles, it is almost totally scentless, hence the name.

CARAWAY

Carum carvi, Linn.
Umbelliferae

Caraway is one of those utility herbs, a plant so pleasant and useful that it's among the best-known and most widely used herbs in almost all parts of the modern world.

Its more obvious uses in the United States include flavoring rye bread, cheeses, and being the base for a German liqueur called "Kummel," which is a syrupy, clear, and colorless coffee-time delight with a strong and pungent bouquet of caraway.

Although it's of only marginal medicinal use, caraway has an enjoyable and distinctive licorice-flavored tang that has won a sizable place for it in kitchens throughout the world.

Old herbal legends associated the quality of retention with caraway. As a result, caraway was an ingredient in love potions as well as an additive to the feed of homing fowl. And true believers held that any object that contained a few caraway seeds would be safe from theft; that, indeed, if any thief tried to steal such an object, the staying power of the caraway would seize and hold him on the spot until the owner reached the scene.

The plant is a biennial with feathery leaves similar to those of fennel and coriander, although caraway does not like to grow near fennel. It should be seeded directly into the beds where it will grow; it does not tolerate transplanting well. Because it is a biennial, plant a new crop each year for a steady supply.

Seeding should be done in early spring for the full biennial cycle of the plant. Spring plantings will produce bushy green foliage, about eight inches high, during the first summer. The foliage will retain its verdancy during the winter. During the second summer, two-foot stalks topped by clusters of white flowers will develop. Seeds will form by midsummer and ripen by the fall. Harvesting time can be shortened if seeds are sown as soon as they're ripe in the fall. In the latter case, some seeds will be produced late the following summer.

Caraway should be harvested as soon as the seeds ripen and darken. Usually they can be separated from the umbel stems by threshing. Dry them in a hot sun or over a low stove heat.

Pay particular attention to weed control during caraway's early months. When the new shoots are about two inches tall, pinch out the smaller ones and allow the remaining plants six to 12 inches of room.

Fertilization is not critical although caraway seems to prefer a fairly heavy soil on the dry side. Some herbalists recommend a planting of caraway to break up and aerate heavy soils.

Some companion gardeners plant peas and caraway in the same row. The peas come up first, and harrowing them in the normal way simultaneously controls weeds that hinder caraway's early growth.

Roots of the mature caraway plant are a delicacy that can be prepared and eaten much like carrots or parsnips. Parkinson also ascribed medicinal value to them. The seventeenth century herbalist advised:

> The roots of Caraway, being boiled, may be eaten as Carrots and by reason of the spicie taste doth warme and comfort a cold weak Stomache, helping to dissolve Wind and to provoke Urine, and is a very welcome and delightful Dish to many.

The leaves, too, can be chopped and added to stews and soups and goulashes to lend caraway's tang to them.

Caraway is said to aid the digestion of heavy starches such as cabbage, turnip, and potatoes. It has aromatic, stimulant, and carminative properties, according to Maude Grieve, who adds that caraway "possesses some tonic property and forms a pleasant stomachic." Caraway seeds, she says, are high in protein and fat content and are used, after the distillation of their oil for commercial products, for cattle feed supplements.

Culpeper said caraway seeds, "once only dipped in sugar, and

Caraway

a spoonful of them eaten in the morning fasting, and as many after each meal, is a most admirable remedy for those that are troubled with wind."

A similar-acting remedy is made by eating one to four drops of caraway oil on a lump of sugar, or in a teaspoon of water.

For a "gripe water" for infants, try a caraway julep made by bruising an ounce of seeds and infusing them for six hours in a pint of cold water. Give one to three teaspoons at a time.

Caraway makes several tasty confectionery treats, among them comfits of sugar-encrusted seeds. Served sometimes as a side dish to dessert fruits, the seeds also can be added to cakes, puddings, and cookies. Use the seeds in apple dishes of almost every kind and in rye and black breads.

Bacon drippings and caraway seeds added to boiled cabbage add a twist of unusual flavor. Try using caraway in the vinegar when pickling beets.

CAROB

Ceratonia siliqua, Linn.
Leguminosae

For thousands of years, the carob tree has flourished in countries bordering the Mediterranean Sea. It bears large, brown pods containing 40 percent sugar and six percent protein. The tree belongs to the legume or bean family and is a handsome evergreen, medium-sized with glossy leaves.

The carob made its United States debut in 1854, when the

U. S. Patent Office distributed 8,000 plants throughout the southern states. Since that time, the development of the carob has been limited mainly to parts of southern California. Many California communities sport very large carob trees today—the result of the work of the California experiment station over 75 years ago. Carob flour, made from the flesh of the pod, is now made in this country from imported pods. This flour has a flavor resembling chocolate and is used, when mixed with wheat flour in making bread, hot cakes, and waffles. Mixed with hot milk, it is an excellent drink.

Carob thrives on a rather warm climate, free from severe frosts and requires at least 12 to 14 inches of rain per year. An average of 23 inches is ideal. On the other hand, carob suffers from too much water, as is shown by the sickly condition of trees planted in wet places, or in lawns which are frequently sprinkled.

The carob requires a near rainless autumn when the pods are reaching maturity. Ripening occurs in September and October according to variety. Harvest is in October to November. Many types of soil, from adobe to sand, are suitable for the carob. Recommended, however, is a rather deep heavy loam with good subdrainage. The root system is very extensive with relatively few fibrous feeder roots.

Carob seeds, when collected fresh from recently ripened pods, germinate readily. They may be planted in beds or flats, and when the second set of leaves is well formed, they are planted in small pots or paper containers. At 12 inches high, the plants are set in boxes four by 12 inches deep, or planted in nursery rows in open ground where there is little danger of frost. When the seedlings have developed a stem three-eights of an inch or more in diameter, they are budded after the fashion of citrus trees.

The budded carob tree, under favorable dry farm conditions should begin to bear the sixth year and produce an average of five pounds per tree. The size of the crops will increase gradually, reaching an average of 100 pounds the twelfth year.

CASTOR OIL PLANT

Castor Bean Plant

Ricinus communis, Linn.

Euphorbiaceae

A tropical ornamental, the castor oil plant has large divided leaves of three to five lobes up to three feet across. It can be used as a foliage screen, for background effect or as a foliage specimen. In northern areas, it is treated as an annual and will seldom exceed ten or 12 feet in height. Because it is very fast growing, it can be very useful in new plantings, providing foliage while slower plants are getting started.

The flowers have no petals and grow in upright panicles covered with dark brown spines. The fruit which follows is a capsule containing three large seeds which are the source of commercial castor oil. The dark shiny seeds are extremely poisonous if swallowed, but can easily be removed from the plant when they first begin to form.

The castor oil plant has long enjoyed the reputation as a fly and mosquito repelling plant and will also rid the garden of moles and gophers. There are several forms which vary greatly in appearance: *Ricinus africanus* has very large green leaves; *R. macrocarpus* has purple-red foliage; *R. cambodgensis* has blackish-purple stems and leaves; *R. sanguinea* is red-leaved; and *R. gibsonii,* a lovely dwarf, has dark red leaves with a metallic luster.

It is a very decorative garden plant, easily grown from seed, which may be started indoors then transplanted to its location when the weather is settled. They will grow in clay or sandy loam, but prefer good drainage.

The oil of the castor bean is one of the best-known laxatives, and perhaps one of the least liked. It is particularly suitable for children and the aged, for it has a gentle action. The drawback is the flavor and odor, both of which are unpleasant. The oil also has seen some external use for skin ailments such as ringworm and itches. The Chinese value castor oil as a laxative, but also use it in cases of difficult childbirth, facial deformities, and stomach cancer.

Castor oil has had a variety of industrial uses, including the manufacture of soap, furniture polish, flypaper, artificial leather and artificial rubber, some types of cellulose, and candles.

CATNIP

Catnep, Catmint
Nepeta cataria, Linn.
Labiatae

Long a source of mysterious and frenzied ecstasy to the feline world, catnip has served the human world at least as well over the centuries as a minor herbal medicine and a major herbal delight.

Before European trade with China began bringing great quantities of fine Eastern tea to the West, catnip tea was a domestic favorite especially among the tea-loving residents of the British Isles.

As a medicine, an infusion of catnip is useful as a tonic, a mild stimulant, nervine, antispasmodic, and emmenagogue. But, of course, this herb is best known for its strange and often hilarious effect on cats.

Nearly all members of the feline species, from the rangiest alley cat to the fiercest mountain lion, are known to have a passionate affinity for catnip. More exactly, they crave the oil that is expressed from a bruised or drying plant.

Maude Grieve, a twentieth century English herbalist, advises gardeners to sow catnip directly in its growing bed, and to take care not to injure the developing plants. With those precautions, Grieve advises, neighborhood cats are unlikely to tune in, turn on and tear up your catnip patch. Her advice is embodied in this old ditty:

> If you set it, the cats will eat it;
> If you sow it, the cats won't know it.

If you own a cat and the two of you have never been on a catnip high together, be sure to include a row for your next planting. The fun begins when you toss a sprig or a few dried leaves to your whiskered bundle of whimsy. Cats delight in

Catnip

rubbing against catnip as though trying to coat themselves with it. They roll on it, tooth it, toss it about with their paws, and rub their faces in it in a comic orgy of delight.

The universal liking that cats have for *Nepeta cataria* is underscored by the fact that the herb's common name in every Western language contains some variation of the word "cat."

The culinary use of catnip seems to begin and end with its tea, which can be served at the end of large meals as a carminative aid. Garnish with a slice of lemon. A variation of this after-dinner treat is candied catnip leaves, made by sprinkling raw sugar on catnip leaves coated with a glaze of equal parts of egg white and lemon juice, mixed gently. Allow the coated leaves to dry at least a day before serving them.

Fortified with honey, catnip tea is used by many as an old-fashion cough remedy. Medicinally, catnip's main use is that of a diaphoretic to induce free perspiration without increasing body heat. Such action is useful in breaking a fever, bringing sleep, and even as a cooler on a hot summer day.

The herb infused also helps nervousness and dispels nervous headaches. Catnip should not be boiled because too much of its highly volatile oil would be lost. Infuse it only.

An adult dose of catnip tea would be two or three table-spoonsful at a time as needed, although taken in large quantities the tea can act as an emetic. Children's doses are two to three teaspoonsful of the infusion, made with one ounce of leaves to a pint of hot water.

For an emmenagogue, though, it's better to use the oil of catnip expressed from fresh leaves. Take one tablespoonful three times a day.

From an English herbalist comes the sobering advice that the root of catnip "when chewed is said to make the most gentle person fierce and quarrelsome, and there is a legend of a certain hangman who could never screw up his courage to the point of hanging anybody till he had partaken of it." Rats are said to be repelled by catnip; so it might be a suitable protective planting around grain crops.

The plant is a perennial with leaves that are almost heart-shaped and grey-green in coloration. The stems are squarish and two to three feet high. Both stems and leaves are coated with downy hairs that overall give a dustblown appearance to the plant. Flowers, pale lavender to pale pink, appear in the leaf axis at the top of the plant from July to September. Insect polli-nation is needed for seed development. The seeds, which closely resemble basil seeds, can be identified by a little white speck on one side.

Either seeding or root division in fall or spring can be used to start catnip. Planting can be done outdoors in late April or early May, or earlier indoors if you're willing to risk bruising the plants and attracting cats while transplanting.

In seeding, rows should be 18 inches apart and plants thinned to 12 inches in the rows. Catnip develops quickly and is easy to grow, but it should have a mulch of hay, straw, or cocoa hulls. It prefers a rich soil, but will do fairly well almost anywhere. In the United States, it quickly escaped captivity and now grows wild in many parts of the country.

Root division can produce up to four new plants from a single growth. Best time to do it is early spring, before the plants get too large. New divisions should be transplanted right away.

Harvesting has to be done as soon as the plants are mature but before they start to turn yellow. Leaves can be stripped off the plant or the entire plant can be cut and dried.

In either case, dry catnip in the shade—not in the sun—so its volatile oils will not be lost. Two or three days will be required for drying.

Cared for, a catnip plant will last for several years . . . your feline friends willing, and that's not likely.

CHERVIL

Anthriscus cerefolium, (Linn.) Hoffm.
Umbelliferae

Brought into Europe from the Levant and the shores of the Mediterranean, chervil is well known to gourmets as the basis of any herbal salad.

For centuries, the tasty herb has been an essential part of most English gardens, where it is said to have been introduced by the Romans. In Southern Europe, it flourishes in the wild although it is native to Asia.

Many people call it "the gourmet parsley," since it has a more delicate flavor than parsley. It is used mostly to add zest to a salad, but the herb has a rich folklore and background in custom.

Pliny said that chervil was a fine herb "to comfort the cold stomach of the aged," and the boiled roots were used as a preventive against plague. In the Middle Ages, people used its leaves to soothe the pain of rheumatism and bruises, and some still eat it today as a cure for the hiccups. Chervil is also supposed to have great qualities of rejuvenation.

In Europe, people eat chervil soup on Holy Thursday as a symbol of resurrection and a new life. Because its scent reminds one of the fragrance of myrrh, one of the offerings at the birth of Christ, chervil is often called myrrhis.

The herb is best known for its use in salads, but it enhances soups, especially sorrel or spinach soup, and adds flavor to fish, eggs, meats, or vegetables. It's often used with oysters.

Evelyn instructed that chervil should never be missing from a salad, since it is exceedingly wholesome and "chearing the spirits."

Culpeper cites a host of medicinal qualities of the herb. Chervil, he said, "is a certain remedy (saith Tragus) to dissolve congealed or clotted blood in the body, or that which is clotted by bruises, falls, etc.: the juice or distilled water thereof being drunk, and the bruised leaves laid to the place, being taken in either meat or drink, it is good to provoke urine, or expel the stone in the kidneys, to send down women's courses and to help the pleurisy and prickling of the sides."

But Gerard warns that "it has a certain windiness, by meanes whereof it provoketh lust." Inwardly or outwardly, he adds, it affects the bladder.

There are two main varieties of chervil, plain and curly. The plants grow to about two feet in height, with small flowers arranged in umbels. The seeds look like tiny sticks, thin and about one-quarter inch in length. Germination takes ten days or longer in the presence of light. The odor is similar to anise or tarragon, and the leaves are somewhat like parsley, but finer.

The gardener can start chervil from seed either indoors or directly outside as soon as the soil can be worked. Since the seeds require light for germination, the seeds should not be covered with soil. However, too much light could dry out the sprouting seed and kill it.

The best method is to make a furrow an inch deep, scatter the seeds evenly, and press them into the ground with the tines of a vertically held rake; water and keep moist until the young plants are visible.

It's also possible to scatter the seeds freely in a small area, tap them into the ground with a shovel and cover them with a cheesecloth. It will probably be necessary to continue watering the seeds right through the cheesecloth until the seeds establish their roots.

Chervil

Then the cheesecloth can be removed, but the soil should still be watered after sundown for another couple of days. Because of the harmful effects of direct sunlight, chervil should be grown in a somewhat shaded area.

Because the plant grows so quickly, indoor germination isn't as important as with other plants, and chervil is more difficult to transplant than most herbs.

The chervil's root is small and long, and the plant should be sown in March or early April and after July for an autumn harvest. The chervil should self-sow generously. If some seedlings are lifted in late summer and put in a cold frame, they'll survive the winter there and in the spring, when the glass is removed, grow to more than two feet and become covered with blossoms. By putting some chervil in a cold frame, fresh leaves can be obtained all year.

Chervil grows much better in cool weather, and thus does better early in the year and towards the end of summer again. In the middle of the summer it goes to seed without a real leaf formation. It's possible to cut the leaves six to eight weeks after seeding. For a continuous supply of leaves, it's best to continually seed the plant throughout the summer, preferably in the shade.

The herb doesn't require much in the way of nutrients, and chervil can easily follow a crop that was fertilized with compost the previous year. Mulching with chopped hay or straw helps keep the soil cool and the plants clean.

The older leaves of chervil obtain a horizontal position gradually and stop growing and start to age. For this reason, the gardener should cut off these leaves first prior to their turning yellow. More leaves will develop from the center until the stalk pushes up, developing into a structure of flowering umbels.

Many gardeners allow one or two plants to fulfill their natural cycle just for the pleasure of watching them grow.

Drying chervil isn't as important a procedure as with other herbs, because the herb is best fresh. Although it dries relatively quickly, it's best to control drying in order to retain full flavor.

If you don't want to miss chervil in the winter, you should either grow some indoors or buy a good commercial brand dried in a glass jar.

Dried chervil should be stored away from light, since the herb will turn yellow or greyish in a short time if exposed to light. It will also pick up the slightest moisture above normal humidity and become stale.

CHICORY

Cichorium intybus, Linn.
Compositae

Chicory is that blue-flowered weed that hems the roadside throughout much of the country. (The blue flowers are always closed by noon.) The leaves resemble those of dandelion sufficiently to have earned it the occasional nickname, blue dandelion. Like dandelion, the plant is the bane of lawn fanatics, for it spreads quickly by sending out runners, and it is tough to eradicate. But chicory is taller than dandelion and loses much of the resemblance in maturity

Because of its tendency to get out of hand, chicory is a plant that must be used cautiously in the garden. It isn't particular about soil, though it does like the sun. It is easily started from seed.

Perhaps the best-known use of chicory is as an additive in coffee. The French are particularly fond of chicory in coffee, and where the French influence dominated here, the preference is seen. The root is used for this purpose and can be used to brew a chicory beverage. Chicory was ascribed a variety of medicinal uses—including a tonic, laxative, and diuretic. Ancient herbals suggest bruised chicory leaves as a poultice for swellings, inflammations, and inflamed eyes· A decoction of one ounce of dried powdered root to a pint of water was recommended for jaundice and general liver ailments. Blanched, the leaves can be used in salads.

CHIVES

Allium schoenoprasum, Linn.
Liliaceae

The hardiness and compactness of this delicate onion-related herb make it an ideal candidate for winter kitchen gardens.

Hardy perennials, chives grow in clumps of small white bulbous roots that send off fine hollow green spears. The tender young spears are harvested and chopped or cut into small segments to grace a wide variety of dishes.

Because chives are difficult to store, many gardeners choose to maintain a fresh supply through indoor gardening.

Chives can be started from seed or purchased already started in young clumps. Seed should be drilled into one-quarter-inch rows as early as the soil can be worked, then covered with fine compost or sifted soil. Tap the covering lightly to assure good soil contact. The plants need rich soil, a fair amount of water, and full sun. Many gardeners border the garden with chives, which develop pretty bluish-pink to lavender flowers.

Early mulching is wise to retain moisture and discourage grass and weeds, which are debilitating competitors for moisture and nutrients. A fish emulsion fertilizer should be added to

Chives

chives to replace nutrients, especially nitrogen, after repeated cuttings.

Chives are an encouraging project for a new herb grower because they develop quickly and produce in profusion· A bed of chives frequently produces more than a family can use but even if that's the case, the tender green spears should be snipped close to the ground regularly to prevent the plants from becoming tough and to help the bulblets develop. Unless there are plans to let the plants flower or seed, cutting should always be done before the round balls begin to develop at the tops of the spears.

The root bulbs develop in clusters, which should be dug up, divided, and replanted every two or three years. Keep the new clusters eight inches apart. Six bulbs to a cluster is about right when dividing.

Maintain a second plantation for chives intended for seed.

To bring a cluster of chives inside for the winter, transplant it into a five-inch pot in late summer and sink the pot into the ground. After the first killing frost, mulch the pot or put it into a cold frame for about 90 days. Chives need this rest period to rejuvenate. Then bring the pot into the house, and put it at a sunny location. Give it water. By January, there will be a fresh supply of chives for harvesting.

If chives are desired between the seasons, chop the spears after harvesting and dry them completely and immediately. Try hanging them in a basket over the stove. Put them in airtight containers immediately, for any trace of moisture will be absorbed by the dried chives, and they'll lose their color and flavor.

A safer way of preserving chopped chives is to freeze a glassful of them at a time.

Native to the Orient, chives have been known for almost 5,000 years, chiefly as a culinary nicety. No extensive medicinal uses ever were developed although chives are said to aid the digestion of fatty foods. Roumanian gypsies used chives in their fortune-telling rites, and clumps of chives were suspended from ceilings and bedposts in chambers to drive away the diseases and evil influences.

Sprinkle chives in green salads and on tomatoes. Add them to sour cream or melted butter as a fine dressing for potatoes, or sprinkle them into soups, sausage dishes, and croquettes.

COHOSH, BLACK

Black Snakeroot, Rattleroot, Squawroot, Bugbane
Cimicifuga racemosa, Nutt.
Ranunculaceae

A tall-growing woodland perennial of the buttercup family, black cohosh is a native of North America. It has a long stalk which splits into several branches, each having long plume-like clusters of strong-smelling, white flowers. The flowers bloom from May to August, ultimately giving way to small, round seed pods. When the stalk is shaken, the seeds rattle within their pods, producing a sound similar to a rattlesnake, thus giving rise to the nickname rattleroot.

Black cohosh is useful as a background plant for a border garden of hardy perennials, or as a member of a wild garden. The leaves are said to repell insects, hence the name bugbane. The plant can be propagated from seed or by root division.

Most prominent as a medicinal plant, black cohosh was widely used by the American Indians, and was particularly important to the Indian midwives. An Indian medicine guide of the late eighteenth century called it "one of our very best remedies in a great many womb troubles," and devoted considerable space to its virtues as an emmenagogue.

Black cohosh is also listed as an astringent, diuretic, alterative, and diaphoretic. As a consequence, it is said to be useful to stimulate the kidneys and to restore the normal functioning of the digestive system. It is also said to be valuable for relieving coughs and reducing the pulse.

The part commonly used is the root, which is gathered during July, August, and September, chopped, then carefully dried. A recommended tincture is made by half-filling a pint or quart bottle with the powdered root, adding diluted alcohol or whisky until the bottle is full, and agitating once or twice a day for two weeks. Doses range from one to thirty drops in a teaspoon of water.

COHOSH, BLUE
Papoose Root, Squawroot, Blue Ginseng
Caulophyllum thalictroides, (Linn.) Michx.
Berberidaceae

A native American, blue cohosh is a hardy perennial found on richly wooded slopes and in hardwood glades throughout the Appalachian region. It grows to three feet in height, with yellowish-green flowers blooming from April to early June and either two- or three-lobed leaves. The "blue" of the name stems from the bluish hue of the foliage and the blue berries which follow the flowers. The rootstock, which is the part used, is matted and knotty.

The uses of blue cohosh were discovered primarily by the Indians, who taught them to white settlers. Though the use of the plant as a folk medicine was wide-spread, the medical establishment didn't admit blue cohosh to the official pharmacopoeias until the late 1800s, and removed it in the early 1900s. Cohosh is a name given the plant by the Algonquins. Other nicknames are derived from its principal use as an aid to parturition.

A doctor reported to the fledgling American Medical Association in the early 1800s:

> The Indians and quacks recommended it in colic, sore throat, rheumatism, dropsies, &c. It partakes of the nature of ginseng and seneka. The Indian women use it successfully in cases of lingering parturition. It appears to be particularly suited to female complaints. It is a powerful emmenagogue, and promotes delivery, the menstrual flux, and dropsical discharges.

He and others urged further investigation of the plant. During its recognition as an official drug plant, blue cohosh was listed as an antispasmodic, emmenagogue, and diuretic.

The roots are collected in the fall, when their chemical constituents are richest. An ounce of the dried and macerated root should be combined with a pint of boiling water to yield a useful infusion. It is given in doses ranging from two to four ounces, three to four times daily.

COLTSFOOT

Tussilago farfara, Linn.
Compositae

Coltsfoot is a curious herb which seems to grow in two distinct stages. Very early in the growing season, the plant develops flat orange flower heads. Only after the flowers have withered do the broad, hoof-shaped, sea-green leaves develop. This habit of growth earned coltsfoot its old name of *Filius ante patrem* (the son before the father).

In England and the Continent, coltsfoot is a fairly common weed. Not surprisingly then, its soil preferences are not distinguished. It does like full sun. It can easily be propagated from root cuttings or seed. Its spreading habits make it an excellent ground cover and account for its wide dissemination.

Because of the two-stage growth, coltsfoot is easily harvested for both its blossoms and its leaves, both of which have medicinal uses. Coltsfoot is usually listed as a demulcent, expectorant, and tonic. But its prime value was as a cough remedy. Indeed, its generic name *Tussilago* signifies "cough dispeller." The old herbalists, as far back as Pliny and Dioscorides, regarded coltsfoot as the best herb for lung and thoracic complaints. A decoction made of one ounce of the leaves in a quart of water boiled down to a pint, sweetened with honey, and taken frequently in teacup doses is recommended for colds and asthma. But the old herbalists usually smoked coltsfoot to capture its curative values. Coltsfoot leaves are the primary ingredient in British herb tobacco, which also contains buckbean, eyebright, betony, rosemary, thyme, lavender, and camomile flowers. The tobacco is reputedly beneficial to sufferers of asthma, catarrh, and other lung troubles.

COMFREY

Knitbone, Knitback, Healing Herb, Ass Ear
Symphytum officinale, Linn.
Boraginaceae

Few herbs have had as many extravagant claims made for them as has comfrey. Known for centuries for powerful abilities as a healer, comfrey was often granted purely miraculous ones as well. Culpeper claimed that comfrey root "is said to be so powerful to consolidate and knit together, that if they be boiled with disseevered pieces of flesh in a pot, it will join them together."

Aside from claims such as these, this showy member of the borage family has, indeed, been used for centuries by herbalists for a wide variety of ailments. Many of its uses are not as radical as the one suggested by Culpeper, but run the gamut from poultices made from the leaves and used to reduce swellings, to teas and infusions of the root used to treat diarrhea.

The mature comfrey plant grows wild, but can be easily cultivated. It is about two to three feet high, erect, and rough and hairy all over. The stem is stout and angular, the root branched, fleshy, spindle-shaped. Roots often grow to a foot in length, an inch or less in diameter, and are internally white, fleshy, and juicy.

The lower leaves are very large (sometimes up to ten inches long), ovate in shape, and hairy—they resemble, in fact, a donkey's ears. The hairs cause itching if brushed. The size of the leaves decreases as they get higher up the plant.

Flower racemes are found at the top of the plant, bearing creamy-yellow or purplish-blue flowers on a stem that curves like a scorpion's tail. Each flower is followed by four seeds in a little cup-like fruit.

Comfrey blooms throughout the greater part of the summer. The first flowers appear in late April or early May and continue until the first frosts. Comfrey, however, is hardy and may not be harmed by the first light frosts. It often continues to produce foliage after other plants have been frost-killed.

Comfrey is beginning to gain some popularity among home-steaders, and many are growing small patches of comfrey on their farms. Comfrey seems, at this point, a difficult and expensive plant to grow on mass farming operations, but is ideal on a small scale. Many are finding it a popular plant, not only for themselves, but for their animals as well.

Comfrey can be raised from plants, crown cuttings containing eyes or buds, and root cuttings. While the first two methods will produce a respectable crop the first year after planting, root cuttings are by far the cheapest method and can be easily ordered through the mail. Although older herbals mention raising com-frey from seed, few growers have had success with this method.

Once established, comfrey is a hardy perennial. The roots will withstand frost down to −40°F. In fact, it is a difficult crop to eradicate. Like horseradish, the roots will produce new plants from any sliver left in the ground.

Cuttings are planted three to six inches deep in a horizontal position. The soil should be well-tilled and manured. Comfrey likes a sweet soil, with a pH of 6.0 to 7.0. Limestone should be applied liberally. Other soil requirements can be met by dressing with ground phosphate rock for phosphates and greensand for potash.

The cuttings should be spaced three feet apart each way. Grasses and weeds should be kept down by cultivation or mulch. Once your cuttings are established, they can be divided for more

Comfrey

plants. The best time to divide is in the spring when the leaves begin to appear above ground.

You can expect a moderate harvest from your cuttings the first year. Cuttings will come into full production in the third year. Some wild claims have been made for yields of comfrey plantings, and it seems to be difficult to determine just how much comfrey you can expect to harvest from a patch of a given size. You should, however, be able to harvest every ten to thirty days throughout the growing season, depending upon weather conditions.

Harvest comfrey just before it blooms. Nutritional and medicinal value seem to decrease once the plant blossoms. Cut the plant with a sickle or knife when the leaves are twelve to eighteen inches high, leaving a two-inch stem stub. It is important not to cut lower than this and damage the newly-forming growth on the crown.

Herbal doctors seemed to have preferred fresh comfrey, giving little value to dried leaves. Nevertheless, the leaves can be dried. Cut the leaves at the end of the day when their food value is highest. Comfrey leaves are tender, so avoid bruising. They should be dried quickly in thin layers in the sun. Allow about two days for the drying to take place, then store in boxes layered between layers of grass hay. Be careful not to shatter or compress the leaves when packing them.

Comfrey root can also be dried for winter use. Clean it carefully (avoid bruising or scraping) and dry slowly in the sun, turning often.

Modern science has established that comfrey is high in calcium, potassium, phosphorus, and other trace minerals. The leaves are rich in vitamins A and C. The virtues of comfrey as a vulnerary—the medieval term for a plant used to heal battle wounds—are due to the amount of allantoin it contains. Medical research has found that allantoin is useful in treating wounds, burns, and ulcers. It is manufactured artificially, and sometimes obtained from fresh extracts from the roots.

Of course, the ancients had none of this knowledge to bolster their remedies. They relied instead on tradition and what worked for them. And comfrey seems to have been a favorite remedy for many ailments.

A decoction of comfrey root, made by putting one quart milk or water in the top of a double boiler, adding one ounce of ground root, and cooking for thirty minutes, was said to be good for dysentery or diarrhea when taken internally. It is also recommended for stomach or intestinal ulcers.

As a remedy for bleeding hemorrhoids or other internal bleeding, one-half ounce of witch hazel leaves were added to the decoction before boiling. Lemon could be added to the decoction for a more pleasing taste. A strong tea made from the roots was used for whooping cough and administered for lung troubles.

Comfrey leaves are also applied externally to swellings, bruises, or broken bones. As Culpeper believed, they are said to hasten the healing of fractures: hence the names, knitbone and boneset. In fact, the name comfrey is thought to be a corruption of the Latin *confervere*, "to heal." The generic name, *Symphytum*, is derived from the Greek *symphyto*, to unite. We now know that one of comfrey's chief effects is to act on the swelling through the allantoin present in the plant.

Culpeper said: "The roots of comfrey taken fresh, beaten small and spread upon leather and laid upon any place troubled with the gout presently gives ease: and applied in the same manner it eases pained joints and tends to heal running ulcers, gangrenes, mortifications, for which it hath by often experience been found helpful."

At times, the entire plant was beaten into a pulp, heated, and applied as a poultice. In this form, it was said to ease the pain of an inflamed, tender, or suppurating part of the body.

In some parts of Ireland, comfrey is eaten as a cure for defective circulation and used to strengthen the blood. Comfrey can be eaten as a vegetable. The first leaves can be used as salad greens, or can be boiled and eaten like spinach. When larger, they become coarse and unpleasant.

The leaves can also be dried, ground, and added to bread or muffins. This is a good way of using another unique component of the plant — vitamin B_{12}. So far, it is the only land plant discovered that contains this vitamin. It is also a good source of lysine, an amino acid lacking in the diets of those who use no animal products whatsoever.

Comfrey root, along with dandelion and chicory roots, can be made into a coffee substitute without the harmful effects of coffee. Roast equal quantities until they are dark brown. Grind and brew as you would coffee.

Comfrey has also been used, with moderate success, as a cattle food. It was first introduced into Britain for this purpose in 1811, and met with only slight success. Although it grew well enough in wet places, it could not be adapted to dry climates. Another problem arises in determining yields. There are hundreds of varieties and strains of comfrey, some yielding a lot of forage and some little.

The English found that cattle did not particularly take to comfrey, although this may have been due, in part, to the fact that they were not used to it. For example, homesteader Nancy Bubel, writing in *Organic Gardening and Farming*, reported on her experiences feeding comfrey to rabbits: ". . . they eat it eagerly as long as no soybeans are in sight. If the rabbits first have a taste of soybeans, lettuce or clover, they'll spoil their appetites for comfrey. We manage their rations so that they get comfrey once a day when they are eager for it, and they clean it up."

Comfrey will not cause scours or bloat in young animals. It is also believed that comfrey will prevent hoof and mouth disease if fed regularly to animals.

CORIANDER

Coriandrum sativum, Linn.
Umbelliferae

One of the most ancient of herbs still in use today, coriander is known to have been cultivated in Egyptian gardens thousands of years before the birth of Christ. Coriander seeds were among the funeral offerings found in Egyptian tombs. And it spread early to Western civilizations, too; the great Greek physician Hippocrates used it in the fifth century B.C.

By the time the herb had reached the Chinese continent, it had acquired a reputation for bestowing immortality and the Chinese herbalists developed several coriander compounds to that end.

Coriander also found itself a cherished place in the most sacred work of Western man: the Bible. There are several Old Testament references to coriander as an herb whose fruit is similar to the mysterious food, manna, that God showered upon the Israelites during their desert trek from bondage. In Exodus 16:31, it is recorded:

> And the house of Israel called the name thereof Manna; and it was like coriander seed, white; and the taste of it was like wafers made with honey.

Coriander, though, is not so divine in all its aspects. The mature green plant, just before it goes to seed, emits a strong odor that some gardeners find highly offensive. Indeed, its generic name is derived from a Greek word, *koris,* that means "bug." And the ancient Pliny described coriander as "a very stinkinge herb." Fortunately, that strong odor gives way to a pleasing aroma as the plant dries. The lasting odor of dried coriander has been described as a combination of sage and lemon peel.

In the Arabian fantasy tales *The Thousand and One Nights,* coriander is mentioned as an aphrodisiac, a use that is somewhat substantiated by more recent confirmation that coriander seeds can be narcotic if consumed in excessive quantities. The same tales tell of coriander being combined with fennel to conjure the devil. In a conjurer's mortar, that may be a likely pairing but in the garden, we're assured by experts on companion planting, the two cannot stand being near each other as coriander hinders the seed formation of fennel.

Coriander was known widely in the British Isles at least as early as the fifteenth century and, most likely, long before that. It was one of the first herbs brought to the New World; a seventeenth century list of herbs grown in New England gardens includes coriander.

The plant is an annual with slender, erect stems bearing finely divided leaves. It reaches a height of one to three feet. Coriander needs only moderately fertilized soil, but it cannot stand constant moisture. Because of its marked liking for well-drained soils and relatively dry climates, most of the commercially produced coriander is grown in arid areas of the world. Morocco is a major producer.

Delicate umbels of flowers, lavender to pale mauve, form late in June.

Seeds germinate in darkness. They should be planted outside in drills a half-inch deep and nine inches apart. Because coriander prefers light, warm and dry soil, a relatively warm and dry spring will give you a late April start. A less favorable season may cause you to wait until May for planting.

Coriander doesn't transplant well, so it should be sown directly in its bed. If you do find it necessary to try a risky indoors start, plant in March and transplant in May. As much as coriander dislikes being near fennel, it welcomes anise as a neighbor and will benefit the formation of anise seeds.

Some English gardeners make a common planting of coriander and caraway in the same row. Caraway is a biennial whose

Coriander

first-year growth is small and close to the ground, and poses no threat to the young coriander shoots. In the second year, caraway is given the row to itself.

In any event, weed control is important while the early coriander fights to establish itself. By mid-August, it should be able to dominate its competitors, however, and even mulching should be unnecessary.

Coriander attracts a great variety of pollinating insects to the garden. The swirl of activity around it may well be alone worth all the trouble of growing coriander—as if there weren't a very good herbal reason besides!

Act swiftly to harvest the coriander when the fruits turn light brown. The small fruits, which envelope the seed, are an eighth-inch in diameter, globular, and will part into halves when they're dried and rubbed between the palms. It's this part of the plant that's most used in medicines and cookery.

If the fruit balls aren't snatched at the right time, the fast-dropping coriander will reseed itself.

Coriander is said by herbalists to have stimulant, aromatic, and carminative properties, although in modern times its chief medicinal use has been to disguise the disagreeable taste of active purgatives.

Its commercial uses now include the flavoring of foods and liqueurs and some confectionery uses, including the fortification of inferior-grade cocoa. The crushed fruit and seed are sometimes used in rich cakes, custards, and jellies. Along with the sugar-coated seeds of anise, caraway, and celery, coated coriander fruits are used in multicolored cake sprinkle to decorate baked goods. In Peru and Egypt, it's common to put coriander leaves into soups and broths.

This herb imparts a wonderful spiciness to sausage and red meats. In pickles and beet salads, it makes a different and tasty addition.

COSTMARY

Chrysanthemum balsamita, Linn. (syn. *Tanacetum balsamita,* Linn.; *Pyrethrum balsamita,* Wild.)
Compositae

Although not always the easiest herb to find, costmary is well worth the extra effort required to track it down. Its practical uses are enhanced by a charming appearance and sweet fragrance, and its history is filled with fascinating tales from all over the globe.

The name of this sweet-smelling herb combines the Latin word *costus,* for "oriental plant," with "Mary" the mother of Jesus. Although in medieval France we find that costmary was called "Herbe Sainte-Marie," other historical references identify it with Mary Magdalene as often as with the Virgin Mary. This aromatic herb has always had a special place in Christianity. In Colonial times, the costmary leaf served as a bookmark in the bibles and prayerbooks of many devout churchgoers. When the long sermon grew boring and drowsiness set in, the sleepy listener treated himself or herself to the minty flavor of the costmary leaves in an effort to stay awake. Thus, the nickname "Bible leaf" grew popular.

Originally found in the Orient, costmary was introduced into England in the sixteenth century, where it soon became extremely popular. In 1578 Lyte commented that it was "very common in all gardens," and Gerard, in 1598, confirmed the popularity of this herb when he said "it groweth everywhere in gardens." Not nearly as familiar today, it is nonetheless an important and precious part of many modern gardens.

Though closely related to tansy, costmary carries a soft, balsamic fragrance which is more aromatic than that of the tansy. Culpeper calls costmary the "balsam herb." Its shiny, pear-shaped, light green leaves are from six to eight inches long with finely-toothed margins. The two to three foot long stems are stiff with short, sturdy, and slightly downy branches. Although attractive all year long, costmary is particularly charming in the spring when it bears clusters of small, pale yellow, buttonlike flowers. Another herb similar to costmary is maudlin, spelled "maudeline" by Parkinson and "maudeleine" by Gerard. Parkinson tells us that although maudlin is smaller than costmary, its fragrance is sweeter. Treasured for what Gerard calls "their sweet floures and leaves," maudlin and costmary were both often used to make "sweete washing water."

There are so many useful ways to make costmary a worth while addition to your garden. Parkinson writes of its uses as a spicy flavoring in ale, from which comes the name alecost or alecoast. In salads and in pottage, fresh costmary leaves lend a sweet aroma and taste, and the lingering fragrance of dried costmary makes it a fine dried herb for potpourri. Dainty bundles of lavender and costmary were commonly made by colonial women "to lye upon the toppes of beds, presses, etc., for sweet scent and savour." It can also be used to sweeten the air of closets and drawers, to make a delicious tea and to enhance the flavor of German sausage. In the garden, costmary keeps the weeds out, acts as a green background for spring flowers, and forms a beautiful, slow-growing edging. It is a wonderful landscaping plant.

Medicinally, costmary is known for its astringent and antiseptic properties. Until 1788 it was listed in the British pharma-

Costmary

copoeia as an aperient, particularly useful in the treatment of dysentery. Culpeper reported that costmary:

> . . . provoketh urine abundantly, and moisteneth the hardness of the mother; it gently purgeth choler and phlegm . . . cleanseth that which is foul, and hindereth putrefaction and corruption; . . . and it is a wonderful help to all sorts of dry agues. It is astringent to the stomach, and strengtheneth the liver and all the other inward parts: and taken in whey, worketh more effectually. Taken fasting in the morning, it is very profitable for pains in the head, that are continual; . . . It is very profitable for those that are fallen into a continual evil disposition of the body, called cachexia, but especially in the beginning of the disease. It is an especial friend and help in evil, weak, and cold livers. The seed is familiarly given to children for the worms, and so is the infusion of flowers in a white wine given them to the quantity of two ounces at a time; it maketh an excellent salve to clense and heal old ulcers, being boiled with oil of olive, and adder's tongue with it; and after it is strained put a little wax, rosin, and turpentine to bring it to a convenient body

Gerard, writing even before Culpeper, said that "the Conserve made with leaves of Costmaria and sugar doth warm and dry the braine and openeth the stoppings of the same; stoppeth all catarrhes, rheumes and distillations, taken in the quantitie of a bean."

Among its other uses, costmary was suggested as part of a very old remedy for "Aqua Composita," a kind of consumption. It is also mentioned in recipes for "Oynment" to heal "bruises, dry itches, streins of veins and sinews, scorchings of gunpowder, the shingles, blisters, scabs and vermine."

Costmary is a perennial plant which is propagated only by the division of roots since there is no seed. You must buy a plant to begin. Existing plants can be divided each spring. It spreads fairly easily and shouldn't give any problem. The growing is easy. The soil requirements are minimal fertilization. The soil type is not important; costmary will grow in sandy soil as well as in heavy clay soils. Costmary does, like other herbs, prefer a well-drained soil and will not thrive in areas where the soil is poorly drained and standing water is common. Mulching is unnecessary and really not possible because the costmary spreads above the ground in the same way that peppermint does. Unlike peppermint, however, costmary retains much more of the bush form, containing itself in more limited space.

The harvesting should be done before the leaves turn yellow. Harvesting in small amounts is recommended. Many leaves grow close to the ground, very few on stems; harvesting, therefore, has to be done almost leaf by leaf. The leaves take only a short time to dry at a temperature of about 100°F. Once they are dried, there's no problem in storing the plant or the leaves for a very long time.

Finding a nursery which carries costmary may be a problem. But when you do find costmary, add it to your garden. The rewards will be great.

CUMIN

Cuminum cyminum, Linn.
Umbelliferae

Cumin is native to the eastern Mediterranean, especially the upper reaches of the Nile. It follows that it was known early to the Persians, Egyptians, and Hebrews, and its use followed civilization around the Mediterranean and into France and England, though it has never become so popular in the northern countries as it has always been in the Near East. At one time, when pepper was rare and expensive, the Romans substituted cumin for it. In the time of Christ, the value of the cumin had increased until it had become negotiable in payment of taxes.

Cumin needs four warm months to mature its seed, so it is better grown in the south than in the northern states, although a crop may be matured in the north if plants are started early indoors. Seedlings should be planted outside in warm sandy loam when the spring has grown really warm. Plants are low and sprawling, because their weak stems will not support the weight of the large heads of flowers and seed. When they are planted outside, the seed is sown at the rate of 16 to 20 seeds to the foot, and the plants are not thinned. A thick growth helps support the heavy heads and keep them off the ground. Like most of the carrot family, cumin plants have finely divided foliage and lavender-white flowers.

Seeds ripen late in the fall. When the heads begin to turn brown, they should be cut and dried indoors. When thoroughly dried, they may be separated from the heads by rubbing between the hands. Seeds are small and may be separated from most of the chaff and stems by being strained through a sieve.

Seeds are used to flavor cheese, bread, cookies, sausage, meats, vegetables, fish, and game. When ground, they are sometimes among the ingredients of curry powder and chili powder.

DANDELION

Taraxacum officinale, Weber.
Compositae

Dandelion is a weed. At least to the harried farmer, the lawn fanatic, and the average person dandelion is a weed. But dandelion has a long and interesting history as a medicinal plant and foodstuff. That yellow-flowered, toothy-leaved plant infesting lawns, vacant lots, and open fields is not always what it appears.

In many areas, the springtime sight of solitary figures roaming open weedy fields, bag or basket in hand, occasionally stopping to uproot a dandelion plant, is familiar. It's usually an older person who still recalls the delight of a dandelion salad or dandelion vegetable dish. For a salad, the leaves should be picked before they reach maturity, otherwise they will be too bitter. They should be blanched before using. An alternative is to boil or steam the leaves and serve them as you would spinach.

The roots are valued more than other plant parts for medicinal uses. In some areas of Europe, dandelions were purposefully cultivated for the roots, which were collected and dried during the second year of growth. The most recent herbals suggest dandelion is merely a simple bitter and mild laxative, but it has been credited as a diuretic, laxative, hepatic, antiscorbutic, sialagogue, tonic, aperient, alterative, and stomachic.

A tea said to be "efficacious in bilious affections" and "much approved of in the treatment of dropsy" is made by infusing an ounce of dried dandelion root in a pint of boiling water for ten minutes. Decant, sweeten with honey, and, during the course of the day, drink several glassfuls.

In Chinese medicine, dandelion is regarded as a blood cleanser, tonic, and digestive aid. It is ground and applied as a poultice to snake bites.

You may not want to cultivate dandelion, though it has been done. However, you might think better of it, knowing that the ancients viewed its wide distribution in nature as a sign — in keeping with the Doctrine of Signatures — that it was a cure-all. The bilious yellow flower was a sign that the plant was good for liver complaints. Even the name of the plant is apparently drawn from its appearance, though there is some disagreement as to which part of the appearance. The name dandelion is a corruption of the French *Dent de Lion,* or lion's tooth. Some suggest the jagged, toothy leaves prompted the name. Others attribute the name to the resemblance of the flower to the golden teeth of the heraldic lion. Still others see some leonine characteristic in the roots. You might give a closer look next time you dig one up and decide for yourself.

DILL

Anethum graveolens, **Linn.**
Umbelliferae

Dill is a hardy, annual plant that visually resembles fennel in so many ways that the herbalist Culpeper said the likeness "deceiveth many."

Life fennel, dill develops a spindly tap root, although dill roots are not usable. Dill also develops a round, shiny green main stem like fennel, but while fennel commonly shows many stems from a single root, there's seldom more than one on a dill plant.

Dill is prolific and if a few are left to seed themselves, a gardener will have his entire season's supply of dill without replanting.

It displays feathery branches along the main stem, which tops in a cluster of umbels with yellow flowers appearing at the tip of each umbel several weeks after planting. Seeds are attached to the umbel tips in pairs.

The plant likes moderately rich, loose soil, and full sun. Because young plants are difficult to transplant, start dill outdoors either by rows one-quarter-inch deep, or by broadcast sowing, or by drills ten inches apart. Cover the new seeds with a light soil blanket. Germination takes place in ten to 14 days at about 60°F.

Both leaves and seeds are used. If plants are to be harvested before going to seed, plan successive replantings from April through mid-July. For pickling — dill's major culinary use — seeding should be done in early May.

Leaves are harvested about eight weeks after seeding, with the outer leaves cut first, always close to the stem. Dry them within a day or two, in the shade, by placing them on fine screen or paper. Use a low oven to complete the drying, if necessary, for dill leaves will lose their color and flavor if drying time is prolonged. Seal them in a tight jar. Freeze them fresh as an alternative to drying.

Plants left to mature will grow to two to three feet, develop the flower-tipped umbels and eventually go to seed.

Dill

For pickling, harvest the flowering umbels and a few leaves.

For oil and fragrance, of course, the seeds are desired. Wait until they're light brown, then cut the umbels, dry them in the sun a few days, and shake loose the seeds. Do cutting in the early morning hours when seeds are less likely to be shaken loose accidentally and lost.

Seeds yield their oils to infusions of hot water or spirits. Bruise them first.

In the vegetable garden small quantities of dill may be sown in the corners and allowed to mature and bloom for honeybees. It is a good herb to grow with cabbage, and, when lightly sown, with carrots, cucumbers, lettuce, and onions. It should never be allowed to mature when sown with carrots, for it has a severely depressing effect on them when it is matured.

The medicinal uses of dill, too, closely resemble those of fennel. A decoction of dill in white wine is "a gallant expeller of wind and provoker of terms," Culpeper says. Dill water is used as a "gripe water" against flatulence in babies.

Good, too, for easing swelling and pains, dill is said to increase milk in nursing mothers and even to cure ulcers. In the

Middle Ages, dill was held to be a powerful charm against witchcraft. The sixteenth-century poet Michael Drayton wrote of a woman,

> "Therewith her Vervain and her Dill
> That hindereth witches of their will."

A 1640 recipe for pickling cucumbers with dill is as follows:

"Gather the tops of the ripest Dill and cover the bottom of the vessel, and lay a layer of Cucumbers and another of Dill till you have filled the vessel within a handful of the top. Then take as much water as you think will fill the vessel and mix it with salt and a quarter pound of allom to a gallon of water and poure it on them and press them down with a stone on them and keep them covered close. For that use I think the water will be best boyl'd and cold, which will keep longer sweet, or if you like not this pickle, doe it with water, salt and white wine vinegar, or (if you please) pour the water and the salt on them scalding hot which will make them ready to use the sooner."

Dill vinegar is easier to make. It simply requires soaking a few dill leaves in vinegar for a few days.

In France, dill is used to flavor cakes and pastries. More likely, you'll want to add its chopped leaves to soups and salads. Creamed chicken and plain cottage or cream cheese take on a tangy snap with the addition of a few chopped leaves. Try it in steaks and chops, too.

DITTANY, FALSE or WHITE

Fraxinella, Gas Plant, Burning Bush
Dictamnus albus, Linn.
Rutaceae

A notably long-lived perennial, false dittany resents transplanting. Sow seeds in open ground as soon as ripe in fall, to sprout in spring. It is a frost germinator. Dittany has dark green, shining compound leaves, and showy flowers in loose terminal spires. The volatile oil from the flowers is emitted as a vapor on sultry summer evenings and if a match is lit, will flash. The white flowering variety has a lemon fragrance; the pink is more fragrant, but less lemony and has the added scent of almond and vanilla. According to Parkinson, it was used against contagious diseases and pestilence.

DOCK

Rumex, various species
Polygonaceae

Dock is a name applied to a group of broad-leaved wayside weeds. As the generic name, *Rumex,* is shared with the sorrels, the docks obviously have a lot in common. Both sorrels and docks have pot-herb uses, but the docks generally are less palatable. The docks also have much in common with ordinary garden rhubarb, and can be used as substitutes for it.

R. crispus, yellow or curled dock, is probably the dominant variety. The plant grows one to three feet in height, and the broad six to ten inch leaves have crisped edges, hence the specific name. The deep root makes the weed hard to eradicate, but it is the root which is used. Collected late in the summer and into autumn, the roots are split, dried, and stored for use as a gentle tonic, astringent, laxative, and alterative. In various compounds, it is useful in treating skin eruptions and itching. A simple ointment for such use is made by boiling the root in vinegar, then mixing the softened pulp with lard or petroleum jelly.

R. obtusifolius, round-leaved dock, the common variety, is used today mostly in wool dyeing. The root yields a yellow dye. But the leaves have also been used as dressings for blisters, burns, and scalds. Round-leaved dock is generally somewhat taller than yellow dock and has generally somewhat larger leaves, with rounded ends.

Other docks include: patience dock *(R. alpinus),* a six-foot tall plant with large, long, pointed leaves; sharp-pointed dock *(R. acetus),* a common plant similar to round-leaved dock, but with pointed leaves which are narrower and longer; red or water dock *(R. aquaticus),* with an appearance and properties not unlike yellow dock; and great water dock *(R. hydrolapathum),* the largest of the docks, with a height exceeding six feet in some cases and one- to three-foot lancet-shaped dull green leaves, which has an affinity for riverbanks.

DOGWOOD

Cornus florida, Linn.
Cornaceae

The dogwood is a beautiful American, small (ten to thirty foot tall) tree that blossoms each May with an abundance of snowy-white flowers. The flowers are followed by a few red berry-like fruits that contain a two-seeded nutlet. It has a grayish trunk bark and reddish branch bark.

The dogwood is a lovely ornament, and a variety of species make a dogwood suitable for most any American climate. *Cornus florida* is a southern species, and the one most frequently noted for its medicinal properties. The dogwood prefers an acid soil, and will thrive in any mixed or semi-shady spot.

The Indians were the first to use this American native for healing, and the white settlers were quick to add it to their folk medicine. Although the bark was the principal part used, both the flowers and fruit have also been used. The Delawares, Alabamas, and Houmas of Louisiana all used the inner bark to make a febrifuge tea. "It is good in low continued forms of fever, where the patient is greatly exhausted," reported one nineteenth-century Indian folk herbal.

During the Civil War, dogwood was one of several native plants which provided a substitute for quinine, which is obtained from the bark of the cinchona tree, a Peruvian native, when the South was cut off from outside sources of supply.

C. florida was listed as a bitter tonic and astringent in the *United States Pharmacopoeia* from 1820 to 1894 and in the *National Formulary* for two decades during the twentieth century. Two other dogwood species *C. circinata* and *C. sericea* were listed for much the same uses at the same time.

EGYPTIAN ONION

Top Onion
Allium cepa var. *viviparum*
Liliaceae

Most people are familiar with the onion, a plant which is unremarkable as a plant but quite remarkable as a food and seasoning. But few are familiar with the onion family's curiosity, the Egyptian onion, a plant that is remarkable as a plant and no less so as a food and seasoning.

The most curious thing about the Egyptian onion is that it develops bulbs at the top of its slender green shoots, as opposed to the typical onion, which develops its bulb at the bottom. The bulbs are set in the ground and send up shoots typical of the onions. But instead of a seedhead, the Egyptian onion develops a bulb, which sends up its own shoot, which develops a bulb and so on. Of course the weight of the several stages of bulbs eventually bends the plant to the ground, where the stalk-end bulbs can take root and establish themselves as new plants.

The onions are plants worthy of herbalists' attentions, and the Egyptian onion might be the variety best suited for one interested in the plant more as an herb and less as a vegetable. The plant is usable in every way that the common onion is usable, and it is an interesting garden plant as well, making an arresting back border for a culinary garden.

The onions generally have some background as valued herbs. Like their relative garlic *(Allium sativum),* onions were a favored food of the Egyptian slaves. According to the Greek historian Herodotus, nine tons of gold was given in payment for the onion consumed by the slaves building the great pyramids. The Egyptians themselves held onions in high regard, for Pliny reports that they "make their oaths" by garlic and onions. They regarded the brittle brown skin which envelops the onion bulb as a symbol of the universe.

Later, Europeans had superstitions about onions, too. One practice was the suspending of onion slices in each room to purge "evil spirits" from a house. The slices were collected and burned daily. One herbalist, Dr. Fernie, recorded a story attributing the immunization of a London household to the plague to a sack of onions. A similar story recorded by another herbalist attributes the immunization to garlic. The conflicting stories serve to demonstrate the inherent similarities of the two herbs. Culpeper noted under his entry for garlic that for most ailments, onions served as well as garlic.

The ancient herbalists did have some good words for onions. Parkinson, for example, said onions had many uses, "so many I cannot recount them, everyone pleasing themselves, according to their order, manner, or delight." Gerard listed a variety of applications. He said they "do bite, attenuate, or make thinne, breake winde, provoke urine . . . they open passages that are stopped . . . the juice sniffed up into the nose, purgeth the head . . . stamped with salt, rue and honey, and so applied, they are good against the biting of a mad dog. . . .The juice annointed upon a pild or bald head in the sunne, bringing the hair again very speedily. . . . Onions sliced and dipped in the juice of Sorrell will take away a fit of the Ague."

Evelyn reported: "Boiled they give a kindly relish, raise appetites, corroborate the Stomach, cut Phlegm, and profit the Asthmatical."

Culpeper, noting that the onion is "so common and well known that it needs no description," listed most of the applications that the other herbalists listed and added a few of his own. The onions, he said, "increase sperm, especially the seed: they kill worms in children, if they drink the water fasting wherein they have been steeped all night. Being roasted under the embers, and eaten with honey, or sugar and oil, they much conduce to help an inveterate cough, and expectorate tough phlegm." He continued, "The juice is good for either scalds or burns. Used with vinegar it takes away all blemishes, spots, and marks in the skin; and dropped into the ears, eases the pains and noise in them. Applied also with figs beaten together, helps to ripen and break imposthumes, and other sores."

His entry continued, "Onions are good for cold watery

Egyptian Onion

humours, but injurious to persons of bilious habit, affecting the head, eyes, and stomach. When plentifully eaten, they procure sleep, help digestion, cure acid belchings, remove obstructions of the viscera, increase the urinary secretions, and promote insensible perspiration. . . . Onion bruised, with the addition of a little salt, and laid on fresh burns, draws out the fire, and prevents them blistering. The use is fittest for cold weather, and for aged, phlegmatic people, whose lungs are stuffed, and breathing short."

Quite a number of medicinal applications of the onions still are listed in herbals. A simple onion tea is listed as a diuretic. The antiseptic properties of the onions may be put to use by mascerating the bulb and applying it to sores, boils, and the like as a poultice. There are a surprising variety of folk cures which are onion-based.

Warts are said to be eliminated by the daily application of salted onion. The same application is said to take the heat out of scalding burns. Calluses can be removed, it is said, through a curious onion treatment. Fresh onions are cut in half, then steeped for at least three hours in strong wine vinegar. The onion halves are then securely bound to the calluses and left overnight.

In the morning, the surface layer of the callus will be sufficiently softened to permit it to be scraped or picked away. Repeat the process until the callus is wholly removed. A reputed cure for athlete's foot is onion juice. Merely rub the juice between the toes two or three times daily until the condition disappears.

For sprains, mix a finely chopped onion with sugar, spread on a cloth and wrap around the sprained joint. A variation on this remedy is to mix a tablespoon of olive oil with a finely chopped onion and apply the mixture as a thick poultice. A third variation calls for a poultice made from a chopped onion and salt.

Onions are also reputed useful in cases of asthma, bronchitis, and other respiratory ailments. Just the odor of the onion is prescribed for some such ailments, although it most often suggested that a raw onion be made a part of the diet until the ailment is gone. A croup remedy is made by thinly slicing an onion, and sprinkling sugar on each slice. The syrup which this concoction yields should be taken in teaspoon doses every fifteen minutes until the croup is gone.

Other onion cures can be cited for earaches, gall stones, protruding piles, headaches, and skin blemishes. Most seem centered about the vegetable garden onion, rather than the curious Egyptian onion, but the qualities are very much similar.

In the kitchen, the Egyptian onion is serviceable in all the dishes in which one would use onions. They are particularly good for pickling. Moreover, the stalks of the Egyptian onion may be diced and used as a substitute for chives.

Since Egyptian onion has no seed, it has to be started from the little onion bulbs, which can be started any time of the year. The little onions are very hardy, and if the plant is not taken care of, these onion bulbs bend down to the ground over winter and, in spring, sprout anew. The growing of the plant is easy, simply because it is so rugged and frost hardy.

The Egyptian onion grows in almost any type of soil, but needs some fertilization if a good formation of little onion bulbs is to be expected. The best fertilizer is a compost not too rich in nitrogen, such as a weed or leaf compost. Manures should be avoided.

The bulbs and stalks may be harvested throughout the growing season. The bulbs will generally make their appearance in early July and can be used fresh immediately or allowed to dry on the plant before harvesting. When dried to a dark brown, the bulbs store very well, better in fact than the common garden variety. The stems would, of course, be used fresh.

As mentioned, Egyptian onions present an arresting appearance in the herb garden, but they can also be of value in a vegetable garden. Planted with carrots, they will help repel the pesty carrot fly. They like to grow with beets and camomile, and, in good soil, they are helped by summer savory and lettuce. Don't plant onions with peas or beans, however, for they will inhibit the growth of them.

ELDER, AMERICAN or COMMON

Sambucus canadensis, Linn.
Caprifoliaceae

This is a large, rather coarse, deciduous shrub that grows rapidly and can reach a height of eight to 12 feet in a few seasons. The elder leaves are large, dark green. It is most handsome in bloom during June and July, with creamy-white, umbel-like flower clusters up to ten inches across with a sweet, heavy scent. Later it hangs heavy with purplish-black berries. Elders are very effective planted in groups. It is hardy, and while not particular about the location, it does especially well in rich, moist soil with some shade. It can be propagated by cuttings of bare shoots in autumn, or it may be started from seed. Elder should be pruned in late autumn or early spring before growth begins.

All parts of the elder are useful: the flowers, berries, leaves, bark, and root. The berries are prized for making wine, pies, and jellies. Elderflower fritters can be made from either fresh or dried flowers. A delightful tea is made from the dried blossoms, and it is helpful for colds and to promote sleep. Elder has been used for many medicinal purposes, in skin lotions, facials and packs, and as an antiseptic wash for skin disease.

Elder was widely used by the American Indians, who applied

the bark as an antidotal poultice to painful swellings and inflammations. There was some use of a bark tea to ease parturition and of a tea made from the dried flowers as a febrifuge. The elder berries were listed in the official pharmacopoeias for a few years during the nineteenth century and the flowers for a nearly century-long period spanning the nineteenth and twentieth centuries. The flowers were listed as mildly stimulant, carminative, and diaphoretic.

Some old Indian folk medicine guides listed the bark and flowers as diuretic, purgative, and emetic, depending upon the dosage. In one guide, the author, one J. I. Lighthall, wrote:

> The old fogy idea of cutting the bark up and down, reversing its medical action, that is, vomiting and purging, is all bosh. It is all owing to the size of the dose, and not the way the bark is cut. In large doses it will vomit, and in smaller ones act as a gentle purgative. Any superstitious reader doubting this will be convinced of the fact by trying it on their own bodies. We obtain positive facts in reference to the action of medicine in different doses, by trying them on ourselves. I speak from experience, not book reading.

Lighthall repeated a number of the common Indian uses for elder, but added that a tea of the flowers had a diaphoretic effect when taken hot, a diuretic effect when taken cold, and that a tea of the bark, taken in tablespoon doses three or four times daily was a mild purgative, while a dose of three to four swallows every five minutes would produce an emetic effect.

Indians called elder the "tree of music" and made flutes from branches cut in spring and dried with the leaves on. Large shoots were used for arrow shafts.

Bruised leaves, rubbed on the skin will keep flies away. It is said to protect garden plants from insect pests. An elder planted near the orchard will lure birds away from other fruit with its berries. A decoction of the leaves will keep caterpillars from eating plants on which it is sprayed; it is also used as a spray for mildew. Elder aids in fermentation of compost and creates humus in the soil around it which can be valuable used in other plantings.

ELECAMPANE

Inula helenium, Linn.

Compositae

Elecampane is a striking herb, tall, erect, and beautiful. It is a sturdy, almost unbranching plant, generally rising between four and five feet, but ranging as high as ten feet. Its huge, tapering leaves, broad at the base, pointed at the apex, are offset by small, daisy-like flowers of orange disks bordered with a shaggy fringe. Elecampane is not a native of the United States, but has been thoroughly naturalized, having come here with the earliest immigrants.

Provided a moist, shady spot, it will grow well in any garden soil, though the better the soil, the better the plant. The seed germinates in about fifteen days and may be sown in the spring or when ripe in a cold frame. Elecampane may also be propagated by root division in spring or by offsets of one bud and eye taken from the parent plant in fall.

Horseheal and scabwort are two of the nicknames elecampane derived from its early medical uses. A decoction of elecampane is said to heal scabs on sheep, hence the name scabwort. Likewise, elecampane was reputedly effective in cutaneous diseases of horses, hence, horseheal.

The part used is the thickened root, which is generally gathered in the fall of its second year. The dried, crushed root is an ingredient in many compound medicines. It is rarely used alone. Its action is diuretic, tonic, diaphoretic, expectorant, antiseptic, astringent, alterative, and gently stimulant. American Indian herbalists found it to be particularly useful in bronchial and lung ailments. One Indian remedy for such troubles was made by combining a half-pound each of elecampane root, spikenard root, and comfrey root. The roots were mashed well, combined with a gallon of water which was boiled down to a quart. The liquid was poured off into a half-gallon container. Eight ounces of alcohol and a pint and a half of honey were added. The recommended dosage was a teaspoonful every two hours.

ELM, SLIPPERY

Sweet Elm, Indian Elm
Ulmus rubra, Muhl. (syn. *Ulmus fulva,* Michx.)
Ulmaceae

A deciduous native of central and northern portions of the country, the slippery elm is a slim, wide-branching, flat-topped tree, occasionally used for street planting. The dark brown bark is deeply furrowed, rough, and scaly. The under bark is a ruddy brown; the innermost layer is buff white and aromatic and is the portion used medicinally. The rough leaves are a deep yellowish, olive green, lighter beneath. It blooms in March and April; the winged, round fruit or seed ripens in spring in two to four years.

Elms may be used as street or lawn trees. They are propagated by seeds sown as soon as ripe, also by layering and greenwood cuttings.

The inner bark is very mucilaginous and has been used and known as one of the more important healing plants. The powdered bark is used as a nutritious gruel or food and is recommended for its soothing and healing action for inflammations of the stomach, bowels, for bronchitis, and as a poultice for ulcers, wounds, burns, boils, and inflamed surfaces. It has been made into lozenges for cough and sore throat.

Relief of inflammations of the digestive tract may be realized by taking a decoction of slippery elm bark. Steep two or more ounces of the bark in a quart of boiling water for an hour or more. After straining, the decoction may be taken freely in tablespoon doses. The same decoction is said to be useful as an enema. A lighter decoction, one ounce of the cut bark to a quart of water, has been recommended as a vaginal douche.

EUCALYPTUS

Blue Gum Tree
Eucalyptus globulus, Labill.
Myrtaceae

There are many very useful and ornamental varieties of eucalyptus, some of them very hardy. The tall blue gum *(Euca-*

lyptus globulus) is used for windbreaks, large, wide branching varieties for shade, and small trees for ornamental shade and lawn trees. The leaves are generally long, narrow, gray-green or bluish on slender, drooping branches. Some varieties produce lovely blossoms in abundance which are a valuable source of honey nectar.

The eucalyptus is a heavy feeder and should not be planted too closely to other plants which might suffer from depletion of nutrients.

Silver dollar is a variety very popular for home landscape, not too large but very attractive. It has colorful foliage from silvery white to pink and reds at various seasons and is valued for dried flower arrangements. The leaves are round with the stem going through the center. Eucalyptus are propagated by seed sown under screens.

Insects are repelled by its aromatic oil, which is also used medicinally. One teaspoon of the oil in one-half pint of warm water, rubbed into the skin, is a powerful insect repellent for man or animals. Dried, finely powdered leaves are used as an insecticide.

The leaves and the oil distilled from them are the elements of eucalyptus used medicinally. The plant is said to have antiseptic qualities, which accounts for its use in treating ulcers and open wounds. The dried and powdered leaves have been inhaled in cases of bronchial inflammations and similar ailments. The oil and infusions of the leaves have been used also in cases of fevers, muscle spasms, croup, and spasmodic throat troubles. Care must be exercised to avoid large doses of eucalyptus, as it may produce indigestion, nausea, vomiting, diarrhea, muscular weakness, and related effects.

EYEBRIGHT

Euphrasia officinalis, Linn.
Scrophulariaceae

Eyebright is a tough but elegant little plant. It's a fairly common British weed, rarely domesticated in the United States. It is an annual, growing two to eight inches in height, having deeply-cut leaves and numerous, small, white or purplish flowers varigated with yellow.

Eyebright is somewhat difficult to grow, since it requires a symbiotic relationship with grass to survive. The eyebright roots send out tiny suckers, which attach themselves to the roots of grasses, drawing a measure of nourishment for the semi-parasite from the grass.

The medicinal use of the plant, as the name suggests, was for eye ailments. An infusion is made by putting an ounce of the herb in a pint of boiling water. When cooled, the infusion should be used to bathe the eyes. Eyebright has also been used in combatting hay fever.

FENNEL

Foeniculum vulgare, Mill.
Umbelliferae

Portly herbalists might find it wise to develop an interest in fennel for, in the words of the old master herbalist Culpeper, all parts of the fennel plant "are much used in drink or broth to make people lean that are too fat." It is not the sort of plant that gardeners will want to integrate in *their* gardens, however, for it is the prime exception to the rule that herbs have a positive effect on surrounding plants.

Fennel is a biennial with a tendency to become a perennial where soil and climate are favorable. Its main tap root is usually finger-thick, white, and fleshy, with smaller horizontal side roots attached. An equally thick main stem of a highly polished green appearance extends vertically to be capped by a small cluster of umbels the first year. In the second year, more main stems develop from the root and develop a multitude of umbels with tiny yellow, five-bladed flowers. Seeds of light to dark brown form in pairs at each bloom. Large feathery leaves of dark green adorn the main stem, which can reach four or five feet.

Fennel must be started from seed, which can be sown outside as soon as the soil can be worked. It prefers moderately fertile soil with adequate calcium and much sun. Avoid constant moisture.

Fennel

Sow lightly in a bed or in drills six inches apart. Keep moist until two thin seed leaves are plainly visible. Germination takes place within two weeks. Thin to six inches.

Fennel must be located with due regard of its neighbors, as noted. It has a decidedly harmful effect on bush beans, caraway, tomatoes, and kohlrabi. On the other hand, it is harmed by certain plants: coriander will prevent the formation of seeds if planted too close, and wormwood planted too close (within four feet) cuts germination and stunts the growth of fennel plants.

At the end of the first year, northern gardeners should dig up the tap roots along with about three inches of stem. Treat them like carrots and potatoes: put them in sand in a humid, cool cellar or outside in a coldframe or trench. In the spring, shorten the roots a bit and plant them 36 inches apart. The fennel will reach its full height and bloom. Harvest seeds as they turn from green to light brown. Morning hours are best to avoid unnecessary seed losses.

Fennel flowers will attract pollinating insects but the powdered plant is used as a flea repellent around kennels and stables.

The ancient Greeks and Anglo-Saxons snitched on their fast days by nibbling a little fennel, which reduced the appetite.

With carminative and purgative qualities, fennel "expels wind, provokes urine, and eases the pains of the stone and helps it to break," Culpeper advised.

Fennel also can be a mother's friend. Leaves and seeds boiled in barley water increase the yield of mother's milk and make it more wholesome. And fennel is the basis for a concoction called "gripe water" used to correct flatulence in infants.

One of the herb's chief medicinal qualities in olden times was its supposed ability to improve eyesight. The early nineteenth-century poet Longfellow wrote of it:

> Above the lower plants it towers,
> The Fennel with its yellow flowers;
> And in an earlier age than ours
> Was gifted with the wondrous powers
> Lost vision to restore.

Seeds are the most-used part of the plant for oil extraction. The seeds yield their oil when distilled in water. Infusions work with hot water but even better with alcohol.

Leaves are used as both a garnish and a flavoring for salads, stews, and vegetables. Boiled with salmon and mackerel, it lessens the oily indigestibility of those fish. Fennel stalks are added to the fire beneath fish in some French kitchens.

The fennel stalk, stripped of its skin and dressed in vinegar and pepper, makes a tasty celery-like salad that is popular in the plant's native Mediterranean area. The Italians call the dish *carlucci* and claim it calms and aids sleep.

FEVERFEW

Chrysanthemum parthenium, (Linn.) Bernh. (syn.
Pyrethrum parthenium, Smith; *Matricaria parthenium,*
Linn.)

Compositae

Feverfew is a hardy biennial to perennial with a daring list of curative claims. A member of the daisy family, feverfew grows freely in fields and untended ground. Reaching as high as two to three feet, it bears golden-green leaves, and white daisy-like flowers, which have inspired people to nickname the herb bride's button or bachelor's buttons. In June, these inch-wide flowers completely cover the plant. The yellow center of the flower is distinguished from the conical camomiles by its flatness. Gerard described the leaves of what he called "featherfew," a variation of the name, as being "tender, diversely torne and jagged, and nickt on the edges. . . ." Unlike some of the sweeter herbs, feverfew emits a strong odor and possesses a bitter taste. The burning taste of the root explains why this herb is classified in some sources as a *pyrethrum,* derived from the Greek *pyr* (fire).

In the past, this versatile herb has offered numerous and varied benefits to humanity. It was once considered effective in cleansing the atmosphere and warding off disease. To combat insects, a tincture made from feverfew mixed with one-half pint of cold water will keep away the gnats, mosquitos, and other pests. But if the insect bites, it's helpful to know that feverfew has the power to "relieve the pain and swelling caused by bites of insects and vermin." Worth noting in particular is the fact that bees find the odor and taste of feverfew highly repulsive.

In Finland, feverfew was administered as a tonic for consumption and its stimulant nature made it a good emmenagogue. Culpeper advised that:

> The powder of the herb taken in wine, with some oxymel, purges both choler and phlegm, and is available for those that are short-winded, and are troubled with melancholy and heaviness, or sadness of spirits. It is very effectual for all pains in the head coming of a cold cause, the herb being bruised and applied to the crown of the head: as also for the vertigo, that is, a running or swimming of the head.

For opium addicts suffering from overdose, feverfew would provide relief, Parkinson claimed. The Italians discovered it a tasty companion to fried eggs. Cotton Mather of colonial New England recommended feverfew sprinkled with rum and applied hot to relieve the pain of a toothache. Victims of coughing, wheezing, and difficult breathing found that feverfew with honey eased the discomfort. The herb was fried with wine and oil and applied externally to eliminate colic. An infusion of feverfew flowers was believed to reduce the sensitivity to pain which highly nervous people experience.

According to Culpeper, feverfew is commanded by Venus, and thus addresses many of its healing powers to the ailments of women. He observed that feverfew is considered to be "a general strengthener of their wombs, and to remedy such infirmities as a careless midwife has there caused . . ." When boiled and drunk

Feverfew

in white wine, feverfew "cleanses the womb, expels the afterbirth, and does a woman all the good she can desire of an herb." Among its many old, familiar names, "Maydes Weed" refers to the use of feverfew as a laxative for "young women suffering from suppression and inclined towards hysteria."

A hardy plant, feverfew needs very little attention. It may be grown and handled like camomile, for the many medicinal uses or for the dainty blossoms it bears. The best time for planting is April, although during the autumn it is also possible. Although feverfew is not difficult to grow in almost any soil, a well-drained, loamy soil, well-nourished with manure offers best results. To protect the fragile young plants from the hoe, it is recommended that weeding be done by hand in the early stages of growth.

Feverfew is propagated in three ways: by seed, by root division, and by cuttings. February and March are the most favorable months for sowing the seeds if that method is chosen. It is recommended that they be thinned out to two to three inches between each plant so that in June they will be hardy and ready to be transferred to permanent quarters on some rainy day in early June. Each plant should be spaced a foot or more apart, leaving two feet between the rows. Soon the plants grown from seed will be firmly established in the soil.

Propagation by division of the roots is done when the roots are most active, often in March. With a sharp spade or knife, they are sectioned into from three to five large parts.

A third way to begin new feverfew plants is by taking cuttings from the young shoots which spring from the bases of mature plants. The heel of the old plant should be attached to these new shoots since it will facilitate rooting. When the cuttings are ready for insertion, any time from October to May, shorten the foliage to three inches and plant firmly in a bed of light, sandy soil in a shady spot. Cover the top of the bed with sand and drench with water. Beware of snails and slugs which can be combatted by sprinkling the plants with soot, ashes, or lime. To protect the feverfew cuttings from black fly, sprinkle them with pepper.

The plants to be harvested may be gathered most any time at the peak of their maturity. The technique may require some practice, however. According to Gerard, feverfew was most effective against the fever or ague if it was gathered with the left hand as the name of the victim was spoken aloud and with nary a glance behind.

FOXGLOVE

Digitalis purpurea, Linn.
Scrophulariaceae

Foxglove is the source of a most famous plant-derived medicine, digitalis. It is, without question, a true medicinal plant.

But foxglove is also a favorite garden plant, having two-inch long thimble-like flowers in a one-sided spray. The flowers develop on an unbranching three-foot stalk, surrounded by the medically valuable leaves.

The leaves are picked in the second year just as the plant

begins to flower. The drug derived from the leaves is used primarily as a blood circulation stimulant and for heart diseases. (It should be noted that digitalis can have deleterious effects and should be used only under proper supervision.) Curiously enough, the ancient herbalists tended to use foxglove for external uses. It was not until 1775 that an English doctor, having heard of internal uses from a folk healer, investigated its benefits on a scientific basis.

Foxglove is grown from seed, though the germination is somewhat uncertain. Seeds must be sown annually to maintain an annual bloom. The soil should be rich and moist. The plants should be fertilized annually with compost and mulched in fall to prevent winterkill.

GARLIC

Allium sativum, Linn.
Liliaceae

Garlic is a ruffian with a heart of gold. It has a wealth of talents—serving man in the kitchen, the medicine chest, and the vegetable garden—yet it is totally undistinguished of appearance and its smell is coarse and offensive. Throughout history, and even today, garlic is the herb many associate with people they'd rather not know. Perhaps it is best characterized as the herb of the common man.

Garlic has a long history, and it has always been tied to the working man, nearly always distained, despite its good works. Its origin is unknown, though it is believed to have spread into the Middle East and Europe from somewhere southeast of Siberia. The Chinese have known and used garlic for centuries, as have the Jews and Arabs. Garlic was mentioned in the *Calendar of the Hsai*, a Chinese book dating back 2,000 years before Christ, is known to have been used by the Babylonians around 3,000 B.C., and is a part of the ancient Hebrew Talmudic law, which stipulates it be used in certain dishes and on certain occasions.

Since these early evidences, the appearance of garlic in man's written record has been repeated again and again, with the same general information set down and the same general attitude evident: garlic will heal many different ailments, but it smells terrible.

The object of these mixed feelings is a small, vigorous relative of the onion. Like all the onions, it is a spare, functional plant, having a bulb sending up a few, thin sprouts. Garlic's strap-like leaves grow to a foot or two in length, and surround a slender flower stalk which develops a globular cluster of tiny white blossoms. There's so little fanciness to it that some herbalists leave it out of their gardens. But the heart of garlic is underground.

It is there that the pungent-tasting and smelling bulb develops. It is a segmented globe, each segment called a clove. There are generally eight to twelve cloves to a bulb. With very rare exceptions, these cloves of garlic are all that see use. (One herbalist suggests harvesting the garlic tops for use in salads of all kinds.)

Garlic is relatively easily cultivated, though it does require a fairly long growing season. As early in the spring as possible, the bulb is split into its component cloves, and each is planted separately. Each should be planted about two inches deep and about six inches from its neighbors. Garlic will grow in most any soil, though it prefers a moist, sandy soil. A dressing of well-rotted manure or compost is helpful, but any raw manure is definitely not. Sun is important; a cold, damp growing season can hinder the garlic's development seriously. Weeds too can crowd out garlic, so don't let them get the upper hand.

Garlic set out in March should be ready for harvest in August to September. Gather the bulbs after the leaves wither. They can be spurred to ripeness by bending the stalks to the ground in late summer. Once harvested, the plants may be braided together by their leaves and hung to dry. Or they can be popped into an old nylon stocking or net bag and, again, hung up to dry. If you are going to try the greens in a salad, gather and use them fresh.

Though garlic is seldom used today for the purpose that made it a historical figure, it nevertheless is a major crop in some areas. California produces the most garlic, but it is also produced in major quantities in Texas, Louisiana, and other states with the warm, sunny climate so suitable for cultivating the herb. In 1960,

$1.8 million worth of garlic was grown in the United States. Most of this garlic goes into the cookpot or salad bowl, but some of it turns up in organic gardens, repelling bugs. A garlic bulb is relatively expensive, but then a little goes a long way.

Moderation is the byword in the culinary use of garlic. Begin, as most cookbooks suggest, by rubbing a clove of garlic around the salad bowl or the saucepan. As the taste for garlic develops, increase the dosage. Eventually, you will be using whole cloves.

A salad benefits from garlic. Cut a clove and rub it around the inside of the bowl. To spark a soup, chop a garlic clove finely and add it. A joint of lamb, mutton, or pork is improved in tenderness and flavor by the addition of garlic. Skin a few cloves and insert them in incisions made in the meat. Cook and serve. A simple method of experimenting with garlic seasoning on any dish is to use garlic salt, a powder made from dried garlic cloves and available in most health food stores. A strong concoction is garlic butter, made by blending together a quarter pound of butter and four mascerated garlic cloves.

The problem with garlic always is the smell. If you like garlic, you might also get to like parsley, which is said to clear the air you exhale. Simply chew a sprig or two at the end of a garlic-rich meal. Milk, too, is said to be an antidote to the garlic smell, though many a cow has tainted its milk — from the farmer's standpoint, anyhow — by munching a bit of wild garlic.

The smell, while being the herb's weak point, is unfortunately inextricably tied to its strong point, the herb's essential oil. The oil is what makes the herb valuable in so many ways, and it is what makes the smell which earned garlic the sobriquet "stink-weed" in days past. The oil is a mixture of substances which are mainly allyl sulfides; the basic active principal is called "allicin." The potency of the oil is such that it is claimed that the garlic odor will taint the breath of one who rubs the cloves on the soles of his feet.

While today's herbalist probably wouldn't be inclined to so treat his feet, the herbalist of old was. Cotton Mather, a leader in the New England colonies, reported that garlic cloves were bound to the feet of smallpox victims. Putting garlic cloves in the shoes of whooping cough sufferers was another clove-to-foot

Garlic

remedy. Other of the old-time garlic remedies were similarly quaint, but these should not blind one to the actual positive effects of the herb.

Organic gardeners, for example, long believed that garlic has a positive effect in the garden as a deterrent to insect pests. To some this sounded silly, but a bit of folklore developed around this use in the last few decades. Some gardeners spotted garlic in amongst their vegetables most susceptible to insect damage, while others used the garlic cloves as an ingredient in homemade insect sprays. And within the last few years, scientific research has verified garlic is effective as an insecticide and insect repellent.

Most reassuring has been a report from England on the research of David Greenstock of the Henry Doubleday Research Association. Greenstock has been experimenting on a scientific basis with garlic and has developed a number of varieties of garlic-based insecticides which are effective against a variety of insects, from the malaria mosquito to cockchafer larvae, without being harmful to livestock or humans. Generally, the smell is credited for garlic's power as a garden guardian, and that's not far from wrong. Greenstock attributes the herb's power to the allyl sulfides, which are the source of the smell.

An easy do-it-yourself recipe from Greenstock is: Take three ounces of chopped garlic bulbs and let them soak in about two teaspoonfuls (50 cc.) of mineral oil (toilet paraffin) for 24 hours. Then slowly add a pint of water in which three-fourths of an ounce of oil-based soap (Palmolive is a good one) has been dissolved, and stir well. Strain the liquid through fine gauze, and store it in a china or glass container because it reacts with metals. Try it against your worst pests, starting with a dilution of one part to 20 parts of water, then going down to one to 100.

Historically, however, garlic's primary positive qualities have been related to health. It has a long list of medicinal uses. The peasants, slaves, and others who have used garlic throughout history have often done so because they believed it was vital to their health. There was a time in this century, for example, when herbalists were drawing parallels between the Bulgarians' use of garlic and their longevity. Pills have been made from garlic and marketed as a dietary supplement.

Medicinally, garlic is a diaphoretic, diuretic, expectorant, and stimulant. For centuries garlic has been a common European remedy for colds, coughs, and sore throats. A syrup of garlic is made by pouring a quart of boiling water over a pound of sliced garlic cloves, allowing the mixture to brew about 12 hours, then stirring in sufficient sugar to produce a syrup. Vinegar and honey may be added and are said to improve the syrup. The garlic smell may be masked by bruising a bit of sweet fennel seed or caraway seed and boiling it for a short time in vinegar, then adding the decoction to the syrup.

A syrup recommended for children troubled by a cough but not inflammation is made by melting an ounce and a half of sugar in an ounce of raw garlic juice (the juice squeezed from the garlic bulb).

These folk remedies are not without medical approval. A number of experiments have been conducted and the results reported are interesting. In the March, 1950 issue of *Medical Monthly*, a German magazine, Dr. J. Klosa reported that garlic oil kills dangerous organisms without attacking other organisms vital to the body. Klosa experimented with a solution of garlic oil and water, sometimes adding fresh extract of onion juice, which enhanced the solution's effectiveness. Studies by Dr. F. G. Piotrowsky of the University of Geneva revealed that blood pressure was effectively lowered in 40 percent of his hypertensive patients after being treated with garlic. In the July 1, 1948, issue of *Praxis,* Dr. Piotrowsky reported that garlic opens up blood vessels, thus reducing pressure. He also noted that dizziness, angina pains over the chest, and headaches often disappear with garlic therapy. More recently, Polish scientists reported from Warsaw in 1969 that bacteria which resist other antibiotics, including staphylococci, succumb to a pulverized garlic preparation. Scientists in the Soviet Union reported in 1972 the production of an actual pharmaceutical antibiotic, allicin, which they say destroys only specific harmful germs, leaving natural bacteria untouched.

The reports from the Communist-bloc countries confirm what had been effectively demonstrated through centuries of application, perhaps on a most formal basis in World War I: garlic is an antiseptic. The use of garlic as an antiseptic has, of course, passed into history as medical science has "progressed," but for years it was used in hospitals and by herbalists. During World War I, there was a boom in the garlic commerce, and the herb is credited with saving thousands of lives. Pads of sphagnum moss were sterilized and saturated with water-diluted garlic juice. When applied to open wounds, the garlic helped control suppuration.

Among the other ailments, garlic is said to remedy rheumatism, whooping cough, and intestinal worms. Garlic cloves were bruised and mixed with lard and the resulting ointment rubbed on the chest and back to cure whooping cough. The garlic syrup was said to be effective against rheumatism, as was simply rubbing the ailing joint with garlic. For intestinal worms, raw garlic juice, or milk which had been boiled with garlic was suggested. For baldness, a lotion was made by macerating several bulbs in a quart of wine or alcohol.

The ancients and the early herbalists had a wider variety of medicinal uses for garlic, but it is hardly surprising, given the proven effectiveness of garlic, that it was so highly regarded in history.

The ancient Egyptians held garlic in great esteem, invoking its name, as one might that of a deity, in the taking of oaths and, in some areas, refusing to eat it because it was too sacred. It was, however, an important part of the diet of the Egyptians' slaves, who reportedly refused to work when it was withheld. The Greeks too had a certain religious awe for garlic; they placed garlic on piles of stones at crossroads as a supper for Hecate, the triple goddess (Phoebe in heaven, Diana on earth, and Hecate in hell); but they also refused entrance to the Temple of Cybele to anyone who had garlic on his breath.

"When Satan stepped out from the Garden of Eden after the fall of man, Garlick sprang up from the spot where he placed his left foot, and Onion from that where his right foot touched." Such is the legend some herbalists attributed to the Mohammedans.

Homeric legend has garlic saving Ulysses from the fate of companions who were changed into pigs by Circe.

Garlic has appeared in writings of all sorts, from the epics of Homer, to the herbals of all ages, to the plays of William Shakespeare. Theophrastus and Pliny the Elder recorded much of what we know of garlic's uses in the ancient Egyptian and Greek civilizations. Aristophanes, the Greek playwright, wrote that garlic juice would restore lost virility, and told of famous athletes who made garlic a part of their training diet. Hippocrates, the medical pioneer, classified garlic as a sudorific, diuretic, and laxative. The Greek philosopher Aristotle wrote: "It is a cure for hydrophobia and a tonic, is hot, laxative, but bad for the eyes."

A number of Roman writers held garlic in equally high regard, Virgil ("essential to maintain the strength of the harvesters"), and Galen ("poor man's treacle") among them. But not all did. Horace called it "more poisonous than hemlock" and told of how he got sick eating it. He recorded that the smell of garlic was viewed as a sign of vulgarity. Fifteen centuries later, William Shakespeare was to record much the same observation.

The Renaissance herbalists generally had much to say for

garlic, much of it picked up from their ancient and medieval predecessors. Gerard quoted Galen at some length. Parkinson reported it to be the "poor man's treacle," a heal-all.

John Evelyn was more effusive:

> Garlick, Allium; dry towards Excess; and tho by both Spaniards and Italians and the more Southern People familiarly eaten with almost everything, and esteemed of such singular Vertue to help concoction, and thought a Charm against all Infection and Poyson (by which it has obtain'd the Name of the Country-man's Theriacle) we yet think it more proper for our Northern Rustics, especially living in Uliginous and moist places, or such as use the Sea; Whilst we absolutely forbid it entrance into our Salleting, by reason of its intolerable Rankness, and which made it so detested of old that the eating of it was (as we read) part of the Punishment for such as had committed the horrid'st Crimes.

Culpeper noted that "Mars owns this herb." He listed a variety of applications for garlic, adding that "for all those diseases the onions are as effectual. But the garlic," he continued, "has some more peculiar virtues besides the former, viz. it has a special quality to discuss inconveniences, coming by corrupt agues or mineral vapours, or by drinking corrupt and stinking waters; as also by taking wolf-bane, hen-bane, hemlock, or other poisonous and dangerous herbs. Authors quote many other diseases this is good for; but conceal its vices. Its heat is very vehement; and all vehement hot things send up but ill-savoured vapours to the brain. In choleric men it will add fuel to the fire; in men oppressed by melancholy, it will attenuate the humour, and send up strong fancies, and as many strange visions to the head; therefore let it be taken inwardly with great moderation; outwardly you may make more bold with it."

Culpeper, of course, in listing the vices of garlic failed to mention the most commonly cited, its smell, making him one of the few writers who neglected it. But he did voice a widely-held belief that garlic was best suited for mild-tempered folk.

A virtue of garlic that these herbalists either overlooked or simply didn't know about was its reputation as a preventative of the plague. One legendary commendation of garlic concerns the Great Plague which swept England in the mid-seventeenth century. One Chester household was immunized from the plague, it is said, because garlic was stored in the building. A related story has the French clerics, who used garlic, ministering freely to the needs of the plague victims without contracting the disease, while English clerics, who didn't use garlic, were quickly cut down.

The most famous story of garlic and the plague tells of "Four Thieves Vinegar," which is a vinegar infused with garlic. According to one version of this legend, four thieves confessed to plundering the bodies of victims during the plague which swept Marsailles, France, in 1721. They protected themselves by imbibing vast quantities of the vinegar. In another version, the thieves are condemned men released from prison to help dispose of the thousands of bodies. Ultimately, they gain pardons by revealing how they carried out their assignment without contracting the plague themselves. Of course, the garlic vinegar was their secret.

The legends and stories, of course, do go on and on. Bull-fighters carry garlic to prevent the bulls from charging. Jockeys in Hungary used to carry garlic to prevent another horse and rider from getting in front of them. In India, garlic is worn for protection against evil spirits and spells. But perhaps the most familiar is the one that has dragged garlic down, the one voiced by so many, including William Shakespeare: "And, most dear actors, eat no onions nor garlic, for we are to utter sweet breath."

GENTIAN

Yellow Gentian, Gentian Root, Bitter Root
Gentiana lutea, Linn.
Gentianaceae

Gentian is a native of the mountainous regions of Europe. It has long been a recognized medicinal herb, chiefly a tonic, being first listed in old Arabic and Greek herbals and having made appearances in herbals and pharmacopoeias to this day. It is said to have been named for Gentius, a king of Illyria, who first discovered its tonic qualities.

Many varieties of this perennial are cultivated for rock gardens and woodland settings. *Gentiana lutea* is the recognized medicinal species. The stem is three to four feet tall, leaves oblong, bright, pale green with large yellow flowers that have a faint aromatic fragrance. Gentians are frost germinators and require a cool situation, with good drainage and ample amounts of humus and compost. Very small seeds are slow germinating and should be as fresh as possible.

The dried root and rhizome are the parts used medicinally. It was long regarded as a splendid tonic to invigorate digestion and purify the blood. A gentian root tonic was made by filling a pint bottle half-full of the dried root, filling it with a half-water, half-alcohol mixture, and allowing it to stand for fourteen days. A teaspoonful was taken before meals. The plant was also said to be helpful in fevers and general debility.

An American gentian, *G. catesbaci,* commonly known as blue gentian, habits swampy areas from Virginia to Florida. It grows between one and two feet tall and has a blue, club-shaped blossom. Never an official drug plant, blue gentian was nevertheless used by the Catawba Indians for back aches. The roots were steeped in hot water and the decoction applied to the painful area.

GERMANDER

Teucrium, various species
Labiatae

There are several varieties of germander, all fine bordering plants for the small garden. *Teucrium lucidum* is a hardy perennial with small, stiff, glossy dark green leaves which lends itself to clipping as a low hedge. It grows about one to one and a half feet tall. *T. chamaedrys,* commonly known as wall germander, is a low, creeping variety which makes a good ground cover. It is hardier than *T. lucidum,* and its leaves will turn reddish in autumn and in dry weather. *T. scorodonia,* known as sage-leaved germander, is a hedge-like plant which draws its common name from its grey-green, sage-like leaves. A fourth variety, *T. scordium,* is a creeping plant with an affinity for marshy, damp places, hence its common name, water germander.

Germander can be started from seed, but the germination

takes as long as thirty days. Perhaps a better method is to start plants from cuttings early in the growing season. The plants may be divided in the fall. The soil should be rich, light, and moist. A sunny spot is preferred but not essential.

Aside from its place in the landscaped garden, germander has a history of medicinal uses. A decoction of the herb has been taken as a remedy for gout. It is often listed as a diuretic, and each variety has different uses.

GINGER, WILD

Asarum canadense, Linn.
Aristolochiaceae

Wild ginger is native to North America. It was used by the American Indians before the first explorers came to this continent. The roots were used in much the same way as ginger was used in Europe, to disguise tainted meat. It was also used as a flavoring in hominy. The root can be used as a carminative and for spasms of bowls and stomach, and as a stimulant for colds.

Wild ginger once grew profusely through North American woods, but is now becoming quite scarce. It is a low, spreading plant with heart-shaped leaves which covers the ground in moist, rich woodland. In early spring it bears purple-brown flowers that resemble dark campanula bells and lie on the ground. It is a better subject for the wild garden than for the herbiary, but may be grown in dappled shade beneath shrubbery at the back of the herb border. Propagation is by root division.

GINSENG

Panax quinquefolium, Linn.
Araliaceae

Ginseng may be the most fascinating wild herb. It's a plant cloaked in mystery and superstition. It evokes visions of mountain men, inscrutable Orientals, clipper ships, fortunes made and lost overnight. It is almost irrevokably tied to the past, and yet it may be an herb of the future.

Put briefly, ginseng is a plant whose root is valued by the Chinese above all other botanicals as a cure-all. Their centuries-old esteem for the plant's root provoked incredible market demands, astronomical prices, overharvesting, largely ill-fated cultivation schemes, and a lingering curiosity. Today, the root remains as important in Chinese folk medicine as ever, as expensive as ever, as untamed as ever, and as mysterious as ever.

Ginseng is an easy plant to be suspicious about. Although the Chinese have used extracts of ginseng root for a thousand years or more as a general tonic, curative, strength-builder, and aphrodisiac, there has until recently been no evidence of a scientific character that ginseng really does the things the Chinese say it does. Moreover, the greatest value is placed upon the root that is primate-shaped, that is, one with a trunk and extremities approximating arms and legs. It smacks of the doctrine of signatures, and indeed, it is believed by some that the shape of the ideal root suggested it as a panacea for man. The shape, incidentally, prompted the Asiatic species of *Panax* to be named *schinseng*, Chinese for man-shape, from which the anglicized ginseng is obviously derived.

Outside of China, ginseng historically has been denigrated by the established medical authorities, although it has been widely used in folk medicine. "It would be difficult to find any plant with a reputation so disproportionate to its actual virtues," was and is the typical judgment of respectable, responsible authorities. But in Russia today, scientists are researching many ideas and substances that are thought to be part of the "lunatic fringe" by scientists here. As a part of this research, the Russians have been working to find the true medicinal value of plants, and they have been trying to promote a plant of their own, *Eleutherococcus senticosus*, which they claim has characteristics very much like ginseng. I. I. Brekhman, MD, author of a book on that plant, recently made these rather interesting comments about it:

> By its pharmacological properties, *eleutherococcus* is in many features similar to ginseng. It is a stimulant, increasing the general tone of the organism, normalizing the arterial pressure and reducing an elevated blood sugar level. Owing to its capacity to strengthen the

Ginseng Root

protective forces of the organism and to increase resistance against various adverse effects, *eleutherococcus* may be regarded as representative of those rare substances which possess an adaptogenic action, and contribute to the realization of its adaptive, 'protective' reaction of the organism.

In other words, they say that *Eleutherococcus* helps people resist the bad effects of stress more effectively.

This research may eventually substantiate the long-held belief that ginseng is indeed "the queen of medicinal herbs," as a Chinese doctor has called it.

The ginseng story must begin with the ancient Chinese medical texts. Among the properties attributed to ginseng in these texts are alterative, tonic, stimulant, carminative, and demulcent. In the traditional Chinese medicine, which is the accepted medicine of today's China, ginseng is "a tonic to the five viscera, quieting animal spirits, establishing the soul, allaying fear, expelling evil effluvia, brightening the eye, opening up the heart, benefiting the understanding, and if taken for some time it will invigorate the body and prolong life." Moreover, it was and is regarded as an aphrodisiac wholly capable of prolonging sexual potency far into the golden years of senior citizenship.

Perhaps as much for the latter as for any of the former properties, ginseng became an extremely desirable commodity. One emperor declared himself the sole ginseng dealer, buying all that was harvested, keeping the best for himself, and selling the remainder at a fat profit. The demand eventually outstripped the supply and prompted widespread overharvesting.

Early in the eighteenth century, it was discovered that *P. quinquefolium,* an American plant, was nearly identical to *P. schinseng* and the harvesting and ultimately the overharvesting of American ginseng began.

P. quinquefolium is a small plant ranging between ten and twenty inches in height when mature. It likes shady ravines, gentle north slopes, and other spots with light, well-drained soil, rich in leaf-mold from hardwood forests. It thrives in such conditions across the eastern half of North America, from Quebec to Manitoba, south to Arkansas and Alabama. Ginseng grows very slowly, the seed taking as long as eighteen months to germinate, the sprout taking another three to six years to mature. It begins with two leaves, each with five lobes (hence the specific name *quinquefolium,* or five-fingered leaf). In the third year it develops a third leaf and a few small greenish-yellow flowers which are followed by a cluster of red berries containing the seeds.

All during this development, the plant's root is expanding ever so slowly, each year adding a growth ring. In a mature plant, the root is two to three inches long and a half to a full inch thick. The larger the root, of course, the more valuable it is. But the older it is, as determined by the number of rings, the more valuable it is too.

The Asiatic ginseng is somewhat larger, but it has the same general appearance and growth characteristics.

It wasn't long after the discovery that a common North American plant was a valuable export commodity that foragers, Indians and white settlers alike, were combing the forests. One observer wrote:

> The trade which is carried on with it here (in Canada) is very brisk, for they gather great quantities of it and send them to France, whence they are brought to China and sold to great advantage. . . . During my stay in Canada all the merchants in Quebec and Montreal received orders from their correspondents in France to send over a quantity of ginseng, there being an uncommon demand for it this summer. . . . The Indians especially travelled about the country in

order to collect as much as they could and sell it to the merchants at Montreal. The Indians . . . were likewise so taken up with this business that the French farmers were not able during that time to hire a single Indian, as they commonly do to help them in the harvest. [Ginseng] formerly grew in abundance round Montreal, but at present there is not one single plant of it to be found, so effectually have they been rooted out. This obliged the Indians this summer to go far within the English boundaries to collect these roots.

As the commerce developed, use of it seemed to develop too. Several American Indian tribes used it, but there is evidence to suggest that they picked up its use from white settlers. It was variously used as a remedy for headaches, cramps, female troubles, shortness of breath, croup and coughs, fevers, rheumatism, sores, general debility, and, of course, impotency and infertility. Despite these uses of the root by the Indians, Dr. Benjamin Barton recorded his conviction that they did not "so highly esteem the Ginseng as their Tartar brethren in Asia do."

And despite fairly common usage of ginseng by the naturalized Americans, it never got beyond the secondary list of the official pharmacopoeias, where it ranked for forty years in the mid-nineteenth century. Nevertheless, those Americans that did believe stories of ginseng's powers and used the root were as fervent in their belief in its powers as the Chinese. One colonist wrote:

> The Root of this is of wonderful Vertue in many Cases, particularly to raise the Spirits and promote Perspiration, which makes it a Specifick in Colds and Coughs. . . . I carry'd home this Treasure, with as much Joy, as if every Root had been the Graft of the Tree of Life, and washt and dry'd it carefully.

Given the relatively immense demand for the root and the frailty of the plant, it is surprising it lasted the nearly two centuries it did before the toll of overharvesting began to show. Throughout the eighteenth and nineteenth centuries, foragers combed the likely spots collecting the root for sale to dealers in New York, Cincinnati, and Knoxville. In 1876, well over a half-million pounds of the dried roots were exported for an average price of $1.17 a pound. The warlords in Chungking and Hangchow paid a much stiffer price for what they considered the medicine *par excellence,* the treatment of last resort.

But the boom couldn't last. Economic depressions prompted many mountain folk to forage the Appalachian hills and Ozark hollows, digging up "seng." As the root became scarce, the price skyrocketed. The peak of the wild ginseng traffic, on which careful records were kept by the U. S. Department of Commerce and Labor, came in 1913 when 221,901 pounds were exported. The average price paid that year for the root was $7.50 a pound, with a total export value for the year reported at $1,665,731.

Today, the wild ginseng trade is but a shadow of its former self. The only wild ginseng left, it is said, is growing in snake-infested corners of the woods which are frequented by only a handful of determined wild-plant collectors.

A few farsighted people did see what was happening, however, and sought to cultivate the profitable plant. George Stanton of Fabius, New York, is generally considered to be the father of the cultivated ginseng industry. As a sickly young man in 1885, he went seng digging for the exercise, and soon thereafter got the idea of trying to grow the plant for profit. Eventually he became well known and successful as the proprietor of the George Stanton Chinese Ginseng Farm, the first of many such entrepreneurs.

There are places where you can buy 1,000 ginseng seeds at prices ranging from $8.50 to $55, depending on whose advertisement you answer. And at least one company sells 100 "Strong Planting Roots (1 year Seedlings)" for $16.75. That same catalog lists eight companies still in the business of buying ginseng root, although the extent of the trade has dwindled. The U. S. Department of Commerce figures show that only 119,246 pounds of ginseng were grown or collected in 1969. But although the amount produced is small, the price the root sold for is indeed interesting—an average of $42 a pound!

Dealers in the roots and seed will send out pamphlets telling briefly how to establish a ginseng garden, but probably the best source of information is *Ginseng and Other Medicinal Plants* by A. R. Harding, originally published in 1908 but currently available in a paperback reprint (Emporium Publications, Boston).

The book is also valuable because it doesn't try to create the false idea that ginseng is a sure-fire cash crop. Even across a gap of six decades, A. R. Harding comes across as a level-headed chap who seems genuinely interested in not misleading people.

"Ginseng is truly and wholly a savage," he says at one point. "We can no more tame it than we can the partridge. We can lay out a preserve and stock it with ginseng as we would with partridges, but who would stock a city park with partridges and expect them to remain there?" The wildness of ginseng soon becomes apparent to anyone who tries to grow it. Few plants of practical value, in fact, present a greater challenge to the grower, but likewise few plants have remained as popular and valuable over a span of centuries as has ginseng.

The basic problem with ginseng is that it will grow only in deep, cool shade on fertile soil that is not "pushed" to fertility with soluble fertilizers. Some say that ginseng undoubtedly would thrive better in a rich, well-drained loamy soil that had not been "used up" at all by regular cropping. Getting the right kind of shade is the main challenge, though. Tree shade is best, because the air under it tends to be both cool and moist. But most commerical growers build shade structures of wood slats, about six feet off the ground. They are more convenient, but according to some experts, such artificial shade is not as good for the plants as natural tree shade.

Another problem with ginseng is that it takes a long time to grow into a marketable root. "The seed of ginseng germinates in 18 months," Harding says. One of the manuals offered by a modern ginseng company even advises that 24 months is not out of line for sprouting, in some cases. But if you get stratified seed, that has been pre-cooled in a refrigerator for several months to simulate wintering, the time of germination could be much shorter. Of course, you can also buy plants, but even so you will have to wait four, five, or even six years for a usable crop of root.

There is also a risk that the kind of soil you have will not produce the best grade of ginseng root. "Soils and fertilizers have a marked influence on products where taste and flavor are important, as with tobacco, coffee, tea, certain fruits, etc.," A. R.

Harding says. "This is true of ginseng in a very marked degree," he continues. "To preserve the flavor which marks the best grade of ginseng, by which the Chinese judge it, it is essential that the soil in the beds should be as near like the original forest soil as possible. Woods earth and leaf mould should be used in liberal quantities. Some little bone meal may be added, but other fertilizers are best avoided to be on the safe side."

Regardless of all the risks and frustrations that a ginseng grower faces, ginseng is a plant worth knowing. Many people have become ginseng fanciers. There has always been a small market for the roots in U. S. health food stores, but now the trend is really up. Almost every store carries a selection of ginseng products in various forms and packages. The instant granules are the most popular, but ginseng liquid is also widely used. The cost is high, but the value is there even if you judge ginseng only on its flavor. After all, you have to pay 15 cents or more these days for a bad cup of coffee in a restaurant. Ginseng tea snaps you to attention in a subtle way, clearing the sinuses with a faint licorice-like aroma, and leaving you with the relaxed feeling of satisfaction which only a truly great hot beverage can produce.

And as you sip your ginseng tea, you can ponder the mystery surrounding the curious root, its history, and its aura.

GOLDENROD

Solidago, various species
Compositae

The goldenrods represent a large and difficult genus of the daisy family, there being more than 80 species, all but one of which are found in the United States. One type of goldenrod or another is undoubtedly familiar to all.

But one in particular, *Solidago odora,* is worthy of specific mention, since it has traded off the showiness of the other goldenrods for a scent, making it the one true fragrant goldenrod. It grows from 18 to 36 inches in height, having a relatively low-key flower head on its solitary stem. Each flower-head has but six to eight blossoms. The narrow leaves are mildly anise-scented.

The flowers of this goldenrod are aperient, tonic, and astringent, and an infusion of them is said to be beneficial in gravel, urinary obstructions, and simple dropsy. The leaves, when infused one teaspoon to a cup of boiling water, act as an aromatic stimulant, carminative, and diuretic.

The American Indians made good use of the many goldenrods in their folk healing. The uses were as numerous as the varieties of the plant. The Zunis chewed the blossoms, slowly swallowing the juice to relieve sore throats. The Alabamas used the roots as a poultice on aching teeth. Several tribes used infusions of the flowers and leaves for fevers and chest pains. The Meskwakis used the blossoms in a lotion for bee stings and other painful swellings. While many of these properties were picked up by the white folk healers, only *S. odora* was listed in the *United States Pharmacopoeia,* being included in a secondary list from 1820 to 1882 as a stimulant, carminative, and diaphoretic.

As showy plants, the goldenrods are worthy members of the ornamental garden. And the leaves and flowers of some varieties yield a yellow dye, permitting the herbal dyer to capture the color for year-round enjoyment.

GOLDEN SEAL

Hydrastis canadensis, Linn.
Ranunculaceae

Golden seal is one of America's justly famous wild medicinal herbs. The plant was first discovered and used by the Indians, principally the Cherokees, adopted into the white folk medicine, admitted to the official pharmacopoeias, foraged nearly into extinction, then dropped from favor.

The herb rarely exceeds six inches in height. It consists of a single main leaf and two five- or seven-lobed secondary leaves. The seeds develop in raspberry-like fruits which appear in heads, usually during July. The parts used, however, are the rhizome and roots.

Originally a plentiful plant in America's virgin forests, it is somewhat difficult to find today. It can be found in rich, well-

drained, forested highlands east of the Mississippi River, particularly in the Appalachian region. It has been cultivated to
some extent, but as golden seal is a sensitive wild plant, it is a
frustrating and often unrewarding venture. The approach taken
in cultivating ginseng is usually followed when growing golden
seal.

The common name golden seal is derived from the rich
golden color the root stains everything it touches. The Indians
used it to dye themselves and their clothing yellow. They also
used it as an insect repellent.

The generic name *Hydrastis,* derived from two Greek words
meaning water and to accomplish, is a clue to the principal
medicinal property of the root. It is a general tonic for the
mucous membranes. An Indian folk healer wrote in the
nineteenth century:

> This root is one of the Indian's favorite remedies; and medical
> men of the present age recognize it as one of the standard remedies for
> many pathological conditions or diseases of the human body. Too much
> cannot be said of this valuable agent, that has been veiled in darkness
> to the medical world so long. I consider it one of the kings of diseases
> of the mucous membrane. It is unsurpassed by any known remedy.

Despite the writer's claim, golden seal was already well known in
the medical world, and indeed had been officially listed as a drug
plant, by the mid-1800s. As early as 1798, Dr. Benjamin Barton
had recorded its medicinal virtues.

Golden seal served as a remedy in cases of gastro-intestinal
and nasal catarrh and in inflammations of the membranes of the
vagina, uterus, and urethra. It has also been used to remedy
dyspepsia. Combined with bicarbonate of soda, it is a useful
mouthwash, providing relief of sores in the mouth and inflammations of the throat. It has been used in eyewash preparations.

The dried rhizomes and roots of golden seal were first listed
in the *United States Pharmacopoeia* in 1831, being dropped in
1842, then relisted in 1863, remaining an official drug plant until
1936. The relative popularity of the herb nearly doomed it, for
it brought foragers as much as $1.50 a pound at a time when most
medicinal plants were worth only two to five cents a pound.

Diligent growers and removal from the official drug list probably saved the plant from total extinction.

In recent years, golden seal has been experiencing a revival of interest. It is used as a home remedy for stomach ailments and as a laxative.

HAWTHORNE

English Hawthorne, Haw, May, May Blossom
Crataegus oxyacantha, Linn.
Rosaceae

A very showy, deciduous bush or small tree, growing to 15 feet, this is the plant for which the ship *Mayflower* was named. It has white flowers in May followed by bright red berries in September. Branches are spiny and even when leafless, are picturesque in effect. They are excellent in a shrubbery border, their lines carrying the vision from lower shrubs upward to the trees in the background. They are frequently grown as hedges and also make excellent lawn specimens.

Hawthornes grow readily in most any soil. They are propagated by division of young roots or by cuttings made in September and set in a cold frame. They can be started from seed, however germination may not take place until the second or third year.

Hawthorne is originally an English plant. It has been used widely as a hedge, but it has also escaped cultivation and is seen in waste places and untilled fields. It has been naturalized in the United States, as well as some other countries.

Aside from its ornamental uses, hawthorne has been valued as a heart tonic, and this value has been increasingly studied in recent years. Promising results have been reported in connection with a variety of heart ailments, including angina pectoris and abnormal heart action. It is also said to be effective in stemming arteriosclerosis, commonly known as hardening of the arteries. The berries of the hawthorne are used, being dried and reduced to a powder. Doses range from three to fifteen grains three to four times daily. But the powder may also be made into a tincture by combining a pint of grain alcohol and an ounce of the hawthorne berry powder. The tincture is given in doses ranging from one to fifteen drops. Though non-toxic, hawthorne can produce dizziness if taken in large doses.

Hawthorne has also been used in treating arthritis and rheumatism, and for emotional stress and nervous conditions.

HELLEBORE, FALSE

Adonis
Adonis vernalis, Linn.
Ranunculaceae

Growing six to twelve inches high with delicate, finely cut leaves, false hellebore produces large yellow flowers of about ten to 20 petals in May or June. Adonis may be grown from seed sown in spring or early fall, or root divisions in spring. It prefers light, sandy soil.

False hellebore's primary medicinal virtue benefits those with heart troubles. It has an action similar to digitalis, though it is said to be far more powerful. It has been used in cases where digitalis failed. False hellebore is listed in some herbals as a poison, and all herbalists recommend it be used only under a doctor's direction.

An insecticide is made from the roots and sold in the form of a dry powder (Hellebore). It is potent only when fresh, and although rather expensive, is used on ripening fruit and vegetables. It is a slow stomach poison for insects and especially useful against currant worm and all chewing insects such as beetles, caterpillars, grubs, cutworm, and grasshoppers. Usually mixed with flour or hydrated lime and used as a dust, it can also be mixed with water for a spray, about one ounce to two gallons of water.

A near relative of false hellebore, *Adonis autumnalis,* is also sometimes called false hellebore, as well as pheasant's eye and red camomile. It is a European native, growing about a foot-high and having finely cut leaves and small scarlet flowers.

HEPATICA

Liverleaf, Noble Liverwort
Hepatica acutiloba, DC.
Ranunculaceae

Hepatica is a small herb of the buttercup family whose three-lobed, leathery evergreen leaves are shed for new ones after flowering. Blossoms, often fragrant, appear very early in spring. They may be white, pinkish-lavender, or purple. These natives of open, rich woodlands can be easily transferred to the wild garden. They require neutral soil, rich in humus, and can be propagated by division of root or seeds *Hepatica acutiloba* has three pointed lobes; *H. americana* (or *H. triloba*) has rounded leaves which are maroon in winter.

Hepatica is a mild mucelagenous astringent, made into an infusion or tea for coughs and colds.

HOLLY

Ilex aquifolium, Linn.
Aquifoliaceae

Hollies are well known for their glossy, evergreen leaves and red berries, used extensively for Christmas greens. The English holly is not as hardy as native species, but will survive winters of southern New York state. It is more beautiful than some of the other varieties as it bears larger, denser clusters of berries. The holly is highly prized as an ornamental in the garden, is used in border shrubbery, as hedging, or a small specimen tree.

Hollies are slow growing and do best in rich, rather moist soil. Plants can be purchased from nurseries either in containers or balled. They should be moved in spring before new growth starts, or in late summer. When transplanted, a daily spraying with the garden hose for several weeks will prove beneficial.

Propagation is by cuttings of ripened wood, placed in a cold frame and kept well moistened. They may also be started from seed, which requires stratification and germinates the second year.

The leaves and berries are used for medicinal purposes. The

leaves are astringent and are used in fevers and rheumatism. The berries are used in dropsy.

HOP

Humulus lupulus, Linn.
Moraceae

The hop is a native of Europe and western Asia, and is commonly known as a principal ingredient in beer. It was not always used in beer, but it has been long used medicinally as a tonic, diuretic, and sedative.

Hopped ale was first brewed in Europe late in the Middle Ages, and was introduced into England in the fifteenth century. It has been cultivated as a commercial crop ever since, its culture being spread wherever conditions are suitable. The female flower, which resembles a globe artichoke, is the part used by brewers. It yields essential oils and resins which give the hop its aroma and beer its taste. The male flowers, incidentally, are born on separate plants and have a quite different appearance than the female flowers.

A perennial vine, the hop produces new shoots each spring which grow rapidly, extending as much as thirty feet before dying down to near ground level at the end of the season. In cultivation, the hop is generally trained up a framework of poles and wires, making it a good screen plant for summer. The vines are usually propagated by cuttings of young shoots from the crown, but they can also be started from seed.

HOREHOUND

Marrubium vulgare, Linn.
Labiatae

The perennial horehound, native to England but adaptable to almost any climate, has been respected since ancient times for its wide variety of uses, from flavoring candy to curing colds to counteracting poisons.

Although it is found in the greatest quantities in England,

particularly the southern counties, it grows throughout Europe and has been transplanted to the Western Hemisphere without difficulty.

The herb seems to thrive in poor, dry ground where other plants can't survive, although it's only half hardy in severely cold climates. It flourishes in the wild.

The plant is bushy and produces annual branching stems from one to two feet in height. Whitish flowers are borne on the wrinkled leaves, which are covered with white, felted hairs, giving the plant a woolish appearance. The plants have a musky smell which is diminished by drying and which eventually disappears when kept. Horehound flowers from June to September.

Called an herb of Mercury by Culpeper, the hoarhound was used widely as a medicine by the Egyptians, Greeks, and Romans The Greeks often used it as an anti-spasmodic drug and as an antidote for the bite of a mad dog, hence its common name, hoarhound.

There are various theories for the origin of the Latin name.

Some scholars believe it was named after Maria urbs, an ancient town of Italy, but most attribute its name to the Hebrew Marrob, a bitter juice. The herb is one of the five plants which the Jews took for the feast of the passover.

The Egyptians called it variously the seed of Horus, bull's blood, and eye of the star.

Used by the ancients as an antidote for many poisons and an anti-magical drug as well as a cure for respiratory diseases, the herb gained fame for curing a long list of ailments through the centuries.

Some ancient values include a cure for a snakebite, an ointment for wounds and itches, a fly repellant, and a worm killer. With honey, the leaves were said to cleanse ulcers, and the juice was considered excellent for clearing the eyesight, either by dropping it directly into the eyes or sniffing it up through the nostrils.

But the most popular use is for clearing the lungs. According to Gerard, "Syrup made of the greene fresh leaves and sugar is a most singular remedie against the coughing and wheezing of the lungs . . ." and Culpeper claims the herb "helpeth to expectorate tough phlegm from the chest, being taken with the roots of the Irris or Orris. . . ."

Horehound

In addition, Culpeper said, hoarhound "purges away yellow jaundice; and with the oil of roses, dropped into the ears, eases the pain of them.

"It opens obstructions of both the liver and spleen and used outwardly cleanses, abates the swollen part and pains that come by pricking thornes, with vinegar, it cleanses and heals tetters."

Culpeper and other authorities also recommend the herb for women to increase the menstrual flow, and in childbirth, to help expell the afterbirth. It is also considered a laxative in large doses.

To make a good syrup for coughs and colds, mix one half ounce each of horehound, rue, hyssop, licorice root, and marshmallow root with a quart of water; boil it down to a pint and a half of liquid, strain, and give in half-cup doses.

Or, a horehound tea for colds can be made by pouring boiling water on the fresh or dried leaves, one ounce of the herb to a pint of water.

For a more pleasant tasting syrup than above, boil one-fourth cup of dried horehound with two cups of water for ten minutes, then strain the mixture after five minutes. Combine one part of the horehound mixture with two parts of honey and stir until smooth.

Horehound drops can be made by combining the above mixture (without honey) with two cups of raw sugar. Place the sugar in a small, deep saucepan and stir in one-eighth teaspoon of cream of tartar, then add the horehound mixture. Stir until the sugar has dissolved, then cook over a low heat until a drop of the mixture in cold water becomes a hard ball. Pour on a buttered dish and cut into cough-drop sizes when it's half hardened. Keep in a cool place until used.

The herb gardener generally doesn't need much horehound because of its great potency. The best method for starting to grow the herb is indoors from seed. Old plants should be divided and planted at a distance of 20 inches.

Horehound needs a warm, sunny location to grow properly, but the soil can be dry and of low fertility and still be used for growing. Weeding in the early stages of growth is, of course, of major importance, but mulching will have little effect on the plant. If mulch is used, it should consist of materials which are able to hold or raise the soil temperature.

Horehound is harvested by cutting all growth three inches above the ground. In the northern part of the United States, two or more cuttings a year are possible, and the plant should remain productive for several years.

To preserve the herb, it should be chopped and dried within a short time and sealed tightly in a jar.

HORSERADISH

Armoracia lapathifolia, Gilib. (syn. *Amoracia
rusticana,* (Lam.) Gaertn., Mey. & Scherb.)
Cruciferae

Horseradish, so named to distinguish it from the edible radish, has been famed for its medicinal qualities from the most ancient times. The Greeks knew it as *Raphanos agrios* (wild radish), and it served them and countless other herbalists as a stimulant, laxative, plaster, diuretic, and antiseptic. It was also used as a cure for scurvy. (Modern science has again proved the wisdom of the ancients by discovering that horseradish is a source of vitamin C.)

Horseradish, however, is much more familiar to use as a condiment; the chief ingredient of a tangy sauce for fish or meats. This use of the root is a comparatively recent one: Gerard, in 1597, spoke with wonder of the German practice of eating horseradish sauce with fish and meat. In 1657, Coles wrote that the root, "sliced thin and mixed with vinegar is eaten as a sauce with meat, as among the Germans." However, he made it clear that the practice was not one a gourmet would adopt. Horseradish root was also eaten by the French. The old French name for the horseradish was *Moutarde des Allemands,* indicating that they had learned its use from their German neighbors.

Horseradish is a perennial. The plant develops large, green to yellow-green, elongated leaves that attain a height of up to two feet. It has been cultivated since the earliest times and may have originated in Hungary.

The plant develops no seed, and propagation is by root cuttings only. Cuttings should be made from straight roots and should be six to seven inches long and include a bud—although any piece of root will develop buds and shoots. For this reason, horseradish should be planted in a corner of the garden that will be kept strictly for horseradish. If you decide to eradicate your horseradish bed, make sure that every piece of root is removed from the ground. Any left in the soil will develop into a plant.

Horseradish prefers wet, clay soil and must be planted early for a good fall crop. The ground should be deeply tilled in January and well fertilized with rotted manure or compost. Planting is done in February. Plant your root cuttings twelve to fifteen inches deep and twelve to eighteen inches apart each way. The horseradish bed should be weeded regularly. Early mulching will help.

Expect to harvest your crop in the fall. Wash the roots and store them in damp sand in a root cellar. They should last through the winter and can be grated fresh as needed.

The roots can also be left in the ground and dug when needed. In this case, mulch as you would for beets or turnips.

In the spring, you will find that you can also harvest and eat the first leaves that appear from the crown. Use them in salads,

Horseradish

chopped fine and mixed with other salad greens. They may also be boiled and mixed with other boiled greens—their taste is too strong to serve alone.

When you harvest your first horseradish root, you will find that it has no odor. Horseradish root contains two chemical components that are responsible for the characteristic smell and taste: sinigrin, a crystalline glucoside, and myrosin, an enzyme. Sinigrin is decomposed in the presence of water by myrosin, and a volatile oil allyl isothiocyanate is formed. This oil is chiefly responsible for the taste and smell of horseradish. Since myrosin and sinigrin exist in separate cells of the root, they do not normally come into contact with each other until the root is bruised or cut.

On exposure to the air, the root loses its color and volatile strength. It should never be boiled, but always used raw and freshly-grated.

Horseradish was of great value to the ancient herbalists as a plaster. Culpeper said, "If bruised and laid to a part grieved with the sciatica, gout, joint-ache, or hard swellings of the spleen and liver, it doth wonderfully help them all." Scraped horseradish applied to chilblains and secured with a light bandage is said to help cure them.

Horseradish when infused in wine will stimulate the nervous system and promote perspiration. It serves much the same purpose when used as a condiment with meat or eaten as a relish with vegetables. To use it as a condiment, grate one cup of horseradish root and mix it with one-fourth cup vinegar. (A blender serves as a quick way to grate the root.) You may try mixing other herbs with the horseradish; dill or mustard would go well with meats.

Horseradish has also been used as a cosmetic. An infusion of horseradish in milk makes an excellent cosmetic for the skin and helps restore freshness and color to the cheeks. Horseradish juice, mixed with white vinegar and applied externally, is supposed to remove freckles.

Horseradish juice and vinegar, well diluted with water and sweetened with glycerine, were used to relieve whooping cough in children. A dose of one to two spoonsful was administered at a time. A syrup for hoarseness was made by infusing one dram of freshly-scraped horseradish root with four ounces of water in a closed vessel for two hours, and then adding double weight of sugar. The dose was a teaspoonful or two repeated occasionally.

Horseradish was also employed as a remedy for worms in children. Coles said: "Of all things given to children for worms, horseradish is not the least, for it soon killeth and expelleth them."

HYDRANGEA

Hydrangea arborescens, Linn.
Saxifragaceae

A deciduous shrub of the saxifrage family, hydrangea grows as a native in central and southern areas of this country, since it can stand only a few degrees of frost. A shrub from four to ten feet high, it has almost heart-shaped leaves three to six inches long. Long lasting rounded clusters of white flowers appear in June and July. The name seven barks refers to the peculiar characteristic of its stem bark, which peels off in seven thin layers of different colors.

Hydrangeas thrive best in rich, moist soil, but will grow under varying conditions. Shoots should be cut back severely and weak growth thinned for good flower heads. They are propagated by cuttings of half-mature shoots, rooted under glass, also by hardwood cuttings. Good plants can be grown from cuttings in one year. They can also be layered and divided.

Hydrangeas were used by the Cherokee Indians. A mild diuretic and cathartic, it was considered a valuable remedy for removal of stone and gravel in the bladder.

HYSSOP

Hyssopus officinalis, Linn.
Labiatae

Hyssop is historically known as a holy herb, used for cleaning sacred places. The herb also has many medicinal uses and flavors an excellent tea.

Hyssop was used by the Egyptians to cleanse lepers, and the herb is often mentioned in the Bible as a purifier. Hyssop is a name of Greek origin, adopted from the Greek *azob* (a holy herb), because it was often used to clean the temples and other sacred places.

In Psalm 51:7, David says in a prayer, "purge me with hyssop and I shall be clean," and in John 19:29, hyssop is mentioned at the crucifixion. "There was a vessel full of vinegar: and they filled a sponge with vinegar and put it upon hyssop and put it in His mouth. . . ." Some scholars, however, believe the hyssop mentioned in the Bible is not the herb known today, and the controversy has never been settled. Throughout the history of the church, hyssop has been revered for its cleansing powers. When Westminster Abbey was consecrated, hyssop was sprinkled on the altar.

Historically, hyssop was a familiar herb. The Elizabethan herbalist Gerard noted simply that he didn't want to bore the reader by describing familiar plants. Dioscorides, in his day, had done the same.

Culpeper reported, "The herb is Jupiter's, and the sign Cancer. It strengthens all the parts of the body under Cancer and Jupiter." His listing of the medicinal virtues of hyssop covered all of those typically attributed to the herb.

> Hyssop boiled with honey and rue, and drank, helps those that are troubled with coughs, shortness of breath, wheezing, and rheumatic distillations upon the lungs; taken with oxymel, it purges gross humours by stool; with honey kills worms in the belly; and with fresh new figs bruised, helps to loosen the belly, and more forcibly if fleur-de-lys and cresses be added thereto. It amends and cherishes the native colour of the body spoiled by the yellow jaundice, and taken with figs and nitre, helps the dropsy and spleen; being boiled with wine, it is good to wash inflammations, and takes away the black and blue marks that come by strokes, bruises, or falls, if applied with warm water. It is an excellent medicine for the quinsy, or swelling in the throat, to wash and gargle it, when boiled with figs; it helps to cure toothache, if boiled in vinegar, and the mouth rinsed with it. The hot vapours of the decoction taken by a funnel in at the ears, eases the inflammations and singing noise of them. Being bruised with salt, honey, and cumin seed put to it, helps those stung by serpents. The head anointed with the oil kills lice and takes away the itching of the head. It is good for falling sickness, expectorates tough phlegm, and is effectual in all cold griefs, or diseases of the chest and lungs, when taken as a syrup. The green herb bruised with sugar, quickly heals any cut or green wounds, if properly applied. The pains and discolourings of bruises, blows, and falls may be quickly removed by a cataplasm of the green leaves sewed in a linen cloth, and put on the place.

A perennial shrub native to Europe and temperate Asia, the herb was easily transferred to America and grows wild in many states.

An essential oil derived from the green portions of the plant are used in making perfumes, especially English eau de cologne.

Hyssop tea is made by pouring a pint of boiling water over an ounce of the green tops and is considered excellent tasting.

It was used by some monks and the Trappist fathers in the preparation of some liqueurs. The recipe book of John Nott, a cook to the Duke of Bolton, written in 1723, recommends hyssop

Hyssop

water for a good complexion. He calls for six spoonsful of hyssop juice in ale every morning.

Externally, the herb is recommended for curing rheumatism and for bruises and contusions. It is also supposed to help cuts promptly.

Hyssop tea and an infusion of hyssop is considered useful in chest diseases and coughs, colds, hoarseness, fevers, and sore throats. It's thought to be especially good for loosening phlegm.

A common infusion is made by simmering two ounces of hyssop in one quart of water for 15 minutes. The brew should then be strained and mixed with a little honey.

Aside from its medicinal uses, hyssop can be used in salads, where it adds a bitter, minty taste. It's also occasionally used in soups, stews, fruit cocktails, and fruit pies.

The companion planter will find some value in hyssop. Planted near grapevines, it increases the yield of the vines. Planted near cabbage, it lures away the cabbage butterfly. Hyssop tea is said to be useful against bacterial diseases of plants. It should not be planted too close to radishes, however.

If nothing else, the herb adds beauty to any garden. The fragrant, attractive plant is extremely hardy and can grow up to three feet. The leaves are thin and long, and have a shiny green color and strong scent when brushed. The flowers form in the leaf axles and according to variety, are blue, pink, or white. The blue variety is most commonly used as a medicinal herb.

The seeds, having a long, oval shape, are dark brown to black and germinate in darkness within ten days at a temperature of 70° F.

Hyssop is best started indoors from seed because it is a slow grower. If direct seeding outdoors is desired, it should be done as early as weather permits. Older plants can be divided early in the spring and re-set at a minimum distance of 12 inches.

The main requirements for growing hyssop are a dry and sunny location and a soil with good calcium reserves. Many gardeners choose the herb as an herbaceous border because it responds well to pruning and makes a beautiful showing when in flower. The blue variety, which is more vigorous and hardy than the other two, is considered to be the most beautiful by most gardeners.

For a hedge, the distance between plants should be kept at 12 inches, while a space of two feet is best for general planting. In case the seeds are sown outside, hoeing, weeding, and thinning will be necessary during the first three weeks, followed by mulching once the plants have reached a height of six inches.

In most cases it will be most convenient for the beginning herb grower to buy a few plants of hyssop unless he intends a long hedge. For tea alone, a few plants will produce enough material to last the whole year.

Like other tea herbs, hyssop can be used fresh and green from the garden. Otherwise, the harvesting takes place when the first flowers are about to open. This step should not be delayed since hyssop tends to become woody within a short time. (The oils and flavors of all herbs, of course, are in the leaves and green stems and not in the wooden parts.)

In order to encourage fresh growth, the cutting should be done close to the ground. Should the harvest be too woody, the leaves should be stripped off the branches. A liquid fertilization with fish emulsion fertilizer is advisable after each harvest.

For drying, the stripped leaves are dried whole, while the soft growth can be chopped with the stem and dried in warm shade. Drying is generally completed in two days.

JACOB'S LADDER

Greek Valerian, Charity
Polemonium caeruleum, Linn.
Polemoniaceae

A perennial growing two to three feet with feather shaped leaves, Jacob's ladder has bright blue flowers with yellow stamens. It grows easily in rich loamy soil with good drainage and is started from seed or root division. The plant is diaphoretic and astringent. *Polemonium reptans,* abscess root, has creeping roots, grows six to twelve inches, and has white or light blue flowers that droop in loose clusters. The root is used for fevers, inflammations, pleurisy, coughs, colds, and bronchial and lung complaints.

JOE-PYE WEED

Purple Boneset, Queen-of-the-Meadow
Eupatorium purpureum, Linn.
Compositae

A perennial of easy culture, this herb grows five to six feet and thrives in ordinary light garden soil. It may be grown from seed or root division in spring. It has rose, or rose-purple flowers in large open clusters, and it will grow on low marshy ground and can be naturalized in the wild garden. It was named after an Indian doctor named Joe Pye who used it medicinally— the astringent root is used for diarrhea, the flowers are diuretic and tonic.

JUJUBE

Zizyphys vulgaris, Lam.
Rhamnaceae

The jujube is a very ornamental deciduous shrub or small tree, hardy as far north as Massachusetts. The leaves are small, oval, alternate, and smooth. They are a light green in color, growing on long, slender, somewhat prickly, drooping branches.

A graceful, delicate looking tree, it is grown for its ornamental value and edible fruits. The smooth, shiny fruit is reddish-brown, about the size and shape of a date. Its texture is similar to apple, with a sweet taste somewhat like a cross between apple and date. They are wrinkled and brownish-red when dried. The fruit can be used fresh or dried and is often used for a confection.

The jujube is propagated by seed and root cuttings. A bare-root tree may be obtained from nurseries in early spring, and will probably be a slender, top-less whip, but in a few short months it will develop its long, drooping, graceful branches. It can bear some fruit the first year. Jujube grows well in average garden soil in a sunny location. To produce sizeable fruits, it should not be too dry while the fruit is forming.

It is mucilagenous and pectoral and was used in the manufacture of pectoral lozenges, however, it is seldom used for this purpose today.

JUNIPER

Juniperus communis, Linn.
Pinaceae

Small or medium evergreen trees or shrubs of the pine family, many types of junipers are used in landscaping, making some of the best ornamentals. Junipers are hardy, attractive, and varied in form. Leaves, needle-like, are mostly gray-green or blue-green, with berry-like blue fruits, which take two years to ripen and are harvested in autumn. Leaves and shoots can be collected any time of year.

A strong aromatic scent emanates from all parts of the shrub. Berries taste slightly bitter-sweet, fragrant, and spicy. Junipers are hardy even in the coldest areas. They prefer dry, sandy, or gravelly soil with full exposure to wind and sun. They will tolerate average garden conditions but resent shade and wet ground.

Among the varied forms, there are dense, columnar trees; medium sized, rounded shrubs; irregular bush forms; and creeping prostrate types. Irish and Swedish junipers are tall, narrow, and quick growing; the Greek and Chinese are very compact, slow growing. Pfitzers are irregular, massive types. California juniper may reach heights of 40 feet, and shore juniper and japonica are spreading ground covers.

This is a most important group of ornamentals used in landscaping—as foundation planting, for accent, for mass, for ground covers. Propagation by seed is extremely slow. They will not germinate until the second or third year. Most varieties can be started from cuttings. Tips four to six inches long are cut in August, the needles are stripped an inch or so from the butt and placed in a coldframe bed of sand four or five inches deep. Water thoroughly, cover with glass, and keep shaded. They will be rooted by the following summer. Most varieties can be found in nurseries in cans or balled.

In the past, juniper was regarded as a magic shrub to use against devils, evil spirits, and wild animals. It is mentioned in the Bible as a symbol of protection. Its aromatic scent made it a popular strewing herb, and shoots were burned to disinfect the air in a room. Berries are used in making gin. They are an excellent seasoning for game, marinades, poultry, and sauerkraut. They will take away the strong gamy taste to which some people object in venison, wild duck, or other undomesticated animals. Before roasting parboil the meat in a beef stock to which lemon, bay leaves, and about four to six juniper berries have been added.

Juniper is considered one of the most useful medicinal plants. Stimulating for appetite and digestion, helpful in coughs and to eliminate mucus, it has a diuretic effect, stimulating the functions of kidney and bladder. A strong tea of the berries is considered an excellent wash for the bites of poisonous insects, snake bites, dog bites, and bee stings.

Korean Mint

A useful infusion of the berries may be prepared by soaking several tablespoons of berries in water, then adding them to a pint of boiling water, leaving them to infuse for a half-hour or more. It is recommended that the infusion be taken in four doses during the course of the day.

KOREAN MINT

Agastache rugosa
Labiatae

Korean mint is a hardy perennial herb, little known, yet pleasing as a tea herb. The root system is strong and draws on the entire depth of soil. Square stems bear serrated leaves, and the lavender to violet flowers develop in the leaf axils, resembling flowering cattails. The seeds, when ripe, are of light to medium brown color and of oval shape. Good seed germinates in darkness within ten days at a 70° F temperature.

Korean mint is best started from seed, indoors in early March, if possible. Germination is easy and fast, and the young seedlings are large enough to handle for easy transplanting. After the plant is established, transplant to a soil in good fertility with a high organic matter content. Given these conditions, the plants will grow five feet tall during the second and following years. Early mulching will give good results, above all because it preserves the precious moisture which the plant likes. Aside from these fundamentals, there is little else this herb needs; it competes well with weeds, attracts insects, and, as a single bush, makes a grandiose showing.

For home use, it is advisable to use the leaves only when making tea. The stem is heavy and tends to become woody early in the year. Leaves may be picked off the plants and used for tea any time during the growing season. For a future tea supply the whole plant should be cut before the flower spikes develop, though for mere beauty leave at least one plant untouched, allowing it to flower. The harvested branches are stripped and the leaves dried whole without chopping. The single leaves dry relatively fast in warm shade and are finished if they break when crushed.

LAMB'S QUARTERS

White Goosefoot, Pigweed, Wild Spinach
Chenopodium album, Linn.
Chenopodiaceae

Lamb's quarters is one of the gardener's most persistent adversaries. But the gardener would do well to let the weed grow and harvest it along with other foodstuffs, for it is a palatable and nutritious plant. Moreover, the weed, so long as it doesn't get out of hand, is a companionable plant for the garden, thanks to its long taproot.

Chenopodium album is a relative of garden spinach and a blood brother of Good King Henry *(Chenopodium bonus-henricus)*, a more domesticated potherb. The plant is erect, growing one to three feet high, with wedge-shaped leaves and densely flowered spikes. The color is somewhat silvery, hence the specific name *album* and the common name white goosefoot.

The plant grows wherever there's rich soil, and it particularly

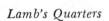

Lamb's Quarters

likes manure piles and compost heaps. Since most regard it as a nuisance, it is easily gathered where it grows. One presumably would neither want nor need to cultivate it.

Both the foliage and the seeds are edible. The greens may be eaten raw in salads or cooked as a vegetable. The greens are rich in vitamins C and A (richer than spinach) and in calcium. The vitamin C content explains the value the Indians ascribed to it as an antiscorbutic. The seeds are collected and ground into a meal after drying, the meal being used to make bread. The seeds may also be eaten raw.

LAVENDER

Lavandula, various species

Labiatae

Lavender in today's world is so well known that its name is instantly associated, not only with the delicate sweet fragrance of its oil, but with the specific mauve-like hue of its tiny petals. It hasn't always been so widely recognized. Known since ancient times, lavender was popular among the pre-Christian Greeks and Romans as a scent for baths and soaps. From that use probably came the generic name *Lavandula,* from the Latin *lavare* (to wash).

In the Dark Ages, though, the sensuous joy of lavender condemned it to relative obscurity behind a host of other herbs that came to prominence because of their religious significance or their medicinal efficacy. Although lavender did enjoy some medieval medicinal applications, it wasn't until Tudor England —the late Renaissance—that lavender's celebrated fragrance once again became joyously and guiltlessly its *raison d'etre.*

Today, the herb supports one of the largest herbal industries in the world, with centers of cultivation for commercial use being in England and France.

There are three basic species of lavender, and each has several varieties. Most widely known in America is English lavender *(L. vera),* also known as true lavender because its oil is of the highest, most fragrant quality. That quality also makes it the most highly valued for commercial production, although spike lavender *(L. spica)* produces a greater volume.

Mrs. M. Grieve, a twentieth-century English herbal expert, wrote that flowers of spike lavender yield three times as much oil as those of English lavender "but it is of a second-rate quality, less fragrant than that of the True (English) Lavender, its odor resembling a mixture of the oils of Lavender and Rosemary."

She added that oil of the third main species, French lavender *(L. stoechas),* has an odor that's "more akin to Rosemary than to ordinary Lavender." The French lavender, though it lacks the attractive sweetness of the English lavender and the copious oil yield of the spike lavender, lays probable claim to historical note. Mrs. Grieve wrote that the French lavender "was probably the lavender so extensively used in classical times by the Romans and Libyans as a perfume for the bath." So each of the species has its own claim to importance.

To decide which variety to grow in your garden, decide whether the main object will be the flowers or the leaves. If it's the flower you want most, the English lavender is your plant. For leaves, the spike lavender will produce a broader leaf and more oil.

All the lavenders are shrubby perennials. English and French lavenders prefer sandy, coarse, even rocky soils that are warm and moderately fertilized. Spike lavender tends to prefer alluvial soil. They all like a sunny location.

Because all the lavenders are natives of the warm Mediterranean climate, they may be difficult to establish in American gardens. English lavender, though, should fare the best; it is the hardiest of the three varieties undoubtedly because of its acclimatization to the temperate British Isles over at least the last 400 years.

Leaves of all the species are light green-grey, resembling those of rosemary. English lavender carries the narrowest leaves, and sometimes is referred to as the narrow-leafed plant. French and spike lavender, then, have broader leaves.

Flowers of the famous lavender hue form in June and July in spikes at the top of the plant. French lavender flowers tend to be a darker hue than those of the other species.

Seeds, which form later in the season, are a shiny dark greyish-brown and generally rather difficult to germinate. They take up to four weeks to sprout, and they have a very low percentage of survival. Lavender started from seed should be planted inside in February because of its long germination time. The Munstead variety has been bred to provide a fairly quick germination period, and that type may give the best results.

Or, lavender can be started by taking August cuttings, which will form productive young plants by the next spring. English lavender winters best of the three species, but all should be afforded some protection against killing frosts. A southern exposure would help, and a windscreen is almost a necessity.

The lavender spot in the garden should be neutral to alkaline in acidity. Add lime if the pH level is more than four. Mulching is not necessary, in fact not even desirable, for it lowers the soil temperature to the discomfort of the plant. Fertilizing is of minor importance, and if the soil is so devoid of nutrients that

Lavender

it just has to be enrichened, use only well-rotted compost or manure, never fresh.

Harvesting leaves is not critical, but flowers must be taken just before they open. They lose their aromatic properties quickly after opening. Both flowers and leaves are dried in shade at 90° to 100° F. They dry well and pose no storage problem.

Lavender's medicinal properties in the old days were said to be aromatic, carminative, and nervine with especial emphasis on the plant's soothing effect on nerve disorders. "It profiteth them much that have the palsy if they be washed with the distilled water from Lavender's flowers," advised Gerard in 1597. A hundred years after that, a popular herbalist said a lavender tincture, "if prudently given, cures hysterick fits though vehement and of long standing." Lavender water has been used for centuries as a home remedy for hoarseness and sore throats, and oil of lavender is a traditional balm for sore joints and toothaches. Up until the First World War, oil of lavender was used as an antiseptic for wounds as well as a vermifuge. Grieve suggests that part of the reason for the decline in lavender production in the early twentieth century was that so many English acres under lavender were diverted to food production during the war and never reverted to lavender.

Lavender has only minute use in the kitchen although Queen Elizabeth I was known to have been fond of lavender conserve.

One of lavender's finest uses today is in sachets and pillows to perfume linen. Said to repel moths, flies, and mosquitoes, a folk formula for making a room-sized insect repellent is to absorb a few drops of lavender oil on a cotton ball, then suspend it from the ceiling.

The dried flowers alone, sewn into a linen pillow, can be tucked among dainty linens to impart to them a lovely scent. For lavender water, add a drop of musk and an ounce of lavender oil to one and one-half pints of mild white wine. Shake well, leave to settle for a few days, then shake again and pour into airtight bottles. Or add two ounces of refined essence of lavender to one and one-half cups of good brandy for a powerful concentrate of lavender water.

A pleasant lavender vinegar is made by mixing six parts of rosewater, one part spirits of lavender, and two parts of vinegar. Or steep fresh lavender tops in vinegar for a week, shaking the mixture each day. At the end of the week, filter the lavender vinegar and store it in airtight bottles.

LAVENDER COTTON

Santolina
Santolina chamaecyparissus, Linn.
Compositae

Lavender cotton has the density, texture, and color necessary for successful use in knot gardens and other starched and formal herb gardens. Its spreading branches, which range as tall as two feet, have very fine blue-gray leaves, said by some to resemble coral. It has small, yellow flowers, but these are usually trimmed off. *Santolina viridis,* or green santolina, is a similar plant in a contrasting color.

Plants can be grown from seed, although rooting cuttings is perhaps a better method. Santolinas like the sun and dry feet, so a light dry soil is the best medium. Santolinas are not terribly hardy, and protection from snow is necessary for survival.

Although the garden use is the santolinas primary one, the leaves are reputed to have value as a moth repellent, and a perfume oil has been extracted from them (though their natural fragrance isn't particularly pleasant).

LEMON BALM

Balm, Sweet Balm, Garden Balm, Honey Plant
Melissa officinalis, Linn.
Labiatae

Lemon balm, so named because its crushed foliage smells like lemons, has a venerable history of use as both a healing herb and as part of a drink to ensure longevity. Shakespeare mentions it in *The Merry Wives of Windsor* as a strewing herb, used to make the house smell more festive and inviting to one's guests.

Long before Shakespeare's time, however, the Greeks were using lemon balm in their own way. In the *Materia Medica* of Dioscorides, we find that lemon balm was used against scorpion stings, insect, and dog bites. Pliny believed that the power of lemon balm was so great that "though it be tied to his sword that hath given the wound, it stauncheth the blood." Gerard, summing up the opinions of Pliny and Dioscorides, says, "Balm, being applied, doth close up wounds without any perill of inflammation."

Lemon balm is not only fragrant and useful, but it is also very prolific and can be easily grown. A native of Southern Europe, it has escaped into the wild and can sometimes be found growing wild in the United States and England.

Lemon balm is a fairly hardy perennial. The root system is short, but dense, and the stem square and branching. The plant seldom grows more than a foot tall indoors, but may reach three or four feet outside.

Leaves are heart-shaped or broadly ovate, yellowish-green,

and generally one to three inches long, growing smaller toward the top of the plant. They are covered with stiff hairs on the top surface. The flowers grow in loose, small bunches from the axils of the leaves, and are bluish-white or yellow. Lemon balm flowers from May until October. After pollination, long, oval, dark brown-black seeds appear.

Lemon balm can be easily started from seed. If left alone, the plant will reseed itself in the garden. It can also be started in a greenhouse or in pots in the house. To start the seeds in a greenhouse, press them into fine, friable soil in a seedpan. When the seedlings are an inch tall, they should be thinned to two inches apart. When they have reached four inches, they can be set out. Allow two feet on all sides.

Cuttings and root divisions are also acceptable and easy ways to start lemon balm. Root divisions can be made in spring or fall by dividing the roots into small pieces with three or four buds to each piece. Plant the pieces two feet apart. If you're making your root divisions in the fall, allow plenty of time for the plants to become established before the first serious frosts.

Lemon balm should be planted in fairly fertile, friable soil in partial shade. Although the plants will grow in sunlight, they will do much better in the shade. Allow two feet on all sides between plants, since they tend to spread sideways. Weed until the plants are well established. An early mulching with hay or straw will prevent the herb from becoming too soiled.

Water during dry periods to guarantee continued growth of the plants and prevent yellowing of the leaves. In the fall, cut off all decayed growth from the roots. Although the roots are hardy, mulching with pine or spruce branches or leaves during the winter will greatly improve chances of survival.

Harvesting lemon balm is easy, and it is possible — in fertile, well-watered locations — to obtain as many as three cuttings a season. Lemon balm should be harvested before it flowers for optimum fragrance, although a good deal of its odor will be lost in even the most careful drying. To harvest, cut off the entire plant two inches above the ground. Be careful to avoid pressure

Lemon Balm

of any kind if packing the herb in boxes or cartons, and try to avoid bruising either the stem or the leaves when you are harvesting the plant.

Balm should be carefully dried within two days of picking —it has a tendency to turn black unless it is dried quickly. Do not harvest if dry sunny weather is not predicted for several days. Drying is best done in the shade at temperatures between 90° to 110° F. It's best to use trays or sieves for drying the herb, rather than tying it in bunches on a string. If you plan on using your lemon balm for tea, dry both leaves and stems.

Lemon balm is an attractive plant to bees — as the early Greeks recognized. In fact, its present scientific name derives from the Greek word for "bee." Gerard recommended planting lemon balm around bee hives, and also suggested rubbing the inside of the hive with balm to prevent swarming and to encourage other bees to join the hive. A Spaniard, Ibn Al Awam, suggested that a mixture of lemon balm and honey or sugar be smeared over the inside of a hive to make it an attractive home for a new swarm — but he quotes other writers who say that it will have the exact opposite effect.

Cows are also supposed to take to lemon balm. If planted in pastures, lemon balm is said to promote the flow of milk in cows.

Many remedies have been ascribed to lemon balm. Gerard says, "Bawme drunk in wine is good against the bitings of venomous beasts, comforts the heart, and driveth away all melancholy and sadnesse."

Dioscorides suggested drinking an infusion of wine and lemon balm and applying the leaves to an infected part of the body — such as an insect bite or the bite of a mad dog. Lemon balm is also a component of a drink given to sufferers of fever, as suggested by Francatelli's *Cook's Guide:* "Put two sprigs of Balm, and a little woodsorrel, into a stone-jug, having first washed and dried them; peel thin a small lemon, and clear from the white; slice it and put a bit of peel in; then pour in three pints of boiling water, sweeten and cover it close."

"Claret Cup. One bottle of claret, one pint bottle of German Seltzer-water, a small bunch of Balm, ditto of burrage, one orange cut in slices, half a cucumber sliced thick, a liqueur-glass of Cognac, and one ounce of bruised sugar-candy.

"Process: Place these ingredients in a covered jug well immersed in rough ice, stir all together with a silver spoon, and when the cup has been iced for about an hour, strain or decanter it off free from the herbs, etc."

Balm tea can be made by pouring one pint of boiling water on one ounce of the herb. Infuse for 15 minutes, cool, strain, and drink freely. You may wish to add honey or lemon peel. In fact, a balm-honey tea is the tea to which amazing powers of longevity were ascribed. John Hussey of Sydenham, England, who lived to the age of 116, breakfasted for 50 years on balm tea sweetened with honey, and herb teas were the usual breakfasts of Llewelyn, Prince of Glamorgan, who lived to 108.

The tea is generally used to induce perspiration and cool patients who have fevers. It was also used with salt to heal sores and ease the pains of gout.

Lemon balm has its culinary uses as well. Leaves can be added to salads or to fruit salads for a pleasant, subtle flavor. A few leaves will improve the taste of a cup of tea.

Homemade wine can be made from the leaves of lemon balm. According to an old recipe from *The Recipe Book of Richard Briggs,* a cook at the Globe Tavern, The White Hart Tavern, and the Temple Coffeehouse in London, balm wine can be made in the following way: "Take twenty pounds of lump sugar and four gallons and a half of water, boil it gently for one hour, and pour it into a tub to cool; take two pounds of the tops of green balm, and bruise them, put them into a barrel with a little new yeast, and when the liquor is nearly cold pour it on the balm; stir it well together; and let it stand twenty-four hours, stirring it often; then bung it tight, and the longer you keep it the better it will be."

LEMON VERBENA

Lippia citriodora, Kunth.
Verbenaceae

Lemon verbena, like Dixieland jazz and Coca-Cola, is a native of the Americas that has spread from there throughout the world. That makes it a distinct rarity, at least in the European- and Mediterranean-centered world of herbs.

Actually, it's a native of South and Central America where it still thrives best today, especially in Peru and Chile. It was a latecomer to North America, where it is difficult to establish.

Europe was introduced to lemon verbena by Spanish conquistadors who found space among their cargoes of gold booty for a few emigrant plants.

Probably because of its American and relatively recent parentage, lemon verbena is lacking in the lore and traditional apothecary uses that surround most herbs. It has limited use in the kitchen.

Its primary role seems to be as a domestic houseplant grown for its pleasing scent of fresh lemons.

For that pleasure, however, there's a price to pay in care

Lemon Verbena

and work, for the lemon verbena is a tender plant that needs constant attention.

In the North American climate, lemon verbena is a tender perennial shrub that must be protected from all frost. Starting the plant is a problem because its seed formation is infrequent and spotty. Greenhouses that handle exotic plants commonly maintain lemon verbena bushes from which they'll cut you a slip around March. If you have a bush, you can take cuttings in August provided you maintain the mature bush in a rich, well-shaded area and keep it moist. The mature plant tends to wilt when cuttings are made, and the cuttings themselves are hard to establish.

Once rooted, though, the bush grows easily and will develop to maturity in one season.

Be sure to bring lemon verbena indoors before the first frost. Indoors, the plant should be fed well-rotted compost or manure every two weeks. Its leaves should be misted or washed weekly with room-temperature water.

Lemon verbena is a deciduous plant; in other words, it loses its leaves in the fall, so don't be concerned when you bring the shrub indoors and it promptly molts its leaves. They'll come back, although the indoors leaves are more apt to be a yellow-green color than the grey-green of outdoor foliage.

Flowers generally form in little white clusters at the end of the branches. Seeds, however, are rare.

Harvesting the leaves can be done almost anytime although waiting until late summer will give you maximum enjoyment of the aromatic properties of the plant. Strip the leaves off a shoot, or cut the whole shoot and chop it and the leaves. Dry in the shade.

The leaves generally may be substituted for lemon or mint in recipes for poultry, fish, and stuffings. It makes a pleasant tea, too.

Lemon verbena is believed to possess properties of a stomachic and antispasmodic although it never gained widespread use in herbal medicine.

LINDEN

Limeflowers, Basswood
Tilia, various species
Tiliaceae

Linden is a well-known tree, commonly used along avenues and entrance driveways for the uniformity it produces. It will attain a height of 50 feet or more, with dense, attractive foliage. The leaves are perfectly heart-shaped, four to seven inches long, coarsely double-toothed. They produce an abundance of fragrant white to yellowish flowers, which are attractive to bees. The fruits or seeds are, about the size and shape of a pea and are commonly called "monkey-nuts."

The trees are generally pyramidal in form, the dark, brownish-gray bark is scored with elongated perpendicular fissures.

Lindens are all hardy and thrive in rich soil. They require moisture, but not too much. Leaves will drop in warm weather if they are too dry. Seeds require two years to germinate. They can be propagated by layers or cuttings.

The fiber of the wood was previously used for making strong ropes. Linden flowers and leaves are an old household remedy for nervousness, colds, headache, and indigestion. A hot infusion is used to check diarrhea. It was also used in a hot bath to promote sleep. Linden flower wine is used as a tonic to stimulate appetite and aid digestion. Foliage can be dried like hay for winter feed for animals.

LOBELIA

Indian Tobacco
Lobelia inflata, Linn.
Campanulaceae

Lobelia is said to be the discovery of Samuel Thomson, the father of the patent medicine, who tried it first on a friend while mowing a field. "He first fully satisfied himself that it had emetic properties," one record of the event says, "by coaxing his partner, who was mowing with him in the field, to chew the green plant, which he did, and became deadly sick and relaxed, and upon drinking some water he vomited and rapidly recovered from its effects, and felt better afterwards than he did before."

The record tells two tales, one of Indian tobacco's first use by a white man, and the other of the hazards of blind herbal experimentation. There is no clearcut agreement among herbalists and doctors as to the propriety of using Indian tobacco; some contend the herb is potentially poisonous, others dispute that claim. But it is a fact that Thomson himself was sued in the death of a patient to whom he had prescribed Indian tobacco . . . and found not guilty.

The focus of this controversy is an annual plant, growing up to three feet tall, having numerous oval-shaped leaves. It is distinguished by its violet to whitish flowers, which bloom between July and October, giving way to seed-bearing fruits. It is commonly found in open fields throughout the eastern half of the United States.

Lobelia inflata is but one of several species of the genus named for botanist Matthias de Lobel which was used medicinally by the Indians. It is, however, the only one to be recognized as an official drug plant. *L. siphilitica* was once regarded as an emetic, purgative, and antisyphilitic, hence the specific name. *L. cardinalis,* commonly known as the cardinal flower, was believed to have the same properties as *L. inflata,* though to a lesser degree.

The dried tops and leaves of Indian tobacco were listed as official drug botanicals from 1820 to 1936, and appeared in the *National Formulary* until 1960. Expectorant and emetic properties were ascribed to the plant.

The plant is currently the subject of intensive research. Scientists are trying large-scale cultivation of the plant, for it is the source of the alkaloid lobeline and a number of other drug substances. Lobeline, like nicotine, acts as a stimulant in small dosages, but as a nerve depressant and poison in large doses, hence the danger of experimentation.

LOVAGE

Levisticum officinale, Koch.
Umbelliferae

An ancient cure for a variety of diseases, lovage is enjoying a surge of popularity both in the United States and Europe for salads, soups, pies, candies, and for itself.

Native to the Balkans and the Mediterranean area, lovage was introduced to much of Europe and to Great Britain by the Romans.

Both the Greeks and the Romans used the herb as a medicine, and in the Middle Ages it was used as a cure-all for most illnesses. In Central Europe, women wore lovage around their necks when meeting lovers, and the herb was often put in love potions as a guarantee of everlasting devotion.

Lovage has been used for disorders of the stomach and feverish attacks in case of colic and for flatulence in children. It was also used for gravel, jaundice, and urinary problems.

Culpeper recommended the herb, saying that a liquid, extracted by boiling the herb in water, "being dropped into the eyes taketh away their redness or dimness. . . . It is highly recommended to drink the decoction of the herb for agues. . . .

The distilled water is good for quinsy if the mouth and throat be gargled and washed therewith. . . . The decoction drunk three or four times a day is effectual in pleurisy. . . . The leaves bruised and fried with a little hog's lard and laid hot to any blotch or boil will quickly break it."

The herb was also added to baths, probably as a deodorant.

Today the herb is used primarily for salads and other dishes; in some countries, especially England, lovage leaves are used to make candy. Oil from the plant is occasionally mixed with tobacco for flavor.

The tall, hardy perennial reaches six feet in ideal conditions, with roots that average one inch thick and grow irregularly in different directions. Its diameter can measure as wide as four or five feet. The dark green leaves resemble those of celery but have an entirely different aroma.

The stalks and leaf stems are hollow tubes with the flower stalks growing above the leaf mass, developing true umbels at the tips with light yellow flowers.

When ripe, the seeds are dark brown and grow in pairs like the dill. The best germination begins in darkness, within two weeks.

Lovage is extremely easy to grow. The seeds may be sown in the spring, but it's preferable to sow them in late summer, when they ripen, and transplant the seedlings to their permanent location later in the autumn or very early in the spring.

Only a few plants are needed because its growth is more abundant than most other plants. As the plants get older, they should be divided every fourth year to keep them vigorous, preferably very early in the spring when the first shoots push through the soil. The plant can live 20 years or more when cared for in this fashion.

Almost every location in the garden is suitable for lovage. One plant could be placed in a corner, even a shaded one. The only areas to avoid are spots that are too sunny or too dry. The fertility of the soil needs to be high, and heavy fertilization with manure compost and lime is advisable in order to achieve optimum results.

Even high soil moisture is beneficial, but not to the extent of standing water or poor drainage. Heavy mulching with hay or straw is well received by the plant, partly because of the increase of soil life and earthworms in particular, which digest the mulch and keep the soil supplied with calcium. Top dressing during the season with compost or drenching the soil around the lovage with a fish emulsion solution aid in vigorous growth.

If the leaves should ever turn prematurely yellow, it is a sign of lacking nutrients or water, or both.

Fresh leaves should be picked all year around in small amounts for soups, gravies, or salads. Obviously, the older leaves should be used first to avoid yellowing, cutting each one off close to the ground. A family will rarely be able to consume the leaves as fast as they grow, leaving the only alternative to cut the plant off about two inches above the ground before the leaves turn yellow and useless.

Since one leaf with stem is often more than two feet long, it is advisable to cut small leaflets off the ribs before attempting to dry them. The stem parts hold so much water it would take days to dry the whole; but the leaf parts alone will dry within two days, in warm shade. Lovage should be dried until it is crisp enough to crush in your hand. It should be stored in a closed container away from light. It tends to yellow with age, even when dried, and becomes useless after one year.

MADDER
Dyer's Madder
Rubia tinctorum, Linn.
Rubiaceae

Madder is a plant known almost exclusively as a dye plant. The long fleshy roots, when dried and milled, yields a variety of colors — red, pink, brown, orange, black, lilac, and purple — depending upon the mordant used. Madder has been raised commercially for its dye value.

Medicinally, madder has been used in experiments to deter-mine the characteristics of bone growth, since it dyes, in addition to textiles, bones, milk, and urine. It has been reputed to be effective in dropsy and jaundice, but not widely.

The plant develops a long (as long as eight feet) spiny stalk the whorls of spiny leaves, but, because of the weakness of the stalks, the plants generally lie along the ground. In its second year, the plant develops tiny yellow star-like clusters of flowers on spikes which top the stalks.

Madder is most easily started from root divisions, since it is a spreading plant, sending up new plants wherever its root surfaces. It can be started from seed. It likes a light, sandy soil and lots of sun.

MANZANITA

Arctostaphylos, various species
Ericaceae

These large, distinctive, evergreen shrubs are native to the west and northwest, growing wild from northern California to Alaska. Of the three most common species the green leaf *(Arctostaphylos patula)* and the grey leaf *(A. mewukka)* or Indian manzanita are large, crooked-branched shrubs from three to six feet high with smooth, red wood which is frequently used for dry decorations. The leaves are about two inches long, oval shaped, and leathery. It is a very decorative shrub for the garden, with drooping panicles of attractive but small, urn-shaped pink or white flowers, followed by round berries in shades of red or pink.

Probably the best known is *A. uva-ursi,* kinnikinnick or bear-berry, a prostrate species with rooting branches. A trailing evergreen, it reaches a height of six inches and will eventually spread to 15 feet. The reddish branches contrast with small bright-green leaves that take on a bronzy tone in fall. Once established, it makes an excellent ground cover for banks, either in full sun or partial shade.

All three of the manzanitas will tolerate poor soil, which can be quite gritty, providing there is adequate drainage. They object to lime in the soil, and require little attention and rarely need summer watering once established.

Plants may be found in some nurseries. Cuttings of mature growth root readily under glass in a mixture of sand and peat. It is best to establish them in pots before setting out. They may be started from seed, which is soaked in concentrated sulphuric acid three to five hours. Sow in gritty sand in early spring; it may take a year to germinate.

Manzanita has been used in America and Europe as early as the thirteenth century. Leaves are picked in late summer. Indians made many uses of this plant, ranking next to acorns for food value. Leaves were used for smoking; berries were eaten raw, cooked, or ground into a meal for porridge. Cider made from berries is a fine drink and they were also used for making jelly.

A strong decoction of leaves is applied warm for relief of poison oak, poison ivy, rashes, and shingles. Both fruits and leaves were used for their astringent properties, for relief of bronchitis, kidney ailments, dropsy and female disorders.

MARJORAM

Majorana hortensis, Moench (syn. *Origanum majorana,* Linn.)
Labiatae

Of nearly 30 varieties of marjoram, sweet marjoram is without a doubt the most popular among herb gardeners in the United States. Many of the others, as a matter of fact, are so obscure and ill-suited to the United States that anyone short of a botanist can expect to encounter them only in textbooks.

Other varieties that are suitable for use as seasoning in cookery include *Origanum onites* (pot marjoram) and *O. heracleoticum* (winter marjoram).

Wild marjoram, *O. vulgare,* historically has been used more in the medicinal applications of the marjoram family than for kitchen purposes.

Several varieties share many characteristics of the herb commonly called oregano. In a few cases, the common properties are so close that confusion reigns over whether the plant is a marjoram or an oregano.

Heinz Grotzke, for example, says *O. heracleoticum* is oregano while M. Grieve lists it as winter marjoram. And *O. vul-*

gare, according to Grieve, is wild marjoram; other herbalists have accepted it as oregano. Still others have dubbed *O. vulgare* British marjoram because it flourishes in those isles.

There seems to be no disagreement, though, that the plant designated *O. majorana* by Linnaeus and *Majorana hortensis* by Moench is sweet marjoram and nothing else.

Sweet Marjoram is a tender perennial in its native Portugal and similar Mediterranean climates, but in North America it's impossible to keep the plant alive through even the mildest winter. So consider it an annual that must be started anew from seed each year.

The dense, shallow root system of sweet marjoram can utilize no more than the top few inches of soil, and so a fairly rich humus is desirable. The plant's square stems grow upright to about 12 inches. Stems are surrounded by a profusion of branches bearing oval, slightly fuzzy leaves with short stems. White or pink flowers appear in mid-summer but are almost entirely covered by small leaves that form a little ball at the end of each stem. Seeds are light brown. They look like small nuts and reach a mature size of one millimeter. Under diffused light, they take eight days to germinate.

Because the seeds are so small, it's almost impossible to tend them properly outside. So sweet marjoram should be started indoors in March in flats. Pat them lightly into well-sifted soil, which should be kept moist. Weeds are fierce competitors with young marjoram; keep them under strict control if they're evident during marjoram's slow early growth. Transplant when the soil has warmed.

Outside, the plants should be spaced six to eight inches although they can be placed in three-plant clumps if the shoots are still small. Five such clumps should provide enough sweet marjoram, both fresh and dried, for a year's use.

Well-rotted compost — never fresh manure — should be supplied to impart a pleasant flavor to sweet marjoram. Regular hoeing is essential to control weeds; in fact, this plant can be "hoed to maturity" and will respond to hoeing in the same way that other plants respond to heavy fertilization. For that reason, mulching should be delayed until two weeks before the first harvest. The ideal mulch is cocoa hulls followed by chopped hay or straw.

The first harvest comes at the time the green ball-like tips appear at the ends of the stems, although for early use some young shoots may be pinched off. When flowers appear, the whole plant should be cut back to an inch above the ground to stimulate a second growth.

That second growth, lush and fuller than the first, is really the main crop. Cut the plants again when flower heads form the second time.

For drying, place the cut plant on fine screen or paper and put it in a warm, dry, shaded area. When dry, rub the plant through a fine screen. Leaves will powder and sift through the screen; the woody stems will remain behind. Sweet marjoram, unlike some other herbs, retains its full flavor when it's dried.

Traditionally, sweet marjoram has been a symbol of youth and beauty and happiness. Legend has it that the plant is a transfiguration of a handsome youth once in the service of King Cinyrus of Cyprus. One day he dropped a vessel of sweet perfume. In terror of displeasing the king, he swooned into unconsciousness and soon was transfigured into the sweet marjoram plant to grace the palace forever after.

William Shakespeare, who knew his herbs well, immortalized the attributes of the plant in *All's Well that Ends Well*. In Act IV, Scene V, there's this repartee:

> *Lafeu:* " 'Twas a good lady, 'twas a good lady:
> we may pick a thousand salads,
> ere we light on such another herb."
> *Clown:* "Indeed, sir, she was the sweet-marjoram
> of the salad,
> or, rather, the herb of grace."

The "herb of grace," though, was a typically scampish, double-entendre that actually compared the lady in question with rue, an herb whose disagreeable qualities are in stark contrast to the sweetness of marjoram.

An even earlier literary tribute to marjoram was paid by

Marjoram

Virgil who, in his *Aeneid,* wrote of being "where the sweet marjoram, breathing its fragrance, surrounds him with flowers and soft shade."

The French, too, cherished the sweetness of the herb. It was custom to tuck a few sprigs of it away in hope chests and drawers of linens.

Oil of sweet marjoram was used as a polish for furniture and as the main ingredient in sweet English washing water. The tea-loving English also steeped leaves of sweet marjoram, sometimes mixed with those of mint, for a different kind of tea.

In the kitchen, use marjoram with green vegetables, turkey, pork, lamb, or eggs. Potpourri, too, is enlivened by this tangy herb, whose fresh tops are sometimes added to home-brewed beer for an unusual snap. Sprinkle a few cut-up leaves of fresh marjoram on lightly buttered whole-wheat bread and broil it slightly for flavorful herb toast.

Or mix one part of sweet marjoram to three of brown sugar to make a tasty dressing for roast leg of lamb. Stick a few whole cloves into the roast, too.

O. vulgare, or wild marjoram, has been preferred over sweet marjoram for medicinal uses. They include the relief of nervous headaches (an infusion of the fresh leaves) and a toothache remedy (a few drops of the oil on a bit of cotton). Used as an emmenagogue and mild tonic, wild marjoram is stimulant, carminative, and diaphoretic.

The herbalist Gerard said marjoram is a good measure:

against cold diseases of the brain and head. . . . The leaves dried and mingled with honey put away black and blue marks after stripes and bruises, being applied thereto. . . .

There is an excellent oyle to be drawn forth from these herbes, good against the shrinking of sinus, cramps, convulsions and all aches proceeding of a cold cause.

For headache or nervousness, mix equal parts of marjoram, sage, catnip, and peppermint. Steep one teaspoonful in a cup of hot water for five minutes. Sip a cup slowly every hour until relieved. Omit the sage for a good stomach soother.

MAY-APPLE

American Mandrake
Podophyllum peltatum, Linn.
Berberidaceae

A prolific native in many areas, this herb pushes its stumpy stem up through the ground in spring, slowly unfolding the wide, flat, yellowish-green leaves which are lobed, shield-shaped, and die down in mid-summer. Hanging from the fork of the stem is a waxy-white, cup-like flower, followed by an oval, lemon-colored fruit, about two inches long, called the "apples." These are edible only when fully ripe with a flavor reminiscent of strawberry. Found in low, shady lands, rich woods and fields, it can be used for open banks or under trees in partial shade in the wild garden planting. It likes rich, moist soil and is easily increased by division or seed (This is not the old-world mandrake).

The root is cathartic, emetic, alterative, and antibilious. It has an influence on every part of the system, stimulating the glands to healthy action and should be used for this purpose in small, frequent doses. Larger amounts are purgative.

MEZEREUM

Daphne
Daphne, various species
Thymelaeaceae

Daphne is valued chiefly for its fragrant flowers. It does best in well-drained sandy loam, well supplied with leaf mold. Propagation is by seeds, cuttings, and layers.

Daphne mezereum is a neat little deciduous shrub, growing to about three feet, with fragrant pink or lilac-purple flowers in winter and early spring before the leaves appear. In summer it has scarlet fruits. *D. mezereum* var. *album* has white flowers and yellow fruit.

D. laureola (spurge-laurel) is an evergreen shrub, with a sweet-scented fragrance, growing up to six feet with large, shining green leaves and yellowish-green flowers in very early spring. It grows best in partial shade and moist soil.

Daphne is diuretic and cathartic, and acts favorably in scrofula and rheumatism. The bark, root, and root-bark are used.

MINT

Mentha, various species
Labiatae

To the average person, the word mint probably evokes visions of candy or chewing gum, not visions of coolly-scented green plants. But there were green plants before there were any other mints, and those green plants have a long and colorful history as well as a place as the most economically significant herb today.

The mint family, Labiatae, is large, having about 160 genera which include the thymes, sages, marjorams, and basil, hyssop, horehound, rosemary, lavender, lemon balm, and many other familiar herbs. But the true mints are the many members of the genus *Mentha,* and it is those herbs which are of concern here. The best known of the mints are spearmint and peppermint, the two most common flavors of chewing gum. Other mints include the apple mint, orange mint, water mint, curly mint,

Corsican mint, and dozens of other species, varieties, and odd hybrids.

As members of the same genus, the mints share a common background and some common characteristics. The most significant of the latter are their square stems and opposite leaves (meaning simply that each leaf has one opposite it on the stem). Most are rampantly spreading perennials which habit moist, rich-soiled areas throughout the world. Originally natives of the Near East, the mints spread across the globe, thanks in part to their growth characteristic but also to the great esteem in which they were held by all who came in contact with them. There is no better evidence of this than the number of literary references to the mints, in the Bible, in Chaucer's writings, in the herbals of all ages, in Greek mythology.

The generic name *Mentha* was first connected with the mint plant by the Greek philosopher-scientist Theophrastus more than 300 years before Christ. He based the connection on Greek mythology. Mintho, the story went, was a beautiful nymph who was loved by Pluto, god of the underworld. Persephone, who had been abducted by Pluto to reign with him over his domain, became jealous and changed Mintho into a fragrant and lowly plant which to this day waits at the shady edges of Pluto's dark world. The plant, of course, is the mint.

In another myth, the fragrant leaves were used to clean and deodorize a table set by an old couple for strangers travelling through their country. The strangers turned out to be the gods Zeus and Hermes, disguised. They richly rewarded Philemon and Baucis, the old couple, for their hospitality, but lay waste to the country at large, for the other citizens had snubbed the strangers. Mint, as you might have guessed from the story, was widely used for the purpose to which Philemon and Baucis put it. It was, and remains, an important aromatic.

The mints can be used in preparing fragrant baths and as ingredients in potpourris, sachets, and other fragrant bags. A room can be scented simply by hanging a bunch of mint in a doorway. This is a common practice in India and other hot countries, for the fragrance lends the impression of coolness.

These uses derive from the use of mint as a strewing herb. Spread across the floors of churches and temples, the herbs, bruised by the feet of worshipers and penitents, cleared the air of the unpleasant odors many brought with them. This practice spread from the public place to the private; houses throughout Europe were thus aerated.

Mint was also used in cooking and food preparation, as much for its cooling effect as for its carminative, stomachic effect. In the Middle East, mint-laced salads are popular to this day. The mint has been used as a condiment, garnish, and to make beverages.

It is impossible to pinpoint a single most common use of mint. There's mint tea, mint jelly, or mint sauce, all everyday commodities. There are as many ways to make mint sauce, it seems, as there are cooks making it. A very simple approach is to combine a cup of well-chopped mint leaves with just enough boiling water to thoroughly moisten them. After the mass has cooled, stir in a cup of orange marmalade. If you have a blender, combine the juice of half a lemon, a scant half-cup of water, two tablespoons of raw sugar, and a packed cup of fresh spearmint. Blend until smooth, chill for about an hour, and serve. Mint tea is made as is most any herbal tea, by infusing about an ounce of the dried herb in a pint of water (when using the fresh leaves, more than an ounce may be required to brew a satisfying tea).

But there are some relatively uncommon ways to use mint. Mix chopped mint leaves with cream cheese and spread it on whole-grain bread. Mix a cup of chopped leaves in a salad, tossing it well, and dressing it with oil and vinegar. Fresh green peas can be perked up by stirring two tablespoons of minced mint into each quart of the vegetable. The ingenious cook can find a variety of dishes that benefit from a dash of mint.

The medicinal virtues of the mint have drawn remarks throughout history. The ancient Chinese herbals listed mint. Pliny the Elder commented, "The smell of mint stirs up the mind and appetite to a greedy desire of food." The Elizabethan herbalists had much to say about it, Culpeper alone listing forty distinct ailments for which mint was a good remedy.

Gerard commented: "The smelle rejoiceth the heart of man, for which cause they used to strew it in chambers of places of recreation, pleasure and repose where feasts and banquets are made. . . . It is applied with salt to bitings of mad dogs. They lay it on the stinging of wasps with good success." And echoing Pliny he said, "The smell of minte does stir up the minde and the taste to a greedy desire of meate."

Parkinson wrote: "Mintes are sometimes used in baths with balm and other herbs as a help to comfort and strengthen the nerves and sinews. It is much used either outwardly applied or inwardly drunk to strengthen and comfort weak stomackes."

Given the usefulness of the herb, it is not surprising that it was among the first travellers to America. It quickly rooted itself in the American soil, as it did everywhere it went. Today it is a commercial crop as well as a common, and sometimes pernicious, weed.

As a wild plant, mint provides enjoyment for food foragers everywhere. According to America's foremost forager, Euell Gibbons, wild mint can offer a continuing education in the variations in mint. Mint often cross-pollinates, producing variations, most of them small, from plant to plant. For the grower, this means a cutting or root division must be used to ensure getting the desired plant variety. For the botanist, it means a continuing challenge. One botanist, Dr. Edgar Anderson, wrote more than 35 years ago of the difficulties associated with classifying mint plants:

> It is difficult to grow mints without losing faith with botanists. No amateur expects to be able to name all the plants of his garden accurately and well, but he does expect that a professional botanist should be able to do so. Yet if he submits his mint collection for determination, the results are almost inevitably disappointing. If the work is done honestly, some of the mints will be left quite unlabeled, and other names will be followed by a question mark. Our amateur will be even more discouraged if he consults a second botanist and then finds, as he most certainly will, that the two sets of names do not agree.

Gibbons says anyone can experience one manifestation of

mint variations simply by tasting a plant from every mint patch happened upon. Each one will have a slightly different taste, some good, some bad. "If the first sprig of wild mint you taste doesn't exactly delight you," Gibbons says, "don't thereby conclude that you don't like wild mint. Keep searching, and eventually you will find a mint that is exactly tailored to your tongue."

The American mint grower probably doesn't share the feelings of Gibbons, botanists, or amateur mint growers. The commercial mint grower, and there are many of them in the upper Midwest and the Northwest, is interested only in predictability. The grower is interested in a mint that will grow in abundance and yield through distillation a vast quantity of oil of a consistent quality. These growers are meeting the industrial needs for the oil of the two dominant mints, spearmint and peppermint. The oil and its constituents are used in medicines, culinary preparations, cigarettes, cosmetics, toiletries, and, of course, candy and chewing gum. The extent of the industry is seen in the government statistics from 1961. More than 43,000 acres in Indiana, Michigan, Wisconsin, Oregon, and Washington were planted to peppermint, yielding an average of 50 pounds of oil per acre. Almost 25,000 acres in Indiana, Michigan, and Washington were planted to spearmint, yielding an average of almost 53 pounds of oil per acre.

Clearly, peppermint, *M. piperita,* is the most useful of the mints. It can be used in many of the culinary applications already described, and it has a history of medicinal use. It has been listed for more than 140 years as an official drug plant. Used in a variety of compound medicines, it often serves only to make disagreeable preparations palatable. Of itself it has strong antispasmodic action. Most herbals list it as a stimulant, stomachic, and carminative. It has been used in cases of flatulence, colic, cramps and other muscle spasms, dyspepsia, cholera, diarrhea, and a variety of other ailments.

A recommended home remedy for colds and flu is prepared by infusing equal quantities of peppermint and elder flowers (boneset or yarrow may also be added). The tea may be taken freely.

Peppermint

A drink of a peppermint-milk infusion is said to provide relief of abdominal pains. Insomniacs are said to find relief in an infusion of two parts peppermint and one part each of rue and wood betony.

In the garden, peppermint can be a worthy companion. Planted or strewn between cabbage plants, it protects them from the white cabbage butterfly. It must be watched carefully, however, to keep its spreading tendency in check. Most herb gardeners keep peppermint, and the other mints as well, in a separate bed to prevent it from crowding out other herbs.

Peppermint has a shallow root system and seems to channel all its rooting energies into the formation of runners which form below and, more abundantly, above ground. The pointed, oval leaves are attached to square stems of a purplish-green color which extends to the undersides of the leaves, particularly in case of the strong "Mitcham" variety. The small flowers are violet and form at the far ends of the shoots only. The seeds are very small, round, and dark brown. Germination takes place in diffused light within ten days. The viability of the seed declines rapidly after the second year.

The only sensible way to establish a good peppermint bed is to purchase a plant or two. Peppermint has been selected for oil content and flavor and is reproduced vegetatively to retain the desired strains. Though peppermint seed germinates well, it must be remembered that plants from seed do not come true to parent plants and constitute a wide variety of different strains. On the other hand, the breeder enthusiast might see a challenge to develop his own special variety.

The chosen strain, or the purchased variety, is reproduced from cuttings or stolons, another name for the runners of the mint. Either way is simple and quite often more successful than desired, meaning that a mint bed can easily get out of hand. Peppermint requires a soil in good fertility and tilth, high moisture holding capacity, and should be free of weeds, especially grasses or clovers. The spacing of individual plants should be at least two feet because the runners will fill in this distance within one year. As soon as the runners begin to spread, hoeing has to be entirely replaced by hand weeding. Mulching can be done only in form of a thin layer in order not to interfere with the development of the shoots which grow out of the nodes of the runners or stolons. The main purpose of the mulch material in this case is to keep the plants clean. Up to three cuttings are possible each year. After the final harvest in fall, all exposed roots and runners are best covered with a one to two-inch thick layer of compost or well rotted manure. This will protect the plants from frost damage and at the same time fertilize the peppermint for the following year.

The time for harvesting is judged by the flowering tendency and the yellowing of the lower leaves. As soon as either or both stages have been reached, the entire plant, including the shoots of runners, is cut one inch above the ground. No stems with leaves should be left after the harvest because they could become host for disease. A layer of compost in fall also covers all crop residues and aids in their decomposition. The second or third harvest will be smaller and may be done as soon as plants are large enough to handle.

The best quality of peppermint is achieved by stripping the leaves off their stems, and drying the leaves whole in warm shade.

Spearmint, *M. spicata,* while somewhat less potent than peppermint, is the mint most people think of as "mint." It is the mint most commonly used in juleps, sauces, and jellies, and it is useful chiefly for these purposes. It does have some effect as a carminative, stimulant, and antispasmodic, but to a lesser degree than peppermint. It is sometimes used as a child's remedy in the same preparations that peppermint would be used in to remedy an adult's complaint.

In Mexico and much of the great Southwest, spearmint is known as yerba buena. And the people there use it the same way spearmint users everywhere else use the plant.

M. spicata grows in erect, unbranched plants rising as high as three feet. It has smooth, bright green leaves with unevenly toothed margins. The flowers, which appear in July or August, vary from almost white to a deep purple and are clustered on a single flower spike. It is most easily differentiated from peppermint by its taste and by the lack of down on the leaves. It is cultivated in much the same way as peppermint.

The apple mint, *M. rotundifolia,* is often found hanging about dumps, compost heaps, and waste places. It is small, unassuming plant, not difficult to please as to sun or shade and soil fertility. It has soft, gray-green woolly leaves, somewhat round, as its specific name suggests, and gray-white blossoms, shading to pink or pale purple.

Pennyroyal, *M. pulegium,* is treated separately.

Bergamot or orange mint, *M. citrata,* is notable for its distinctive, citrus-like fragrance. Its rounded, broad leaves are dark green with a hint of purple. The undersides of the leaves often have a reddish hue, and in spring the entire plant is distinctly reddish-purple. Easily cultivated, it adds an interesting fragrance to the herb garden, and, harvested, to tea-time and potpourris.

Egyptian mint, *M. niliaca,* has leaves that are so velvety that English children call them "fairy blankets." This is a tall mint, growing to three or four feet in height, and it is thought to be a hybrid between apple mint and either spearmint or long-leaved mint *(M. longifolia).*

Water mint, *M. aquatica,* bears its flowers in little rounded balls at the tips of the stems and in the axils of the uppermost leaves. The leaves are egg-shaped, have stalks, and are somewhat hairy. One well-known variety of water mint has crisped or crinkled leaves and is sometimes called *M. crispa.* There are also forms of other mints that have crisped leaves. *M. citrata,* mentioned above, is often classified as a form of water mint.

Corsican mint, *M. requieni,* is a delightful little creeping plant with minute, rounded leaves, forming an almost moss-like mat. When lightly brushed it emits a very strong, pleasing odor of mint. It is sprinkled in late summer with little lavender blossoms. Corsican mint reportedly is used to flavor liqueurs, and is delightful as a ground-cover for small spots.

It thrives in moist shade, but will also grow in the sun. Since it does not survive cold winters unless well covered by snow, it is better to keep indoors in pots over winter. Propagation is by division.

M. viridis, known simply as mint, is a hardy perennial plant, found growing in abundance along the roadsides in many places. It is often grown in gardens, however, and is used in soups, sauces, and salads very generally. It is of the easiest culture. It is increased by divisions of the root, and planted at distances of a foot apart; it quickly forms a mass, which may be cut for many years without renewal. It is grown to a considerable extent in hotbeds, in the same way as lettuce. Its treatment there is very simple, being merely to lift up the roots in a solid mass, placing them on the three or four inches of earth in the hotbed, and to water freely as soon as it begins to grow.

MORMON TEA

Ephedra nevadensis, Wats.
Gnetaceae

The earliest written record of Mormon tea appeared in the Badianus manuscript — a 1552 herbal highlighting Mexican plants. Written by an Aztec medicine man, the book was translated into Latin and the original copy today resides in the Vatican.

Known to early settlers of the American West as "squaw tea," *Ephedra nevadensis* was favored by the Indians for its reputed health-giving properties. Speculation goes that the drink took on the name Mormon tea because it was an excellent substitute for Mormon-scorned coffee or regular tea.

A Chinese variety of Ephedra known as "Ma-Huang" was used in the Far East for over 2,000 years and, according to *Chinese Folk Medicine* by H. Wallnofer, it was revered for almost all the same health-giving qualities as its Western cousin.

Early pioneers brewed this tea as a remedy for colds and kidney disorders as well as a blood purifier or "spring tonic." They ground the dried stems and mixed the powder with pinon pine sap to concoct a salve to soothe open sores on people and animals alike.

A modern recipe for brewing this herb tea reads like the directions for ordinary tea. Pour a cup of boiling water over about a tablespoon of dried stems and allow to steep for at least five minutes. If you're using fresh stems, be more generous, as fresh tea is not as concentrated as the dried form. Strain and sweeten with honey to taste. A cure-all or not, Mormon tea proves a pleasantly refreshing beverage.

The plant itself is often called joint fir because of its resemblance to a fir bush with jointed stem-like needles. Olive drab in color, it rarely has leaves; rather its tube-like stems serve the leaf's function. Early Mexicans called the stems "canutillo," meaning little tubes or pipes.

Mormon tea seems to grow best in higher altitudes and prefers rocky, alkaline soil. It needs very little moisture, as evidenced by the U. S. Bureau of Plant Industry's pre-World War II attempts to use all seven western Ephedras as ground cover in arid areas of California and Arizona.

MUGWORT

Artemisia vulgaris, Linn.

Compositae

Mugwort — famed for the protection against fatigue, sunstroke, wild beasts, and evil spirits it offered travelers — got its name because it was once used in place of hops to flavor beers. The dried flowered plant was boiled with malt liquor and this liquid added to beer. It was used for this purpose among country people in England until quite recently.

It has also been suggested that the name of the herb has been derived from *moughte* (maggot), because from Greek times the plant has been regarded as useful in driving away moths.

Wherever its name came from, mugwort has been surrounded by legends and superstitions for centuries. A crown made from sprays of the plant was worn on St. John's Eve to protect the wearer against evil possession. In Germany and Holland it is known as St. John's plant, and it is believed that if mugwort is gathered on St. John's Eve, it will give protection against diseases and misfortunes. It is said that John the Baptist wore a girdle of mugwort in the wilderness, and that the powers of the plant protected him against harm there.

In China, mugwort is hung up during the time of the Dragon Festival (fifth day of the fifth moon) to ward off the evil spirits. It is also used as a *moxa* — an herbal preparation placed on the skin and ignited to cauterize ulcers, ease pain, and restore sensation to numbed limbs.

Mugwort is a tall plant — it commonly reaches three feet in height, and may grow to seven feet under the best conditions. Its stems are angular and of purplish hue. The leaves are smooth and dark green on top; they are covered with a cottony down underneath, and are light grayish-green.

The flowers are in small, oval heads. They are pale yellow or reddish and are arranged in long, terminal panicles. The seeds that form after pollination are light gray, small sticks about one millimeter by one-quarter millimeter in size.

Mugwort is closely related to common wormwood, but can be readily distinguished by its pointed leaves and by the fact that the leaves are lightly colored only on the under-surfaces. It also lacks the oil of the wormwood.

Mugwort is easily raised from seed. Germination of the seeds takes place at fairly low temperatures — from about 55° F to 60° F and is fairly fast. However, since the seeds are so small, the best way to start mugwort is indoors for transplanting outside. Mugwort can also be reproduced by dividing old plants, or by buying a live plant from a grower. Both of these methods yield faster results.

Because the plants may reach a height of six to seven feet under the best conditions, it is best to plant them near the perimeter of the garden where they will not have to compete with other plants for space or sunlight. Once established, mugwort will spread rapidly unless it is cut back.

Plant mugwort in moist and well-fertilized soil. It should be well-composted, and cultivated or mulched until established.

Harvesting depends on the part to be used. If you are brewing tea from the mugwort, harvest before it flowers. Mugwort is also used as a seasoning for goose when it has flowered, but before the flowers fully open. Dry leaves or flowering buds in the shade. They dry well and retain color well.

Mugwort root, collected in the fall, is also used as a remedy. Roots should be free from rootlets and washed with cold water. Drying is begun in the open air: spread the roots thinly and don't let them touch. When somewhat shrunken, they must be finished in a drying room or shed or in a stove under a low heat. Drying should take two weeks or more. The root is not dried until it is brittle, snapping when bent.

Astrologers regarded mugwort as a plant under the influence of Venus, and recommended it for treating ailments of women. One of its chief uses was to stimulate the menstrual flow, often when combined with pennyroyal and southernwood.

It was also used to stimulate perspiration.

Mugwort was administered as an infusion, prepared in a covered vessel using one ounce of the herb to one pint of boiling water. Administer in one-half teaspoonfuls, while still warm. The infusion may also be taken cold as a tonic in similar doses three times a day.

Mugwort was also recommended for palsy or epilepsy. Gerard said, "Mugwort cureth the shaking of the joynts inclining to the Palsie." Withering reports that a dram of the powdered leaves given four times a day cured a patient who had been affected by hysterical fits for many years.

Mugwort

The flowering buds are used as a stuffing for geese during roasting. The dried leaves are also used as a tea, and were used quite extensively at a time when tea was costly.

Culpeper, recommending that the tops of the plant be used freshly gathered, reported: "A very slight infusion is excellent for all disorders of the stomach, prevents sickness after meals and creates an appetite, but if made too strong, it disgusts the taste. The tops with the flowers on them, dried and powdered, are good against agues, and have the same virtues with wormseed in killing worms. The juice of the large leaves which grow from the root before the stalk appears is the best against the dropsy and jaundice, in water, ale, wine, or the juice only. The infusion drank morning and evening for some time helps hysterics, obstruction of the spleen and weakness of the stomach. Its oil, taken on sugar and drank after, kills worms, resists poison, and is good for the liver and jaundice. The root has a slow bitterness which affects not the head and eyes like the leaves, hence the root should be accounted among the best stomachics. The oil of the seed cures quotidians and quartans. Boiled in lard and laid to swellings of the tonsils and quinsy is serviceable. It is admirable against surfeits."

MULLEIN

Verbascum thapsus, Linn.

Scrophulariaceae

Mullein is another of those naturalized weeds which deserves a place in the garden. It was introduced in the United States as a garden plant, but quickly escaped and spread across the nation. It was brought here in the first place because of its medicinal values; it has served for centuries as a demulcent and emollient, being used, paradoxically, for both diarrhea and constipation, and was especially valued as a remedy in bronchial and lung ailments.

The plant is a striking one, with a tall, flower-studded spike arising from a thick stake of leaves. Mullein is a biennial, and the flower stalk does not develop until the second year. In the first year, the large, woolly leaves develop and they persist over the winter. The flower stalk, with its yellow blossoms, rises from four to eight feet in the second year. Both leaves and blossoms have use.

Dried, the leaves have been smoked to ease throat congestions. Dried and powdered, the leaves are used in soothing infusions. A popular remedy called for boiling an ounce of dry powdered leaves in a pint of milk for ten minutes, straining the infusion carefully (to remove the hairs which give the leaves their woolly character), stirring in a teaspoon of honey and serving warm, a wineglassful at a time. The infusion is useful primarily as a remedy for coughs, but it has also been suggested for diarrhea and constipation. The flowers usually are steeped in olive oil for several weeks, and the resulting ointment used on bruises, frostbite, hemorrhoids, and even aching ears.

Mullein is easily established in the garden. The seeds germinate in about ten days, and the resulting plants will ultimately self-sow freely. Mullein grows well in poor soil.

MUSTARD

Brassica, various species
Cruciferae

Both kinds of mustard have been used as condiments for many centuries. Use of the seed is thought to have dated back to the time of the Greeks, who also used the plant's green leaves as a potherb and salad.

Black mustard is a hardy annual which grows to a height of four feet, even in poor soil. But when grown for its seed, black mustard must be kept fairly moist and well-nourished.

White mustard is more often grown in the garden for its seed. It is a plant that grows to a height of eighteen inches, and its leaves are useful for salad. It may become a pest, because it self-sows freely, so it is inadvisable to plant it in the regular vegetable garden or flower border.

When grown for the seed, which is used in pickling and as a peppery condiment, pods must be picked before they are entirely ripe, or they will shatter and the fine seed will be lost. Pods are spread on muslin to dry, and are crushed to remove seeds and hulls. The seed must be further crushed and milled to remove the fine hulls before they are used. Commercially, mustard seed is ground to a flour to provide dry mustard. This process, however, is beyond the scope of home gardeners and is not recommended.

NASTURTIUM

Tropaeolum majus, Linn.
Tropaeolacae

Nasturtium is one of the most familiar companion plants used by the organic vegetable gardener. The low, viney plant with its saucer-like leaves and bright-colored flowers attracts some pests and repels others. Both the leaves and flowers are edible and are, in fact, a tasty ingredient for fresh salads.

The genus *Tropaeolum* includes more than 50 annual or perennial plants, mostly climbing. Common nasturtium *(T.*

majus) is a tender annual, and one of the most popular annuals because of its showy flowers in many shades of red, orange, and yellow. Large varieties climb as high as ten to twelve feet. Dwarf varieties grow in low, compact, rounded bushes slightly less than one foot high and about a foot in diameter. These forms are excellent for bedding.

Common nasturtium is a native of South America, and is sometimes known as Indian cress, a reference to the Peruvian Indians who made good use of it. It made its way from the land of the Incas to Europe by way of conquering Spaniards and pirating Englishmen, first appearing in English gardens at the very end of the sixteenth century.

The common name nasturtium should not prompt one to confuse *T. majus* with the botanical genus *Nasturtium*. The most common of the latter clan is *N. officinalis,* commonly known as watercress. The only real connection between watercress and nasturtium is the taste, and nasturtium is sometimes regarded as a substitute for watercress. The name *Tropaeolum* is derived from the latin *tropaeum,* for trophy, and was an allusion to the shield-like leaves and helmet-like flowers.

Nasturtium is most useful in cooking and in the garden. The entire plant has a spicy, yet delicately pungent flavor. Both the flowers and young leaves are fine for salads and sandwiches, used in the same manner as lettuce. The seeds also make a fine snack, and the Chinese have relished pickled nasturtium seeds for centuries. Simply gather seed clusters when about half grown, leaving some of the stem still attached. Clean them and put them in a jar, covering them with freshly boiled cider vinegar. Tightly seal the jar and store in a cool place.

Another technique for pickling the seeds involves gathering them as soon as the blossoms are gone from the plants. Soak them for three days in cold salt water, changing the brine each day. Prepare a pickle of nutmeg, peppercorns, horseradish, and vinegar, warming but not boiling the mixture. Drain the seeds, place them in a jar, add the warm pickle, and seal.

The medicinal use of nasturtium over the years has been almost nonexistent. Pliny the Elder reported: "A sluggish man should eat Nasturtium, to arouse him from his torpidity." And it

Nasturtium

is said the juice of the plant is an effective remedy for itches.

The primary use of nasturtium remains in the garden. It is, as noted, a popular ornamental flower, and it is an even more popular companion plant. Companion planters report it is particularly useful in keeping vegetables and fruits susceptible to aphids clear of the pest. Nasturtium does this by attracting the aphids to itself, thus providing a single clean-up spot for the organic gardener. In addition, nasturtiums repel the white fly and the squash bug. An infusion of the plant, made by covering the plant with water in a pot, bringing it just to boiling and immediately taking it off the heat, can be cut four to one with water and used as a spray.

Nasturtiums do best in a sunny, well-drained location. When planted in a shady spot or in wet ground, they tend to produce a large growth of foliage with relatively few flowers. Since it is a viny plant, enough space should be allowed so it can hang down a bank or slope, or even be allowed to climb over a compost heap. The soil should be quite fertile.

The seeds should be sown outside as soon as the danger of

frost has passed. Cultivate the soil well. Cover the seed with about an inch of soil and firm well. Thin plants to about a foot apart. If the soil is poor and hard, spade it deeply, adding several inches of finished compost to the surface. Harvesting can take place at most any time, the leaves and flowers being used fresh.

NETTLE, STINGING

Urtica dioica, Linn.

Urticaceae

Nettle is like a beast with a heart of gold. It makes good eating, and it has a variety of healing virtues, but its embodiment turns away many. For stinging nettle has come by its name for good reason, as knows anyone who has had a run-in with it.

Stinging nettle is a familiar plant inhabiting roadsides, vacant lots, and waste places. It's a perennial with persistent, spreading roots. It is heart-shaped, has finely toothed leaves, and its one- to two-foot stems are covered with downy hair and with venomous spines. Each spine is a hollow needle filled with venom which is released whenever the plant is brushed. The venom stings like a bee and produces a red rash. (Dock is an antidote; the leaf is bruised and the juice rubbed on the nettle sting. It is said that wherever nettle grows, dock grows.)

Happily, the virulent qualities of nettle are destroyed by cooking or drying the plant. Simply boiling or steaming the foliage can produce a satisfying vegetable, but nettle is more tasty when made a part of some fancier dish. Old herbals contend that nettles are useful in weight-reducing diets.

A variety of cosmetic properties were attributed to nettle. Nettle water was reputed to be an excellent wash to clear the complexion and give brightness to the eyes. Boiling the entire plant in a mixture of vinegar and water, then adding eau de cologne was supposed to produce a good hair lotion. Combing the hair with expressed nettle juice was supposed to stimulate hair growth.

The plant did, of course, have many medicinal properties attributed to it. It was said to be anti-asthmatic and was used in bronchial and asthmatic ailments, as well as consumption. The seeds were recommended as antidotes to venomous bites and stings and such poisonous plants as henbane, hemlock, and nightshade. A novel use of the plant was as a counter-irritant in rheumatism cases. The afflicted person was "whipped" on the rheumatic joint with whole plants. The idea was that the pain of nettle stings would make the sufferer forget the pain of the rheumatism.

OREGANO

Origanum, various species
Labiatae

Oregano is the mystery plant of the herb world. There is no agreement as to which species of the genus *Origanum* is referred to by the common name oregano. Heinz Grotzke says oregano is *O. heracleoticum,* while a number of other authorities refer to *O. vulgare* as oregano. Still a third group of authorities cites the two species without attaching the common name oregano to either; these authorities call *O. heracleoticum* winter marjoram and *O. vulgare* wild marjoram.

The old herbalists offer little help to the layman. They tend to refer to all the species of the *Origanum* genus as "organy." One recent herb book relates the common name oregano to this early term implying that it was a name used only for the plant *O. vulgare.* In another book, Helen M. Fox relates her experiences trying "to find exactly which plant is 'oregano,' used as flavoring in the South and in Mexico." She reports that in Mississippi she was shown dwarf origanum and in Mexico *Majorana hortensis* (sweet marjoram), in both cases being told the plant was oregano.

A curious element of the mystery is that the plants, though of the same genus, are quite different.

O. heracleoticum is a perennial native to Greece and the Island of Cyprus. It isn't fully acclimated to harsh winters, so in the northern area of the United States, it should be treated as a tender perennial. A dense system of fine roots produces a

Oregano

low growing, almost creeping plant with very hairy leaves. The flower stalks grow erect, about 12 inches tall, and develop at their ends small clusters of white flowers. The seeds are light brown and particularly tiny.

O. vulgare is also a perennial, also a native of the Mediterranean. It, however, is quite hardy. The plant is erect, rising to two feet in height. It has dull, gray-green, oval leaves, far less hairy than those of *O. heracleoticum.* The flowers can be pink, white, purple, or lilac.

But in these descriptions lies something of a clue. Adelma Grenier Simmons, who identifies *O. vulgare* as oregano, notes, "The most flavorsome oregano is a small-leaved, almost trailing plant with white flowers. It is easily overrun by the coarser types and needs to be kept separate and wintered inside." Grotzke says that the color of the flowers is "the best guide to distinguish the two varieties of *Origanum.* Oregano always has white flowers." And it is he who asserts that the tender, creeping, small-leaved, white flowered *O. heracleoticum* is the true oregano. The botanic identity aside, the appearance of the best oregano for culinary use should be clear.

The flavor is the heart of oregano's usefulness, for it is duely famous as a seasoning herb. The fame is due primarily to its use in pizza pies, spaghetti sauce, and other tomato dishes. Sparingly add the leaves, fresh or dried, to any of these dishes. Oregano is also a flavorful garnish for beef or lamb stews, gravies, soups, salads, or tomato juice. *O. heracleoticum* is limited to such uses, but the capacities of *O. vulgare* are more ranging.

O. vulgare has an ancient medicinal reputation, the Greeks having used it both internally and externally, as an antidote to narcotic poisoning, convulsions, and dropsy. The Elizabethan herbalists noted these properties, and added many of their own. Culpeper, for example, wrote: "It strengthens the stomach and head much; there is scarcely a better herb growing for relieving a sour stomach, loss of appetite, cough, consumption of the lungs; it cleanses of the body of choler, . . . and helps the bites of venomous beasts. It provokes urine and the terms in women, helps the dropsy, scurvy, scabs, itch, and yellow jaundice. The juice dropped into the ears, helps deafness, pain and noise in them."

More recent herbalists have listed it as mildly tonic, diaphoretic, carminative, stimulant, and useful as an emmenagogue. They have noted that its warming qualities have made it useful as a liniment and rubefacient. A frequently mentioned toothache remedy is oregano oil. Moisten a bit of cotton with a few drops of the oil and place it on the aching tooth. A warm infusion of oregano is said to spur the fever and eruption of measles and to be helpful in cases of nervous headache. The ancient Greeks made warm poultices of the leaves to apply to painful swellings, and even twentieth century herbalists have recommended such use.

Because of the strong balsamitic odor of the whole plant, it has had some use in potpourris, sachets and aromatic waters, although it takes a secondary role to sweet marjoram in such applications. The flower tops of the plant are said to yield a dye, though one of limited durability. It dyes wool purple and linen a reddish-brown.

If the mystery has aroused your curiosity, perhaps you would like to try cultivating some oregano. The plant can be started from seed or through the use of cuttings. The real trick seems to be getting the seed or a cutting from a true oregano plant. In any case, the plant is easily started using the standard practices for the approach used.

The demand of oregano on soil fertility is modest, though good drainage and tilth are essential. Planting outside with a distance of twelve inches between plants should be delayed until danger of frost has passed. Hoeing and weed control are important; mulching with cocoa hulls or hay helps to keep the plants clean. Water requirements are minimal and generally supplied by average rainfall.

As soon as the white flowers appear, oregano is ready for harvest, unless of course, continued picking for fresh use during its growth never allowed it to flower. Even then oregano should be trimmed about six weeks after planting, cutting off all shoots to within one inch from the growing center. This practice stimulates dense, bushy growth.

In addition to inside drying, oregano is one of the few herbs which may be dried outside in the sun after harvesting without losing much of its properties. It dries very fast due to its "hot" nature. Rubbing the dried material through a fine screen will prepare the oregano for culinary use.

PARSLEY

Petroselinum hortense, Hoffm.
Umbelliferae

One of the best known herbs, parsley is also one of the most effective and versatile. Pliny considered the bright green biennial one of the most important of his time for its medicinal values. Today, parsley is mostly used as a decorative herb, but it has high nutritional and medicinal value which is unfortunately overlooked.

Parsley is believed to be indigenous to Sardinia, Turkey, Algeria, and Lebanon, where it still grows wild. The Romans are credited for bringing the herb to England, and the English carried it and cultivated it throughout the world.

The Greeks believed the god Hercules chose parsley for his garlands, and consequently it was woven into crowns for victors in the athletic games. Greek warriors used to feed it to their horses before races with the belief that it would help them run faster. At Greek banquets, chaplets of parsley were worn to absorb the fumes of the wines and to help the men from becoming inebriated. It was also used to subdue the odor of garlic, onions, and other smelly foods.

Theocretus wrote:

> At Sparta's palace twenty beauteous maids
> The pride of Greece, fresh garlands crowned their
> heads
> With hyacinths and twining parsley drest
> Graced joyful Menelaus' marriage feast.

On the other hand, the Greeks also were believed to have associated parsley with oblivion and death. According to Greek legend, parsley sprang up where the blood of the Greek hero Archemorus had spilled when he was eaten by serpents. Because of this legend, a common expression was that if you were "in need of parsley," you were seriously, almost hopelessly, ill. The Greeks also used the herb to make wreaths for their graves. As the parsley became transplanted onto the ground around the graves, it made a beautiful carpet of green.

Parsley is slow to germinate, and the superstition growing around this fact was that before it came up, it had to go to Satan and back seven times. Some believed that only a witch could grow it and that a fine harvest was assured only if it were planted on Good Friday or by a pregnant woman. Transplanting parsley was never done, because it was said to displease the herb and bring bad luck to the household of the offender.

The medicinal uses for parsley, through the ages, were almost endless. Parkinson said "the rootes boiled into broth help open obstruction of the liver, veines and other parts . . . . The rootes likewise boiled with leg of mutton . . . will have their operation to cause urine."

Gerard agreed that parsley was just the thing to "take away stoppings and provoke urine," either in a broth or by eating the seeds. He added that parsley seeds "waste away winde, are good for suche as have dropsie, draw down the menses, bring away the afterbirth; they be commended also against the cough, if they be boiled or mixed with medicines for such a purpose. . . . They are also good to be put into clysters against the stone or torments of the guts."

That wasn't all, of course. Harris claimed that the bruised leaves were used successfully to cure bites and stings of insects, and the seeds could be used to kill vermin in the hair. He also said it was poisonous to birds. Certainly not to rabbits, however, who love parsley more than any vegetable. Turner had a dandy use for parsley. If thrown into a fishpond, he instructed, it would "heal the sick fishes therein."

Culpeper recommended parsley for most of the above uses, and added several of his own. Being under the dominion of Mercury, it was very comforting to the stomach and was good against the falling sickness. If the leaves were laid on the eyes, it helped to ease swelling and pain, and dropped into the ears with a little wine, it would ease earaches. "If used with bread or meal, or fried with butter," he said, "and applied to women's breasts that are hard through the curdling of their milk, it abates the hardness and takes away the black and blue marks coming of falls or bruises."

Some of these uses may be questionable, but parsley's value as a diuretic is still highly regarded today. In Greek, the word parsley means "stone-breaker."

The herb is a rich source of calcium, thiamin, riboflavin, and niacin. It abounds in vitamin A, and has more vitamin C than an orange. Because of its richness in vitamins, some consider it excellent to ease the pain of arthritis. A useful infusion is made by pouring one quart of boiling water over a cup of firmly packed parsley, both leaves and stems. Allow to sit for 15 minutes, then strain through a coarse cloth and bottle immediately. Cool quickly and keep under refrigeration. Parsley is also useful for eliminating bad breath.

In the first year, the biennial herb develops a multitude of green leaves on long stems until the winter halts its growth.

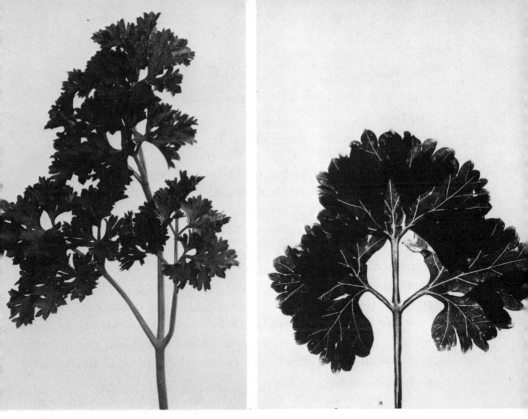

Parsley

White roots of various thicknesses, depending on variety, penetrate the soil to a depth of a foot. Flower stalks, reaching a height of over a yard, develop the second year, with greenish yellow flowers on clusters of umbels. The seeds are greyish brown and germinate within three weeks.

Since the herb gardener is generally interested only in the leaves, the plant is usually planted each year and considered as an annual. The superstition about the hazards of transplanting parsley are based on the fact that parsley doesn't transplant well. Thus the gardener should plant the herb outside, where it's supposed to grow.

Traditionally, parsley is transplanted in rows where it forms an attractive border to a garden. Early and shallow seeding will aid successful germination, even without watering.

The best type of soil for parsley is a fertile humus soil with good moisture holding capacity. Well-rotted compost is excellent fertilizing material, worked into the soil with a hoe or by rototilling. The gardener should avoid manure, however, because this would attract flies and could result in infestation of maggots.

Naturally, weed control is important, but especially with parsley because it develops so slowly at first. It's a good idea to hoe around the herb on a weekly basis until a hay or straw mulch takes over control of the weeds.

Because parsley is primarily used fresh, it is usually picked almost daily in the summer months. The larger outer leaves should be cut or broken first, always close to the core of the plant, without leaving parts of stems attached. Parsley can also be harvested by cutting the whole plant about an inch above the ground. Be sure not to damage the growing point, however.

The harvested plant should be dried in its entirety in the shade, in a short time. It may be necessary to finish the drying in the oven. Once dried, parsley should be crushed and stored in a tight container. Keep it away from moist places.

Curiously enough, this widely-known and much-used herb has had a long history of identity troubles. Gerard preferred the name *Apium hortense* for the plant he identified as garden parsley. The more commonly used name for that plant was *Petroselinum,* a name believed to have been ascribed to the plant by Dioscorides, the Greek herbalist and physician. The name was meant to distinguish parsley from celery. Both were selinons, and celery was called *heleioselinon,* or marsh *selinon,* and parsley was called *petroselinum,* or rock *selinon.* Gerard's contention was that the plant he was talking about wasn't the same plant the Greeks called *Petroselinum.*

In 1764, Linnaeus named the plant *A. petroselinum.* Later botanists reclassified and renamed it *Petroselinum lativum* and *Carum petroselinum. P. hortense* is the current name.

P. crispum is a widely cultivated and used curly-leaved variety of the parsley. It is a very old variety, having been mentioned in the writings of Pliny. It has very similar properties to *P. hortense,* but is somewhat less hardy.

PASSION VINE

Passiflora incarnata, Linn.

Passifloraceae

There are many varieties or species of this beautiful climbing vine, noted for its unusual flowers, usually crimson, purple, and white. It is grown as an ornamental suitable for warmer parts of the country. Some varieties produce edible fruits used in jelly and juices. It is propagated by seed, stolons, or cutting. It prefers to grow in fibrous loam with leafmold. Plant and leaves are used as an antispasmodic and sedative, useful in nervous ailments, for headaches, and to promote rest and sleep.

PENNYROYAL, ENGLISH

Mentha pulegium, Linn.

PENNYROYAL, AMERICAN

Hedeoma puleogioides, (Linn.) Pers.

Labiatae

There are two pennyroyals, an American pennyroyal and an English pennyroyal, which appear to have little in common, yet their utilitarian characteristics are very much the same.

The English pennyroyal has the better standing in the herbal literature, since it emanates from the right part of the world for that. But the American pennyroyal probably has as long a history of use, by the Indians and later by the white settlers.

American pennyroyal is a purely American plant, found from the Atlantic coast west through the Dakotas and south to Texas and Florida. It is a branched annual, growing about a foot tall. Like all the mints, it has a square stem with tiny opposite leaves. Tiny flowers bloom in the leaf axils.

Its minty smell earned it the name smelling weed among the Onondagas. Its reputed ability to help suppressed menstruation earned it the name squaw mint in other tribes. Because it was a common plant in most regions of North America, it was familiar to a great many Indian tribes, and a variety of uses were recorded. The Chickasaws soaked the plant in water, then placed it on the forehead to relieve itching and watering eyes. The Mohegans made a stomach-warming tea of it. The Catawbas made a cold remedy from it. White settlers reported using pennyroyal as a diaphoretic, antispasmodic, febrifuge, and for arthritis. A nineteenth century Indian folk healer wrote:

> The hot tea of the plant is a very efficient remedy for all cramps and pains and colic. It is an active sweat producer, or, in medical terms, an active diaphoretic. Good for colds and cramping. . . . Good for pains in the stomach and colic in babies. I prefer the tea from the plant over and above all other forms and modes of preparation. It is harmless, and there is no danger of giving too much.

A recommended treatment of colds, fever, and influenza involved having the suffering victim soak his feet in a very hot footbath while drinking a cup or two of pennyroyal tea. He was then tucked into bed under several blankets to keep him sweating until the fever broke.

These various Indian and folk uses eventually provoked the attention of the medical profession. American pennyroyal was an official drug plant from 1831 to 1916, being used as a stimulant, carminative, and emmenagogue. From 1916 to 1931, pennyroyal oil was official, listed as an intestinal irritant and an abortion-causing agent.

The most obvious tie with English pennyroyal is American pennyroyal's unofficial property as an insect repellent. The Indians and white settlers alike rubbed their exposed skin with a handful of crushed pennyroyal leaves to protect themselves from the stings and bites of mosquitoes and gnats. It was this quality in English pennyroyal that earned it its common name, and the settlers undoubtedly tied its name to the American plant which had the same smell and action.

English pennyroyal is an official member of the mint family, being of the genus *Mentha* (which, of course, American pennyroyal is not). It is a totally insignificant plant, staying low, creeping along the ground. Only the lavender-blossomed flower stalk rises above the ground. The leaves are tiny.

But very early on, English pennyroyal was noticed because it seemed to have the power to drive away fleas. Pliny remarked on it, and Linnaeus selected a specific name indicative of this power in naming the plant, *pulex* being the Latin for flea. Both its old botanical name, *Pulegium regium,* and its old common name, Pulioll-royall, are references to the insect repelling properties of the herb, and indications that even royalty had problems with body lice.

English pennyroyal is not a native of England, despite its name, but rather a native of the Near East, from whence it spread across the cooler parts of Europe and north to Finland. Both the Greeks and the Romans used and valued the little herb, and Pliny, for example, listed a considerable number of disorders pennyroyal was said to remedy.

The most famous of the English herbalists all remarked on the plant, with Culpeper, for example, noting:

> Drank with wine, it is good for venomous bites, and applied to the nostrils with vinegar revives those who faint and swoon. Dried and burnt, it strengthens the gums, helps the gout, if applied of itself to the place until it is red, and applied in a plaster, it takes away spots or marks on the face; applied with salt, it profits those that are splenetic, or liver-grown. . . . The green herb bruised and put into vinegar, cleanses foul ulcers and takes away the marks of bruises and blows about the eyes, and burns in the face, and the leprosy, if drank and applied outwardly. . . . One spoonful of the juice sweetened with sugar-candy is a cure for hooping-cough.

Culpeper's contemporaries generally echoed his sentiments toward pennyroyal.

More recent English herbals have listed pennyroyal's properties as carminative, diaphoretic, stimulant, and emmenagogic. It is also said to be antispasmodic and stomachic. These properties, it is worth pointing out, parallel the properties listed for American pennyroyal. As with American pennyroyal, the herb is generally administered in the form of an infusion, one ounce of the herb to a pint of boiling water, in teacupful doses.

Both American and English pennyroyal are inhabitants of the herb garden, though the former is a common wild plant in most areas of the United States. It can be found in spots with dry, acid soil and full sun. The garden conditions should duplicate, as well as possible, the natural conditions American penny-

American Pennyroyal

royal likes. Since it is an annual, it must be started from seed. The seeds are slow to germinate, but once the plant is established, maintaining it should be no problem, as it self-sows freely.

English pennyroyal may be started from seed, which germinates in the dark at a temperature of 65 to 70 degrees, but it is slow to germinate and takes a long time to establish itself. English pennyroyal, as a perennial, is best started from cuttings or root divisions. It roots very easily provided it's kept moist enough at all times. As the pennyroyal creeps on the ground, it forms roots wherever the stem touches the ground, which makes it rather easy to subdivide an older plant and make new plants.

The growing of pennyroyal is similar to that of any other mint. It likes a rich soil, but would also grow in the shade. It likes a good water supply and especially a high humus content in the soil. If the humus condition is poor, pennyroyal will develop a light green yellowish appearance and look starved. Thus, the application of good manure compost is most important. The harvesting of pennyroyal is harder than that of many other plants because the plant grows so low and because the size of the leaf is so small. It's very often difficult to harvest the shoots without getting some soil or some stones or some leaves or some other growth too. For the home garden it is easier because only one or two shoots are needed to flavor a meal. The plant should be used fresh as long as it is available, but can also be dried in the shade, preferably before chopping. The dried herb should be stored, as should all dried herbs, in tightly sealed, non-metallic containers.

Sown into sachets and fragrant bags, either of the pennyroyals will repel the moths and lend your clothing a minty aroma.

PERIWINKLE

Running Myrtle

Vinca minor, Linn.

Apocynaceae

A very useful plant for ground cover, periwinkle is very hardy, thrives in shade, and is one of the best plants to grow beneath trees and other areas where a carpeting effect is desired. It has shining evergreen leaves and pretty blue flowers in spring. *Vinca major* is larger, taller, and faster growing and can be used to quickly cover shaded banks. This herb is propagated by root divisions and cuttings. Medicinally, it was used as an astringent and nervine.

PIPSISSEWA

Ground Holly, False Wintergreen

Chimaphila umbellata, (Linn.,) Bart.

Pyrolaceae

This small evergreen of the heath family has shiny, leathery, dark green leaves in irregular whorls. The fragrant flowers, from white to rose-pink or light purple, rise above the leaves in a cluster of four to seven blossoms. The fruit is an erect five-celled capsule.

Found mostly in northern areas, it prefers an acid soil, rich in leafmold. The creeping root-stalk makes it a desirable ground cover around conifers and other broad-leaf evergreens. They are propagated by soft wood cuttings, taken when the leaves are half-grown.

The variety *Chimaphila maculata* has varigated foliage and very fragrant white flowers.

It is used in long-standing rheumatic and kidney ailments. The medicinal properties are listed as astringent, alterative, diuretic, and tonic.

PLANTAIN

White Man's Foot, Great Plantain
Plantago major, Linn.
Plantaginaceae

Plantain is considered by many today to be a weed, but its great reputation in the herbal lore earned it notice in some of the world's great literature, as both Chaucer and Shakespeare mention the plant in their writings. It is known all over the western world, having spread widely from its European origins. The American Indians, for example, found it spreading wherever the European went, and called it "white man's foot."

There are many varieties of plantain, there being more than 200 genera in the family Plantaginaceae. The most familiar, *Plantago major* or common plantain is characterized by its ribbed, ovate leaf and its spiked stalk with purplish-green blossoms. It has a short rhizome with many long, straight yellow roots. The roots, leaves, and seeds have seen herbal use.

While the Indians may have given it a somewhat pejorative name, they discovered important uses for it. They used the leaves in vulnerary poultices and on stings and bites. A tea they administered for kidney ailments. But their uses were antedated by similar uses the Europeans made of it. Culpeper noted, for example, "Briefly, the plantains are singular good wound-herbs to heal fresh or old wounds or sores, either inward or outward." And Shakespeare had characters in at least two plays recommend plantain leaf for a "broken skin."

POINCIANA

Poinciana, various species
Leguminosae

Perhaps not as well known for its medicinal values as some of the other shrubs, the beautiful poinciana ranks with the showiest trees and shrubs when in bloom. A delicate looking plant, it grows on a slender, single stalk with a wide spreading top of feathery, mimosa-like foliage and clusters of brilliant red and yellow flowers with conspicuous, long red stamens. The two most common varieties are *Poinciana pulcherrima,* dwarf poinciana, or Barbados flower-fence, so called as they are frequently planted along a fence line; and *P. gilliesii,* found growing in many arid regions of California and often referred to as the desert bird of paradise. They are native to warm regions, although they suffer no damage in temperatures as low as 20 degrees.

Poinciana thrives in poor, sandy, dry soil. It will grow in most garden soils if not overwatered. Once established, it does not require summer watering. In windy areas, the slim stalks should be staked or supported to keep them erect, especially while plants are young.

Plants are easily started from seed, which should first be soaked in warm water, then sown in sandy soil. It will grow from 12 to 18 inches a year and can reach a height of ten feet.

A purgative is derived from the leaves, which are also used as a tea for liver infections. Decoctions of the flowers are used as a wash for eye inflammations and ulcers of mouth and throat. No insect pests or diseases have been observed on the poincianas.

POKEWEED

Poke, Poke Root, Pigeonberry, Inkberry, Pokeberry
Phytolacca decandra, Linn. (syn. *Phytolacca americana*)
Phytolaccaceae

Pokeweed is one of the more important Americans in the plant world. It is a wild plant, rarely if ever cultivated, but it is known all over America and in many European countries. It has been used in a variety of medicinal applications, as a food-stuff, and as the botanical name and several of its common names indicate, as a dye plant.

One of the most curious uses of the poke color was to dye wines. It was a practice said to have been discontinued in Portugal because the poke spoiled the taste and in France because it was outlawed. The juice of the berry is a beautiful purple and can be used to dye textiles, though it is somewhat short on durability. The name *Phytolacca* comes from the Greek for plant (phyton) and crimson lake (lacca), an apparent reference to the plant's dye qualities.

The leaves, if gathered in spring or early summer, are edible and the first shoots of spring can be eaten like asparagus. But the plant develops toxic properties with maturity and should be regarded as poisonous. The medicinal uses are many, but again, the dosages must be carefully followed, for overdose can cause vomiting, convulsions, and death.

Various tinctures, ointments, and poultices have been made of poke and used in cases of glandular swelling and chronic rheumatism. It has been valued too as an emetic and alterative, largely because of its slow action. One recommended alterative is an infusion of one tablespoon of the cut berries or root with a pint of water. The infusion is taken in tablespoon doses.

POMEGRANATE

Punica granatum, Linn.
Punicaceae

Pomegranate is a popular garden bush in warm areas. It is a lovely plant with thick vigorous green foliage and brilliant orange-red flowers. The fruit ripens in September and October and is about the size of an orange, has a dark red, hard rind filled with juicy seeds. There is a dwarf form frequently used for hedges.

The plant is propagated mainly by hard wood cuttings taken in spring, and also by seeds and layers. The pomegranate prefers to grow in deep, heavy loams.

Bark from the root and stem and the rind of the fruit have been used medicinally. In China, the fruit rind is still used, being considered an astringent, tonic, laxative, and vermifuge. It is used for rheumatism and is made into a lotion for inflammation of the eyes. It is considered a specific for removing tapeworm and is used as a gargle for throat irritations. Fruit rinds were used for tanning leather. The fine Cordovan leathers were prepared this way. The juice is used for making wines and jelly.

POPLAR

Populus, various species
Salicaceae

The poplars are fast growing, soft-wooded, deciduous trees of the willow family. Leaves are alternated, followed by catkins. Poplars grow readily in any soil, and because of their rapid growth, are often planted in dry regions for windbreaks. They are easily propagated by seed or hardwood cuttings.

American aspen, or white poplar, is a small tree with slender, alternating branches. The broad leaves are heart-shaped, whitish with white veins, and hang on such slender stalks that they flutter restlessly. The trunk and limbs are silvery white. It should be planted against dark-leaved trees or evergreens to benefit from the full beauty of form and coloring. The autumn foliage is a clear yellow, a lovely addition to a woodland setting.

Buds, leaves, and bark are used for their soothing, balsamic qualities—as a wash for burns, cuts, and scratches. The bark is regarded as a universal tonic and can take the place of Peruvian bark or quinine. It may be freely given for cases of debility, indigestion, fever, and kidney and liver ailments.

Balm of Gilead *(Populus balsamifera)* is a strong growing tree with a balsamic fragrance. It makes an excellent shade tree for the lawn. Buds are boiled in olive oil, cocoa fat, or other good oil and make an excellent salve. The buds and bark are a stimulating tonic. The buds are used for colds, coughs, stomach and kidney ailments, and as a gargle. To dissolve the resin, the buds are soaked in alcohol before being used for a tea.

POPPY

Papaver somniferum, Linn.

Papaveraceae

Opium poppies are native to Greece and the Orient. They were grown by the Greeks, Romans, and early Chinese primarily for their seed, which was used in cooking and as a source of oil. A variety of poppy with very flavorful seed has been developed by the Dutch from a combination of *Papaver somniferum* and *P. rhoeas,* the corn poppy. This poppy is widely grown in India, Turkey, and Persia, both for seed and for opium. The seed does not retain any of the narcotic properties, which are present only in the green seed pod.

Opium poppy is an annual which grows about one foot high. Its four-petaled white flowers are tinged with blue and grow to four inches in diameter. It requires a long growing season, and cannot be matured in the north unless plants are started indoors. This is a precarious undertaking, because the roots are very sensitive and resent transplanting. Seed may be sown in pots and the whole root ball is transferred to the garden when the weather has become warm. Six inches to a foot should be allowed for each plant, depending on variety. Soil should be rich and moist, but above all, sunny. Poppies bloom very indifferently in the shade.

Pods should be allowed to dry on the plant, but must be caught before they turn their saltcellar-like openings to the ground to spill their seed. Drying can be finished on muslin indoors. When the pods are crisp, seed may be removed by rubbing the pods between the palms. The tiny seed can be separated from the chaff by putting it in a coarse strainer and shaking.

Poppy seed is used principally for baked products of all kinds. It is also one of the main ingredients of commercial birdseed mixtures. Oil from crushed seed is used as a substitute for olive oil.

POTENTILLA

Five-Fingers, Five-Leaf Grass, Cinquefoil
Potentilla, various species
Rosaceae

These hardy little herbs of the rose family can be found in a variety of forms and colors. Generally, from six to 18 inches high, they are common in this country growing on meadow banks, hillsides, and open grounds. They thrive in a sunny location and prefer sandy soil, but will grow in most garden soils. They are easily increased by seeds or root division. Cinquefoil can be used in beds and borders; some species are useful for bare banks and in the rockery.

Silvery cinquefoil is a very lovely species from five to 12 inches high. Little yellow flowers are clustered at the ends of branches. The undersides of fern-like leaves are covered with fine silvery wool, contrasting the dark green upperside. It blooms from May to September, and the root was used for red dye. *Popentilla reptans* has a slender creeping stem with leafstalks one to two inches long, five leaflets joined near the base, about two inches across with prominent veins below, and scattered hairs on veins and margins. It spreads by runners.

The whole top of potentilla is used as an astringent and febrifuge, as a mouth wash, lotion, for diarrhea, piles, and sore throat.

PURSLANE

Portulaca oleracea, Linn.
Portulacaceae

Purslane is familiar to most gardeners, for it is a very common garden intruder. Those gardeners who would root it out for the compost heap would do well to save it for the salad bowl, for purslane is actually cultivated as a potherb. It is a fleshy annual whose many branches and tiny green and reddish leaves,

Purslane

reddish stems, and minute yellow flowers spread rapidly along the ground. Both stems and foliage are meaty and oily.

A native of India and Africa, purslane was introduced into Europe as a salad plant during the fifteenth century. The old herbals list many medicinal applications for purslane. Culpeper, Gerard, Parkinson, and others agreed it was a good refrigerant, serving in ailments of heat—fevers, inflammations, and the like. The expressed juice of the plant, taken with honey or sugar was said to relieve dry coughs, shortness of breath, and immoderate thirst. For fevers and inflammations of the eyes, purslane was bruised and applied externally.

But the most common use of the succulent herb was in salads. It is a particularly nutritious food. It was widely cultivated in Europe, and travelers to the New World took specimens with them. The new Americans cultivated the little herb, but it quickly escaped from their gardens and spread across the land. It was something of a surprise to Samuel de Champlain's men to discover the Indians had no use for it, rooting it out of their corn patches much as Americans still do.

PYRETHRUM

Chrysanthemum cinerariaefolium, Vis.

Compositae

Pyrethrum is the source of the "safe" insecticide of the same name which is widely used by organic gardeners. The flowers are dried and powdered; the powder is best used alone, but it has served as a base for more toxic and dangerous pesticides.

The plants themselves are not only pretty but useful, since the quality which makes the powdered flowers useful to the gardener makes the plants valuable in the garden. The flowers are white or pink daisy-like blossoms topping stems reaching as high as two feet.

Pyrethrum is hard to start from seed; it should be started in a sterile planting medium. Once established, the seedling should be transplanted to a limy soil in a sunny spot. Regular cultivation is important to eliminate competition from weeds. Avoid excessive watering. In the spring, the plants may be increased by root division.

The root of the word pyrethrum is the Greek word for fire, *pyr.* The reference is apparently to either the color of the flowers or to a use of the plant as a febrifuge. Curiously enough, though a genus *Pyrethrum* exists, the plants commonly known as pyrethrums are members of the *Chrysanthemum* genus.

ROSE

Rosa, various species

Rosaceae

Roses have been known throughout the northern hemisphere as far back as literature records. Early poets of Greece, China, and Persia all sang praises of the rose. Dried roses have been found in Egyptian tombs. An indication of its antiquity is the fact that the name for a rose is almost the same in every European language.

To the herbalist, the rose is best known as an aromatic—one of the best aromatics—and as an ornamental. But it has also been used medicinally and is a useful plant in cooking.

There are probably more different kinds of roses than of any other plant considered an herb. Linnaeus, in 1762, described 14 rose species, a number which he soon increased to 21. After Linnaeus had pointed the way, other botanists followed with more and more complete classifications. John Lindley in 1820 described 76 species and sub-species. In recent years Professor Alfred Rehder at Arnold Arboretum classified 296 species.

Species described by botanists are pure strains. They do not include crosses, hybrids, doubles, bud mutations, and sports. The latter varieties, though not recognized by academic botanists as separate species, account for 95 percent of the roses listed in current catalogs. It has been estimated that through the latter half of the nineteenth and the first half of the twentieth century at least 16,000 varieties of roses were developed. Each year sees a new crop of hybrids presented to the gardener.

The herbalist is probably interested in very few of these 16,000 varieties. One of the very best is *Rosa damascena,* a principal ancestor of many of the hybrid perpetuals we have today. It is said to have first appeared in France at about the time of the Crusades. This rose was the source of the very best attar of roses. The whole bush is graceful, growing about three feet in height. The flowers come in many colors ranging from pale pink to deep red and pure white. A second important rose is the Provence rose, *R. gallica.* It has deep red blossoms appearing one to three on a branch. It grows two to three feet tall and has stocky branches.

These two kinds of roses bloom but once a year, but they are historic roses, fragrant and beautiful, well worth having in the garden.

Another interesting rose is the rugosa *(R. rugosa),* a hardy shrub rose which bears many attractive fruits, or hips, in fall. The hips are a rich source of vitamin C. The rugosa grows six to 15 feet tall, will endure heat, cold, dryness, sandy or clayey soil, and even salt sea air. Its flowers are single, double, or semi-double, in white, pink, and red. The rugosa is a native of China, Korea, and Japan. Because it is a distinct species, it can reproduce itself from seed.

The rose petals are the aromatic heart of the plant. The petals have been harvested and processed for their oil for centuries, with the French and Bulgarians producing the leading attars of roses. A technique for extracting attar of roses on a home scale is outlined in Chapter Four. The chapter also covers the use of rose petals in potpourris, sachets, and other aromatic items.

While the rose is undoubtedly best known for its fragrance, it is also a valuable culinary herb. Many have heard of rose hip tea, but the fruit of the rose can be used in a variety of ways by the imaginative cook. An extremely rich source of vitamin C, the rose hips are the fruit of the rose. After petals drop in the fall, the hips appear as pods of various sizes and colors. Most varieties of roses have hips the size of a pea or a marble. Many are green; some orange and red.

The great majority of American gardeners think that rose hips have no value, except possibly as an accent in flower arrangements. But concentrated in the hips of some varieties of roses is nature's richest source of vitamin C. Several common hips are as much as *60* times richer in vitamin C than oranges. The pleasant flavor of hips is both fruity and spicy. In the early fall the large bushes are covered with the orange and red fruits. Some people enjoy eating them fresh—right off the bush. Most often, though, they are collected, trimmed, and cooked lightly before being used in a variety of recipes.

Because the elusive vitamin C is difficult to hold through a drying process, rose hips are not easily prepared in powder form. The best idea is to make an extract or puree of them. This can then be stored with a minimum loss of food value, and used throughout the year by the tablespoonful or in fruit juices, salads, soups, and sauces.

Regardless of what you are making, follow these few rules when preparing rose hips:

1. Trim both ends of the rose hip with a pair of scissors before cooking.
2. Use stainless steel knives, wooden spoons, earthenware or china bowls, and glass or enamel saucepans.

3. Cook quickly with the lid on so there will not be much loss of vitamin C.

4. After the hips have been cooked the required time, strain out the spines and seeds or break them down by rubbing the cooked pulp through a sieve.

To prepare an extract of the rose hip, one must first chill the hips to inactivate the enzymes which might otherwise cause a loss of vitamin C. Remove blossom ends, stems, and leaves, then quickly wash the hips. For each cup of rose hips bring to a boil one and one-half cups of water, then add the rose hips, and simmer 15 minutes. Let stand in a pottery utensil for 24 hours. Strain off the extract, bring it to a rolling boil, add two tablespoons of lemon juice for each pint, and pour into jars and seal.

A rose hip puree may be made as follows: Take two pounds of rose hips and two pints of water. Stew the berries in a saucepan until tender. This will take about 20 minutes, and the lid should be kept on. Then press the mixture through a sieve and the result will be a brownish-tinted puree of about the same consistency and thickness as jam.

In Sweden, rose hip soup is a popular, healthful dish. It's easy to make: The hips are ground and boiled for ten minutes, then strained and again brought to a boil and thickened with four level teaspoonsful of potato flour (you can use soybean or whole wheat flour) which has been prepared with two cups of cold water. This soup can be served hot or cold.

The rose also has been used medicinally. The red rose has been listed as an official drug plant, the petals being used primarily to mask unpleasant odors in medical preparations. The Renaissance herbalists all reported on roses.

Despite its other uses, however, the rose is primarily an ornamental herb for today's gardener. Many gardeners devote their space solely to roses. Roses require sun, free circulation of air, and porous, well-drained, acid soil with a pH of five to six. Full sun for eight hours a day is best, but six hours' sun, provided they are morning hours, are sometimes sufficient.

The best plants to buy are two-year-old, field-grown, budded stock. Roses may be planted in fall or spring. Most nurseries dig their roses in the fall, store them through the winter, and ship in spring. If they are purchased in fall and held over for spring planting they should be heeled in at the bottom of an 18-inch trench, covered with loose soil, and mulched after the ground is frozen.

Soil should be trenched and prepared to a depth of 24 inches for best results with roses. Experiments have proved that roses planted in more shallowly prepared soil will give equal results with those in deep beds during the first year, but after the second year the roses in 24-inch beds are superior.

In preparing a rose bed, the top spade's depth of soil is removed and saved, the lower spade's depth then removed and discarded. In its place, a mixture of one-fourth rotted manure and one-half humus is mixed with the top loam. The mixture is then returned to the bed and permitted to settle for two weeks before planting.

A hole slightly larger in diameter than the spread roots of the plant should be dug deep enough barely to bury the bud graft when planting. Soil is mounded cone-shaped in the center of the hole, and the plant seated upon it. If any of the roots are damaged, they should be pruned back of the damage. Long straggly roots also are cut back and the tips of most others removed. The hole is half filled with soil and a pail of water poured into it, to wash soil among the small rootlets. When the water has seeped away, the hole is filled to garden level and tamped around the plant. Canes are then pruned to six to eight inches above soil level.

Roses are seldom grown from seed because seed-grown plants will revert to species. It is possible to propagate species from seed, but this requires more work than most gardeners are willing to do for the results achieved.

Several methods of handling rose seed, which is contained in the hip, are suggested. One is the "ripening" method. Hips are mashed to make a pulpy mash, permitted to ferment at about 40° F for 60 to 120 days, then washed and layered in humus in a flat or flower pot, and placed outdoors on the north side of a building to refrigerate.

A second method is to remove the seed from the hip and, without fermenting, to place it in leaf mold or peat moss in a flat or pot outside. Weathering during the cold months seems to help the seed to germinate. A third, and simpler method, is to plant the seed directly in the garden in the fall. If this method is adopted, seed should be sown about an inch deep, and six inches apart. After germination plants may be moved to stand a foot apart and permitted to grow for two years before taking their place in the shrubbery border.

A practical method for propagating roses true to the parent is by cuttings or slips. Cuttings are taken from the most healthy plants, and are made at a point where the cane breaks with a snap. If it bends, the wood is too tough. If it crushes, it is too green.

The cuttings may be set directly into an existing rose bed, or may be started in a corner of the garden where they will receive morning sun only. Cover them with glass jars, pushing the jars securely into the soil, then water well. It is not necessary to water them too often, because the moisture which condenses inside the glass jar will keep them sufficiently wet.

If the cutting forms roots, new shoots will appear within three or four weeks. Jars are not removed until the cuttings have roots enough to supply plenty of moisture to the leaves— possibly not until the following spring. Cuttings may be made any time from June until the first frosts. If they are made during July or August, it is well to shade them from the afternoon sun.

Roses need plenty of water when the season is dry, but it should be supplied at weekly intervals in quantities large enough to reach the deepest roots rather than in small daily doses. Mulch may be spread around the plants when the weather becomes hot and dry, to conserve moisture. Compost, buckwheat hulls, ground corn cobs, straw, decayed or shredded leaves, or lawn clippings may be used. If peat moss is used, it should be moistened before it is applied. It is advisable to mix a nitrogenous fertilizer with the mulch, particularly if corn cobs are used.

A formula developed especially for spring and summer rose feeding contains the following: two parts fishmeal, two parts dried blood, one part cottonseed meal, one part wood ashes (if soil is very acid), one part phosphate rock, and one part green-sand. The first three ingredients supply nitrogen; wood ashes supply potash; and phosphate rock and greensand provide phosphorous. Application of this fertilizer may be repeated in monthly doses, ending August 1 in the north, September 1 in mid-sections, and October 1 in the south.

Most bush roses need winter protection in areas where temperatures fall below 10° F. It is standard practice to mound the soil around the plants to a depth of at least eight inches. After the soil is thoroughly frozen and field mice have found their winter quarters elsewhere, a mulch of straw, leaves, or garden refuse mixed with manure may be filled in between mounds. Further protection is seldom necessary, unless the plants are exposed to drying winter winds. Burlap held by stakes may be used to shield the bed from strong winds.

Winter cover should be removed before growth starts in the spring. Mulch should be raked away, and the winter's manure may be cultivated into the top layer of soil. The bed is then left to bake under the warm spring suns to kill spores of fungus diseases until the time arrives for covering with the summer mulch.

Bedding roses are pruned in the spring when new shoots are about one-fourth inch long. Dead wood—all wood with brown, dried, or shriveled bark—is trimmed off first. The plant is then inspected for injury, and any canes injured by the winter winds or ice are trimmed back. Next rough, gnarled branches with weak twigs, and thin weak shoots are removed. Then the remainder of the branches are shortened by one-third of their length if many flowers are desired, or two-thirds length for larger but fewer blossoms.

ROSEBAY, DWARF

Alpine Rose
Rhododendron hirsutum, Linn.
Ericaceae

A hardy evergreen shrub growing only about one and one-half feet tall, it has hairy oblong leaves and rosy-pink blossoms, preferring a shady-moist location and slightly acid soil. It can be well utilized around conifers. Propagation is by seed, layering, suckers, and occasionally cuttings.

Leaves were used as a stimulant, diaphoretic, and diuretic.

ROSEMARY

Rosmarinus officinalis, Linn.

Labiatae

Among patricians of the herbal society, rosemary ranks as one of the noblest. Steeped in religious traditions, rosemary has a place as a symbol of fidelity and remembrance in two of the holiest of Christian ceremonies: the wedding and the funeral. Its more temporal uses as a medicinal and culinary herb are dazzling in number and variety. And it's a beautifully decorative addition to any garden.

The most common variety, *Rosmarinus officinalis,* is a perennial evergreen shrub that grows to a height of two to four feet. A native of the balmy Mediterranean, rosemary sometimes reaches six feet in warm climates and good soil. Legend holds that the rosemary bush grows to six feet in 33 years—the stature and life of Christ—and then, in obeisance to Him, ceases its vertical growth so as never to stand higher than He did.

Rosemary can be started by seeding, cuttings, or layering. Seeding usually is avoided because of the low percentage of germination. Commonly only one to five of every ten seeds planted will germinate. And it may take up to three years to produce a cuttable bush from seed. For gardeners who have no choice but to seed, planting should be done indoors in light, rich, and well-drained soil as early as January. Save at least one plant for cuttings in subsequent years.

Cuttings are sprouted by taking a six-inch end tip of new growth and burying its lower four inches in sand or vermiculite, or along a shady border of the garden. August is the best time. If the cuttings are planted outside, cover each one with an inverted water glass. They'll be ready to transplant in two to three months.

To layer new sprouts, just weight one or two of the lower

Rosemary

branches of a mature bush beneath the soil.

Rosemary will develop into a highly ornamental bush with a woody stem and boughs of evergreen needles that are dark green on top and lighter on the undersides. Blue flowers, light to dark, form at the tips of branches in the spring. The flowers are white on the more obscure variety *Rosmarinus officinalis* var. *alba*. Otherwise, there is little difference.

Another legend attributes the delicate blue of the *officinalis* flowers to the Virgin Mary. As this one goes, Mary draped her azure cloak over a white-bloomed rosemary bush during the flight from Egypt, whereupon the noble plant embraced the hue of the Virgin's garment.

The name rosemary sometimes is said to be a similar Virginal tribute. More likely, the name is a derivative of the Latin *ros* (dew) and *marinus* (of the sea). The plant's native habitat was among the misty hills of the Mediterranean seasides.

Rosemary flourishes with occasional watering although it requires well-drained soil, slightly alkaline. It cannot stand to be dehydrated, and that danger exists especially indoors.

A word of caution to growers north of Virginia: rosemary cannot stand heavy frosts. It can be left outside year-round, but it must be protected. The best is to plant along the south face of a wall where plastic or glass winter greenhouses can be constructed around the plant. Burlap or a bushel basket can be substituted if necessary. Plants also can be brought inside for the winter, but then care must be taken to supply enough room and enough moisture for the roots. Spray the branches every few days, too. Both the blue and white *officinalis* varieties cannot stand temperatures below around 27° F. The danger point for *Rosmarinus prostratus,* a creeping blue-flowered variety, is a few degrees higher.

R. prostratus, in addition to making a bright and fragrant soil-retention covering for banks, is a lovely indoor ornamental when planted in a hanging pot and allowed to cascade over the sides.

All varieties prefer sunny or semishady locations.

It's uncertain how rosemary was dispersed from its Mediterranean homeland. One theory holds that Roman conquerors brought it to northern Europe and England with them. Another says the Crusaders brought it home after adopting it from their Saracen foes, who used it as a balm for their wounds.

European herbalists quickly bestowed on rosemary a reputation for having the ability to strengthen the memory. That attribute, no doubt, gave rise to the use of rosemary as a symbol for constancy. Rosemary sprigs, dipped in scented water, were woven into bridal bouquets or exchanged by the newlyweds as a token of their troth. Or, richly gilded and bound in multicolored ribbons, the sprigs were presented to the wedding guests as reminders of virtuous fidelity.

At funerals, rosemary sprigs were tossed into the grave as a pledge that the life and good deeds of the departed would not soon be forgotten.

Of rosemary, the seventeenth century poet Robert Herrick wrote:

Grow for two ends, it matters not at all,

Be't for my bridal or my burial.

Shakespeare's Ophelia, mourning Hamlet's madness in Act IV, Scene VI of *Hamlet,* laments:

There's rosemary, that's for remembrance;

pray you, love, remember;

and there is pansies, that's for thoughts.

Medieval herbalists bedecked rosemary with wonderous abilities to cure nervous afflictions, and even to restore youth. William Langham in the sixteenth century prescribed: "Seethe much Rosemary and bathe therein to make thee lusty, lively, joyfull, likeing and youngly."

Bankes Herbal adds: "Make thee a box of the wood and smell it and it shall preserve thy youth."

In a practical vein, rosemary indeed was used extensively in manufacturing a favorite Renaissance instrument: the lute.

As a curative tonic, elixirs of rosemary extract were said to be of value, in the words of Parkinson, "inwardly for the head and heart; and outwardly for the sinews and joints."

Inwardly were taken various decoctions including rosemary tea and wine and diluted Hungary water, a powerful distillate said to cure stiffness of the joints when rubbed externally.

Tea is made by infusing a pint of water with one ounce of young rosemary tips or a heaping teaspoon of dried leaves. Taken with the juice of half a lemon and a touch of honey, the tea is said to alleviate headaches and help the restless get to sleep at night.

Rosemary wine can be made according to an ancient recipe by soaking a handful of six-inch tips in half a gallon of white wine for a few days. Modern-day vintners, though, probably would do well to keep the white wine in the refrigerator; it spoils quickly.

From a 1759 recipe book comes a formula for spirit of rosemary. "Gather a Pound and a half of the fresh Tops of Rosemary, cut them into a Gallon of clean and fine Melasses Spirit (probably dark rum), and let them stand all Night; next Day distill off five Pints with a gentle Heat. This is of the Nature of Hungary-water, but not being so strong as that is usually made, it is better for taking inwardly. A Spoonful is a Dose, and it is good against all nervous Complaints."

Hungary water itself, according to legend, was invented by a gnarled hermit to cure his queen, Elizabeth of Hungary, of paralysis of the joints. The water, actually a powerful distillate of rosemary oil in alcohol, is rubbed on the sore and lame areas.

What is thought to be an elaboration on the original Hungary water formula is offered in a 1732 herbal. Take a handful of foot-long tips and chop them into inch-long slivers. Add them to a gallon of brandy. Add almost as much myrtle as rosemary, and let the concoction stand three days. Then distill it to an oily reduction.

Culpeper says a "coarser way" of making Hungary water is to add a few drops of oil of rosemary to spirits, possibly vodka. Pure oil is available commercially, but Culpeper suggests filling a narrow-mouthed bottle with flowers, covering the mouth with a fine cloth and inverting the bottle into a waterglass. When set in the sun, the solar heat will drive the oil from the flowers, and it will collect in the lower glass "to be preserved as precious for divers uses, both inward and outward . . . ."

A pleasant sachet and insect-chaser can be made from equal parts of rosemary, lavender, and ground lemon peel.

For a pleasant mouthwash, infuse one-third of a teaspoon each of rosemary, anise, and mint in a cup of water.

One ounce each of rosemary and sage infused for 24 hours in a pint of water makes a pleasant hair tonic that can be used on dandruff. After infusion, strain the liquid and add a teaspoon of powdered borax.

A delightful, nonburning incense can be had by mixing a handful of crushed rosemary and a like amount of juniper berries in a pan of water. Heat well and stir, then keep the mixture on a radiator in winter or in sunlight during summer. The aromatic emissions were used for centuries in French hospitals and courts to ward off disease. It's called the *incensier* method.

Culpeper recommended burning rosemary "to expel the contagion of the pestilence."

It hardly needs to be mentioned that rosemary has a major

place in the modern kitchen as a tangy herb to flavor beef and veal, pork, lamb, poultry, soups, stuffings, sauces, and salad dressings. It can be purchased in the form of dried and chopped leaves. But if it is available fresh, cuttings from the new growth can be laid directly on roasts and poultry to add garnish as well as flavor.

RUE

Herb-of-Grace, Garden Rue, Herby Grass
Ruta graveolens, Linn.
Rutaceae

Rue—the herb of grace—has been used as an herbal medicine for thousands of years. It was prescribed for at least eighty-four different ailments in Pliny's day. Its generic name, *Ruta*, derives from a Greek word meaning "to set free," indicating ancient belief in its potency to relieve maladies and illnesses.

Rue was famous as an antidote to poisons of all kinds. Gerard wrote: "If a man be annointed with the juice of rue, the poison of wolf's bane, muchrooms, or todestooles, the biting of serpents, stinging of scorpions, spiders, bees, hornets and wasps will not hurt him." Rue is said by some to have been the main ingredient in the poison antidote of Mithridates, the king of Pontus, who experimented with poisons and their antidotes. When he tried to commit suicide by poisoning himself, he found that he was unable to die from the poison (some sources attribute this immunity to herbs of the genus *Eupatoria*). He finally persuaded a slave to stab him to death. Rue is used in China today to counter poisons and is recommended for malarial poisoning.

Rue is a hardy evergreen perennial, native to southern Europe. The stem, in the lower part, is woody, and the leaves are alternate and bluish-green in color, and bi- or tri-pinnate. The foliage is very aromatic, emitting a powerful—and, to some—disagreeable odor. The taste is bitter.

The flowers are greenish-yellow in terminal panicles, blossoming from June until September. The seeds that form after pollination are grayish.

Rue

Rue is easily propagated from seeds, unlike many herbs. Seeds should be started indoors in February for May planting outside. When the seedlings are about two inches high, they may be planted outdoors, allowing 18 inches each way between plants. Rue should be planted in the sunlight for best results, although the plants will do fairly well anywhere.

Rue can also be propagated by cuttings or rooted slips made in early spring. Cuttings should be planted in the shade until well-rooted, when they can be transplanted into a permanent, sunny location.

Rue can be harvested several times a year. Harvest leaves (the part of the plant used in herbal remedies) before the flower forms. After the first cutting, top dress the plant with good compost or organic fertilizer to stimulate a second growth.

The herb is usually used fresh, but it can be dried in the shade and stored in an airtight container to avoid loss of quality.

Rue's nickname, "herb of grace," lends holy connotations to the herb. Brushes made from rue were, at one time, used to sprinkle the holy water at the ceremony preceding High Mass.

It was also called the "herb of Repentance," presumably because of this same use. Ophelia, in *Hamlet,* refers to this use of the herb when she says, "There's rue for you and here's some for me; we may call it herb of grace o' Sundays."

Presumably the herb's use in the Church led many during the Middle Ages to believe that it was a powerful defense against witches. Rue was commonly used to ward off spells— although the Greeks used it for the same purpose. It is said that rue was the herb given by Mercury to Ulysses to free him from the charms of the witch Circe.

Rue has been regarded from the earliest times as successful in warding off contagious diseases, and preventing the attacks of fleas and other noxious insects. For ages, rue was an important part of the bunch of aromatic herbs carried by judges into court as a safeguard against the fevers, diseases, and pests prisoners had picked up in the jails. It was often strewn in the court, and sprigs of rue were placed on the dock benches to disinfect them. Gerard gives an interesting recipe for a disinfecting paste made from rue: "The leaves of rue eaten with the kernels of Walnuts or figs stamped together and made into a masse or paste, is good against all eville aires, the pestilence, or plague."

Ruewater was sprinkled about the house to kill fleas. And it was also placed or grown near stables or around manure piles to repel flies.

Culpeper recommends it for sciatica and pains in the joints. For these purposes, the affected area was commonly "annointed" with rue. Culpeper also recommends the following:

> . . . the juice thereof warmed in a pomegranate shell or rind, and dropped into the ears, helps the pain of them. The juice of it and fennel, with a little honey, and the gall of a cock put thereunto, helps the dimness of the eyesight.

Leyel said that rue "bestows second sight, and it certainly preserves ordinary sight, by strengthening the ocular muscles." This use of the herb—to bestow second sight—is ancient. Pliny tells us that Greek painters used rue to achieve a second sight and to relieve their eyes after working long hours in dim light. It was used for similar purposes during the Middle Ages.

Both the fresh and dried plants are used in compounding

herbal remedies, although the latter is less powerful. One common use for rue is as a tonic with sedative qualities in colic, and as a stimulant for the circulation. It is also taken to prevent aging. For this purpose, an infusion of one teaspoon of the dried herb to a cup of boiling water is made.

The medicinal virtues of rue are due to a volatile oil found in glands distributed over the entire plant. Oil of rue is made from the fresh herb, and may be administered in doses of from one to five drops. The oil may, however, cause allergic reactions in some people. If you develop a long-lasting rash similar to poison ivy rash, it is best to avoid handling or using rue.

Rue is little used as a condiment because of its strong taste. However, the Italians sometimes add a few chopped leaves of rue to salads. Rue leaves are also eaten to refresh the mouth and relieve giddiness, hysterical spasm, or nervous headache.

If you've got some doubt as to where to obtain rue, remember that the Greeks believed that rue stolen from a neighbor's garden did better than a plant acquired honestly.

SAFFLOWER

Carthamus tinctorius, Linn.
Compositae

Safflower is an important annual with dark-green and shining leaves with prickly orange hairs on margins somewhat resembling thistle in foliage and form. The flowers are made up of clusters of green bracts, topped by tufts of deep yellow florets, turning orange as they mature. They are very ornamental when grown in clumps. Seeds ripen in August and look like curious white teeth with stained ends. The seeds are the source of safflower oil. Dried blossoms are used as a substitute for saffron for coloring chicken gravy, soups, and pickles; the orange coloring is water soluble. From the same blossom a resinous red dye is used for dying silk or mixed with talc for rouge. This plant was found in the Egyptian tombs. It grows in poor, dry soil, in full sun. Sow seeds in April where they are to grow as they do not transplant well.

SAFFRON

Crocus sativus, Linn.

Iridaceae

Saffron is the herb that provides late season color to the garden. As the weather turns cold and the trees begin shedding their leaves, the lovely lilac flowers of the saffron appear. Without the flowers, the plant itself is undistinguished, having narrow, grass-like leaves.

The saffron flower, in addition to providing garden distinction to the plant, holds the useful element: the stigma. Each flower has three scarlet-orange stigmas which are collected and dried and used to dye a variety of foodstuffs. They have also been used to dye textiles. Medicinally it is a carminative, diaphoretic, and emmenagogue.

It is best to purchase saffron plants, since new plants won't blossom for three years. Moreover, saffron must be hand-pollinated to get seed, so the best method of propagation is bulb division. The bulbs can be divided annually or only once in three years. But whichever method is used, the plants shouldn't remain in the same spot more than three years. The corms are planted in late July to early August. Place them six inches deep and six inches from any neighbor. The soil should be light and rich, the location sheltered.

If you expect to collect the stigmas, be sure to plant thousands of saffron, for 60,000 stigmas weigh only a pound. Obviously, the dried material is very expensive, and, as might be expected, the stigmas are often adulterated—or stretched—with arnica or calendula petals or safflower florets.

SAGE

Salvia officinalis, Linn.

Labiatae

Sage the Saviour enjoyed widespread popularity as a virtual panacea for all ailments of the body when herbal medicine was practiced universally.

Fortunately, the decline of herbal medicine didn't leave this pleasant herb in present-day obscurity, for as the medicinal use of sage waned, its role in cookery increased.

Nevertheless, sage still has a place in herbal medicine. Although there are few who still hold that sage can cure tuberculosis and treat snake bites effectively, it is said to be of value in reducing nervous headaches and sore throats.

The plant's very name is an offshoot of its once-held power to work such a salutory effect on the human body that it prolonged life itself. An ancient Latin proverb, dating at least to the early Middle Ages, goes: *Cur moriatur homo cui Salvia crescit in horto?* (Why should a man die when sage flourishes in his garden?)

The generic name *Salvia* means "health" or "salvation." The specific name *officinalis* indicates that sage was among herbs of medicinal value listed in the official pharmacopoeia. Indeed, sage was listed officially in England and America.

A Mediterranean native, sage was scattered throughout Europe in the back sacks of Roman legionaires. Centuries later, when East-West trade developed, European sage became a highly prized export item that was worth three or four times its weight in Chinese tea.

The seventeenth century herbalist Gerard said sage "is singularly good for the head and brain, it quickeneth the senses and memory, strengtheneth the sinews, restoreth health to those that have the palsy, and taketh away shakey trembling of the members."

Sir John Hill, another herbalist, agrees with Gerard about sage's strong tonic property. Sage, Sir John wrote, "will retard that rapid progress of decay that treads upon our heels so fast in the latter years of life, will preserve the faculties and memory, more valuable to the rational mind than life itself without them; and will relieve under that faintness, strengthen under that weakness and prevent absolutely that sad depression of spirits, which age often feels and always fears, which will long prevent the hands from trembling and the eyes from dimness and make the lamp of life, so long as nature lets it burn, burn brightly." He

Sage

did not suggest whether sage might also improve the syntax.

In the ninth century, a European herbalist proclaimed: "Amongst my herbs, Sage holds the place of honor; of good scent it is, and full of virtue for many ills."

It was, and is, a popular plant. In reality, there are more than a dozen varieties of sage with varying colorations, leaf shapes, and life cycles. *S. officinalis,* being the most popular, is the one discussed here.

Even the *S. officinalis* will vary in coloring and leaf markings from plant to plant. If you should happen to cultivate a plant whose markings please you, propagate others from that plant by cutting or pegging. Plants started from seed, even seed from the treasured growth, often will not be consistent in markings.

The typical *S. officinalis* is a foot or more high with a squarish stem and rounded-oblong leaves supported by short stems. Purplish flowers appear in August in whorls at the upper end of the plant. The leaves and stems are coated with stubbly silver-grey hair that has earned the plant the Arabic nickname of "camel's tongue."

Sage is a hardy perennial that will withstand most American winters, but it should not be allowed to outlive three or four years because of the tendency of its stems to become woody and tough. Each spring, the woody growth should be trimmed away. Sage is easy to start from seed because the seeds are large and can be spaced and observed well in their early growth. Indoor seeding will get the plants started four weeks earlier than outdoors planting. Place seeds a foot apart in March for inside planting, or in April outside.

Decisive factors are a sunny, wind-protected area with neutral soil, a good calcium supply, and plenty of moisture, especially in the early stages. Compost can be applied, but fresh manure should be avoided because it produces an undesirable flavor in the herb.

Because sage likes a well-aerated soil, early spring hoeing and cultivation are important. Use cocoa hulls for summer mulch.

Crucial factors in determining how sage will fare over the winter are how the last fall harvesting is accomplished, and when. It should be no later than September, and only leaves and stems high up on the plant should be taken. A light September harvest is all that will be possible the first year. In subsequent years, at least two cuttings will be available.

Dry the leaves in the shade until they're crisp. For tea, just break them up by hand. For seasoning, rub them through a fine screen. The flavor keeps well after drying.

Experts on companion planting suggest placing sage near rosemary. They say the two herbs stimulate one another. Sage also will protect cabbage from its insect enemies and make it more digestible. Young cucumber and grass shoots, however, are inimical to sage and their growth could be stunted by a nearby sage bush.

The old herbalist Culpeper said sage is "of excellent use to help the memory, warming and quickening the senses." He said it's also "profitable for all pains in the head coming of cold rheumatic humours, as also for all pains in the joints, whether inwardly or outwardly."

Maude Grieve, a twentieth-century herbalist, said an infusion of sage can be prepared "simply by pouring one pint of boiling water onto one ounce of the dried herb, the dose being from a wineglassful to half a teacupful, as often as required, but the old-fashioned way of making it is more elaborate and the result is a pleasant drink, cooling in fevers, and also a cleanser and purifier of the blood.

"Half an ounce of fresh sage leaves, one ounce of sugar, the juice of one lemon or one-quarter ounce of grated rind, are infused in a quart of boiling water and strained off after half an hour." She added a Jamaican variation in which lime juice is substituted for the lemon juice.

That sage tea, said Grieve, "is highly serviceable as a stimulant in debility of the stomach and nervous system and weakness of digestion generally."

A superstrength distillate of sage tea is used not only to heal brushburns but as a tinting agent to darken greying hair.

Sage, rubbed daily on the teeth, is said to keep them sparkling white.

A finely sage-flavored wine can be made using a modern version of an old recipe. Decide yourself whether the wine will be taken sparingly as a tonic or in somewhat greater measure as a pleasantly exotic beverage with meals.

There were no electric blenders in 1796 when the recipe was first published, but allow yourself that one convenience. Use it to blend a cup of fresh sage leaves into half of a quart bottle of Claret or good Burgundy. Run it on high speed for a couple of minutes, until the sage leaves have been pulverized and suspended throughout the *vin rouge*. Then return the sage wine concentrate to its original bottle and *voila!*

Use finely crushed sage leaves to flavor cheeses and sprinkle it over buttered bread. Use it to flavor sausages, fowl, and pork; one of its properties is that sage aids the digestibility of heavy, greasy meats.

Use it sparingly at first because it has a heavy, almost dominating flavor. To tone sage down, some cooks say that parsley added in large measure to the sage will take the edge off its pungency.

For a unique after-dinner mint, brush egg white diluted with a bit of water over fresh sage leaves. Sprinkle powdered sugar lightly over the leaves. In addition to making an interesting light dessert, the sage mints will bring the herb's carminative property to the aid of distressed diners.

An early nineteenth-century recipe for sage and onion sauce recommends: "Chop very fine an ounce of onion and a half-ounce of green sage leaves, put them in a stamper with four teaspoonsful of water, simmer gently for ten minutes, then put in a teaspoonful of pepper and salt and one ounce of fine breadcrumbs. Mix well together, then pour to it a quarter-pint of broth, gravy or melted butter, stir well together and simmer a few minutes longer. This is a relishing sauce for roast pork, geese or duck, or with green peas, on Maigre Days."

Sage is no stranger in today's cookbooks, either. You'll find it mentioned often in any book that believes an herb rack is to be used for more than decorating a blank wall in the kitchen.

ST. JOHN'S WORT

Hypericum perforatum, Linn.
Hypericaceae

St. John's wort is another of those roadside herbs. It is a perennial which grows to a height of one to three feet and having bright sun-like flowers and unusual black-spotted leaves. The specific name *perforatum* is a reference to the leaf spots, which appear to be holes but which are actually subsurface oil glands.

The source of the most common name is open to speculation. Some tie it to a relation between the flowers and St. John the Baptist's birthday, which was the summer solstice; others relate it to the blood red oil the leaf glands contain—St. John's blood it is sometimes called (though it is also called Mary's sweat). The somewhat mystical religious ties of the plant are clear, however, and the plant was reputed valuable in exorcising evil spirits. The generic name *Hypericum* is from the Greek, meaning "over an apparition."

It has been used as an astringent, nervine, and aromatic. Some valued it as a vulnerary. Others used it for coughs, lung ailments, and particularly in urinary troubles. An infusion of one ounce of the herb to a pint of boiling water was prescribed in wineglass doses.

SALAD BURNET

Sanguisorba minor, Scop. (syn. *Poterium sanguisorba,* Linn.)

Rosaceae

Burnet is a bushy perennial that grows 12 to 24 inches tall and produces nearly evergreen, fernlike foliage. The bruised leaves taste and smell somewhat like cucumbers.

The flowers in each head bear crimson-tufted stigmas with long, drooping filaments. Burnet flowers in June and July. Both the flower and leaf-stalks are a deep crimson color. Turner in his *Newe Herball* in 1551, describes the plant as follows:

> It has two little leives like unto the wings of birdes, standing out as the bird setteth her wings out when she intendeth to flye. Ye Dutchmen call it Hergottes berdlen, that is God's little berde, because of the colour that it hath in the topp.

Salad burnet was formerly used as a fodder plant in the British Isles, but it has fallen out of use there. Its ability to remain green on poor soil throughout the winter adds to its value in the salad garden—it is a long-lasting source of fresh greens.

Salad burnet is easily grown from seed, and can be grown in all parts of the United States, with perhaps some difficulty in southern Florida and along the Gulf Coast. A single mature plant produces one-half cup of fresh leaves for the first harvest and one-quarter cup each week thereafter.

Burnet needs full sun and does best in soil with a pH of 6.0 to 8.0. Sow the seeds one-half inch deep outdoors in late fall or early spring. When the seedlings are about two inches

Salad Burnet

high, remove smaller ones. Allow 12 to 15 inches between plants.

Burnet begins growing in March and can be harvested until after the first snowfall. The leaves should be picked when young and tender. Remove flower stalks to encourage the development of new leaf growth. Burnet often grows spontaneously from seeds dropped by mature plants, and these plants can be transplanted in your garden.

The leaves are used fresh, but can be dried. When dried, they lose some of their cucumber flavor and are a bit more nutlike. They should be dried rapidly in the shade to retain as much of their color as possible.

Burnet always had its place in the herb gardens of former times. Bacon recommends it to be set in walkways together with wild thyme and water mint to "perfume the air most delightfully, being trodden on and crushed."

It was much used in salads and in wines, being the "pimpernella" essential in the best French and Italian salads. It was also used in drinking cups, like borage, to slightly flavor the drinks. One generic name, *poterium,* comes from the name of a Greek drinking cup, the *poterion,* and refers to this use of the herb. Gerard spoke of this use of salad burnet when he said, "It is thought to make the hart merry and glad, as also being put into wine, to which it yeeldeth a certaine grace in the drinking."

The older herbalists recommended burnet for a number of complaints. Pliny suggested a decoction of the plant with honey for several disorders, and it was said to protect against the Plague and other contagious diseases. Burnet had a reputation as a healer of inward and outward wounds when it was used as a drink or in an ointment, and it was used by the Tudors to cure gout and rheumatism.

Dodoens recommended this use of the herb:

> Made into powder and dronke with wine, wherin iron hath bene often quenched, and so doth the herb alone, being but only holden in a man's hande as some have written. The leaves stiped in wine and dronken, doth comfort and rejoice the hart, and are good against the trembling and shaking of the same.

Gerard suggested the juice of burnet taken in a drink as "A speciall helpe to defend the heart from noysome vapours and from the infection of the Plague or Pestilence, and all other contagious diseases for which purpose it is of great effect . . . ."

It is still regarded as a styptic, and an infusion of the whole herb is employed as an astringent. It is also a cordial and promotes perspiration.

The fresh leaves may be used for salads, vinegars, cream cheese, drinks, seasoning green butters, and as a garnish.

SALSIFY

Tragopogon porrifolius, Linn.
Compositae

Salsify—sometimes spelled salsafy—is a potherb, grown for its root. The root is harvested, stored, and cooked much as one would carrots or beets.

The plant is fairly easily grown, provided the seeds are well watered from the time of sowing until the seedlings are well established. The seeds should be sown early. For the roots to form properly, the soil must be open and friable.

SARSAPARILLA

American Sarsaparilla, Wild Sarsaparilla
Aralia nudicaulis, Linn.
Araliaceae

Sarsaparilla root was one of the foremost patent medicine ingredients during the heyday of the botanically-based cure-all elixirs. It is perhaps fitting that it should have been so used, for it was a native American plant, never mentioned in the European or Oriental herbals.

Most people recognize the name sarsaparilla, undoubtedly associating it with the soft drink of that name. While the beverage is flavored by a sarsaparilla plant, it is a tropical variety of the genus *Smilax.* This genus also is the source of the aromatic drug named sarsaparilla.

Aralia nudicaulis does have an impressive history as a wild herb, though. The Indians were the first to use the plant, of course, but the white settlers were not slow to recognize its virtues. It was perhaps best known as an alterative, but other properties were ascribed to it as well. "The bark of the roots, which alone should be used in medicine, is of a bitterish flavor, but aromatic," wrote one early American. "It is deservedly esteemed for its medicinal virtues, being a gentle sudorific, and very powerful in attenuating the blood when impeded by gross humours."

The use of it in patent medicines was wide-spread and lead to the sale of many adulterated products under the sarsaparilla name. "Such . . . is the furor for swallowing it," erupted one irate doctor, "that the manufacturers employ steam engines in its preparation, and these syrups and extracts of sarsaparilla are becoming among the chief exports from the commercial emporium and [a sufficient quantity] will soon be made here to supply all creation with physic for a century to come." The demand for, and thus the production of, sarsaparilla physics was spurred by such reports from folk healers as this:

> I saw a case of scrofula caused by a bad vaccine virus.
> The flesh seemed as though it would fall from the bones, and the physicians that were in attendance gave her up and said she would have to die. The mother made a strong syrup or tea of sarsaparilla root and

made her drink it instead of water. It did the work. She got well.

The problem was, of course, that not all the medicines sold as sarsaparilla medicines were strictly that. Nine proprietary sarsaparillas were analyzed at the Connecticut agricultural station in 1911 and were determined to comprise yellow dock, burdock, sassafras, poke root, wintergreen, licorice, senna, black cohosh, prickly ash, stillingia, mandrake, and a variety of other botanicals and chemicals, plus a shot of the namesake medicine.

Such abuses undoubtedly contributed to sarsaparilla's removal from the official drug plant lists, where its effects were noted as stimulant, alterative, and diaphoretic.

The plant involved in all this controversy is a very low-growing, single-leaved perennial with a tremendously long yellow root. The leaf is divided into three parts, each having five leaflets from two to five inches long. The flowering stalk bears clusters of whitish flowers from May to June, followed by round almost-black berries. The root is collected in the autumn. When dried, it may be infused, one teaspoon to a cup of boiling water, to make a refreshing drink.

SASSAFRAS

Sassafras albidum, (Nutt.) Nees (syn. *Sassafras officinale*, Nees & Eberm.)
Lauraceae

Sassafras is an American herb, with its lore deeply interwoven in the history of the continent.

It is a tree found all along the Eastern seaboard, growing in the south as tall as 100 feet. But in the north, sassafras does poorly, rarely developing more than a shrubby growth. In any case, sassafras has many slender branches, with broadly oval leaves and inconspicuous greenish-yellow flowers. The bark is smooth and orange brown.

The tree's value is found in the root bark, although in some regions the leaves have been used as a condiment. An oil is distilled from the root bark which is used in drugs and as a flavoring. The root bark is dried, chopped into tiny bits, and used, one teaspoon to a cup of water, to make a flavorful tonic tea.

Historically, sassafras was regarded as the remedy for syphilis, as well as a number of other ailments. Columbus is said to have sensed the nearness of land from the strong scent of sassafras. Its formal discovery is generally attributed to Spaniards exploring Florida. The tree and tales of its values learned from the Indians were carried to Europe. Ultimately, sassafras became one of the first commercial exports from the new land.

SCENTED GERANIUM

Pelargonium, various species
Geraniaceae

The most striking thing about the scented geraniums is their incredible variety. They just may be the most delightfully varied aggregation of plants in the herb world. There are hundreds of varieties, more than enough to stagger anyone interested in cataloging them.

Curiously enough, the scented geraniums aren't geraniums, though they are related through botanical family membership. The scented geraniums all share an elongated seed case resembling a stork's bill, a resemblance which lead to the generic name *Pelargonium.* They share, too, qualities of scent, color, and form unsurpassed in the botanical world. All are half-hardy, leafy semi-shrubs.

All herbal writers speak of the remarkable scents of these herbs, some liltingly, others more matter-of-factly. The fragrance remains for each to experience before true understanding can be achieved. For the strength and variety of pelargonium fragrances are indeed remarkable. And the scents are the dominant herbal virtue of the plants.

Of course the pelargoniums have a colorful history as houseplants, but they were houseplants chiefly because of their fragrance. Herbalists given to such things wax nostalgic about grandmothers and Victorian mansions and brushing the gargantuan rose geraniums, thereby releasing its strong rose fragrance. The Victorian Era was the heyday of the pelargoniums, but there are pockets of revived interest today.

The pelargoniums were first introduced to an expanding world civilization in the seventeenth and eighteenth centuries by sailors who stopped off while rounding the Cape of Good Hope. In the fashion typical of the spread of herbs, pelargoniums sprouted all over Europe and eventually made their way to America. The plant then as now was popular simply as a pretty, fragrant houseplant.

The French did find commercial value in several of them, when it was discovered that they could substitute for attar of roses in perfume making. Since that discovery, the perfume makers have grown large amounts of scented geraniums in North Africa and southern France. About one pound of leaves will produce a gram of oil. Three ounces of oil dissolved in alcohol serves as an essence that is one of the principal ingredients in scented soaps, perfumes, and potpourris. And of course the leaves themselves find a place in homemade potpourris.

The ingenious cook can find a variety of culinary uses for the various scented geraniums. Perhaps the most familiar is the use of rose geraniums in apple jelly to make rose geranium jelly. One places two or three rose geranium leaves in the bottom of a jelly glass and pours in hot apple jelly. It is as easy as that. Rose geranium sugar is made, similarly, by layering the herb leaves with the sugar. Rose geranium tea is fragrant and refreshing. The challenge for the true pelargonium lover is to experiment with the many varieties. The rose geranium is cited here merely because it is the most popular of the pelargoniums.

Little is made of the medicinal values of the pelargoniums. One herbal reports most pelargoniums have astringent properties and says they have been found valuable in dysentary and for ulceration of the stomach and upper part of the intestines. A folk remedy for an aching head was to bathe the head in geranium vinegar. But apparently little more has been made of them in the medical regard.

The pelargoniums are all started from cuttings. The growing presents no particular problems. The small plants should be set outside during the summer, where they will develop rapidly and produce a large amount of leaves. Since they are quite tender, they must be brought inside during cold, winter months.

Cuttings should be taken in early fall, using a sharp knife to cut just below the node where the leaf grows from the stem. Four- to five-inch cuttings should be taken from the larger varieties and three-inch cuttings from the smaller ones. The cuttings are then inserted into clean sand, deep enough to hold them erect and spaced so as to permit free air circulation. Keep the cuttings well watered and shaded for several days, gradually introducing them to sunlight. After two or three weeks, the cuttings should be sufficiently well established to survive transplanting to individual pots, preferably two to three inches in size. The more vigorously growing varieties will have to be retransplanted into four-inch pots as their roots fill the small pot.

When transplanting the pelargoniums outside, they should be placed in a spot with fertile soil, high in humus. They must be well watered to develop properly.

The scented geraniums, of course, can be kept in containers, and moved back and forth from indoors to outdoors as the climatic conditions change. By so doing, some very impressive-sized plants can be developed—the kind grandma had in her Victorian mansion. Grown indoors, the plants need all the sunlight they can get, regular watering, and relative coolness in winter, no more than 72 degrees. They should be planted in boxes or pots at least five inches deep, preferably twice that. Use a good potting mixture to assure adequate drainage and fertilize the plants occasionally with a manure or fish emulsion tea.

Insects present no problem. The scented geraniums are very resistant to insect attack. Moreover, the companion planter may find white-flowered scented geraniums valuable to have in the vegetable garden. Folklore holds that the plant attracts Japanese beetles, which eat the flower and die. It is certainly worth experimenting, for even if it doesn't work (or isn't needed), the scent and form of the pelargonium is a welcome addition to any garden.

The leaves of the pelargoniums can be used fresh, and will be if you cultivate them in containers indoors. The main harvest

Scented Geranium

of those grown seasonally outdoors should be before the slightest frost, as the plants are highly sensitive and die off at the first touch of frost. Leaves so harvested should be dried in the shade. Dried well they will store well.

The real problem with growing pelargoniums is selecting particular varieties to grow. Without doubt, the basic scented geranium is the one commonly called the rose geranium, *P. graveolens*. This is a large plant with deeply cut gray-green leaves, lavender flowers, and a rose-like fragrance. It will grow to three feet in height unless pruned regularly. Within this species there are a stunning number of varieties: *P. graveolens* var. *camphoratum* or camphor rose, the Gray Lady Plymouth, the Lady Plymouth, the Little Gem, the variegated mint-scented rose, and so on and so on. It is said there are more than fifty varieties of *P. graveolens,* about a dozen of these being easily available.

There are many other species of pelargoniums, each with its distinctive leaf-shape, color, and flower. *P. fragrans* or the nutmeg geranium has small, smooth, gray-green leaves, spreading branches, sprays of small white flowers, and a pungent nutmeg-like fragrance. *P. torento* or the ginger geranium has roundish leaves with sharply toothed margins, darkly marked lavender flowers, and a ginger-like aroma. *P. nerosum* or the lime-scented geranium is quite similar to the ginger geranium, but has small, darker foliage and, naturally, a lime-like scent.

There are a variety of lemon-scented geraniums, two of the most common being *P. limoneum* or lemon geranium and *P. melissinum* or lemon balm geranium. The former has fan-shaped, toothed leaves, and is strongly scented of lemon. The latter has a light green leaf which resembles that of a maple tree and small lavender flowers. It smells like lemon balm. And it is one of the fastest-growing pelargoniums.

Two other interesting pelargoniums are the peppermint geranium and the attar of roses geranium. The peppermint type, *P. tomentosum,* has large, flat, downy-covered leaves. It is strongly aromatic in the tradition of its namesake. *P. capitatum,* the attar of roses type, has divided foliage and pinkish flowers. It is sometimes referred to as the oak-leaf geranium, a name properly applied to *P. quercifolium,* or the rose-scented, oak-leaf geranium. In any case, the resemblance of the fragrance is obvious.

The listings above, of course, ignore the dozens of varieties existing within each species designation, as well as the scores of other species. If nothing else about the pelargoniums is striking, its numbers are.

SEA HOLLY

Eryngium maritimum, Linn.
Umbelliferae

A beautiful, very hardy perennial, sea holly grows one foot tall with broad, spiny, grayish-blue leaves and pale blue flowers surrounded by spiny bracts. The flowers are frequently dried for winter bouquets. They should be planted in light, rich soil, in an open sunny location. It is an excellent plant for the rock garden. Seed should be sown as soon as ripe. They can also be propagated by division. The root and leaves are used for uterine irritation and bladder diseases, glandular deficiencies, as a nervine, and tonic. Roots are nutritious and can be candied for a confection. They are rich in minerals, especially iron, magnesium, silica, and iodine.

SENNA

Cassia, various species
Leguminosae

The cassias are common in tropical countries and several varieties are hardy as far north as New England. Well known for their medicinal value, they are also grown as ornamentals. They are grown from seed, preferring sandy loam and sun.

Cassia marilandica, American or wild senna, is a hardy perennial growing four feet. The leaves are composed of eight or ten leaflets which are oblong, smooth, and narrow. The bright yellow flowers bloom from June to September. Leaves for medicinal purposes are gathered while the plant is in bloom. It is a most important cathartic and with some herbalists, ranks equally with the foreign sennas.

C. fistula, purging cassia, is a small tree from India with evenly pinnate leaves. It has long racemes of showy yellow flowers and pods one to two feet long. These are the cassia pods used commercially and are mildly cathartic. The leaves and flowers are also purgative, and the bark is used as an astringent.

A useful infusion of any senna can be made with two ounces of the leaves to a pint of boiling water. The leaves should steep for at least an hour, then be strained off. Wineglassful doses should be given every few hours until the purging action is experienced.

SESAME

Sesamum orientale, Linn.
Pedaliaceae

Sesame is native to Africa and the warmer parts of Asia. Earliest records show that sesame seed was a staple food and oil source in China, Japan, and India, and was also used in ancient Greece. The Egyptians and Persians of Biblical times ground it into a kind of flour, from which they made bread. The Romans crushed the seed and used it like butter for a spread on bread. Today it is still used as a bread spread, the oil being used in the manufacture of some oleo-margarines.

Sesame is a strong, slender annual growing to 18 inches, with slender, dark-green leaves and inch-long flowers, resembling foxglove, which lie along the square stem. It is a warmth-loving plant which will only mature its seeds in our southern states and Hawaii, though it may be started early in pots in the north and planted in the garden for decorative purposes.

Seed is started early enough in spring to allow it a growing season of 90 to 120 days of hot weather. Plants are thinned to stand six inches apart. Full sun and moderately rich soil are required. Planted as close as this, the plants grow thick and bushy and shade the soil under them.

Seed pods are picked in fall just before the first frost causes them to shatter. They are spread to complete their drying on trays, then are shaken out of the pods, hulled, and winnowed.

If used in large enough quantities, sesame seeds are a very good source of vitamins C and E, of calcium, and of unsaturated fatty acids. The seeds are used in many baked products, needing to be baked or roasted to bring out their nut-like flavor. In the Orient, they are often mixed with honey and dried fruits to make a sweetmeat.

SKIRRET

Sium sisarum, Linn.
Umbelliferae

Skirret is an old time potherb. It is a Chinese native, naturalized in Europe and occasionally seen in the United States. Under favorable conditions, the plant grows to three to four feet in height. It is topped with umbells of white flowers. The part of the plant which is used is the root, which resembles clusters of little parsnips.

The plants are most easily increased by dividing the root each spring. They can be grown from seed, but germination is a sometimes proposition.

The root is cooked as a vegetable. It is supposed to be a valuable addition to the diet in cases of chest ailments.

SORREL

Rumex, various species
Polygonaceae

You'll have to look hard to find so noble and useful a common weed as the sorrels. In a figurative sense, you'll have to look hard, that is. In a literal sense, you won't have to look hard at all if you don't purposefully tend the sorrels in your garden. They'll try to root themselves in deeply and, showing the bad manners of their low breeding, they'll reseed themselves frantically in an aggressive attempt to take over the rest of the plot.

But the sorrels really are noble and useful in the kitchen, where they've found roles ranging from a surrogate spinach to the chief ingredient in the French delicacy *Soupe aux herbes.*

Of the most commonly cultivated of the sorrels, the broad-leafed French sorrel *(Rumex scutatus)* dominates the narrower-leaved garden sorrel *(R. acetosa)* because of the former's broader, meatier, and more tasteful leaves. In most other respects, though, they're identical.

In general, the sorrels are closely related to the docks, but they seem to be more palatable than their weedy cousins. Both the sorrels and the docks are of the genus *Rumex,* a Latin allusion to the spear-shaped leaves of the genus.

Of a different genus altogether is a plant whose common name is wood sorrel. Probably lumped in with the sorrels because it tastes quite similar, wood sorrel *(Oxalis acetosella)* bears absolutely no botanical kinship to the sorrels.

What wood sorrel and the real sorrels share is the same high content of the chemical salt, binoxalate of potash, which imparts a highly acid taste to the sorrels, docks, and wood sorrel. Common garden rhubarb similarly has a high concentrate of that salt and, as a result, an acid taste.

French sorrel likes a dry, friable soil in a sunny location. Garden sorrel, though, prefers plenty of moisture. They both have developed a high-flown taste for rich soils, considering their low-born status.

Both species may be grown from root divisions made in the

spring or fall, but the sorrels are hardy, frost-resistant plants and can be started easily from seed. Seed should be planted outside in March or April, or earlier indoors, in rich moist soil. When the shoots reach one or two inches, thin them to six inches. Mulch as soon as possible, especially if you're growing garden sorrel. That will hold moisture and prevent the topsoil from crusting, a condition that the sorrels abhor.

Stalks of small bell-shaped flowers, usually yellow-green with purple veins, will form early in the spring and be in bloom by May. Seeds form rapidly and, if not harvested immediately, will set themselves for a new crop of little sorrels the same summer. Gold finches and purple finches will help keep the sorrel seed under control. It's a favorite food for them. But you'll probably have to do your part, too. Removing the seed pods from the plants also will tend to rejuvenate the plant so it will keep producing green leaves for your kitchen well into the fall.

Sorrel leaves can be harvested any time the plant is growing. Use fresh leaves if you can; drying them does not preserve their distinctive citrus-like flavor. The following is a unique suggestion for preserving sorrel leaves. It's based on an eighteenth-century French prescription. Drive the water from sorrel leaves by lacing them with plenty of salt and frying them very slowly with a generous stick of butter. After the water has evaporated, turn off the stove and allow the sorrel butter to become tepid, then ladle it into jars. Allow the mixture to cool thoroughly, then seal each jar with a layer of pure melted butter, cover it with an airtight cap and refrigerate.

Another traditional sorrel recipe is for the sweet-and-sour sauce that imparted one of Garden sorrel's common nicknames— "Green Sauce"—to it. The recipe, which comes from the English countryside, requires beating sorrel leaves to a mash and adding sugar and vinegar. It was used as a sauce dressing, much like apple sauce, beside cold meat, fish, and fowl. The English herbalist Gerard, in his 1597 treatise on useful plants, said such a "Greene Sauce is good for them who have sicke and feeble stomaches . . . and of all sauces, Sorrel is the best, not only in

Sorrel

virtues, but also in pleasantness of his taste." The favored species in England at that time, though, probably was French Sorrel, it having succeeded garden sorrel about the time of Henry VIII whose reign ended in 1547.

Peasant cooks also made it common kitchen practice to tie sorrel leaves around tough cuts of meat in the belief that the leaves' acidity would tenderize the meat.

Boiled sorrel leaves are a succulent substitute for spinach. Remove the stalks, and place the leaves in a saucepan. A cast iron saucepan, or one with a cast-iron core, is best for cooking vegetables because the cast iron distributes heat evenly over the lowest of flames. Cover the leaves with a minimum of water and simmer slowly for half an hour, turning the sorrel frequently. Strain the leaves, but save the juice. Chop the leaves finely, return them to the juice, and add pepper, salt, and butter to suit your own taste. Stir for another ten minutes over a low fire, and serve.

The renowned French provincial *Soupe aux herbes* is a heavenly blend of herbs and vegetables, the perfect illustration that a vegetarian's diet absolutely need not be a drab one. One variant of the epicurean highlight begins by melting a quarter-pound stick of the best butter in a large saucepan. In it soften, but do not brown, the following: one cup of fresh French sorrel leaves, and six leeks or four shallots or one medium onion. Add six chicken bouillon cubes and eight cups of water. Cover the pan and cook over medium heat for 30 minutes. Cut back the heat, then stir in four potatoes that have been boiled, pared, and cubed. Add a sprig or two of rosemary; one ten and one-half-ounce can of cream of chicken soup; one ten and one-half-ounce can of cream of mushroom soup; and one and one-half cups of cream or one fourteen and one-half-ounce can of evaporated milk. Simmer but do not boil. Use parsley, chives, or any other garnish you like. The recipe serves eight to ten people.

As an ingredient in green salads, sorrel lends "so grateful a quickness to the salad that it should never be left out." That was the advice of John Evelyn in 1720. He added that a sorrel salad "renders not plants and herbs only, but men themselves, pleasant and agreeable."

Irish peasants commonly used sorrel leaves as a side dressing to fish and milk, and it was believed throughout Europe—probably with some accuracy—to be a tonic against scurvy.

Some religious historians hold that the ternate leaves of sorrel, rather than those of clover, were the instruments St. Patrick used to illustrate the Trinity. That school holds sorrel to be the original shamrock.

Medically, sorrel is said to have diuretic, antiscorbutic, and refrigerant properties and is given to reduce fevers and to quench thirst. Herbalists caution against sorrel for persons with gout and rheumatism for its acid composition is believed to aggravate those conditions.

Nicholas Culpeper in the mid-1500s wrote:

> . . . all the Sorrels are under the dominion of Venus. It is useful to cool inflammation and heat of the blood in agues, pestilential or choleric, or sickness and fainting, arising from the heart; to quench thirst and procure an appetite in fainting or decaying stomachs; for it resists the putrefaction of the blood, kills worms, and is a cordial to the heart, which the seed does more effectually, because it is more drying and

binding, and thereby stays the fluxes of women's courses, or flux of the stomach.

An outmoded use for extract of sorrel leaves is as a stain remover on linen cloth. Related to that was an ancient Chinese belief that sorrel juice could remove freckles. The *Rumex* genus is well known to the Chinese, for in 2,000 years of weed-like wanderings it has spread throughout the world.

SOUTHERNWOOD

Artemisia abrotanum, Linn.
Compositae

Southernwood is a relative of wormwood and tarragon and mugwort and all the other artemisias, but its relationship to wormwood is particularly close in that it is regarded in Europe as the southern variety, hence the name. Like wormwood, it is a five- to seven-foot ornamental shrub and has been used quite widely in landscaping. Its foliage is finely divided, gray-green in color. It has a lemon odor, though varieties having camphorous and tangerine-like odor exist.

Southernwood cuttings are easily rooted, and this is the way to establish the plants. Its soil requirements are not remarkable. It is a quite hardy plant.

Southernwood is said to ward off moths and another pest of a different sort, drowsiness. In the days of long, tedious church services, the worshipers steeled themselves with southernwood and lemon balm. Branches placed in chests and closets are said to steel clothing against moths. Southernwood is also used in aromatic objects, in sweet baths, and aromatic waters. Medicinally, southernwood is astringent, anthelmintic, and deobstruent.

SPEEDWELL

Veronica officinalis, Linn.
Scrophulariaceae

This small perennial creeps over the ground, and roots form at joints of woody stems and send up branches three to ten inches high. Leaves are opposite, soft and hairy, and grayish green. Flowers arranged in spires bloom from May to July in shades of blue. They are hardy, free-flowering, and thrive in light shade or open sunny locations. They can be easily grown from seed or by division, and are good plants for the rock garden or for ground covers.

A tonic, alterative, and diuretic, it is used in cough, catarrh, and for skin diseases.

SUMAC

Rhus, various species
Anacardiaceae

The sumac is a decorative ornamental, with compound leaves that turn brilliant scarlet in the fall. The small flowers in panacles are followed by bunches of red, berry-like fruit. They grow well in poor, dry soil and can be massed on a dry hillside. Sumac can be propagated by root cuttings or seed, which is sown in fall, or stored at freezing temperatures for germination in spring.

Root bark and berries of the scarlet sumac are used medicinally for diarrhea, leucorrhea, and febrile diseases. The astringent berries were also used for a gargle. The Indians used the split bark and stems in basket-making and the roots for a yellow dye. They used the crushed leaves as a poultice for skin diseases and a decoction of leaves for venereal disease.

The fragrant sumac is a smaller shrub with aromatic, three-part leaves. The yellowish flowers develop before the leaves and the fruit is red and hairy. The root bark was used in treatment of diabetes, for discharges of kidney and bladder, also for incontinence in both children and aged persons.

Toxicodendron vernix, the poison sumac, is the only moisture-loving species and should be avoided.

SUMMER SAVORY
Satureja hortensis, Linn.
Labiatae

Summer savory is by far the most popular of more than a dozen different species of the aromatic *Satureja* genus.

A hardy annual whose growth tends toward a symmetrical ordering of branches, summer savory can be grown equally well outdoors, where it reaches 18 inches, or indoors where it will be somewhat smaller. Now used almost exclusively in the kitchen, summer savory nonetheless is a member of that herbal group that was held to have medicinal properties in the days when medicine conjured images of steaming infusions and mealy poultices.

Nicholas Culpeper, a late sixteenth-century herbalist, said both summer savory and its cousin winter savory *(S. montana)* are good for "heating, drying and carminative (action), expelling wind from the stomach and bowels, and are good in asthma and other affections of the breast. . . .

"Keep it dry and make conserves and syrups of it for your use, for which purpose the Summer kind is best. This kind is both hotter and drier than the Winter kind."

Both savories were applied to the stings of bees and wasps to ease the pain. Culpeper, as a matter of fact, went so far as to recommend this herb as a remedy for deafness.

Summer savory makes a delightful tea. Make it in the usual fashion of infusing one ounce of the herb in one pint of boiled water. Add one and one-half tablespoons to a quarter-pound of creamery butter for a tangy spread. Egg dishes profit by the addition of summer savory, and so do nearly all kinds of meat, fowl, and green salads.

The ancient Romans used summer savory to flavor vinegar. Virgil, renowned as a beekeeper as well as a poet, made sure his hives had easy access to the herb, for it enhanced the honey.

Roots of the summer savory bush are well-divided and spread laterally through the upper layer of soil. They produce a plant that is equally well-branched above ground, with leaves that are dark green and have the shape of wide needles a half-inch long. It flowers in July by producing light pink to violet flowers in the leaf axles in little bunches of up to five flowers. The nut-shaped seeds are dark brown to black; they germinate in two or three weeks when exposed to light at outside temperatures. Their viability decreases rapidly after the first year.

Savory is a fast grower and is best sown directly in outside rows nine inches to a foot apart, or broadcast and later thinned. Shallow seeding—not deeper than an eighth-inch—is important for proper germination. If top soil dries out quickly, water the seed lightly to keep it moist. Water after sunset to avoid crusting of the topsoil.

Savory is a fast-growing herb that will shade the soil in a short time and so act as its own mulch. Special care should be taken, though, to keep the soil weedfree in its early growth. Weeding can become very difficult if weeds are allowed to develop and tangle themselves around summer savory's early growth. Slight hilling will help to keep the plants upright.

Dwarfed or slow growth will most likely be due to one thing: a lack of water. Savory's moisture requirements are very high, so be sure to keep it moist during dry weather. Indoor pots of summer savory should be hand-sprayed with an atomizer at least twice a week. Moderate fertilization is sufficient, for savory prefers a soil that is light and only modestly nutritious. Avoid fresh manure.

Experts on companion planting have noted that summer savory aids onions in their growth, so it makes a pleasant as well as a useful border around them. It also makes a beneficial neighbor to green beans, both in the garden and in the cooking pot.

Harvesting may begin as soon as the plants are six inches high, and it may continue all summer. The object is to prevent summer savory from flowering, after which leaves will curl and turn yellow and brown. Early harvesting should take just the tops of the plants. The main harvest, done when the plant insists on flowering, should be done as soon as the flowers open. The whole plant should be taken and dried.

Because summer savory is a "hot" herb, drying takes little time. Spread the whole plant on fine screen or paper and allow

Summer Savory

it to dry in warm shade. In a climate with low humidity, especially at night, the savory could even be dried outside in the sun provided the drying would be complete within two days. The leaves also can be frozen, too, but they dry well.

Just a word about the cousin, winter savory, might be in order.

Winter savory is a hardy, dwarf-bush perennial that prefers poor, coarse soil. It does not need as much water as its summer-time counterpart. As a matter of fact, too much moisture will decrease winter savory's wintertime hardiness. Winter savory develops pale lavender flowers a month earlier than summer savory. It is propagated either from seed sown the same way as summer savory, or by dividing its root cluster in April. The vitality of this perennial will decline after a few years, so the wisest course is to raise a new crop by seeding or division every other year. Take clippings as you need them, but be sparing in cold weather.

SUNFLOWER

Helianthus annus, Linn.
Compositae

The sunflower is perhaps one of the most important herbs commercially in the world today, yet very few people think of it as an herb. But the familiar giant, looking much like a colossal daisy, very much an herb, though its past may not be as storied as some.

The sunflower is a native American. The Indians used the seeds as a source of meal, and the Spanish conquerors of South and Central American civilizations found the plant was much reverenced. The Incas of Peru, particularly, made the sunflower a part of their religious practice: the priestesses in the Inca temples of the Sun were crowned with sunflowers and carried them in their hands. Reproductions of sunflowers sculpted in pure gold were placed in many of these temples.

The Spaniards and other visitors to the New World were quick to carry seeds to the Old World, and the sunflower soon spread across Europe. The Europeans apparently didn't put the plant to immediate use. Gerard noted, for example, that the virtues were not known. "There hath not anything been set downe either of the ancient or later writers concerning the vertues of these plants, notwithstanding we have found by triall, that the buds before they be floured, boiled and eaten with butter, vinegar and pepper, after the manner of Artichokes, are exceedingly pleasant meat, surpassing the Artichoke in provoking bodily lust. The same buds with the stalks near to the top (the hairiness being taken away) broiled upon a gridiron, and afterward eaten with oile, vinegar, and pepper, have a like property."

Parkinson, too, reported that the sunflower had no use "in Physicke with us but that sometimes the heads of the Sunne Flower are dressed, and eaten as Hartichokes are, and are accounted of some to be a good meate, but they are too strong for my taste."

Both Parkinson and Gerard acknowledged the ancestry of the plant, referring to it as the Flower (or floure) of the Sunne, the golden floure (or flower) of Peru, or the marigold of Peru. Culpeper didn't acknowledge the plant at all.

The fact that these herbalists knew of no use "in Physicke" shouldn't prompt us to discount the sunflower as a medicinal herb. Grieve's *A Modern Herbal* reports: "The seeds have diuretic and expectorant properties and have been employed with success in the treatment of bronchial, laryngeal and pulmonary affections, coughs and colds, also in whooping cough." At least one American herbal confirms these uses adding that the plant is useful against dysentery, malaria, and inflammations of the bladder and kidneys. The root was used for snakebites, and the Ojibwa Indians crushed it and applied it as a wet dressing to draw blisters. The leaves are astringent and have seen use in herbal tobaccos.

A recommended preparation is made by boiling two ounces of the seed in a quart of water, continuing until only twelve ounces of fluid are left. Then strain the liquid and add six ounces of gin and six ounces of sugar. The preparation is given in doses of one to two teaspoonsful, three or four times daily.

An infusion said to be useful in cases of whooping cough may be made from seeds that have been browned in the oven. The oil might also be used, given in doses of ten to fifteen drops, two or three times daily.

Perhaps one of the more curious home remedies has long been practiced in the Caucasus, using sunflower leaves. It is employed in cases of malarial fever. A large cloth is spread over a bed, and the sunflower leaves are spread over the cloth, then moistened with warm milk. The fever victim then is wrapped up in it. This is said to stimulate perspiration, and the process is repeated daily until the fever breaks.

The sunflower is not particularly remarkable for its medicinal uses or its past. But it is a remarkably versatile commercial plant. Every part of the sunflower has had some economic use. The entire plant can be used as fodder for livestock. The flowers yield a yellow dye. The pith of the stalks can be used to make paper and is used as a mounting medium for microscope slides. Having a specific gravity lower than cork, the pith for years was

Sunflower

used in the making of life preservers and life belts. But the part of the plant which still is of major economic significance today is the seed.

Sunflower seed, used for food by the Indians long before white men reached America, is one of the richest in nutritional value. Seeds are 25 percent protein—putting them on the same protein level as meat. They contain liberal amounts of vitamins, especially A, B-complex, and the sparse E found in their unsaturated oils. The mineral content includes much more calcium than in cottonseed, soybean, or linseed, potassium comparable to raisins, nuts, and wheat germ, the highest rating for magnesium, and more iron than any other food except egg yolk and livers. Sunflower seed meal is highly digestible, has over 50 percent protein. The top-quality oil is rich in lecithin and unsaturated fatty acids, contains 30 percent protein as well as its share of vitamins and minerals.

Already an important crop in Canada, South America, and Russia, sunflower seed is rapidly becoming a major world-wide commodity. Primarily, its market is as a protein-rich feed for cattle, hogs, poultry, and birds—with human-food consumption now increasing tremendously as oil and meal uses are adapted, and as more people become aware of the appealing taste and outstanding nutritive values of the crunchy seeds.

The oil is useful industrially too, being used in making soaps, candles, burning oils, Russian varnishes, and Dutch enamel paint.

The seeds can be used in cooking in a variety of ways. The American Indians ground the seeds into a meal. The journal of Lewis and Clark contains the following annotation from July 1805:

> The Indians of the Missouri, more especially those who do not cultivate maise, make great use of the seed of this plant for break, or in thickening their soup. They first parch and then pound it between two stones, until it is reduced to a fine meal. Sometimes they add a sufficient proportion of marrow-grease to reduce it to the consistency of common dough and eat it in that manner. We . . . thought this a very palatable dish.

The seeds can be used much as you would use nuts. Ground into a meal, they can be used in baking or as a supplement in a variety of dishes. Combine some meal with several eggs to make a breakfast omlet that's a departure from any other you've had. Just blend a cup of sunflower seed meal, four lightly beaten eggs, a half teaspoon of kelp, and a half teaspoon of caraway seeds; pour the blended ingredients into a hot, oiled skillet and brown on both sides. A cook is limited only by imagination in using sunflower seeds.

Sunflower seeds are being sold increasingly as snacks. In Russia and China they are *the* snack. In the United States, the seeds are available already hulled. But in countries peopled with dedicated sunflower seed eaters, the seeds are hulled by fingers and teeth.

Here is how it's done. You first insert the seed between the teeth, the seed standing on edge, still holding on with your fingers until you give it the first crack with the teeth. Then the tendency of the seed, when the pressure of the teeth is removed, is to lie down flat. You quickly insert the lower teeth into the opening you have made in the seed, removing your fingers. The lower teeth exert sufficient pressure to remove the kernel from the shell with the gradual aid of your upper teeth. You will find that your tongue comes to your rescue and helps to push the shells to one side. It is all done in a twinkling. The Russians poke them into one corner of the mouth, with a stream of hulls flowing from the other corner, and they do it fast. They accomplish the act without the aid of the hands, using the tongue and teeth in cooperation.

Some people hull sunflower seeds with their fingers alone, or with a wooden clothespin. The fingers can do an adequate job, sometimes with the aid of a little twisting motion to widen the crack through which entry to the kernel is obtained. Of course, you will not get fat eating hand-hulled sunflower seeds, because your fingers or jaws will get tired before you can overdo the calories. But keep in mind that sunflower seeds are a powerful, rich food, and you don't need to eat great quantities to improve your diet in a significant way. Eating them can be developed into a habit, and the hulling can be a pleasant diversion for idle hands.

From the point of view of the gardener, growing sunflowers is an enjoyable occupation. If you plant the Mammoth Russian variety, you will be amazed at the magnitude of the plant—often reaching over 12 feet in height when grown without competition from other plants. When the plants are young, each morning their heads will turn to face the sun. There are many varieties, including some that do not produce seed. These are used chiefly as ornamental plants in the flower garden. Some resemble giant black-eyed Susans, while still others are huge, beautiful pompons resembling chrysanthemums.

But the most interesting sunflowers are those that produce seed. While these come in dwarf, semi-dwarf, and tall varieties, the best kind for the average gardener or homesteader is the giant sunflower *(H. giganteus),* also called the Indian potato. This is a strong-growing perennial that climbs to 12 feet or more and carries a huge head packed with really big seeds—the type suited for harvesting and eating.

Most popular and widely grown of the giant varieties is the Mammoth Russian, which matures in about 80 days. Besides being the largest and tallest of all sunflowers, it bears big, striped seeds that are thin-shelled, meaty, and rich in both flavor and food value. The plants' towering, husky stalks make excellent screens or field backgrounds. When grown close together, their broad leaves will keep the sun from reaching weeds and can be extremely effective as weed smotherers.

Two additional tall varieties are Manchurian, a late 85-day giant type, and gray stripe, second in head size to Mammoth Russian with heavy-yielding, lighter-colored seeds which ripen in 91 days.

Among the smaller varieties, usually grown as farm silage or oil-supply crops, are three dwarfs: sunrise (71 days), advance (68 days), and arrowhead (62 days); plus two semi-dwarfs: jupiter (67 days, plump black seeds), and Illinois common (73 days, good-yielding choice for home gardeners).

Sunflowers have other garden virtues. They grow very well with mild, organic fertilizers. Also, they have few insect pests, and seldom is there a need to spray them. For giant-sized heads, space the plants at least three or four feet apart, but for production of seed you will want to space them more closely. Giant heads are not as easy to harvest or dry as smaller heads, so crowd the plants a little. Just don't overcrowd them. Overcrowding of any sunflower, especially any of the taller-growing varieties, causes plants to fall in heavy winds. Usually sunflowers are planted on 36- or 42-inch rows, with a seed planted every five or six inches of row length. While they are hardy to light spring frosts, it's a good idea to allow a growing period close to 120 days before the first fall freezes. As the heads grow heavy, the stalks may need support of some kind.

When you approach the problem of harvesting the seed you will do well to note the time when the birds begin to pick out the seed around the rim of the head. Naturally, the outer seeds mature earlier than those nearer the center of the head. Just as soon as about two-thirds of the seeds are well filled, the head may be gathered. If you wait for the center seeds to fill out you may lose the outer ones. The easiest way to harvest this crop is to cut off the heads with a foot or two of the stalks attached and hang them up in an airy, dry place to cure before attempting to separate the seeds from the husks.

Much later, after the rush of harvesting your other garden crops is over, you may remember your collection of sunflower seedheads hung to dry in the attic. The rough stalks have become brittle by now. The fat seeds separate easily as you run your thumb lightly over the surface of the head. They rattle like peas as they fall into the pan you have placed to catch them. The sound gives you a feeling of satisfaction altogether out of proportion to what you thought was the value of the seed being gathered—winter food for the wild birds. You peel a few of the seeds, nibble on them and find them quite palatable.

SWEET CICELY

Sweet Chervil, Sweet Fern
Myrrhis odorata, Linn.
Umbelliferae

Sweet cicely is the herb that just doesn't seem to have a personality of its own. Throughout the writings on sweet cicely are references to other plants it resembles: chervil, ferns, hemlock, and anise. But despite its lack of a distinct personality and its difficulty to cultivate, sweet cicely is nice to have around.

The best of the descriptions of sweet cicely begin by pointing out its branching stems of fern-like leaves which taste like sugary anise and smell like lovage. The entire resemblance of the plant is like hemlock. And so it goes. The resemblances are perhaps unfortunate, but they are true.

Sweet cicely is a thick-rooted perennial, a hardy plant which develops generally to a height of two to three feet, though in isolated cases to a height of five feet. The first shoots are almost triangular, lacy leaves, but as the herb slowly develops it bears many leaves, all downy and white-spotted on the undersides, all heavily scented. In the early summer, usually late May to early June, flat-topped umbels of white flowers appear, followed by unusually large fruits, usually called the "seeds." These are about an inch long and, when ripe, a dark brown to black color.

The seeds are spicy, the leaves have a sugary licorice flavor. All parts of the plant have been used in cooking and in folk medicine. The plant is strongly scented. Curiously enough, though the plant has no recorded history of use for its scent, its botanical name, _Myrrhis odorata_, is derived from the Greek for perfume.

There is some question as to the origins of the plant, though it is commonly listed as a British native. One herbalist reports that in sections of England it is called the Roman plant and suggests that this name may be "a clue to its original intro-duction." In any case, sweet cicely is found throughout Europe and the British Isles and has been naturalized in the United States.

Sweet cicely has a variety of uses in cookery, and it is used for such in most countries in which it is found. The French grant it some importance, often combining it with tarragon. Though once popular in England, it has fallen from favor there. Never-theless, when used in cooking, the results are tasty. The leaves are used fresh in salads, soups, and stews. The seeds go into salads when green and into spicy herb mixtures when ripe. The roots may be eaten raw or boiled.

These culinary uses seem to be of more note historically than any other use. Most of the old herbalists made note of sweet cicely's ability to enhance a salad, with Gerard calling the leaves "exceeding good, wholesome, and pleasant among other sallad herbs, giving the taste of Annise-seed unto the rest." Gerard also pointed out that the seeds were also excellent salad ingredients, "dressed as the cunning Cooke knoweth how," but added that he preferred them boiled and served with oil and vinegar.

The latter dish he considered "very good for old people that are dull and without courage; it rejoiceth and comforteth the heart and increaseth their lust and strength."

The boost for heart and body is not easily obtained, however. Though the herb is not reported to be rare in Europe, it is not overly common in the United States. The difficulty of propagation is the prime factor. The plant is most difficult to grow in southern Florida and along the Gulf Coast.

Sweet cicely is a very particular plant in that the seed is very hard to germinate. A professional herb grower has reported never having been able to germinate a seed "willingly." "If germinated in the greenhouse, it was by coincidence," he said, "because we have always some herb seeds in our compost that we use for potting soil, and it would come up under the bench in the potting soil without any attention."

In theory, the seed is brought to germination through a process of alternate freezing and thawing, but the theory is oftimes a practical failure. Perhaps the best method of propagating sweet cicely is to buy a plant from a grower. Failing this, the seed should be sown in fall. Though the germination rate will be poor, at least a few seeds should sprout and plants develop. The seeds from these plants may be harvested upon ripening and immediately replanted at the base of the mother plant. Or the plants may be divided in the spring. The process will require several years of persistent effort, but the results are rewarding.

In terms of garden environment, sweet cicely prefers shaded, rich, moist, crumbly soil. The soil should be enriched with compost or manure. Mulching, however, is seldom a benefit and sometimes a detriment since it can harbor molds when coupled with the damp shade sweet cicely prefers.

The leaves can be harvested throughout the growing season. Since they remain green from early spring to late fall, they are available fresh over an extended period. A single mature plant will yield about four cups of leaves. The seeds should be harvested green or ripe, depending, of course, upon the intended use. A half cup of seed may generally be taken from a single plant. The roots should be harvested only after the plant has matured sufficiently for the yield to make the harvest effort worthwhile. The plant parts are rarely, if ever, dried.

While this gardening effort will yield a lovely garden plant and a tasty potherb, it will also provide a useful plant for folk medicine. Sweet cicely is listed as an aromatic, stomachic, carminative, and expectorant. The roots seem to be most useful medicinally. Eaten fresh, the root is said to be a gentle stimulant for debilitated stomachs and good for coughs and flatuence. Similar benefits arise from taking an infusion of the root in brandy or water. This infusion is also reported a valuable tonic for young girls.

These qualities are not unlike those listed by the early herbalists, of course. Parkinson recommended candied sweet cicely roots as of "singular good use to warm and comfort a cold flegmaticke stomack," adding that the confection was "thought to be a good preservative in the time of the plague." Culpeper echoed the reports of his fellow herbalists: "The roots boiled and eaten with oil and vinegar, or without oil, does much to please and warm old and cold stomachs oppressed with wind and phlegm, or those that have the phthisis or consumption of the lungs; the same drank with wine is a preservation from the plague: it provoketh women's courses and expelleth the after-birth; procureth an appetite to meat, and expelleth wind: the juice is good to heal the ulcers of the head and face. . . ."

And Culpeper coined the phrase about sweet cicely most popular with latter day herbalists: "It is so harmless you cannot use it amiss."

Gerard, as well as the other early herbalists, lumped sweet cicely with chervil, often calling it sweet chervil or great chervil. While some confusion has since been generated by the association, the descriptions are clear enough. "This groweth very like the great hemlock, having large spread leaves cut into divers parts, but of a fresher green colour than the hemlock, tasting as sweet as the aniseed," wrote Culpeper. "The stalks rise up a yard high, or better, being cressed or hollow, having leaves at thé joints, but lesser; and at the tops of the branched stalks, umbels or tufts of white flowers; after which come large and long crested black shining seed, pointed at both ends, tasting quick, yet sweet and pleasant. The root is great and white, growing deep in the ground, and spreading sundry long branches therein, in taste and smell stronger than the leaves or seeds, and continuing many years."

While the confusion seems all in a name, it makes it clear how sweet cicely has suffered for lack of a clearcut identity of its own.

SWEET WOODRUFF

Asperula odorata, Linn.

Rubiaceae

Sweet woodruff is a beautiful, fragrant, little herb often found in the deepest recesses of the forests, where the sun penetrates only with difficulty.

A native of the forests of Asia and Europe, woodruff has been traditionally used as an ointment and a perfume.

In the fourteenth century, the plant was used in England and the Scandanavian countries to make an herb water for cordials. The plant first appears in print in the thirteenth century, as "wuderove," derived, some scholars believe, from the French "rovelle," a wheel, which refers to the spoke-shaped leaves of the plant.

In France, the plant was called "Muge-de-boys," musk of the woods. In Germany, as early as the thirteenth century, the herb was used to flavor May wine. The Mai Bowle is served today in Germany and in the German sections of American and South American cities on May Day and thereafter for the rest of the month.

Throughout the Middle Ages, woodruff used to be hung in churches and placed in boxes with lavender and roses on special days, such as St. Peter's and St. Barnabas' Day.

It was also used for stuffing beds and placed between the pages of books. Today, it can be kept among sheets and towels to preserve them from insects and provide a pleasant scent.

Gerard suggested it be used frequently indoors to "attemper the air, coole and make fresh the place."

Besides its use as a perfume, woodruff was credited for being a valuable medicine. It was claimed the herb could remove biliary obstructions of the liver and relieve upset stomach. When the fresh leaves were applied to cuts and wounds, they brought relief.

Gerard added that the herb was good for the heart and liver.

A good punch can be made from dried sweet woodruff, or the herb can be used as a flavoring to soda or white wine.

Sweet Woodruff

The perennial herb stands about eight inches tall, with slightly shiny yellow-green leaves in whorls of six to eight around the stem. When crushed, the herb smells of sweet hay and slightly of vanilla. The plant thrives in moist soil.

Woodruff is extremely difficult to grow from the seed, and most gardeners would be well advised to buy the plant from an herb gardener. The most frustrating part of growing the plant from seed is its long germination period, often 200 days. Whether grown from seed or purchased, the herb can be divided and replanted when it has covered an area of two square feet.

The first and foremost requirement in growing the plant is shade, accompanied by a soil that is slightly acid and has a high humus content. The best medium for growth is leaf mold compost; no other fertilization is needed. Occasional weeding might be necessary, while hoeing is out of the question as it might destroy parts of the spreading root system.

Woodruff may be harvested at any time during the growing season. It is different from most herbs in that the lovely fragrance develops only when the woodruff is dried. The green plant itself is almost odorless.

The shoots are cut close to the ground in any quantity desired, or as is most often the case, as much as the gardener feels he can spare without ruining the lovely green carpet the herb produces.

The small amounts that are harvested should be chopped and dried instantly in warm shade.

TANSY

Bachelor's Buttons, Bitter Buttons, Stinking Willie
Tanacetum vulgare, Linn.
Compositae

If tansy has an essential character, it is that of preservation and immortality. Its very name is a derivative of the Greek name *Athanasia* meaning "immortal." Used as an embalming agent from ancient days until the time of the American Revolution, tansy also was used to preserve meat from the ravages of storage in pre-refrigeration times.

Tansy also developed into a symbolic and pragmatic ingredient in the holiest of Christian springtime rites: Easter. Tansy, by the seventeenth century, had been embraced by the church as one of the Bitter Herbs of Passover to be eaten at Eastertime. Tansy cakes became an Easter day tradition symbolizing the Passover herbs.

The more practical side of tansy's role in the Easter tradition was the herb's proclaimed ability to rejuvenate the human body after a long winter of existence on salted meat and fish. Tansy cakes also were said to purify the humours of the body after the sparsities of Lent.

Here's an old recipe for tansy cakes believed to date back to the seventeenth or eighteenth century:

> Beat seven eggs, yolks and whites separately; add a pint of cream, near the same of spinach juice, and a little tansy juice gained by pounding in a stone mortar; a quarter of a pound of Naples biscuit, sugar to taste, a glass of white wine, and some nutmeg. Set all in a

Tansy

saucepan, just to thicken, over the fire; then put into a dish, lined with paste, to turn out, and bake it.

Tansy itself is a hardy perennial that is hard to start from seed but, once established, inclined to take over nearly everything in sight. It might be worth the trouble in the long run to plant tansy in a sunken bottomless container such as half of a clean 55-gallon drum. That'll prevent the aggressive root structure from spreading into neighboring plantings.

The plant consists of a stem, two to three feet high, with fern-like leaves four inches wide and six inches long. Late in summer, heads of flat, round, yellow flowers develop and last several weeks. Leaves alone are used for seasoning and medicine.

Tansy likes modestly fertilized soil with adequate nitrogen. It's best started from purchased plants which can be propagated by dividing the roots or taking slips. Plant young shoots at least a foot apart.

Harvest the leaves at the peak of growth, but avoid yellowing leaves. For tansy tea, however, take the young green shoots and strip the leaves off the stem. Drying the leaves will take about two days in 90° F. shade.

It's interesting to note that the moniker "Stinking Willie" was hung on tansy by the Highland Scots, who considered it a weed. They named the weed contemptuously after a hated Lowlands conqueror.

In Colonial America, a clump of tansy to repel flies, mosquitoes, and ants was hung in many a pantry. In earlier days, tansy was strewn on the floors of English manor houses to repel insects that were attracted to the leavings of feasts and revelry. Adding tansy to the debris apparently was preferred to sweeping it out of the house. In addition, oil of tansy rubbed on the body is said to repel insects.

Medicinally, tansy was said to increase fertility when applied externally and to cause abortions when consumed. It has all the properties of aromatic bitters and was taken in tonics and teas to sooth the nerves, aid digestion, and calm a number of female discomforts such as hysteria, kidney weakness, amenorrhea, and fevers. It was used externally for skin eruptions and sprains.

Among the better-known culinary uses of tansy is in the manufacture of the liqueur Chartreuse. Once used as a substitute for pepper, tansy has a place in salad dressings and omelets. Use it sparingly because it's a powerful seasoning agent.

TARRAGON

Artemisia dracunculus, **Linn.**

Compositae

Tarragon, affectionately known in most Western languages as "little dragon," is one of the handful of herbs that has passed down to us from antiquity. Like rosemary, sage, thyme, and basil, tarragon traces its historic roots back hundreds of years before Christ.

Its use was recorded by the Greeks about 500 B. C.; tarragon was among the so-called "simples"—one-remedy herbs—used by Hippocrates. European gardeners knew tarragon in the Middle Ages, but it wasn't until the end of those dark times that it leaped the English Channel. It entered England during the Tudor reign probably as a preferred gift for the royal herb garden from a Continental monarch. For many years, tarragon was relatively unknown outside the royal garden. It must eventually have made good its escape, though, because it arrived on America's post-Revolutionary shores in the first few years of the nineteenth century.

Tarragon's common name probably is a corruption of the French *esdragon,* derived from the plant's Latin specific name *dracunculus,* a little dragon. It seems likely that the plant earned its "little dragon" tag in the first place because its brown, coiled roots resemble a cluster of small, knarled serpents.

In ancient times, tarragon was thought to be of value in drawing the venom from the bites of snakes and insects and in treating the bite of a mad dog.

In the Middle Ages, it was thought to increase physical stamina, and sprigs of it were tucked into pilgrims' shoes before they set out on their long, fatiguing journeys. English herbalists of the day said that tarragon, taken inwardly, was "good for the heart, lungs, and liver." More specific prescriptions for its medical uses are hard to find.

In the kitchen, though, it has a wide range of uses that begins with the traditional tarragon vinegar. This best-known of tarragon elixirs can be made simply by filling a wide-mouthed bottle with fresh sprigs, then soaking them in fine-quality vinegar of white wine. A delicate-flavored vinegar is important so as not to stifle tarragon's relatively light flavor.

Next to other herbs, however, tarragon can be overpowering. It should be used with discretion in combination with its sisters.

Considered to be one of the fine herbs, as opposed to the robust herbs, tarragon makes a delicious additive to all kinds of white sauces, fish, cheese, eggs, and green vegetables such as spinach, peas, and limas. Cauliflower, too, benefits from a sprinkle of tarragon.

As an ingredient of tartar sauce, the herb is indispensable, and it's almost *de rigeur* in *sauce Bearnaise* as well.

Try this for a heavenly light lunch: to your favorite recipe

Tarragon

for creamy white sauce, add parsley and tarragon. Serve it over poached eggs nestled in shells of the lightest pastry. Accompany with a chilled, light dry white wine, maybe Chablis.

When it comes time to acquire your first tarragon bush, beware! There are two distinct varieties, and some herb houses don't differentiate.

One is desirable, and that's the one we've been talking about. It's commonly called German or French tarragon. Unless you have access to an established bush from which you can take a slip or some roots, you'll have to buy the bush from a commercial herb house. The European variety rarely produces fertile flowers that go to seed.

The other variety is the less desirable Eastern variety, commonly called Russian tarragon. It does not seem to have a separate specific name, but it differs greatly from the Western variety. Russian tarragon produces seeds copiously and seems more vigorous a plant than the aromatic European variety, but it's unfortunately lacking in the oils that make European tarragon such a delight to taste and smell.

A good rule of thumb is just to avoid buying tarragon seed; start your plant from a cutting or root division.

The cuttings can be taken early in spring, after the main plant has begun to show new growth. Place the new slip under an inverted waterglass to keep it warm. Keep the plants about 20 inches apart because tarragon sends out a lateral root structure rather than a vertical one.

Tarragon likes moderate sun in a fertile, well-drained location. Heavy mulching is advisable to improve the soil's capacity to hold moisture, although a thoroughly wet soil won't do.

Fertilize established plants with a liquid solution such as fish emulsion after taking cuttings.

Root division can be done likewise in March or April by dividing the root cluster of a single mature plant into two or three clumps. Mature plants should be divided at any rate every four years to rejuvenate them.

It would be a wise idea to set up a rotation system for dividing some plants each year if you plan to make tarragon a mainstay of your herb garden.

Be very careful if you choose to hoe your tarragon; the bushes' lateral, shallow root structure makes them vulnerable.

With good care, tarragon in the garden will grow to two or three feet. Upright green stalks will carry elongated leaves, green or dark green. Small yellow and black flowers form in August.

Harvest tarragon early in July or when the lower leaves start to turn yellow. This yellowing is a sign either of insufficient fertilization or of aging. In either case, the yellowed leaves will not turn green again, and that's cause enough to gather them before the discoloration progresses. Leave two or three inches of stem.

First cuttings, however, may be taken as early as June. Older plants are more likely to give a heavy first cutting and second, or even third, crops.

Tarragon leaves brown easily, so dry them carefully to avoid that. Strip them from the stem and dry in a warm, dry, shaded, and well ventilated area. The temperature should not exceed 90° F.

When leaves are dry, seal them in tight, dry containers; they'll re-absorb moisture at the first chance.

Tarragon winters well if its beds are covered with straw or hay to protect the roots slightly.

Consider, though, that taking one or two plants inside for the winter will grace your home with the sweet aroma of fresh-mown hay all winter long.

After the last fall cutting, transplant a tarragon root cluster into a pot no less than ten inches in diameter. Leave plenty of room for those roots to spread out. If the potting soil is not sandy, add some light gravel for airiness.

Don't overwater tarragon indoors. It should be allowed to dry out for a day or two before re-watering. Twice-monthly feedings will make it thrive.

THYME

Thymus vulgaris, Linn.
Labiatae

When the time has come to plant even the most meager of herb gardens, the time has come to plant thyme.

Another of the herbs whose beginnings go back two millennia or more, thyme has acquired such a wide usefulness both medicinally and in cookery that it is a mainstay of the modern herbal array.

Traditionally, thyme has been graced with many strong positive associations, not the least of which has been humor. In Renaissance England, when wits were keen and words well chosen, it was said that thyme could hardly enter a conversation between two persons of quick mind without a welter of puns developing. The first allusion to the herb soon became jokingly known as "punning thyme."

From the earliest, thyme has been associated with honey, without doubt because it attracts bees in great profusion. It's common practice in Mediterranean orchards to plant thyme as a ground cover that also attracts pollinating insects to the fruit trees.

Virgil, the ancient Roman poet who also was a beekeeper, praised honey drawn from thyme. Recounting the advice of the first century B. C. philosopher, a later English admirer said Virgil affirmed that thyme "yieldeth most and best honni and therefore in old time was accounted chief . . . [Mounts] Hymettis in Greece and Hybla in Sicily were so famous for bees and honni, because there grew such store of Thyme."

Thyme-based honey still can be had in some Greek import shops in the United States. Those who have tasted it say a flavorful trace of thyme is unmistakable.

Young sheep in the plant's native Mediterranean region often are set out to graze on fields of wild thyme, a feed that many believe enhances the flavor of lamb.

A Biblical association with thyme is the Christ-child's manger. Christian tradition holds with good cause that thyme was among the three or four herbs upon which Mary and the Child bedded in Bethlehem of Judea, and so it has become an herb to be included in Christmas creches. It also has been a favored plant in the gardens of churches and monasteries.

The bee-honey-thyme image lasted through the centuries and bloomed in the European age of chivalry, when thyme flourished as a symbol of strength and activity and bravery. Many a lady embroidered her knight a penant showing a bee hovering over a sprig of thyme.

French Republicans embraced thyme as a symbol of their own courage, and a sprig delivered to the door of a loyal Republican was a silent summons to a clandestine meeting.

In early Greece, thyme signified graceful elegance. One of the highest compliments a suitor could pay his lady was to tell her she was sweet as thyme. In many cases, she was indeed sweet as thyme because oil of thyme was used in those days as a lady's perfume. It still is used in scented soaps and bath oils.

Thyme's generic name *Thymus* is thought by many lexicographers to be a derivation of the Greek *thumus* (courage). Others believe it evolved from an ancient Greek expression meaning "to fumigate." Thyme was considered to have strong antiseptic properties, and it was used as an incense to purify the air. A similar belief was that a hillside of thyme not only sweetened the air near it, but cleansed it of bad vapors as well.

It seems the ancients weren't too far wrong about thyme's antiseptic properties.

Mrs. M. Grieve, an early twentieth-century herbal authority, wrote at length about thymol, a commercially valuable component of oil of thyme as well as several other plants. Commercial processors prefer the Indian plant Ajowan, Mrs. Grieve wrote, because Ajowan oil contains a higher percentage of the desired thymol than does oil of thyme.

Thymol, she reported, was used extensively as a battlefield antiseptic in World War I although the Allies felt a serious shortage early in the war because pre-war production of thymol had been centered in Germany, the enemy belligerent. Production quickly was shifted to England and India, then a part of the Empire, and the English Mrs. Grieve noted with satisfaction that domestic thymol soon was "equal in quality and appearance to that previously imported from Germany."

She said thymol had other uses as a deodorant, local anesthetic, meat preservative, paint for infectious irritations of the skin, mouthwash, and several other germicidal agents.

Thyme, especially thyme tea, is said by herbalists to be aromatic, stimulant, diuretic, carminative, diaphoretic, emmenagogic, and antispasmodic, as well as antiseptic.

If you can't locate thyme honey, which is the delicious base for several herbal remedies, you can make a near likeness using a good domestic honey and thyme tea. To make the tea, make the usual herbal infusion of one ounce of the dried leaves to one pint of boiled water. Allow the infusion to cool to room temperature, then strain it and add a cup of pure honey. Stir until mixed uniformly. This thyme syrup must be refrigerated. Taken in tablespoonful doses several times a day, it's good for sore throats, coughing spells, and colds.

In the kitchen, dried thyme leaves are as nearly universal a seasoning as any herb could be. One recent expert on herbal cookery advocated using thyme "as freely as salt—in other words, in practically everything."

Thyme

It's pleasing in red meat, poultry, and fish as well as almost any vegetable, even the heartier ones.

Botanically, there are many closely related species in the *Thymus* genus. Most of them bear a close resemblance to *T. vulgaris,* a species that itself has at least three varieties: English thyme, German winter thyme, and French summer thyme. They differ mainly in the width of their leaves, being respectively varigated, broad, and narrow.

The different varieties of thyme also are grouped generally into upright and trailing types with *T. vulgaris* being the most common of the uprights and wild thyme *(T. serpyllum)* being foremost among the creeping thymes that make so pleasant a ground cover.

T. vulgaris, common thyme, is usually started from seed although cuttings or root divisions can be substituted. Seeding should be done in indoor flats because a temperature of around 70° F.—unlikely outside in the spring—is needed for germination. The seeds are exceptionally small. It takes some 170,000 to make an ounce. They should be evenly distributed over the seed bed, and covered only lightly or not at all. They should germinate in about two weeks.

After the young plants have taken root, they can be moved outdoors to cooler weather. They should be set nine inches apart in full sun and a sandy, dry soil that is moderately fertilized. Thyme's nutrient requirements are not heavy; most important is to avoid heavy wet soils.

A dense system of fine roots will develop along with a well-branched surface structure of woody stems and branches to which are attached small oval-shaped leaves. The plant will reach eight to ten inches in height. Leaves will be grey-green, and pink or violet flowers will appear in the leaf axils of the tip ends from May to August.

Weed control is important because weeds can be a debilitating competitor for nutrients with the small, slow-developing young thyme. Once the shoots are established, mulching will hold soil warmth and discourage weed rivals.

Open cultivation and hoeing always should be avoided around low herbs because the hoeing and the rain's action on the bare earth will dirty the lower branches of the plant.

Harvest thyme just before flowers begin to open by cutting the entire plant one and a half or two inches from the ground. A second growth will develop, although that should not be cut at all. Harvesting the second growth will reduce thyme's winter hardiness especially if the ground is bare and the temperatures fluctuate widely. If you must have more thyme late in the summer, prune just the upper third of the plant, and then be sure to give it extra attention in the cold months.

Thyme, especially if a second growth is taken, should be mulched or covered over with an earthen blanket for the winter. Like all members of the thyme genus, Common thyme is a hardy perennial but it needs care over the winter to survive the cold months.

After harvesting, lay the entire plant on a fine screen or a sheet of newspaper and dry it in the warm shade. When dried, the leaves will separate from the woody stems upon light winnowing or simple rubbing. Throw the stems onto the compost pile; the leaves alone are usable. Drying is easy, and thyme stores well at low humidity.

If you move your thyme bed to another corner of the garden, be sure to fertilize the plants' old area heavily before planting another herb there. Thyme tends to rob the soil of nutrients.

TOBACCO

Nicotiana tabacum, Linn.

Solanaceae

Tobacco is a pernicious weed to many people, even those who use it. But it can and should be considered an herb, for it has a colorful past and it remains an economic keystone for at least one southern state and an important agricultural commodity in several other states.

There is no solid evidence that the plant was seriously used by the Indians who cultivated it. But the arrivals from the Old World quickly plunged into efforts to turn the plant to economic gain, efforts most notably marked by the introduction of tobacco to England by Sir Walter Raleigh. Then as now, the noxious weed was denounced. King James I offered a "Counterblaste to Tobacco," labelling smoking as "a custome lothsome to the eye, hatefull to the Nose, harmefull to the braine, dangerous to the Lungs, and in the blacke stinking fume thereof, nearest resembling the horrible Stigian smoke of the pit that is bottomlesse."

In time, however, a great many applications developed in folk medicine, and tobacco found its way into the official pharmacopoeias. Gerard listed 25 virtues of tobacco, six of which required the smoking of it. It was said to be a sedative, diuretic, expectorant, discutient, sialagogue, and emetic. The smoke was blown in the ear to relieve ear aches. Suppositories of tobacco leaves were used for "strangulated hernia." The leaves were applied as a poultice to bee stings, swellings, and sores.

An annual growing six feet tall, tobacco is a handsome garden plant. Its broad leaves may be a foot or more in length, and the stem is covered with sticky hairs. The two-inch flowers are white, rose, or purple-rose, borne in racemes.

Tobacco is grown commercially on a large scale in the southern states, as well as in Pennsylvania and Connecticut. There are special varieties for cigarettes, cigars, pipe, and chewing tobacco. All require approximately the same culture.

The seeds are sown in a very rich and friable soil under glass in late winter. The minimum temperature of the hotbed must be 70° F. Some varieties require shading. Probably no crop needs a rich organic soil more than tobacco—fine tilth is of the greatest importance to good growth and health. The plants are set out 12 inches apart in rows three feet apart and cultivated until they cover the soil. The tops are picked off just before flowering to prevent the plants from going to seed. Drying is a process which must be done very carefully in a special curing house.

TREE OF HEAVEN

Chinese Sumac
Ailanthus glandulosa, **Desf.**
Simaroubaceae

The tree of heaven can be used to good advantage where rapid growth is desired, as it will grow ten feet or more in one season, and may reach a height of 60 feet. A tall hedge can be quickly grown by setting trees close together, then topping at the desired height each spring.

A hardy, deciduous tree, it has a tropical appearance with large pinnate, compound leaves resembling sumac. It can be of particular importance in city yards because of its resistance to smoke, dust, and disease.

The crushed leaves and flowers have a strong odor offensive to most insects. It can be propagated by root cuttings, but grows easily and rapidly from seeds, and frequently self-seeds.

The bark and root bark is used as a cardiac depressant, for dysentery, diarrhea, leucorrhea, and to eliminate tape worm.

VALERIAN

Garden Heliotrope
Valeriana officinalis, Linn.
Valerianaceae

Valerian, or garden heliotrope, a perennial member of the Valerianaceae family, is probably the most tranquilizing herb you can grow in your garden.

A native of England but found growing throughout the world, valerian has dark green, serrated leaves grouped in pairs. The plant, which grows three to five feet tall, develops a flower stalk early in the year with fragrant light lavender flowers. Its seed is flat and heart-shaped, and colored either light or dark grey.

Most people find valerian's scent disagreeable, but there are some who like it. In ancient times, an Asian version of valerian apparently had a very pleasant scent. It is believed valerian is the spikenard referred to in the Bible as a perfume brought from the East.

During the Middle Ages, valerian roots were laid among the clothes as a perfume. The herb can intoxicate cats like catnip, but also attracts rats. Legend has it that the Pied Piper of Hamlin carried valerian roots in his pockets when he lead the rats into the river.

But valerian's greatest use is as a medicine. Its historic uses are varied.

Culpeper said the root was under the influence of Mercury, and thus "hath a warming faculty."

He highly recommended the herb for bruises, coughs, and the plague. Others have claimed valerian is useful in treating hypochondria, hysteria, epilepsy, migraine headaches, some forms of fever, and most diseases of the nervous system.

Gerard said valerian was "excellent for those burdened and for such as be troubled with croup and other like convulsions, and also for those that are bruised with falls."

He added that "no broth or pottage or physicall meats be worth anything if [valerian] be not there."

But valerian's chief use is as a sedative. It has remarkable

Valerian

calming effect and is one of the most often used remedies for nervousness and hysteria.

If taken too often or in excessive doses, however, it can cause headaches, spasmodic movements, or hallucinations.

An excellent compound for nervousness is an infusion of one-half ounce each of valerian, skullcap, and mistletoe in one and one-half pints of boiling water, covered and left standing for at least two hours. A tablespoonful can be taken two to four times daily.

Another infusion of one ounce each of powdered valerian, powdered ginger, powdered lobelia, and two ounces of powdered pleurisy root is also considered good as a tranquilizer.

In the garden, valerian makes a handsome and useful border. The utility of the border is for the companion planter, in that it helps most vegetables. It is said to attract earthworms. A recommended garden practice is to make a spray from valerian and to spray plants and soil once a month throughout the summer. The result is supposed to be strengthened plants and an abundance of earthworms.

Valerian seeds don't germinate very easily, and most gardeners would be better off starting the plant from plant divisions rather than seed. If no older plant is available in the garden, the plant will have to be purchased.

Valerian has a peculiar habit of growing out of a "crown," a short, conical root-stock. The crown may develop several years before the sleeve and flower stalks develop.

When dug up, the crown may be transplanted and used to start individual plants. This should be done in March or April, as soon as the crown appears.

The plants very easily overcrowd themselves, so occasional dividing of the plants is necessary to insure good growth. At least every three years, the whole planting should be divided and the plants redug, planted in rows at least one foot apart. The plants should be spaced one foot apart in the row as well.

The root is the most important part of the plant for medicinal purposes, and should be harvested in fall before the first frost. When harvested, the roots should be washed thoroughly to remove all stones and debris and dried.

Drying roots is different from drying leaves. They should be dried at a high temperature, such as 120° F. until the roots are brittle. If they're rubber-like, they should be dried further.

The roots should be carefully stored to keep free from moisture.

VERVAIN

Verbena officinalis, Linn.

Verbenaceae

Vervain is a wayside plant, but one of a magical, mystical past. *Verbena officinalis* is not an American native, though *V. hastata,* a relative, is. Since its introduction here, however, this spiky plant has spread widely, often being found in waste places. An erect plant, it is topped by small purplish-blue flowers.

Vervain has been used as a tonic, diaphoretic, and expectorant, but no strong claims have ever been made as to its efficacy. In China, it is used to induce menstruation, to relieve rheumatism, and as an astringent and vermifuge.

Historically, the plant has been associated with sorcerers, witches, and magic. In ancient times, it was bruised and worn about the neck as a charm against headaches and venomous bites. An old legend reputes vervain to have been used to staunch the wounds of Christ on Calvary.

VIBURNUM

Viburnum, various species
Caprifoliaceae

These widely distributed members of the honeysuckle family rank among the most useful and ornamental shrubs for general planting. They are compact and bushy, with attractive foliage, showy flowers, and decorative fruits. Well suited for shrub borders and roadside planting, they also make handsome single specimens for the lawn.

Viburnums are hardy, not very particular as to soil, but prefer a situation that is not too dry. They may be grown from seed that has been stratified, green-wood cuttings under glass, hardwood cuttings, and layering. Three species of viburnums are recognized for their medicinal value.

Viburnum prunifolium, (Black haw, stagbrush, American sloe) is native to many areas of eastern and central United States; it is a large shrub or small tree with wide spreading branches. The handsome foliage is dark green, leaves are elliptical, and finely toothed, about one to three inches long. The clusters of pure white flowers, from two to four inches broad, bloom from May to June. They are followed by clusters of ovid, blue-black fruits on red stems. The sweet fruit is edible but lacks flavor.

Dried bark of the root is used as a uterine tonic for preventing miscarriage. Also used as a sedative and nervine.

Viburnum opulus (sometimes called *V. americanus* or *V. trilobum* [cramp bark, high cranberry, snowball tree, cranberry bush]) is a large, upright shrub or tree and it usually has several stems from the same root. The leaves have three lobes and are broadly wedge-shaped. Showy clusters of flowers bloom in

June, with the outer blossoms larger and sterile. The large, heavy clusters of scarlet juicy berries remain decorative after the leaves have fallen, until spring. The fruit is very acid, resembles the common cranberry and is sometimes used as a substitute for it.

A handsome plant, native to northern parts of this country and Canada, it grows in low, rich lands, woods, and borders of fields. The bark is used as a nervine and antispasmodic. It is very effectual for cramps, spasms, and convulsions.

Viburnum lentago (sheep-berry, nanny-berry) is also a tall shrub or small tree, has large lustrous leaves, clusters of creamy-white flowers, and juicy black berries. It is distinguished in winter with its long-pointed buds. It is used as a stimulant and diuretic.

VIOLET

Viola odorata, Linn.
Violaceae

An old world species, naturalized in many areas and widely cultivated, violet is found in both blue and white flowering varieties. It should be planted in rich, loamy soil in a sheltered position. Partial shade and moisture are required. Add a generous amount of compost to its soil. The plants multiply by runners, and they also are grown from seed. There are many cultivated varieties. *Viola tricolor* is an all summer blooming variety with small purple and gold flowers. Very easily grown, it self-sows readily. It is commonly called heart's-ease or Johnny-jump-up.

In addition to their ornamental uses in the garden, violets have ornamental uses in cooking. The blossoms have been candied and added to cakes as decorations. The flowers may also be floated in party punch.

The leaves and flowers are said to have antiseptic and expectorant properties. In China, violet blossoms are burned under abscesses in the belief that the smoke will aid in healing sick wounds. The Chinese also use the blossoms in decoctions and poultices.

WAHOO

Burning Bush, Indian Arrowroot, Spindle Tree
Euonymus atropurpureus, Jacq.
Euonymus americanus, Linn.
Celastraceae

Wahoo is a tall shrub, topping 25 feet on occasion, which inhabits moist open woods and river edges from the east coast to Montana. Its most striking appearance is presented in winter, when its pale purple fruits have burst open and been exposed by the fallen leaves, all against a backdrop of glaring snow. It is this appearance which has earned it the nickname burning bush.

The bark of wahoo is gray, its leaves opposite. In June, its purple flowers appear. The fruits develop in October.

The Indians were the first Americans to make use of the plant. The common name, sounding like someone's excited whoop, is credited to both the Sioux and the Creeks. The Indians used a decoction of the bark for uterine troubles and eye ailments. Beaten into a poultice, the bark was also used on facial sores. An infusion was drunk as a physic.

The white settlers didn't take long to pick up the Indian applications of wahoo bark, using it for laxative, diuretic, and tonic effects. Something of a nineteenth-century fad developed, and the bark went into various patent medicines and was extremely popular for a time in England. It was listed as an official drug plant. In 1912, a report was published showing the plant produced a digitalis-like effect on the heart, boosting the herb's popularity as a heart medicine. But four years later wahoo was dropped as an official drug plant, though it continued to be included in the *National Formulary* until 1947.

For medicinal use, the bark should be gathered in the fall. The fruits may be attractive, but they are considered poisonous and should not be used. A decoction is made by boiling one ounce of the bark slowly in a pint of water. When cooled, the decoction is served two to three times daily in wineglassful doses. The bark may also be steeped in grain alcohol to make a tincture, given in five to ten drop doses, usually mixed with water or on sugar.

WILLOW

Salix, various species
Salicaceae

The shrubs and trees of this group are related to the poplars. They come in varied forms, some upright, others weeping, and there are also prostrate varieties. They are hardy, deciduous, and bear flowers in catkins, covered with silky hairs.

The willows are highly valued as ornamentals. The graceful form, lovely foliage, and on some varieties, decorative silvery catkins or "pussies," make them an important feature of the garden design. They also provide a quick growth and can be used as a protective shelter for young slower-growing plants.

They thrive in a moist location and the extensive root system makes them a valuable planting to prevent shore-line erosion. A weeping willow, drooping near a pool, makes an artistic setting. The willows prefer moist locations, but will grow and naturalize readily in most situations. They grow easily from cuttings and may also be grown from seed, which should be planted as soon as it is ripe.

They have been cultivated for basket-making. Indians applied pounded, dry bark to navals of the new-born infant. Bitter, astringent, and detergent, it was also used for diarrhea, to staunch bleeding, and for dandruff. It is used for fevers, rheumatic ailments, and headache. The bark and berries are the parts used medicinally and contain salicin, the prime ingredient in aspirin.

WINTERGREEN

Spiceberry, Teaberry, Checkerberry
Gaultheria procumbens, Linn.
Ericaceae

Wintergreen, as it is most frequently called, is an evergreen shrub of the heath family and is a common plant in woods and clearings from Canada to Georgia. It is a low-growing plant with creeping stems. The broad leaves are elliptical, leathery, glossy green above, and paler below. The nodding white flowers are followed by edible scarlet berries.

The red wintergreen berries were at one time sold as a sort of confection in Boston markets, but they are seldom, if ever, found there now. Leaves of wintergreen were used by the Maine Indians to make a tea. Principal use now is for flavoring candy and chewing gum, which is a pity, because the bright red berries are sweet, tender, and flavorful.

Like most of the heath family, wintergreen needs an acid soil which it finds most often in pine woods. The acidity should be about the same as for trailing arbutus, between pH 4.5 and 5.5. It needs shade and a well-drained, preferably sandy soil. Wintergreen can be propagated by seeds, cuttings, and layers. Divisions may be set out in fall or spring. Beacuse of its strict requirements, it makes a better wild garden subject than one for the herbiary.

It is very difficult to establish plants taken from the woods. Nursery-grown stock is more satisfactory, having been accustomed to artificial conditions. It should be planted on a shady slope and mulched with two to four inches of pine needles.

The leaves are considered a valuable remedy in treatment of rheumatism. It is aromatic, astringent, and a stimulant, used both internally and externally. As a poultice, it can be applied to boils, felons, swellings, and inflammations. The tea is beneficial as a gargle.

Berries and leaves are both used for flavoring, but are not dried. Berries in brandy make a drink like bitters. Oil distilled from the leaves is used for flavoring and for perfume.

The native western variety, *Gaultheria shallon* (sallol) grows to two feet or more and is a good undershrub. Leaves are heart-shaped with panicles of pinkish-white flowers and dark purple fruits. It is used as a tea for a refreshing beverage.

WITCH HAZEL

Spotted Alder, Winterbloom, Snapping Hazelnut
Hamamelis virginiana, Linn.
Hamamelidaceae

Growing as a small tree or shrub, this hard deciduous native is of special interest to the gardener because of the long blooming season—from late fall to early spring. It is vigorous and bushy, with several crooked, branching stems from the same root. Leaves are oval, alternate, somewhat fragrant, and turn yellow and orange in the fall. Fragrant, light yellow flowers with narrow, wavy petals are borne in clusters and appear while the leaves are falling; seeds mature the following summer. The hard-shelled fruits, nut-like capsules or pods, shoot out their seeds like bullets from a gun.

Witch hazels do well in moist, sandy loam and can take shade and moisture. They grow in damp woods in all parts of the country and several species are available as landscape plants in nurseries.

The branches are used as divining rods to detect underground water and metals.

Its medicinal properties are astringent, tonic, and sedative. An old-time remedy still in popular use, a decoction of the bark and leaves is used for a mouthwash and as a vaginal douche to check internal and external hemorrhaging, and for treatment of piles. An ointment was also made for local application. The distilled extract of fresh leaves and twigs was used both externally and internally, and for relief of varicose veins it was applied as a moist compress. For diarrhea, it was administered as an enema. It was used as a wash for tumors, inflammations, bed sores, and inflamed eyes.

An official drug plant, the waters distilled from the bark are sold by the hundreds of thousands of gallons annually. Nevertheless, there is still some disagreement over the efficacy of the herb.

WOAD

Isatis tinctoria, Linn.
Cruciferae

Woad is a biennial with a long history of use as a dye-plant, hence the specific name *tinctoria*. During the first year the plant develops into a rosette of long, narrow blue-green leaves. The second year, stalks grow, rising as much as four feet. Bright yellow flowers develop.

The plant can be grown from seed, and once established, it will self-sow freely. It requires fertile soil, good drainage, and some sun.

Woad was widely cultivated in Britain for the blue dye from the leaves, having been imported there from France and the Roman states. Even in the twentieth century, some commercial use was made of it in dyeing, though as a fixative for true indigo and as a mordant for black dye rather than its color. The leaf and stem had some medicinal use in making plasters and ointments for ulcers, inflammations, and bleeding wounds, though it is too astringent for internal use.

WORMWOOD

Artemisia absinthium, Linn.
Compositae

Wormwood, like its relative mugwort, has been shrouded with superstitions for centuries. It got its generic name from Artemis, the Greek name for Diana, because she discovered the plant's virtues and gave them to mankind. Another story has it that it is named for Artemisia, Queen of Caria, who gave her name to the plant after she had benefitted from its treatments.

Wherever its name came from, wormwood is one of the bitterest herbs known. Its common name comes from its ability to act as a wormer in children and animals. In fact, it was used in granaries to drive away weevils and insects, and was used as a strewing herb in spring to drive fleas away. A strong decoction of wormwood was also used as a wash for the floors of sickrooms to purify them from the illnesses of their inhabitants. The ancients also believed that wormwood was a counter-poison against toadstools, hemlock, and the bites of the sea dragon.

It was used along with marigold, marjoram, thyme, honey, and vinegar as part of a charm taken on St. Luke's Day to receive a vision of one's future mate.

Wormwood is a perennial, and can be quite decorative in the garden. It should not be grown near other plants, however, and it does not make a good companion plant. It contains large amounts of a toxic substance called absinthin, which will wash off the leaves of the plant and into the ground nearby, inhibiting the growth of closely planted herbs or plants. This can be particularly bad in years of heavy rainfall.

The stem of the wormwood is branched, and firm—almost woody at the base. The stem can reach a height of two to two and one-half feet, and is covered with fine silky hairs, as are the leaves. The leaves themselves are three inches long by one broad, thrice pinnate with linear, blunt segments. They are grayish-green and have a distinct odor.

Flowers are small and globular, and are arranged in an erect, leafy panicle. They bloom from July until October with a greenish-yellow tint.

Wormwood is very easy to grow. Soil fertility requirements are minimal, and the only care needed to raise the plants is to weed them. Plants can be propagated from cuttings, by root division in autumn, or by seed sewn in autumn. Seeds can also be started in the house in winter and transplanted outside in the spring. Germination is quick. Allow two feet between plants.

The whole plant is used. Gather it in July and August. Collect the plants on a dry day and dry in a warm room in bunches. Use only the upper green portion for drying—discard the woody stem and the roots. If, after a few days the leaves are dry but the stalk is still damp, hang the bunches near a stove to finish. When dry, rub the herbs through a sieve to remove the coarser stems, and pack immediately in jars. Seal at once to prevent reabsorption of moisture.

Wormwood has been used as a tonic and diuretic, to promote

Wormwood

digestion, and to restore appetite. An infusion of one ounce of the herb to one pint of water was prepared, and given by the wineglassful four times a day. Grieve's herbal says, "A light infusion of the tops of the plants, used fresh, is excellent for all disorders of the stomach, creating an appetite, promoting digestion, and preventing sickness after meals, but producing a contrary effect if used too strong."

The latter is a caution that should be well-observed by the experimenter with herbal remedies. In fact, wormwood in concentrated form is a volatile poison. It produces tremblings, dullness of thought, and convulsions — classic signs of narcotic poisoning. In small doses, it is probably safe, but home experimenters may be well to stay with wormwood as a strewing herb or use it as a natural pest control.

Wormwood is too bitter to have many culinary uses, but it

has been used to flavor beer before the common use of hops. Vermouth is also made with wormwood, as is absinthe. It has been used since ancient times as a way to make wine more intoxicating when they are mixed together. It is also reported that the Germans made wormwood wine.

Of course, wormwood is familiar to many as a vermifuge—perhaps the classic. The dried, powdered flowers are most usually used, although diluted absinthe liqueur is also given.

If used in the garden, wormwood will repel black flea beetles, moths, and protect nearby cabbage plants against the cabbage-worm butterfly. A weak tea bath will discourage slugs if sprayed in the ground in fall and spring. The same spray can be used in storerooms to keep weevils away from stored grains. The tea may also be sprayed on plants to repel aphids, but don't use the spray too often on plants, as it may retard their growth.

There are two other species of wormwood commonly used in herbal remedies, Roman wormwood and sea wormwood. Roman wormwood is much more delicate than common worm-wood, and has numerous, darker, and smaller flowers. Vermouth is made from this species because its flavor is not as bitter as is that of the common wormwood. Sea wormwood grows commonly in salty soils, and is smaller than the common wormwood. Both the sea and Roman wormwoods were used in remedies, but they were considered weaker than the common wormwood.

Dr. John Hill, writing in 1772, recommended wormwood in many forms. "The leaves have been commonly used," he wrote.

> But the flowery tops are the right part. These, made into a light infusion, strengthen digestion, correct acidities, and supply the place of gall, where, as in many constitutions, that is deficient. One ounce of the Flowers and Buds should be put into an earthen vessel, and a pint and a half of boiling water poured on them, and thus to stand all night. In the morning the clear liquor with two spoonfuls of wine should be taken at three draughts, an hour and a half distance from one another. Whoever will do this regularly for a week, will have no sickness after meals, will feel none of that fulness so frequent from indigestion, and wind will be no more troublesome; if afterwards, he will take but a fourth part of this each day, the benefit will be lasting.

YAM, WILD

Colic Root, Rheumatism Root
Dioscorea villosa, Linn.
Dioscoreaceae

The wild yam is a twining perennial found all over the United States and Canada. It has a long, branched, and crooked root which has been used medicinally as an expectorant, diaphoretic, and, in large doses, an emetic. It was officially listed for a time as a diaphoretic and expectorant.

The colloquial names applied to the root stem from southern Negro use of the root for colic and muscular rheumatism. Some Indians used the root to relieve the pains of childbirth, and it is reputed to be particularly helpful in relieving the nausea of the morning sickness so often associated with pregnancy.

There are nearly 150 varieties of *Dioscorea,* many of them developing edible tubers like potatoes. An interesting ornamental variety is *Dioscorea batatas,* sometimes known as the Chinese yam, the red velvet yam, or the cinnamon vine.

A herbaceous, tall climbing plant with slender twining stems, it is useful and decorative where a heavy screen is not desired. It is grown for its large edible tubers, up to three feet long, and its attractive foliage. The leaves are shiny, ribbed, and veined and small clusters of cinnamon-scented white flowers blossom out of the axils of the leaves. Little tubercles form in the leaf axils and, from these, new plants can be started. Easy to grow, they can also be started by seeds, tubers, and cuttings.

YARROW

Achillea millefolium, Linn.
Compositae

If you were a twelfth-century knight at arms, you'd probably carry a pouch of fresh yarrow leaves with you as nature's own first-aid kit.

But being a twentieth-century gardener, you'll undoubtedly want to turn to yarrow instead as a wonderfully decorative border around your garden.

Despite the plant's principal use now for its bright long-blooming flowers, there are still several practical reasons for cultivating yarrow. In companion planting with other medicinal herbs, yarrow—like its cousin tansy—repels Japanese beetles, ants, and flies. In addition, its diaphoretic, styptic, tonic, and astringent properties justify its place in the herbal medicine chest even to this day.

Yarrow gets its generic name *Achillea* from the legend that comrades of the Greek hero Achilles used yarrow to heal their wounds during the Trojan War. The specific name *millefolium* derives from yarrow's feathery leaves, so well divided the plant appears to be thousand-leaved.

Yarrow is a hardy perennial that grows wild and will exist—though maybe not thrive—in almost any grade of soil. It's considered, with some justification, to be a weed by many gardeners.

The flowers of the yarrow plant lend themselves to drying for bouquets. You can choose from among the white, red, orange, and yellow blooming varieties although the white and red seem to be most important and most often cultivated ones for medicinal and culinary use. Orange and yellow are more grown for their floral attributes.

A word of caution when using the white medicinal variety. This variety must be moved annually because it excretes a toxin to the soil that eventually will defeat even its own growth. If you need to have the white medicinal, you might grow it for a season —just long enough to get to know and recognize the plant. Then hunt it wild; it flourishes unattended in almost any area of the eastern United States.

Starting yarrow can be done either from seed or by dividing the root clumps of established plants. Yarrow seed will germinate in light. Sow it on top of fine soil and keep it moist until it germinates. Start it indoors in March so it will be ready for harvesting in June or July. Although fertilization is of minor importance because of yarrow's hardiness, annual applications of bonemeal will promote its growth. Too, yarrow will produce a more pleasing aroma in light, sandy soils than in heavy, clay ones.

For medicinal and culinary uses, cut the whole plant at the peak of the flowering. Chop the stem and leaves and dry them

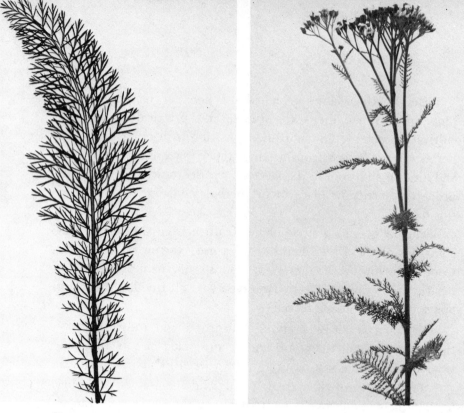

Yarrow

rapidly in 90 to 100° F. Because of its fine division, yarrow will darken quickly if not dried rapidly and thoroughly.

Yarrow used as a companion plant will drive away many common garden insects, and will increase the content of volatile oils in nearby herbs.

Among the reputed conjuring powers of yarrow is its ability to bestow on young squires and maidens a heart-throbbing vision of their future loves. That's accomplished (so tradition has it) by sewing an ounce of the herb into a small square of flannel and putting it under the pillow. Before retiring, the visionary recites this plea:

> Thou pretty herb of Venus' tree,
>   Thy true name is Yarrow;
> Now who my bosom friend must be,
>   Pray tell thou me tomorrow.

During the night, the visionary's true love is supposed to appear in a dream-vision.

A more down-to-earth application of yarrow is for breaking colds and fevers. For that, sip an infusion made by pouring a pint of boiling water over an ounce of yarrow, then adding a teaspoon of honey and three drops of Tabasco sauce. The patient should be heavily covered. This remedy will open the pores and cause profuse sweating to purify the blood of toxins.

Minus the honey and Tabasco, the straight infusion can be used as a shampoo that's said to prevent baldness.

A parallel formula for breaking colds and fevers is to substitute elder flowers and peppermint for the honey and Tabasco.

As a general tonic, yarrow is said to have a salutary effect on the entire nervous system.

The herb throughout the centuries has been used also as snuff, a toothache remedy, and as a substitute for hops in the brewing of homemade beer.

In the kitchen, yarrow occupies only a marginal place. Its usefulness is limited to an occasional stand-in for cinnamon or nutmeg.

YERBA SANTA

Mountain Balm, Holy Herb
Eriodictyon californicum, (Hooker & Arnott) Torrey
Hydrophyllaceae

Yerba santa is an evergreen shrub native to the mountains of California and northern Mexico. The stem of this two to four foot high plant is covered with a peculiar, brown, varnish-like resin. It has thick, leathery, lance-shaped leaves and clusters of bluish flowers.

The herb was widely used by the Indians who knew of it. The leaves were smoked or chewed like tobacco for asthma and were used to brew a tea for colds. An interesting natural mouthwash was made by the Indians, who rolled the leaves into balls, dried them in the sun, then chewed them. The first taste was said to be bitter, but if one soon took a drink of water, the taste would turn sweet and cooling.

In 1875 the wild herb was introduced to the medical profession. It was listed, then dropped, then relisted, and redropped from the official pharmacopoeias. But it is still listed in the *National Formulary* as a useful expectorant.

A GLOSSARY

Abortifacient: A drug which causes abortion.

Alterative: In medicine, this is a substance which gradually alters or changes a condition. Often, it is a medicine that cures an illness by gradually restoring health.

Annual: A plant that completes a cycle of development from germination of the seed through flowering and death in a single growing season.

Anodyne: A medicine that relieves pain.

Anthelmintic: A medicine which expels or destroys intestinal worms. Such medicines are also called *vermifuges.*

Antidote: A medicine which counteracts the action of another, particularly a poison.

Antiperiodic: A medicine which prevents the periodic return of attacks of a disease, such as a period fever.

Antipyretic: A medicine which tends to reduce or prevent a fever. Such medicines are also referred to as *febrifuges* and *refrigerants.*

Antiseptic: A substance that will destroy infection-causing micro-organisms.

Antispasmodic: A medicine that relieves or prevents involuntary muscle spasms or cramps, such as epilepsy, spastic paralysis, painful menstruation, and even "charley horses."

Aperient: A mild and gentle-acting laxative medicine.

Aromatic: A substance with a spicy scent and pungent but pleasing taste. Aromatic herbs are useful for the fragrance, and are often added to medicines to improve their palatability. Just the fragrance and flavor alone can provide a psychological lift.

Astringent: A substance which causes the tissues to contract, thus

628

checking the discharge of mucous, blood, and the like.

Axil: The angle between a leaf or branch and the plant stem.

Balsamic: A substance which heals or soothes.

Biennial: A plant that requires two seasons to complete the growth cycle from germination of seed through flowering and death.

Bitter tonic: A substance with an acrid, astringent, or disagreeable taste which stimulates the flow of saliva and gastric juice. Such tonics are taken to increase the appetite and to aid the digestive process.

Bract: A modified leaf which forms either on the flower stalk or as part of the flower head. Bracts are often mistakenly referred to as flowers.

Carminative: The after-dinner mint is the most familiar carminative. It is a substance which checks the formation of gas and helps dispel whatever gas has already formed.

Catarrh: An inflamation of any mucous membrane, but especially one affecting the respiratory tract.

Cathartic: A laxative or purgative which causes the evacuation of the bowels. A laxative is a gentle cathartic, while a purgative is much more forceful and is used only in stubborn conditions.

Catkin: A downy or scaly spike of flowers produced by certain plants. The pussy on the willow is a familar example.

Cholagogue: A medicine which promotes the discharge of bile from the system.

Composite: A flower actually made up of many separate flowers, complete of themselves, which are united in a single head. This is the characteristic flower of the Compositae or daisy family.

Corm: The bulb-shaped base of certain plants, such as the turnip and the radish. A corm is usually starchy and edible.

Corroborant: Another term for a tonic or other substance which is invigorating.

Counterirritant: An irritant that distracts attention from another, usually an agent applied to the skin to produce a superficial inflammation which reduces or counteracts a deeper inflammation .

Crucifer: Flower of four petals arranged in a cross-like formation. This is the characteristic of the Cruciferae or mustard family.

Decoction: A preparation made by simmering a botanical in water for an extended period. Usually, a decoction is made of hard substances, such as roots, bark, or seeds, since it takes long exposure to heat to extract their active principles. The water is only simmered, however, for vigorous boiling may destroy the vital properties of the plant. Usually an ounce of the botanical is combined with a pint of boiling water, covered, and simmered for a half-hour or more. Some herbalists prefer to use more than a pint to compensate for the liquid lost during the simmering. The preparation is strained and cooled before administration. It should be used immediately for it loses viability rapidly.

Demulcent: Oily or mucilaginous substances which soothe the intestinal tract, providing a protective coating and allaying irritation.

Deobstruent: A medicine which clears obstructions from the natural ducts of the body.

Detergent: In medicine, as in the laundry, a substance used for cleansing.

Diaphoretic: A substance taken internally to promote sweating. Such medicines are also called *sudorifics* and have been used along with sweat baths throughout history to promote general and specific health.

Diuretic: A medicine which promotes the flow of urine.

Emetic: An agent which induces vomiting.

Emmenagogue: A medicine taken internally which promotes menstruation.

Emollient: A substance which, when applied externally, softens and soothes the skin.

Expectorant: A substance that loosens phlegm of the mucous membranes, facilitating its expulsion.

Extract: A medicine or other substance which contains the essence of a plant. Extracts are made in a variety of ways, depending upon the best method of drawing the principles from the plant. *Decoctions, infusions,* and *tinctures* can all be considered extracts in some sense of the word.

Febrifuge: A remedy which helps dissipate a fever. Sometimes called *antipyretic.*

Flatulence: Gas in the stomach or bowels.

Hemostatic: Any substance used to stem internal bleeding.

Hepatic: Any substance which affects the liver, whether helpfully or harmfully.

Herbarium: A collection of dried plants systematically arranged to permit easy study of them.

Hygroscopic: Having the ability to readily attract and retain moisture.

Infusion: An extract of some substance derived by soaking the substance in water. A tea is an infusion. With herbs, the usual infusion is made by combining an ounce of the dried and powdered herb with a pint of boiling water and allowing them to steep for five to ten minutes. This is the simplest and most common method of extracting the medicinal principle from dried botanicals.

Laxative: A gentle cathartic, helps to promote bowel movements.

Mucilaginous: Mucous-like, slimy; offers a soothing quality to inflamed parts.

Nervine: A substance which calms or quiets nervousness, tension, or excitement.

Pectoral: Relieves ailments of the chest and lungs.

Perennial: A plant which continues a cycle of new growth and flowering for many seasons between germination of the seed and death.

Physic: A medicinal substance or preparation.

Poultice: Material applied to the surface of the body as a remedy for some disorder. Usually, a poultice is made of fresh vegetable matter that has been crushed or soaked into a limber mass, then placed between two pieces of cloth for application.

Purgative: A strong cathartic, given to relieve severe constipation. Sometimes synonymous with cathartic.

Raceme: A simple clustering of flowers on nearly equal-length stalks along a stem with the lowest flowers blooming first and the youngest blossom at the top.

Refrigerant: A substance which cools and reduces fever. Seldom used, it is much the same as *febrifuge* and *antipyretic.*

Rheumatism: An ailment characterized by stiffness of the joints or muscles.

Rhizome: An elongated, thickened, usually horizontal, underground plant stem which sends out roots below and shoots above. It is differentiated from ordinary rootstock by the presence of nodes, buds, and occasionally scale-like leaves.

Rubefacient: A substance which, when rubbed into the skin, reddens the skin by attracting blood to the area.

Scrofula: An infection and enlargement of the lymph glands. Thanks largely to modern sanitation, scrofula is no longer common.

Sedative: A medicine which calms the nerves.

Serration: Sawlike tooth. Many herbs have serrated leaves.

Sessile: A term used to refer to leaves and flowers which have no stalk.

Sialagogue: A substance which causes an increase in the flow of saliva.

Soporific: A substance that tends to induce sleep.

Specific: A medicine that has a special effect on a particular disease.

Stimulant: A substance which increases or quickens the various functional actions of the body, such as quickening digestion, raising body temperature, and so on. It does this quickly, unlike a *tonic,* which stimulates general health over a period of time. And unlike a narcotic, it does not necessarily produce a feeling of general well-being, a feeling a narcotic produces by depressing nerve centers.

Stomachic: A medicine which gives strength and tone to the stomach or stimulates the appetite by promoting digestive secretions.

Styptic: A substance that stops or checks bleeding. It is usually an *astringent* which shrinks the tissues, thus closing exposed blood vessels.

Sudorific: A substance which promotes sweating. Much like *diaphoretic.*

Thoracic: A medicine used to remedy respiratory ailments.

Tincture: A solution of organic material in alcohol. Some botanicals will not release their principles to water, hot or cold, so they are soaked in grain alcohol, brandy, gin, vodka, or other spirits, straight or diluted with water. Usually an ounce of the herb is combined with a pint of spirits, or spirits and water, and allowed to steep, with daily agitation, for two weeks. The liquid is strained before use. This type of extract stores well.

Tonic: A substance which invigorates or strengthens the system. Often tonics act as stimulants and alteratives. *Bitter tonics* stimulate the flow of gastric juices, increasing the appetite, and promoting the intake of food, which strengthens and invigorates.

Tuber: An enlarged part of a root or underground stem. The potato is perhaps the most familiar tuber.

Umbel: A cluster of flowers formed by stalks of nearly equal length sprouting from a common center. The individual flowers form a flat or nearly flat surface. This type of flower cluster is characteristic of the Umbelliferae or carrot family.

Vermifuge: A medicine that destroys intestinal worms and helps expel them. Also called *anthelmintic.*

Vesicant: A substance which causes blisters or sores. Poison ivy is a vesicant.

Vulnerary: An herb used in treating battle wounds.

A BIBLIOGRAPHY

Adrosko, Rita J. *Natural Dyes and Home Dyeing*. New York: Dover, 1971.

American Ethnology, Bureau of. *American Indian Medicines*. Washington, D. C.: Smithsonian Institute, 1957.

Andrews, E. D. and Shaken, F. *Herbs and Herbalists*. Stockbridge, Ma.: Berkshire Garden Center, 1959.

Bailey, L. H. *Hortus Second*. New York: The Macmillan Co., 1942.

Beau, Georges. *Chinese Medicine*. Translated by Lowell Bair. New York: Avon Books, 1972.

Beston, Henry. *Herbs and the Earth*. Dolphin Books Edition. New York: Doubleday, 1973.

Blair, Thomas S. *Botanic Drugs*. Cincinnati: Theraputic Digest, 1917.

Brooklyn Botanic Garden. *Dye Plants and Dyeing*. Brooklyn Botanic Garden Handbook No. 46, 1964.

Budge, Sir E. A. Wallis. *The Divine Origin of the Craft of the Herbalist*. London: Culpepper House, 1928.

Carter, Kate B. *Pioneer Home Cures of Common Diseases*. Salt Lake City: Daughters of Utah Pioneers, 1958.

Carter, Kate B. *Pioneer Medicines*. Salt Lake City: Daughters of Utah Pioneers, 1958.

Clarkson, Rosetta E. *Herbs and Savory Seeds*. New York: Dover, 1972.

Clarkson, Rosetta E. *Herbs, Their Culture and Uses*. New York: Macmillan, 1966.

Cocannouer, Joseph A. *Weeds, Guardians of the Soil*. Old Greenwich, Ct.: Devin-Adair, 1964.

Coon, Nelson. *Using Wayside Plants*. Great Neck, N.Y.: Hearthside, 1957.

Coon, Nelson. *Using Plants for Healing*. Great Neck, N.Y.: Hearthside, 1963.

Culpeper, Nicholas. *Culpeper's Complete Herbal*. London: W. Foulsham & Co., undated.

Davenport, Elsie G. *Your Yarn Dyeing*. Pacific Grove, Ca.: Craft and Hobby Book Service, 1970.

Davidson, Mary Frances. *The Dye Pot*. Gatlinburg, Tenn.: by the author.

Dioscorides. *The Greek Herbal*. Oxford: Oxford University Press, 1934.

Emmart, translator. *Badianus Manuscript (1552)*. Baltimore: John Hopkins Press, 1940.

Evelyn, John. *Acetaria, A Discourse of Salletts—1699*. Reprint. Brooklyn: Brooklyn Botanic Garden, 1937.

Fenton, William N. *Contacts Between Iroquois Herbalism and Colonial Medicine*. Washington D. C.: Smithsonian Institute, 1941.

Fernald, M. D., ed. and rev. *Gray's Manual of Botany*, 8th Edition. Boston: American Book Co., 1950.

Fernie, W. T. *Herbal Simples*. London: J. Wright, 1914.

Foster, Gertrude B. *Herbs for Every Garden*. New York: Dutton, 1966.

Fox, Helen Morgenthau. *Gardening with Herbs*. New York: Dover, 1972.

Fox, Helen Morgenthau. *The Years in My Herb Garden*. New York: Collier Books, 1953.

Fox, William. *Family Botanic Guide*. Sheffield, Eng.: Fox & Sons, 1916.

Gibbons, Euell. *Stalking the Healthful Herbs*. New York: David McKay Co., 1966.

Grieve, Mrs. M. *A Modern Herbal*. New York: Dover Publications, Harcourt Brace, 1931.

Hardacre, Val. *Woodland Nuggets of Gold Ginseng*. New York: Vantage, 1968.

Harriman, Sarah. *The Book of Ginseng*. New York: Pyramid Books, 1973.

Harris, Ben Charles. *Eat the Weeds*. Barre, Ma.: Barre, 1968.

Healey, B. J. *A Gardener's Guide to Plant Names*. New York: Charles Scribner's Sons, 1972.

Heffern, Richard. *The Herb Buyer's Guide.* New York: Pyramid Books, 1973.

Henkel, Alice. *American Medicinal Leaves and Herbs.* Washington: U.S.D.A., Bulletin No. 219, Government Printing Office, 1911.

Hersey, Jean. *Cooking With Herbs.* New York: Charles Scribner's Sons, 1972.

Jacobs, Marion Lee and Burlage, Henry M. *Index of Plants of North Carolina with Reputed Medicinal Uses.* Austin, Tx.: Henry M. Burlage, 1958.

Jain, K. K., M.D. *The Amazing Story of Health Care in New China,* Emmaus, Pa.: Rodale Press, 1973.

Jarvis, D. C. *Folk Medicine.* New York: Henry Holt & Co., 1958.

Kadans, Joseph M. *Encyclopedia of Medicinal Herbs.* New York: Arco, 1972.

Kierstead, Salie Pease. *Natural Dyes.* Boston: Bruce Humphries, 1950.

Kirschner, H. E. *Nature's Healing Grasses.* Yucaipa Ca.: H. C. White, 1960.

Krochmal, Arnold. *Guide to Medicinal Plants of Appalachia.* Washington, D. C.: U. S. Agricultural Handbook, Government Printing Office, 1968.

Law, Donald. *Herb Growing for Health.* New York: Arc, 1969.

Leighton, Ann. *Early American Gardens—For Meate or Medicine.* Boston: Houghton Mifflin, 1970.

Levy, Juliette de Bairacli. *Herbal Handbook for Farm and Stable.* London: Faber and Faber, 1963.

Levy, Juliette de Bairacli. *Herbal Handbook for Everyone.* Newton Centre, Ma.: Branford, 1966.

Levy, Juliette de Bairacli. *Nature's Children.* New York: Schocken, 1971.

Levy, Juliette de Bairacli. *Complete Herbal Book for the Dog.* Levittown, N.Y.: Transatlantic Arts, 1971.

Leyel, Mrs. C. F. *Green Medicine.* New York: Faber and Faber, 1952.

Leyel, Mrs. C. F. *Elixirs of Life.* London: Faber and Faber, 1958.

Lighthall, J. I. *The Indian Folk Medicine Guide.* New York: Popular Library, undated.

Loewenfeld, Claire. *Herb Gardening.* Newton Center, Ma.: Charles T. Branford Co., 1965.

Lucas, Richard. *Nature's Medicines.* London: Parker, 1966.

Lucas, Richard. *Common and Uncommon Herbs for Healthful Living.* London: Parker, 1969.

Marks, Geoffrey. *The Medicinal Garden.* New York: Scribner, 1971.

Massey, A. B. *Medicinal Plants.* Virginia Polytechnical Institute, Bulletin No. 30, 1942.

Messegue, Maurice. *Of Men and Plants.* New York: The Macmillan Co., 1973.

Meyer, Joseph E. *The Herbalist.* Hammond, Ind.: Indiana Botanic Gardens, 1939.

Millspaugh, Charles F. *Medicinal Plants.* Philadelphia: John C. Yorston, 1892.

Northcote, Lady Rosalind. *Book of Herb Lore.* New York: Dover, 1971.

Organic Gardening and Farming, eds. *The Organic Way to Plant Protection.* Emmaus, Pa.: Rodale Press, 1966.

Peterson, Roger Tory and McKenny, Margaret. *A Field Guide to Wildflowers.* Boston: Houghton Mifflin, 1968.

Philbrick, Helen and Gregg, Peter. *Companion Plants and How to Use Them.* New York: Devin-Adair, 1966.

Quelch, Mary Thorne. *Herbs for Daily Use.* London: Faber and Faber, 1946.

Rohde, Eleanour Sinclair. *A Garden of Herbs.* New York: Dover, 1969.

Rose, Jeanne. *Herbs and Things: Jeanne Rose's Herbal.* New York: Grosset and Dunlap, 1972.

Scully, Virginia. *A Treasury of American Indian Herbs: Their Lore and Their Use for Food, Drugs, and Medicine.* New York: Crown Publishers, 1970.

Shelton, Ferne. *Pioneer Comforts and Kitchen Remedies.* High Point, N.C.: Hutcraft, 1965.

Sievers, A. F. *American Medicinal Plants of Commercial Importance.* U.S.D.A. Publication No. 77, 1930.

Simmonite, W. J. *The Simmonite-Culpepper Remedies.* London: Foulsham, 1957.

Simmons, Adelma G. *Herb Gardening in Five Seasons.* New York: Hawthorn, 1971.

Simmons, Adelma G. *Herbs to Grow Indoors.* New York: Hawthorn, 1969.

Step, Edward. *Herbs of Healing.* London: Hutchinson, 1926.

Stone, Eric. *Medicine Among the American Indians.* New York: Hafner, 1962.

Thurstan, Violetta. *The Use of Vegetable Dyes.* Leicester, Eng.: Dryad, 1964.

United States Department of Agriculture. *Common Weeds of the United States.* New York: Dover, 1971.

Vogel, Virgil J. *American Indian Medicine.* Norman, Okla.: University of Oklahoma Press, 1970.

Webster, Helen N. *Herbs, How to Grow Them and Use Them.* Rev. ed. Newton, Ma.: Charles T. Branford Co., 1942.

Weiner, Michael A. *Earth Medicine—Earth Foods . . . Of the North American Indians.* New York: Macmillan, 1972.

Williams, Louis O. *Drug and Condiment Plants.* Washington D.C.: U.S.D.A. Handbook, Government Printing Office, 1960.

Woodward, M. *Leaves from Gerard's Herbal.* New York: Dover Publications, 1969.

Wren, R. C. *Potter's Encyclopedia of Botanical Drugs and Preparations.* London: Pitman, 1956.

Youngken, H. W. *Textbook of Pharmacognosy.* Philadelphia: Blakiston Co., 1948.

A LIST OF SOURCES

Herbs and related items are available from a tremendous variety of outlets, and it would be folly to suggest these remaining pages can do anything more than offer some guidelines for making herbal purchases. Included is a list of firms, reputable ones from all indications, which do business by mail.

First place to look if and when you are in the market for herbs is the telephone directory. There are herb farmers and gardeners and dealers in some pretty surprising locations, so don't think you are too backwater to have an herb outlet nearby. Of course most metropolitan centers will have at least one such outlet.

Failing there, the post office may be your next best connection. Practically everything you could want of an herbal nature is available through the mail, even live plants. A great many herb businesses depend on the mail for a major portion of their income, so they are prepared to deal through the mail.

Write to any of these businesses and ask for a catalog or information on what they sell. Certainly you must always be specific about what you want, particularly when dealing with herbs, and particularly when dealing through the mail. If at all possible, use botanical names. (And if the business person doesn't know the botanical names, take it as a warning that you've not found a reliable source.) Shop around, looking not only for the best price, but for the best quality and service too.

Not every business is going to have everything you might want. Most large mail-order seed outlets, like Burpee and George Parks, have a selection of herbs listed in their catalogs, but you'll have to look elsewhere for anything out of the ordinary. Remember, though, that not all herbal plants are universally classified as herbs, so look among the trees, flowers, and food plants in seed catalogs.

There are an increasing number of stores catering to those

who have not the time, space, or inclination to grow their own herbs. You can purchase condiments, teas, medicinal plants, dye plants, aromatics, and all sorts of related products in these stores. If one is nearby, by all means stop in and browse.

If you are interested in more information on herbs, check your local library or bookstore for the books listed in the bibliography which precedes this section. Not all will be readily available. Some are long out of print and are available only in the most extensive (or specialized) library collections.

You may be able to get a line on other herb gardeners in your area through gardening clubs. You can get a listing of the many organic gardening clubs by writing to Organic Gardening Clubs of America, 33 East Minor Street, Emmaus, Pennsylvania 18049. The Herb Society of America has a number of regional chapters, about which you may get some information by writing the society at 300 Massachusetts Avenue, Boston, Massachusetts 02115. The society sells a variety of publications, including its own annual, *The Herbalist*. Just don't write for whatever handouts they have, for there are none. The society comprises people who have demonstrated a long-standing interest in herbs. Membership is by invitation. But if you are interested, get in contact with a regional chapter.

The following list of herbal outlets is as accurate as we can make it. While most of the businesses listed have been in operation for many years, we cannot guarantee they will still be operating at the time you read this. The list makes no pretense of being complete. It is, rather, a starting point, and an effort has been made to include at least one outlet for every variety of herb or herbal product available. The businesses marked with an asterisk (*) are those that say they deal in organically grown herbs.

Aphrodisia
28 Carmine Street
New York, New York 10014
   Unusual botanicals.
      Catalog 25¢.

Black Forest Botanicals
Route 1, Box 34
Yuba, Wisconsin 54672
   Catalog 10¢.

Borchelt Herb Gardens
474 Carriage Shop Road
East Falmouth,
    Massachusetts 02536
    Catalog 10¢.

W. Atlee Burpee Company
P. O. Box 6929
Philadelphia,
    Pennsylvania 19132
    Seeds and plants.

Casa Yerba*
Star Route 2, Box 21
Day's Creek, Oregon 97429
    Seeds and plants.

Caswell-Massey Company, Ltd.
320 West Thirteenth Street
New York, New York 10014
    Catalog free.

Cedarbrook Herb Farm*
Route 1, Box 1047
Sequim, Washington 98382
    Brochure 20¢.

China Herb Company
428 Soledad
Salinas, California 93901

Gardens of the Blue Ridge
Ashford, North Carolina 28603
    Native live herbs.

Greene Herb Gardens*
Greene, Rhode Island 02872
    Herbs, herb plants, seeds.

Hahn and Hahn
    Homeopathic Pharmacy
324 West Saratoga Street
Baltimore, Maryland 21201

Haussmann's Pharmacy
534-536 West Girard Avenue
Philadelphia,
    Pennsylvania 19123
    Unusual botanicals.
    Catalog available.

Heise's Wausau Farms
Route 3
Wausau, Wisconsin 54401
    Growers and dealers in
    American ginseng.

Herbarium, Inc.
Route 2, Box 620
Kenosha, Wisconsin 53140
    Botanical drugs and spices.

Hickory Hollow*
Route 1, Box 52
Peterstown,
    West Virginia 24963
    Herbal products.

Hilltop Herb Farm
Box 866
Cleveland, Texas 77327
    Herbs, herb plants, seeds,
        unusual botanicals.
        Catalog 30¢.

Indiana Botanic Gardens, Inc.
P. O. Box 5
Hammond, Indiana 46325
    Wide variety of botanicals
        and herbal products.
        Catalog 25¢.

Joseph J. Kern Rose Nursery
Box 33
Mentor, Ohio 44060
    Old varieties of roses.

Kiel Pharmacy, Inc.
109 Third Avenue
New York, New York 10003
    No catalog.

Meadowbrook Herb Garden*
Wyoming,
    Rhode Island 02898
    Seeds, plants, herbal
        products.
        Catalog 50¢.

Dr. Michael's Herb Center
1223 North Milwaukee Avenue
Chicago, Illinois 60622
    Complete line of herbal
        medicinal preparations.

Nature's Herb Company
281 Ellis Street
San Francisco, California 94102
    Unusual botanicals.
        Catalog 25¢.

Nichols Garden Nursery*
Pacific North
Albany, Oregon 97321
    Herbs, vegetables, flowers
        and other plants, seeds,
        botanical products.
        Catalog 15¢.

George W. Park Seed Company
P. O. Box 31
Greenwood,
    South Carolina 29646
    Catalog.

Penn Herb Company
603 North Second Street
Philadelphia,
     Pennsylvania 19123
     Dried herbs, seeds, and
       herb products.

Pine Hills Herb Farms*
P. O. Box 144
Roswell, Georgia 30075

Snow-Line Farm
11846 Fremont
Yucaipa, California 92399

Snug Valley Farm
Route 3, Box 394
Kutztown, Pennsylvania 19530
     Wool, mordants, dried dye
       plants, and dye starter
       kit.

Straw Into Gold
5550-H College Avenue
Oakland, California 94610
     Mordants, natural dyes.

Tillotson's Roses
802 Brown's Valley Road
Watsonville, California 95076
     Catalog of old roses, $1.

Well Sweep Herb Farm*
451 Mount Bethel Road
Port Murray, New Jersey 07865
     Price list available for
      seeds, plants, and
      products.

The Woolgatherer
47 State Street
Brooklyn Heights,
     New York 11201
     Yarns and dyes.

World-Wide Herb Ltd.
11 Sainte Catherine Street East
Montreal 129, Canada
     Botanicals.

INDEX